LEARNING AND INNOVATION IN
ORGANIZATIONS AND ECONOMIES

Learning and Innovation in Organizations and Economies

BART NOOTEBOOM

OXFORD

UNIVERSITY PRESS

Great Clarendon Street, Oxford OX2 6DP

Oxford University Press is a department of the University of Oxford.
It furthers the University's objective of excellence in research, scholarship,
and education by publishing worldwide in

Oxford New York

Athens Auckland Bangkok Bogotá Buenos Aires Calcutta
Cape Town Chennai Dar es Salaam Delhi Florence Hong Kong Istanbul
Karachi Kuala Lumpur Madrid Melbourne Mexico City Mumbai
Nairobi Paris São Paulo Shanghai Singapore Taipei Tokyo Toronto Warsaw

and associated companies in Berlin Ibadan

Oxford is a registered trade mark of Oxford University Press
in the UK and certain other countries

Published in the United States
by Oxford University Press Inc, New York

British Library Cataloguing in Publication Data

Data available

Library of Congress Cataloging in Publication Data

Data available

ISBN 0-19-924099-X

1 3 5 7 9 10 8 6 4 2

Typeset by Graphicraft Ltd., Hong Kong
Printed in Great Britain
on acid-free paper by
Biddles Ltd., Guildford and King's Lynn

Preface

AUDIENCE

This book is intended mainly for scholars and students in the areas of economics, management and organization, sociology, and political science. Practitioners, particularly consultants, who seek some conceptual depth in the areas of innovation and organizational change and learning may also be interested. In economics, relevant areas would be innovation and innovation policy, innovation systems, business systems, entrepreneurship, industrial organization, evolutionary economics, Austrian/Schumpeterian economics, institutional economics, networks, governance, organization, economic history. In management and organization they would be organizational learning, organizational behaviour, strategic management, innovation management. In sociology and political science they would be institutions, business systems, innovation systems, networks, structure and agency, social order, sense making.

For universities, the book is aimed more at advanced than at basic courses. It can be used as the main text for courses on organizational learning or organizational change, innovation and innovation policy, innovation management, entrepreneurship. It can be used as a secondary source in courses on organizational behaviour, organizational design, industrial organization, strategic management, business development.

PURPOSE

The purpose of this book is mainly theoretical—to find and to develop theory for the explanation of phenomena of innovation and learning at different levels: innovation systems, organizations, people in organizations. However, to maintain a connection with reality, illustrations, in the form of the 'stylized facts' that we seek to explain, are added throughout the book.

The central issue of the book is: How can stability and change be combined, in technologies, competencies, organizations, and institutions? In the organizational literature this is known as the problem of combining 'exploitation' and 'exploration'. In exploitation, people, organizations, and industries try to use their available competencies and resources efficiently, in order to survive in the short term. In exploration, the aim is to discover and develop new competencies, in order to adapt and survive in the long term. This entails a paradox: exploitation requires coherence, co-ordination, stability, and a certain amount of formalization, while exploration requires that these be loosened and replaced. How can this paradox be resolved? For an answer I will employ several disciplines: economics, sociology, and cognitive science.

STRUCTURE

I have attempted to make individual chapters suitable for independent reading, in so far as this could be reconciled with the coherence needed for a reasonably systematic account. The book starts, in Chapter 1, with a statement of its purpose and scope. This sketches the main themes and lists twenty-two research questions. It puts the book on the maps of the different disciplines used. Finally, it discusses my methodological position: I aim for a realistic theory, but at the same time I employ a social construct-ivist, interactionist theory of knowledge. How can these be combined?

In Part I building-blocks for theory construction are sought from the different disciplines. In the field of management and organization, explored in Chapter 2, the focus is on issues of knowledge and learning. In Chapters 3–5 the focus is on mainly unorthodox streams in economics: Austrian/Schumpeterian economics, the 'resource–competence' view, evolutionary and institutional economics. The resource–competence view is found to be useful for achieving theoretical coherence, especially when it is combined with an interactionist view of knowledge and meaning. In cognit-ive science, in Chapters 6 and 7, I arrive at the 'situated-action' view of knowledge and language, rather than the 'computational–representational' view. It provides the underpinning for the interactionist perspective used in the book.

Part II uses the building-blocks from Part I for the construction of new theory. Chapter 8 develops a theory of learning by interaction. Chapter 9 forms the core chap-ter of the book. It develops a general 'heuristic of discovery', in the form of a cycle, with the claim that this underlies learning and innovation at all levels. Chapter 10 elab-orates the theory, in an attempt to make it more rigorous, by using the notion of a 'script', derived from cognitive science. To the cycle of discovery Chapter 11 attaches a cycle of organizational integration and disintegration.

In Part III the results are used for applications in a theory of innovation systems, in Chapter 12, a theory of organizational learning, in Chapter 13, and answers to the research questions, in Chapter 14. A summary of the book is given at the end.

HISTORY

This book has had an incubation time of thirty-five years. It started when I was a student of mathematics at Leyden University, the Netherlands. I was interested also in philosophy, especially philosophy of knowledge. A fellow student alerted me to the work of Jean Piaget on the development of knowledge in children. I had a strong feel-ing that underlying his theories were fundamental principles of change processes. When later I had children myself I performed the Piagetian play experiments on them, and was much impressed to find that they replicated Piaget's results. I decided that sooner or later I would pursue the intuition that something fundamental and universal lay there and 'only' had to be unpacked.

I made a first attempt in the seventies. I was working on a doctoral dissertation in econometrics, but parallel to that I ventured on a second, philosophical, thesis, in which I tried to develop a general 'logic of change' and to apply it in a theory of science, learning, and language. This failed without a chance under the supervision of a professor of analytic philosophy. No wonder: my project was completely antithetical to his world-view. But I thought the failure was mine, so I shelved the enterprise, happy that I had hedged my bets with another dissertation.

It was only many years later, after many studies of innovation, and finding that several of my ideas had appeared in other people's publications, that I became convinced that I was not wrong, and that the project should be picked up again. This stimulated me to make a shift from economics to studies of management and organization, which were much more receptive to discussions of learning. The time finally seemed right.

But it was still not easy to get on to any stage. The first success was an article published in 1989 in the journal *Human Systems Management*, which does not seem to have attracted any attention at all. An article pleading for plausible theory in economics, in 1986 in the journal *Economics and Philosophy*, preceded this. The second success came with a paper, in 1992, in the *Journal of Evolutionary Economics*, which was probably published only because I presented it under the guise of trying to make static transaction-cost economics dynamic. This provided me with an opportunity to smuggle in the main theoretical foundations for a theory of discovery. I developed an early version of my proposal for a general 'heuristic of learning', and peddled it to some of the more prestigious journals. Their response was that the work was very original, and they were pretty sure this was the way to go, but they could not publish it because it was difficult to recognize and insert in existing thought. Then the paper won me the William Kapp Prize from the *European Association for Evolutionary Political Economy* (EAEPE) in 1996, and I will remain grateful forever for this act of recognition and support. The paper in fact contained a book crammed into it, and it was very difficult to get published, even after the prize. It was finally accepted for a special issue of the *Cambridge Journal of Economics*, published in 1999. Geoffrey Hodgson and Ash Amin had something to do with this, and I am grateful to them. An elaboration of another part of the paper from the journal of evolutionary economics, using Saussure's theory of language, was published in 1992, in a volume of papers from a conference of the EAEPE. The ideas presented in my papers won appreciation from John Foster and Kurt Dopfer, and I am grateful for their feedback and support.

ACKNOWLEDGEMENTS

Over the past few years I have benefited from discussions with a number of people. At the department of management and organization of Groningen University I had constructive discussions with René Jorna, even though, or perhaps because, he was a firm adherent of the computational–representational view of cognition, while I felt more drawn to the situated-action view. I further had inspiring sessions with László Pólos, then at the University of Amsterdam, who had an apparatus of intensional logic that held promise for formalizing my heuristic of learning. We are currently co-operating in an attempt to realize that promise. I had many stimulating discussions at conferences of the EAEPE, conferences sponsored in 1996–8 by the EMOT programme (European Management and Organization in Transition) of the European Science Foundation, a meeting hosted in 1998 by DRUID (Danish Research Unit for Industrial Dynamics), meetings hosted in 1998 and 1999 by the Max Planck Institute in Jena, a workshop in 1999 in Ancona hosted by Antonio Calafati, and a workshop in 1999 in Brisbane hosted by John Foster. The people involved were, among others: Richard Nelson, Sidney Winter, Franco Malerba, Nicolai Foss, Peter Maskell, John Foster, Stan Metcalfe, Kurt Dopfer, Geoffrey Hodgson, Pier Paolo Saviotti, Ash Amin, Maureen McKelvey, Robert Delorme, Ulrich Witt, John Groenewegen, Anna Grandori, Mark Ebers, Antonio Calafati, Jack Vromen, Margherita Turvani, Uskali Mäki, Paivi Oinas, Ekkehart Schlicht.

In the academic year 1998/9 the University of Groningen granted me sabbatical leave, and the Royal Netherlands Academy of Sciences (KNAW) awarded me a fellowship at the Netherlands Institute for Advanced Studies in the Humanities and Social Sciences (NIAS) in Wassenaar. I am grateful to both for enabling me to liberate the story from the confines of a paper and produce a book. At NIAS I had stimulating discussions regarding the project of this book with Benny Shanon, who is a most eloquent opponent of the computational–representational view, Joost van Baak, Professor of Russian literature, who helped me develop my thoughts on language, Vladimir Ivanov, who was translating the work of the Indian sage Bhartrhari from Sanskrit into Russian, and put me on to the work of Bhartrhari, and Maurits van der Molen, who suggested readings in psychology. Special thanks go to the members of the 'Innovation Systems Research Group' at NIAS, of which I was a member: Rogers Hollingsworth, Jerald Hage, Richard Whitley, Frans van Waarden, Marius Meeus, Ernst Homburg, Brigitte Unger, Steve Casper. They were prepared to listen to some of my ideas and to provide useful feedback and suggestions for literature.

I thank Rogers Hollingsworth for comments on drafts of several chapters, Richard Nelson for comments on earlier versions of the chapters on evolution, institutions, and innovation systems, Geoffrey Hodgson for comments on the chapters on evolution and institutions, René Jorna for comments on several versions of the chapters on knowledge and language. Of course none of them bears any responsibility for remaining errors.

In addition to the publications already mentioned, earlier versions of other parts of the book have recently appeared in journals or are currently under review. A combination of parts of the chapter on the heuristic of discovery (Chapter 9) and the chapter on organizational integration and disintegration (Chapter 11) was published in 1999 by Routledge in a volume edited by Anna Grandori, with the title *Interfirm Networks: Organization and Industrial Competitiveness*. An earlier version of the chapter on innovation systems (Chapter 12) was published in 1999 in *Research Policy*. A combination of parts of the chapter on the heuristic of discovery (Chapter 9) and parts of the chapter on organizational learning (Chapter 13) is under review by *Organization Science*. A combination of parts of the chapter on organizational integration and dis-integration (Chapter 11) and parts of the chapter on innovation systems (Chapter 12) is under review by *Organization Studies*. An earlier version of the chapter on inter-organizational learning (Chapter 8) is under review by the *Journal of Management and Governance*.

Contents

Contents

1

Purpose and Scope

This Chapter specifies the purpose of the book, the research questions, the main themes, and the perspectives and disciplines involved. It gives a reflection on the historical roots of some of the issues. It discusses my methodological position. I take a realist view but also employ a constructivist theory of knowledge. How can these two be reconciled?

1.1 PURPOSE AND QUESTIONS

The purpose of this book is to explain the emergence of novelty in organizations and economies. That includes innovation in industries, technology systems or 'innovation systems', and learning in organizations. Those subjects are combined because they must be causally connected, somehow. Innovations are produced by organizations and in that process organizations learn. This paragraph introduces the main themes: innovation, entrepreneurship, industry life cycles, firm life cycles, organizational forms, organizational learning, and the erratic nature of novelty. For each of these themes research questions are specified.

1.1.1 Innovation

The literature on innovation and innovation systems is mostly oriented towards incremental change, building on existing competencies, moving along a 'technical trajectory' (Dosi 1984), according to a 'techno-economic paradigm' (Dosi *et al.* 1988, Freeman & Perez 1989). Incremental change is interspersed with more radical innovations, yielding novel competencies and technical trajectories, or paradigm breaks, in Schumpeterian 'creative destruction' (Abernathy & Utterback 1978). Such phenomena of relative stability (trajectories, paradigms) interrupted by more radical change have also been characterized as 'punctuated equilibria' (Tushman & Romanelli 1985, Gersick 1991, Romanelli & Tushman 1994). How radical innovation, paradigm switches, or punctuation arise remains unexplained. Even in neo-Schumpeterian theory radical innovation is exogenous: a stone thrown into the tranquil pond of equilibrium. The resulting ripples can be studied, but the origin of the stone remains a mystery. Some would say that the search for the sources of innovation would be a search for the philosopher's stone: if we could explain innovation, we could predict it, and that would deny that it is a true innovation. But that is mistaken: one can very well develop a logic, or heuristic, of discovery without claiming to be able to predict its outcomes. This yields the first and central research question for this book. That question entails two others:

Question 1 (the central question): What are the sources and conditions of paradigm switches, punctuations, or radical innovations?

Question 2: How can we identify paradigm switches and punctuations? (Are they the same?) How can we demarcate incremental and radical innovation? How can we operationalize 'discontinuity'?

Question 3: What are the meaning and role of 'paradigms' here?

An example of a series of punctuated equilibria, extending over a long period of time, is the succession of naval 'trajectories', in the fifteenth to eighteenth centuries, punctuated by more or less radically new designs and combinations (Nooteboom & Constandse 1995). I name only a few. One is the triangular lateen sail adopted by the Portuguese from Arabian merchants and combined with the square sails already in use (Mokyr 1990). In sailing, square sails have the advantage of speed when sailing with the wind, while the triangular lateen sail yields wider possibilities for manoeuvring against the wind. The latter allows for sailing in a specific direction in different winds, such as sailing on rivers and entering and leaving ports. Therefore, its adoption greatly reduced the idle time of ships locked inside or outside ports. The best constellation, however, was to use multiple masts for employing both designs (Mokyr 1990). Another example is the Dutch design of the 'flute' ship to reduce deck surface and thereby labour costs and toll levied in the Sont Straits, on the route between the North Sea and the Baltic—which were both in proportion to deck surface—while maintaining payload. The solution was a bulbous shape. Apparently, that shape was inspired by principles of dike construction developed in the lowlands. A third example is British use of teak wood for greater durability, and copper plating on the hull to prevent speed-reducing growth of sea organisms. Punctuations in ship design were accompanied by shifts of dominance from the Portuguese to the Dutch, and from the Dutch to the British.

The example of the succession of naval trajectories is interesting because it illustrates several relevant issues. Dutch ship design entailed a nice example of Schumpeterian 'novel combinations'—of principles of shipbuilding and principles of building dikes. Moreover, the experience in both spilled over to the building of windmills. Together, these activities constituted what, in the terminology of Porter (1990), might be called an innovative 'cluster' of mutually supporting, cross-fertilizing activities (Nooteboom & Constandse 1995). As Schumpeter proposed, radical innovation appears to arise from novel combinations. When, then, can an innovation be called radical? When the distance between the different technologies that it combines is large? What, precisely, does that mean? How would we measure such distance? Or is it radical when it is radical in its consequences? Perhaps the novel combination of sails was 'radical', in the sense that it combined 'distant' Arab and Western technology, but how about the others? Were the novel combinations of principles of carpentry from ships, dikes, and windmills more or less radical? The question thus is:

Question 4: How do novel combinations arise? How are they related to radical innovation and creative destruction?

Schumpeter already indicated that innovations are not only technical but can also be organizational or commercial, opening new markets for inputs or products.

> An example of an organizational innovation is the use by the British of technical drawings and specifications of ship design (de Vries & van der Woude 1995). This turned tacit into explicit knowledge, and thereby reduced transaction costs. It greatly facilitated transactions between designers and builders of ships, allowing an organizational separation between the two, with resulting specialization. It also allowed teaching to apprentices to be transferred from the muddy shipyard to a classroom, and transformed teaching from the transfer of tacit knowledge into the transfer of codified knowledge, documented in technical drawings and blueprints. It helped ship-building to develop from a craft into an industry.

This innovation seems rather trivial in a technical sense, but it certainly was fairly radical in its effects. It is likely to have contributed to the shift of power from the Dutch to the British. It is an organizational rather than a technical innovation, but also serves to show that the two types of innovation are intertwined.

1.1.2   Life Cycles

According to the 'life-cycle theory' of innovation, innovations typically start with a variety of alternative forms and after a process of technical and commercial selection consolidate and converge on some 'dominant design' (Abernathy 1978, Abernathy & Utterback 1978, Abernathy & Clark 1985). The question is:

Question 5: Why does a dominant design arise, and how?

> Examples of dominant designs are the VHS system for video-recording, and assembly-line production of Ford's Model T (Abernathy 1978). Tushman and Romanelli (1985: 198) give the following examples in addition to the Model T: DC3, 370 computer (IBM), and Fordson tractor, which 'all shaped the evolution of their product class for over 15 years'.

A dominant design allows for efficient, large-scale production and division of labour. The dominant design yields standardization at the interfaces between specialized units, within or between organizations, which is needed for division of labour. A dominant design typically yields a period of stability, in which the new technology or paradigm is refined and improved with incremental innovations (Rosenberg 1972) along a technical trajectory. Expanded demand *enables* large-scale production. Increased competition, as a result of the diffusion of proprietary technology and the consequent decline of initial partial monopolies, *necessitates* that such opportunities be utilized for cost reduction. This pressure is absent, however, when competition can be warded off by collusion, protection of proprietary competencies or other entry barriers, or by staying ahead in innovation.

As indicated, a theoretical problem with life-cycle theory is that it does not explain the origins of novelty, or punctuation, and simply assumes that it arises somehow. That yielded Research Question 1. An empirical problem is that, often, dominant designs precede rather than follow innovation. A related question concerns the sequence of science and technology. Science is aimed at understanding and technology at making things work. Sometimes science precedes technology, which is realized as an application of science, but it can just as well be the other way around: technological practice precedes scientific understanding (Nelson 1993). An example is the steam engine, which preceded the theory of thermodynamics. When we look more closely at science, we see that there also tinkering[1] generally precedes systematic understanding, but this is not so visible because the systematic reconstruction *ex post facto* is what gets published.[2] The question is:

> Question 6: How can we explain when and why dominant designs follow or precede innovation, and when and why technology (tinkering) follows or precedes science (understanding)?

After consolidation of an innovation there are familiar phenomena in its diffusion. This is associated with the notion of 'product life cycles'. Novelty takes time to build up, then breaks through (if it survives), in accelerating diffusion, and then levels off at some saturation level, typically according to an S-shaped path, and then sooner or later is replaced by the next innovation (for a survey, see Mahajan & Wind 1986).[3] Typically, the innovation is adapted during diffusion. The question is:

> Question 7: What is the relation between diffusion and innovation? Is diffusion a mere 'working out' of the innovation, or does it also prepare for the next innovation? Does it tend towards equilibrium or does it prepare for ongoing disequilibrium?

A not so well-known example is the development of self-service retailing, which is interesting because it is organizational rather than technical. It also shows how the diffusion of one innovation leads on to the next innovation. Development started with the emergence of small self-service grocery stores with a limited assortment of grocery products, followed by supermarkets, which added fresh foods and non-food items, which were followed by discount stores, and next superstores. In all cases, in most countries the novelty was initiated by small independent entrepreneurs and then taken over by large chain-store corporations (Nooteboom 1984).

---

[1] The term 'tinkering' is proposed in an attempt at translating the very apt French word, 'bricolage'.
[2] There are good reasons for this. Reporting of research aims to show the argumentative structure, as a basis for efficient criticism, in the 'context of justification', rather than to give an account of how insights developed 'in the context of discovery'.
[3] One model of the S-shaped path is the logistic curve, which entails that diffusion proceeds according to a contagion process, by demonstration and/or 'word of mouth'. Another model is a cumulative-probability distribution (e.g. the normal or log-normal distribution), which entails the explanation that reservation prices of different users follow the density of such a distribution, and as a result of cost reductions the price declines and draws in new users according to the distribution.

According to Vernon's (1966) 'product-cycle' model of internationalization, innovation starts in technologically advanced countries, on the basis of the 'push' of cumulative technological advantage and the 'pull' of advanced demand. Later, after standardization and increasing competition, the technology 'trickles down' to less developed countries to be produced there at lower costs. This theory should not be confused with the life-cycle theory of industrial dynamics discussed above, but it is largely consistent with it. The theory suggests that established technology, organizational structure, and management are simply transferred and imposed on the host country. However, recent evidence does not confirm that theory: products and technologies are allowed to vary in host countries, and multinational companies (MNCs) also transfer research and development (R & D). This will be discussed in Chapter 11. The question is:

> Question 8: Why and how do companies internationalize? Is this purely to diffuse innovations or also to develop them?

1.1.3 Entrepreneurship

Creative destruction is effected by entrepreneurs, and a point of ongoing debate is whether it is primarily small, independent, new firms that play this role (Schumpeterian entrepreneur 'mark I') or large, integrated firms (Schumpeterian entrepreneur 'mark II'). Schumpeter expected that in the course of time innovation would shift from mark I to mark II. Schumpeter's argument was that innovation would be increasingly based on specialist, science-based research, which requires division of labour and more or less formalized co-ordination in large laboratories, and implementation in large production systems. The discussion of this theme of industrial dynamics and entrepreneurship is taken up in Chapter 3, and will proceed in later chapters (Chapters 9 and 11). The question is:

> Question 9: When and why are small firms (or 'industrial districts') more successful in innovation and learning than large ones (or multinational enterprises), or vice versa? How do small and large firms relate in innovation and diffusion?

The facts show clearly that small firms adopt innovations produced elsewhere later than large firms (Nooteboom 1994). They also clearly participate less in R & D (Nooteboom 1991, Vossen & Nooteboom 1996), which would favour the mark-II hypothesis. But when small firms do participate, they tend to do so more intensively than large firms (Nooteboom & Vossen 1995). Both results hold true for most 'Pavitt sectors' (Pavitt 1984) of manufacturing industry. The exception is 'science-based' industries, where large and small firms seem to be equal in both participation and intensity. Examples of such industries are biotechnology, electronics, new materials, and instruments. They tend to produce their own product and process innovations internally.

The other sectors are:

supplier-dominated: traditional, often craft-like, industries such as furniture, leatherwork, apparel, printing. Mostly, process innovations come from suppliers;

'specialized suppliers': producers of machinery, instruments, components. Innovations are often developed in co-operation with industrial customers, who in addition to specification of advanced demand also supply technology and know-how;

'scale-intensive': large-scale assembly (cars, consumer electronics, aeroplanes) and process industries (oil, chemicals, steel). The emphasis lies on process innovations, which are internally generated.

There is also evidence that small firms produce more innovation output per unit of input (for a recent empirical indication, see Brouwer 1997). So, if anything, the evidence points to small firms being more innovative, in the sense of having a greater intensity and a greater productivity of innovation when they do engage in innovation.

There is ample empirical evidence. For a survey see Nooteboom (1994). Jewkes, Sawyers, and Stillerman (1958) reported that of sixty-one inventions during the first half of this century only sixteen could be ascribed to large firms. Mansfield (1969) later reported an empirical investigation that the productivity of R & D in the largest firms is lower than in medium-sized and large firms. A study by Schmookler (quoted in Blair 1972) showed that inventions by operating staff took place almost entirely in smaller businesses. An American report on the 'State of Small Business' in 1983 reported that small firms (less than ten people employed) produced two and a half times as many innovations per employee as large firms (Davis, Hills, & Laforge 1985). On the basis of the innovation database of the Science Policy Research Unit (SPRU) in Brighton, Wyatt (1985) claimed that the relative innovative efficiency (innovative output divided by innovative input) of small firms is much higher than in large firms. In a study of innovation data in the US Small Business Administration database, Acs and Audretsch (1990) found a higher average rate of innovation among small than among large firms. The tendency of large firms to hold back on the innovations that they do produce (to protect stakes in existing markets) is reflected in a study undertaken at George Washington University. It showed that firms with more than \$100 million sales or more than 100 patents actually applied only 51 per cent of their patents, compared with 71 per cent for smaller firms (quoted in Weinberg 1990).

Often, small rather than large firms produce innovative applications of new technology, alone or in industrial districts. Often the basic idea or technology is available in large firms, and indeed produced in their laboratories, but is not transformed into novel products and practices.

Examples are: electric light (Thomas Edison), the telephone (Alexander Graham Bell), assembly-line production of cars (Henry Ford), aeroplanes (the Wright brothers), microcomputers (Silicon Valley), computer-aided design (Rothwell & Zegveld 1985), self-service retailing (Nooteboom 1984). The latter study gives a unique illustration of a series of life cycles of retail forms, that were initiated by small firms, who were bypassed by large firms, which subsequently moved on to the next innovation, while small firms stayed on. Both the innovators and the laggards were small firms. Innovating small firms are typically outsiders who are not committed to the existing system. Laggard small firms hang on to residual, specialized market niches that allow for small-scale production.

However, we do observe both mark I and mark II entrepreneurship.

Thus, Saxenian (1994) noted that while in Silicon Valley it is small firms that develop microelectronics, in the Boston area it is large firms. McKelvey (1996*b*) noted that large pharmaceutical companies have survived radical innovations in genetic engineering, and McKelvey and Texier (2000) documented how Ericsson made radical innovations in mobile telecommunication, surviving the corresponding transformation of products, production, and organization.

1.1.4   Life Cycles of Firms

In addition to life cycles of products, production processes, and technologies, there are life cycles in the development of firms. Typically, small, innovative firms, if successful, run into obstacles of development. After an entrepreneurial stage of innovation and convergence of new technology on a dominant design, there is a need to formalize. In order to grow and survive, successful innovators often need to shift from an informal structure and culture to more formal ones. The entrepreneur has to delegate responsibilities and set up procedures of co-ordination and control. With division of labour among dispersed, specialized units it becomes impossible to maintain direct supervision. This bureaucratization often does not fit with the chaotic, charismatic entrepreneurial style that created initial success. Often, the firm cannot successfully take this hurdle, and, then, is often taken over by a more managerially oriented leader or larger firm that has more taste, talent, and experience for a certain amount of bureaucratization. Thus, the takeover of entrepreneurial small firms by large firms can be beneficial to both and to society. But that is not necessarily so. The entrepreneurial drive of the small firm can get stifled in the large bureaucracy. Sometimes innovative firms are taken over to freeze the innovation, allowing the acquiring firm to reap the profits from established products for longer.

> Question 10: How do firms develop, and how can they survive? How does this relate to entrepreneurship?

1.1.5   Organizational Forms

The themes of entrepreneurship, firm structure, and firm development connect with a recurrent and pervasive theme in the literature on organizational forms. Volatile conditions require disintegrated, 'organic' structures of small firms or autonomous units in large firms. Stable conditions require more integrated, 'mechanistic', or bureaucratic organizations, with more or less elaborately, tightly, and formally co-ordinated units of activity (Burns & Stalker 1961, Emery & Trist 1965, Thompson 1967, Lawrence & Lorsch 1967).

More recently, these issues have been studied in surveys of multiple firms as well as case studies of individual firms. Damanpour (1991) gave a meta-analysis of twenty-three survey studies of the correlations of the adoption and implementation of a variety of internally and externally generated innovations with a range of organizational variables. The main outcome was that centralization had an almost universal negative effect, and formalization mostly had a negative effect, with some exceptions for service innovations and innovations in not-for-profit organizations. This confirms expectations on the basis of the considerations given above.

In a case study, Burgelman (1996) tells the story of INTEL Corporation. At first it had a highly decentralized, entrepreneurial structure, with little direction and with co-ordination of initiatives coming up from below. An executive is quoted as follows (Burgelman 1996: 413): 'As the company grew, we tried to replicate the environment that had led to making "correct" decisions by forming relatively small business units and creating a bottom-up strategic planning system. However, that became very unwieldy . . . The system is now more top down'.

The research question is:

> Question 11: How are organizational integration and disintegration related to innovation? How does this connect with the issue of firm size in relation to innovation?

1.1.6   *Organizational Learning*

The preceding themes connect with an emerging debate, in the organizational literature, on organizational learning. A distinction is made between first- and second-order learning (Hedberg, Nystrom, & Starbuck 1976, Fiol & Lyles 1985) or, equivalently, between 'single-loop and double-loop' learning (Argyris & Schön 1978). The first is learning to do existing things better (more efficiently) and the second is learning to do new things (from a new perspective). This is also connected with the notion of 'parametric' change (Langlois & Robertson 1995) as opposed to 'architectural' change (Henderson & Clark 1990). The Austrian economist Hayek distinguished between two kinds of 'spontaneous order': the first kind entailed the operation of rules, the second kind entailed the change of those rules. Holland (1975) and March (1991) distinguished between exploitation and exploration. The first entails efficient use of existing competencies and the second the development of new ones. Exploitation is required for firms to survive in the short term, and exploration is required to survive in the long term. Thus, the literature states that in order to survive now and later the firm must perform both. But this entails a paradox. Exploitation requires the maintenance of existing identity, knowledge, and practices, with a certain amount of control and co-ordination, in a dominant design. Exploration requires their change, with a loosening of control and co-ordination. Exploitation entails a danger of 'inertia' that blocks exploration. First-order learning entails improved exploitation, and second-order learning entails successful exploration. How can one resolve this paradox of stability and change? This is Research Question 12. Volberda (1998) called it the 'flexibility paradox'. Earlier, I called it the paradox of identity and change (Nooteboom 1989). The capability to balance exploitation and exploration is perhaps the greatest challenge and most important task of both management and technology policy. A crucial question thus is how the paradox can be resolved.

> Question 12: How can firms combine first- and second-order learning, or exploitation and exploration?

Question 13: How and why does inertia arise? When is it bad and when not? How is this related to dominant designs?

Question 14: How can inertia be evaded or overcome, to proceed with further innovation or learning?

A famous example of the emergence of inertia is the Ford motor company. Having achieved high economy of scale in standardized assembly-line production, it refused to differentiate its product, in contrast with General Motors, which saw that the market was ready for differentiation (Abernathy 1978). Tushman and Romanelli (1985: 172, 176, 195) tell the story of ATT, which started as an innovative, small, R & D-intensive Bell company in 1974. In the period 1913–76 it developed from local sales 'through a loosely structured organization whose core values centred on flexibility, research and innovation' (p. 176) to 'universal, low cost service as core values, delivered through a vertically integrated and highly formalized structure' (p. 176). The Dutch Philips company has been trying hard, with a succession of new Chief Executive Officers (CEOs), to break through its rigidity, with limited success, leading up to the newest replacement of the CEO by someone from outside the industry (Boonstra).

Several authors (Nonaka & Takeuchi 1995, Choo 1998, Volberda 1998) have considered these questions. The discussion of this theme of organizational learning is taken up in Chapter 2, and will proceed in later chapters (Chapters 9, 10, and 13). Nonaka and Takeuchi pointed out the importance of metaphor in the creation of new knowledge, because it establishes connections between previously unconnected areas of experience.

Question 15: How and when does metaphor work as an instrument of innovation? How does this relate to the notion of innovation through novel combinations?

An example given by Nonaka and Takeuchi is the use of a beer can as a metaphor for the design of a copying machine. Henry Ford did not strike out at random when he employed the principle of the assembly line. He did not invent it out of the blue. He adopted the idea from the mail-order business: clerks sit behind a conveyor belt, in front of shelves of products, to fill boxes moving past according to order lists appended to them. Windmills form an innovative combination of the watermill, which provided the mechanical technology of horizontal shaft, transmission, and gears, and sailing ships, which provided the use of wind rather than water power (Mokyr 1990: 45).

Exploration and innovation require diversity. This is related to the question concerning the role of organizational disintegration: novelty requires looser structures for greater diversity. It is also related to issues of consensus and disagreement.

Question 16: When, and on what, is consensus among top management good for firm performance and when disagreement?

Hrebeniak and Snow (1982) found a positive association between performance and management consensus on the strengths and weaknesses of the firm. Dess (1987) found that in a fragmented industry with sharp competition, performance is positively associated with both consensus on goals and consensus on methods, separately (the conjunction of the two is not needed for success).

Bourgeois (1980) found that performance is positively associated with consensus on means but negatively with consensus on goals. Grinyer and Norburn (1977–8) also found a negative association between performance and consensus on goals. De Woot, Heyvaert, and Martou (1978) found a negative association between performance and consensus on methods. Controlling for differences in the degree to which the environment is turbulent, Bourgeois (1985) found a positive association between performance and diversity in top-management perception of uncertainty, as well as diversity in goals, for all levels of turbulence.

An emerging view in the innovation literature is that innovation arises, in particular, from interaction between organizations (Lundvall 1985, 1988, 1993, McKelvey 1996*b*, Nooteboom 1992*a*, 1999*a*). The question is why this is so, and how it works:

Question 17: What is the role of interfirm interaction in innovation and learning?

Question 18: What are the conditions for learning in collaboration between organizations?

A classic stylized fact is that small, technologically not very advanced firms do not make much use of universities or technological centres, and employ more proximate partners such as customers, suppliers, banks, colleagues (for a survey, see Nooteboom 1994). Cohen and Levinthal (1990) show that collaboration in R & D does not reduce but on the contrary increases internal R & D, to maintain the 'absorptive capacity' needed to utilize the R & D of partners. Colombo and Garrone (1996) find similar results for information-technology sectors. Similarly, on the basis of patenting studies, Granstrand, Patel, and Pavitt (1997) find that firms need to maintain technological diversity even when they engage in outside collaboration. Kleinknecht and Reijnen (1992) and Rocha (2000), however, find no such effect.

The theme of learning by interaction is taken up in Chapters 3 and 8. Issues of learning invite a deeper analysis of theories of knowledge and language, which is taken up in Chapters 6 and 7. There, it will be argued, among other things, that the role of metaphor is closely related to the notion of innovation by novel combinations, and that indeed interaction between people and organizations is crucial for learning.

1.1.7   Erratic Novelty

Novelty is typically unexpected and erratic, with other results than those looked for. This is the 'King Saul effect'. However, while innovation is prone to failure and surprise, and entails much trial and error, it is not blind and completely random; it is serendipitous. Invention occurs only to the prepared mind.

Looking for a better dynamo for bicycle lights, Philips Company hit upon the development of an electric shaver. Bessemer invented his steel-making process while trying to solve problems of a spinning cannon shell (Mokyr 1990: 116). A handful of people stumbled upon X-rays, but Marie Curie was the only one to see what it might mean, and what its implications and uses might be.

Question 19: How random or systematic is novelty? How does it happen that search yields results in unexpected directions? How prepared does one have to be in order to invent? How does this preparation take place?

Another well-known phenomenon is that often attempted innovations that are technically viable and of superior quality are subject to failure for lack of fit with consumer demand; or, perhaps less obvious, for lack of fit with wider technological systems of testing, implementation, or production, or with commercial systems of distribution.

A widely publicized case is the failure of Philips's and Sony's systems for video recording (respectively the 'Video 2000'and 'Betamax'), to the benefit of the technically inferior system of VHS that now prevails. In this particular case the failure was because of unanticipated network externalities in the availability of appropriate software in distribution channels, in the form of pre-recorded video tapes and tapes of appropriate length for recording baseball games. The VHS producers utilized that to gain a first-mover advantage that prevailed over technical superiority.

The lack of fit also includes what is called the 'Leonardo effect' (Mokyr 1990). Leonardo da Vinci conceived many ideas that could not be realized or even tested with contemporary technology, such as his idea of a flying man.

The idea of a submarine first occurred in 1624 (Mokyr 1990: 58). In the seventeenth century the Dutch inventor Christiaan Huygens thought of the principle of the internal-combustion engine, on the basis of exploding small amounts of gunpowder (Mokyr 1990: 73).

Related to this, and part of the general problem of lack of fit, is the phenomenon that often innovations are first applied where their potential cannot be fully realized.

An example is the development of the semiconductor industry (Stoelhorst 1997). It started with the transistor as a substitute for the vacuum tube. But its potential went further: its greater reliability, greater speed, lower power usage and heat dissipation opened up opportunities for much more complex electrical systems. But the manual soldering of the connections between the discrete components formed a bottleneck: it was expensive and generated too many errors. Ultimately, the answer was to make a range of components (resistors and capacitors next to amplifiers) in the same silicon technology, and integrate them in an overall system including connections between them, in an integrated circuit. It was only then that the full potential could be realized.

Question 20: How can we explain fits and misfits of novelty? What are the conditions for survival?

Another stylized fact is that in the beginning innovations often carry a burden of inappropriate leftovers from old practice, or fall-backs on such practice. This might be called the phenomenon of 'hysteresis' (which originally referred to a phenomenon in electricity: the lagging of magnetic effects behind their causes).

An example is that in the transition from the use of wood to the use of iron in civil engineering joints were still made in the form of wedges, needed for wood, while for steel this created an unnecessary complication. When direction indicators were built into cars, they first mimicked hand waving with small, finger-shaped swivelling devices flipping out. Subsequently, when cars obtained lights, little lights were built into the flips, until someone leaped to the idea that a blinking light would serve the purpose, eliminating the costs of construction, wear, tear, and repair of mechanical flips. But sometimes there is innovation in falling back on old practice. Mokyr (1990)

TABLE 1.1   *Research questions*

1. What are the sources and conditions of paradigm switches, punctuations, or radical innovations?
2. How can we identify paradigm switches and punctuations? (Are they the same?). How can we demarcate incremental and radical innovation? How can we operationalize 'discontinuity'?
3. What are the meaning and role of 'paradigms' here?
4. How do novel combinations arise? How are they related to radical innovation and creative destruction?
5. Why does a dominant design arise, and how?
6. How can we explain when and why dominant designs follow or precede innovation, and when and why technology (tinkering) follows or precedes science (understanding)?
7. What is the relation between diffusion and innovation? Is diffusion a mere 'working out' of the innovation, or does it also prepare for the next innovation? Does it tend towards equilibrium or does it prepare for ongoing disequilibrium?
8. Why and how do companies internationalize? Is this purely to diffuse innovations or also to develop them?
9. When and why are small firms (or 'industrial districts') more successful in innovation and learning than large ones (or multinational enterprises), or vice versa? How do small and large firms relate in innovation and diffusion?
10. How do firms develop, and how can they survive? How does this relate to entrepreneurship?
11. How are organizational integration and disintegration related to innovation? How does this connect with the issue of firm size in relation to innovation?
12. How can firms combine first- and second-order learning, or exploitation and exploration?
13. How and why does inertia arise? When is it bad and when not? How is this related to dominant designs?
14. How can inertia be evaded or overcome, to proceed with further innovation or learning?
15. How and when does metaphor work as an instrument of innovation? How does this relate to the notion of innovation by 'novel combinations'?
16. When, and on what, is consensus among top management good for firm performance and when disagreement?
17. What is the role of interfirm interaction in innovation and learning?
18. What are the conditions for learning in collaboration between organizations?
19. How random or systematic is novelty? How does it happen that search yields results in unexpected directions? How prepared does one have to be in order to invent? How does this preparation take place?
20. How can we explain fits and misfits of novelty? What are the conditions for survival?
21. How can we explain hysteresis: old technologies staying on as parts of new technologies?
22. How are all these phenomena of innovation and learning connected between the levels of people, organizations, and innovation systems?

reports the case of aspirin (acetyl salicic acid): it had been discovered and rejected in favour of sodium calicic acid, until a Bayer chemist fell back on aspirin when its substitute caused undesirable side effects.

Question 21: How can we explain hysteresis: old technologies staying on as parts of new technologies?

These issues of fit are taken up, in particular, in Chapter 10.

1.1.8 Summary of Questions

For the themes of innovation, entrepreneurship, industry life cycles, firm life cycles, organizational forms, organizational learning, and the erratic nature of novelty twenty-one research questions have emerged. They follow from the central question concerning the sources and conditions of radical innovation. A multilevel theory is needed which explains how people in organizations learn, and by their interaction produce organizational learning, which results in innovation and the transformation of industries. Thus, one important, final question has to be added:

Question 22: How are all these phenomena of innovation and learning connected between the levels of people, organizations, and innovation systems?

The questions are collected in Table 1.1. Chapter 14 reviews the answers that this book is able to offer.

The phenomena and questions reviewed above might be compared with the 'common patterns' that Malerba and Orsenigo (1996: 66) identified in their survey of the dynamics and evolution in a range of industries, studied by different researchers: cars, semiconductors, biotechnology, computers, aircraft, photolithographic-alignment equipment, and machine tools. They are specified in Table 1.2.

TABLE 1.2   *Common patterns*

Technological discontinuities are followed by periods of incremental technical change and, subsequently, by new discontinuities.

Entry tends to occur in specific periods of evolution, not necessarily only after technological discontinuities.

Processes of industrial concentration and competence-enhancing (Henderson & Clark 1990) technical change are followed by periods of competence destroying technological change.

Processes of specialization, diversification, and vertical integration always take place with various forms and intensity in certain stages of industry evolution.

Government policies and public institutions always play a major role.

Great institutional and organizational differences across countries are present.

Source: Malerba and Orsenigo (1996: 66)

In their discussion of the research agenda, at the end of their survey, Malerba and Orsenigo (1996: 83) arrive at a conclusion that expresses the challenge that I wish to address in this book:

the sort of empirical analysis discussed here needs . . . to be strictly complemented by the development of rigorous theoretical efforts aimed at the understanding of the general mechanisms, if any, which generate the regularities and differences in industrial evolution. Conversely, such an effort raises several fundamental questions related to the basic philosophy, methodology and tools of theoretical analysis and strains the scope of current theoretical models

1.2 PERSPECTIVES

This paragraph reviews the basic notions to be used in an attempt to answer the research questions. They are the fundamental notions of dynamics, revolution, evolution, uncertainty, abduction, institutions, structure, and agency.

1.2.1 *Dynamics, Revolutions, and Evolution*

In his work on industrial dynamics Dosi (1984, Dosi *et al.* 1988) was inspired by Kuhn's (1970) work on scientific revolutions. Kuhn proposed that in science there are prolonged periods of 'normal' science: 'puzzle solving' within the established 'paradigm', punctuated by occasional 'revolutions' of 'paradigm shift'. Dosi's use of the term 'paradigm' derives from his inspiration by Kuhn. However, neither the demarcation of revolutions nor the notion of paradigm is clear. Therefore, I included a question concerning the meaning of paradigms in the list of research questions (Question 3). Masterman (1970) noted that the term 'paradigm' has twenty-one meanings. Among others: exemplar to be followed (this is the literal translation from the ancient Greek), illustrative case, disciplinary framework, basic perspective, criteria of good scientific conduct. An exemplar in economics is Adam Smith's 'pin factory' to illustrate economies of scale on the basis of division of labour.

How do we identify scientific revolutions? This is related to Research Question 2: How do we identify radical innovation?

> Examples of scientific revolutions are those of Copernicus/Galileo, Newton, and Einstein in physics, of Kant in philosophy, of Darwin in biology, and of Keynes in economics. But there are many cases where we hesitate between revolution or mere 'drastic change'. Does Herbert Simon's work on bounded rationality constitute a revolution in economics or business; Karl Weick's work on sense making in organization theory?

Attempts have been made to explain industrial dynamics and innovation by means of evolutionary theory. This is already apparent, in the above presentation, in the use of the notion of 'punctuated equilibrium'. That term is based on the work of Eldredge and Gould (1972) and Gould (1989). Evolutionary metaphors have been used for the theory of organizational development (Burgelman 1996, Tushman & Romanelli 1985, Romanelli & Tushman 1994). More prominently and extensively, they have been used to model industrial dynamics (Veblen 1919, Hannan & Freeman 1977, 1984, Nelson & Winter 1982, Witt 1993*b*, Hodgson 1993, Vromen 1995, Metcalfe 1998). The evolutionary perspective emphasizes the variety of firms, subjected to a 'selection environment' of markets and other institutions, yielding dynamics at the population level of industries. One point of debate is how adaptive rather than passive, or inert, firms are. Are they able to adapt to the selection environment, or to transform it, in order to survive in the long run? In contrast with biology, in economic systems people construct mental or other models of nature and markets, with which they develop speculative arguments, based on experience, about possible futures and possible effects of innovative actions. They think, communicate, and learn. In Chapter 4 it will be concluded that we should turn to theories of knowledge, learning, and language. These are taken up in Chapters 6 and 7.

As indicated before, the different orders of learning (first-order vs. second-order learning or single-loop vs. double-loop learning) are closely related to the distinction between exploitation and exploration. A similar distinction also arises in cognitive science. As formulated by Rose (1992: 138):

To function effectively . . . all living organisms must show two contradictory properties: retain stability—specificity—during development and adult life, resisting the pressures of the endless buffeting of environmental contingency, both day-to-day and over a lifetime. And they must show plasticity—that is, the ability to adapt and modify this specificity in the face of repeated experience . . . To unravel the dialectic between specificity and plasticity and to understand its mechanisms form some of the major tasks of modern biology

Is there perhaps a common conceptual issue underlying all these issues: the relation between incremental and radical innovation, between practice according to a techno-economic paradigm and the breaking of such paradigms, between equilibrium and its punctuation, between first- and second-order learning, between exploitation and exploration, between specificity and plasticity? The working hypothesis of this book is that there is such a common ground. As indicated in the previous paragraph, the central purpose of this book is to make an attempt at developing a general logic, or heuristic, of discovery which underlies both innovation and organizational learning and explains the relation between the two, as well as the relation between exploitation and exploration.

1.2.2 Structure and Agency

Much debate has been spent on what exactly institutions entail, how changeable they are, and how they vary across different countries. There is a literature on 'varieties of capitalism' (e.g. Hollingsworth & Boyer 1997, Whitley 1998), which proposes that institutional differences between different countries are pervasive and durable, and that this will prevent convergence even under pressures of globalization. This issue of the structure and variability of institutions is considered in Chapter 5, and is further developed in the chapter on innovation systems (Chapter 12). A central issue is also how institutions, at the macro level of the 'institutional environment', connect with the micro behaviour of firms, to produce outcomes in terms of innovation and organizational structure. This is also taken up in Chapter 12. It will be argued that the mediating variable is co-ordination, including the governance of interfirm relations. This is connected with the idea, in the literature on innovation systems, that innovations arise from interaction between organizations (Lundvall 1985, 1988, 1993).

The issue of institutions, their role in an economic selection environment, their variability, and the extent to which they can be modified by the behavioural units that they select, is close, if not identical, to the issue of structure and agency in sociology (Archer 1995). How do social and cultural structures condition (enable, constrain) actions, and how do these actions reproduce, elaborate, or transform those structures? In view of this it will be argued that we need to connect economics and sociology. This is further explored in Chapter 5.

1.2.3   Knowledge and Learning

The Austrian economist Hayek recognized that knowledge is distributed, localized, and often largely tacit, and he characterized competition as a 'discovery process' (Hayek 1976). This dynamic-process view of markets is connected with the Austrian assumption of subjectivism: different people not only have different preferences (as all economists would agree), but also have different knowledge. I add, and emphasize, that they have different knowledge even when they obtain the same data or 'information'.

This claim has to be supported by a theory of knowledge, and such a theory will be presented in Chapter 6. It is a theory of knowledge construction in interaction with the physical and social environment. It is in interaction with nature and with others, in markets, organizations, and private contexts, that people construct information from data and develop their own knowledge and views of the world. This yields a useful perspective for the present purpose: it is in their mutual interaction that both people and firms learn and contribute to innovation. This is related to Research Questions 17 and 18. This perspective of interaction as a basis for cognition further strengthens the need to connect sociology and economics.

Interaction between firms can entail both competition and co-operation, and therefore Hayek's view should be extended: it is the market more generally, and not just competition, that constitutes a discovery process. The term 'discovery' is a good one, for two reasons. First, discovery is readily seen to embrace both innovation in markets and learning in firms, and that reflects the aim of this book. Second, it indicates that the greatest challenge is to develop not just a theory of incremental innovation, first-order learning, and exploitation, but to go beyond that to a theory of radical innovation, paradigm breaks, second-order learning, and exploration. The term 'discovery' conveys that ambition. However, some may understand discovery as revealing something that already exists, and that is not the connotation intended here: discovery here includes creation of novelty.

1.2.4   Abduction

While it may be too obvious to require discussion, it should be remembered that discovery entails real or radical uncertainty, in the sense of Knight (1921). In other words, it goes beyond risk, which is associated with a known, closed set of possible alternatives, with a probability distribution attached to them.[4] In fact, the set of options to choose from is open, and often options are discovered or created after, not prior to, action. Options are often options to discover further options. This requires a logic or heuristic of 'abduction' (Peirce 1957): How do we explore options that are unknown? How do we arrive at new hypotheses that have some chance of viability? Of all the novel ways of doing things that we can think of, which should we try, and how do we find out what other, as yet unknown, options there are?

One way to try and deal with uncertainty is to make contingency plans on the basis of scenarios, as in the famous scenario planning by the Shell Oil Company.[5] However, while we can think of many logically possible future worlds, we lack knowledge about their likelihood, we have no way of knowing whether we have thought of all possible futures, and we cannot be certain that the futures we have thought of contain the actual future. If we attach subjective likelihoods to scenarios, we should be aware that they do not satisfy the usual axioms of probabilities. If we are lucky, the future approaches one of the scenarios we constructed sufficiently closely for us to implement the corresponding contingency plan.

In particular, the future is difficult to predict because actions will have unforeseeable consequences and there will be strategic reactions to our actions from others, which are themselves difficult to predict. Interactions in social systems have unforeseeable and unintended systemic effects. We are playing games whose participants, strategies, and pay-offs are revealed only as the game is played, and then shift in the process. Thus, discovery goes beyond search among existing options to include the creation of new options and, as Schumpeter proposed, this creation is often destructive of existing resources and competencies.

To achieve the purpose of this book, the problem of abduction needs to be solved. How can we make steps into the unknown, in exploration, while preserving existing resources in such a way that exploitation is maintained? How do we set about creation with a minimum of destruction? What is the optimal process of discovery? We need a heuristic to move from present competence to novel competence, while surviving in the process. The main task of this book is to develop such a heuristic. This is taken up in Chapter 9. There, I will build on the basic intuition of Peirce's 'pragmaticism' that novelty arises from practice. As Peirce (1957: 239) formulated it: 'Thought requires achievement for its own development.'

---

[4] In the absence of a distribution, the theory prescribes that one should employ a homogeneous distribution: all eventualities have equal probability. This may be revised according to a Bayesian procedure as more information becomes available.

[5] I stood at the cradle of Shell's scenario planning, developing models for the board of managing directors to assess the impact of scenarios and contingency plans to deal with them, in the early seventies, prior to the oil crisis. What actually happened in that crisis came close to one of the scenarios identified.

1.3   DISCIPLINES

This book employs several disciplines. Many people claim that interdisciplinary research cannot yield deep and consistent results. With this book I hope to prove the contrary. The disciplines used are management and organization, unorthodox (evolutionary and institutional) economics, sociology, and unorthodox (situated-action) theory of knowledge and language. There is also a connection with theories of complex adaptive systems, with the topic of self-organization or auto-poiesis.

There are overlapping themes in these disciplines, and they can learn from each other. A secondary aim of this book is to help in their mutual acquaintance, to stimulate novel combinations between them. However, it is perhaps too much to expect the reader to absorb a full range of disciplines. This paragraph is offered only to show the reader what main lines of heritage I pick up from the disciplines he is familiar with. I try to indicate my position on the maps of different disciplines, so to speak. The reader can skip the sections on disciplines he is not familiar with. In a final Section some reflections are given on the historical, philosophical roots of the central issue of stability and change.

1.3.1   Economics

The book is economic in the original sense, as in the work of Adam Smith and Marshall, that it investigates the determinants of wealth and material well-being. As a scholar in the area of management and organization I feel affinity with Marshall's interest in the practical affairs of business. This will be reflected in regular asides, in a contrasting typeface, with illustrations from business practice. Adam Smith is a source of inspiration for his interest in linking economics with psychology, in his 'theory of moral sentiments'. He went beyond the contemporary economist's exclusive preoccupation with the desire to pursue material gain. My focus on learning and the paradox of exploitation and exploration connects with Penrose's attention to the utilization and development of organizational capabilities. As indicated, I share Hayek's view of competition, or more broadly the market, as a discovery process. I also share the Austrian notion of subjectivism: the dispersion and variety of knowledge across different people in different positions. Veblen and Nelson and Winter have been inspirational with their evolutionary view of markets. What Veblen, Schumpeter, Hayek, and Nelson and Winter have in common is their orientation towards economic process rather than the (equilibrium) outcomes of that process. However, in spite of the attractions of the evolutionary view I am inclined to shift the focus to a perspective of self-organization inspired not so much by biology as by social and cognitive science.

The book is not economic in Lionel Robbins's sense of being occupied mostly or exclusively with alternative uses of scarce resources. Rather, it is concerned with the development of novel resources. The analysis does not take rational choice as its basic assumption, but rather investigates the sources and limitations of reason.

1.3.2   Sociology

This book is sociological in the sense that it takes interaction between people as the basis for knowledge and language. I do not adhere to methodological individualism; I recognize that social and cultural structure have an existence and causal efficacy of their own. I do, however, grant that they are the (unintended) result, directly and indirectly, in a hierarchy of effects, of the actions of people. To some, this may not be a denial but a confirmation of methodological individualism, since it accepts the idea that somewhere in time, by some possibly complex set of causal mechanisms, people were the efficient cause of institutions. This book is not sociological in the sense of seeing individual behaviour as completely determined by the social context. It does not adhere to methodological collectivism. I maintain that people yield the only efficient cause there is, and that people have their own individuality in spite of the fact that their identity is determined to a large extent by their interaction with others, in social contexts.

For my perspective of interactionism, G. H. Mead has been an important source of inspiration. For the interaction between structure and agency I was interested for a while in Giddens's structuration theory, until Margaret Archer created doubt with her claim that it neglects the fact that structure and agency interact as separate realities. People are born into specific positions and endowments in a current structure that is largely the unintended consequence of actions of past generations. Next, as agents they may to a greater or lesser extent contribute to the reproduction or change of structure, in their actions in roles embedded in that structure.

This book tries to operate on the basis of 'methodological interactionism'. The crux of this is that people are the only efficient causes there are, but their cognitive and other capabilities of action are constructed in processes of interaction with others, which are conditioned by social and cultural structure. I claim that this resolves a number of problems in economics and provides the basis for a unified behavioural science.

1.3.3   Cognitive Science

My constructivist view of knowledge aligns well with some sources in cognitive science. In developmental psychology these are, above all, Piaget and Vygotsky, with their view that intelligence is internalized action, is constructed from interaction with the physical and social environment. Piaget indicated how cognitive development might proceed in a sequence of stages. Vygotsky indicated, in contrast with Piaget, how the construction of intelligence is socially embedded and supported from the very beginning of child development. This is discussed in Chapter 6 and the stage theory of development is taken up in a stage theory of discovery in Chapter 9.

My view of cognitive development can be summed up as follows: An endowment of genes yields a flexible but still limited ability to construct neural structures. This structuring occurs in interaction with the physical and social environment. Tentative cognitive structures are reinforced by success in that interaction. This is the basis for cognition and language, which yield a basis for action, which affects the environment. This social embedding provides a link with, and a cognitive underpinning for, the interactionist perspective taken in this book.

In my philosophy of language a central source is (the later) Wittgenstein, with his pragmatic notion of 'meaning as use' and his notion of 'family resemblance' among members of a class. Meanings are not fixed outside practice but are disambiguated and constituted in practice. As a result they are not universal and closed but context-dependent and open to change. The notion of family resemblance entails that members of the class that constitutes the reference or 'extension' of a concept do not necessarily share essentialist characteristics that define the class, but typically have characteristics that may be shared pairwise, without any characteristics being shared by all members. Typically, there will be a prototype, and class membership is judged by resemblance to the prototype. This notion is connected with the notion of an 'exemplar', which is one of the meanings of the term 'paradigm'. The prototype serves as a 'default', i.e. a temporary standard that may shift when it is systematically contradicted. In linguistics, an important source for me was Ferdinand de Saussure, with his distinction between the intersubjective order of language ('*langue*') and creative, deviant, individual parlance ('*parole*'). However, while primarily Saussure had a structuralist interest in the former, I am primarily interested in the latter: how idiosyncratic parlance can shift intersubjective meaning. As will be discussed in Chapter 7, this relates to the notion of the 'hermeneutic circle', from the work of Gadamer and Ricoeur.[6]

All this aligns well with the emerging, unorthodox, situated-action view in cognitive science, discussed in Chapter 6. This view entails that, rather than being available prior to action and outside of context, mental structures ('representations') and meanings are formed by context-specific action. Thereby they are context-dependent, and are subject to shifts triggered by context-specific, idiosyncratic action. I propose and will argue that this connects with the sociologist's issue of structure and agency, the evolutionary economist's issue of selection and adaptation, and the management scholar's issue of exploitation and exploration, and that it provides a basis for a better understanding of all three.

1.3.4   A Field of Literature

It was noted above that industrial innovation and organizational learning must be causally connected somehow, and that we need several disciplines to deal with them. However, the corresponding streams of literature are only weakly connected. Insights in innovation and learning are fragmented and spread across a wide field of literature,

---

[6] As will be argued in more detail in Chapter 7, I propose that the crux of the hermeneutic circle is as follows. Sentences (or discourses) are constructed by selecting elements from existing 'paradigmatic repertoires' of concepts and combining them according to compositional rules, but, in the juxtaposition of words (or sentences) in specific, context-bound sentences (or discourses), novel connections between meanings shift paradigmatic repertoires.

with different, largely disconnected streams that focus on different aspects, aggregation levels, and perspectives from different disciplines. Some of these are:

- studies of organizational learning in the literature on management and organization
- 'population ecology' in sociology
- studies on innovation in the literature on evolutionary and neo-Schumpeterian economics
- a related literature on innovation systems, to which sociologists also contribute
- a literature on institutional economics which studies the boundaries of organizations, interorganizational relations, alliances, and networks and the way in which these form the basis for such systems of innovation
- connected to that, a wider literature on networks which taps both economics and sociology
- a marketing literature which is especially strong in the diffusion of innovations
- a literature on system dynamics, complex adaptive systems, and computational methods for the modelling of dynamic processes
- different literatures in cognitive science

It is impossible for any single scholar to embrace the whole of this literature, and hazardous to attempt a survey: that would inevitably contain gaps. Parts of this voluminous literature are explored in Part I, in a quest for building-blocks to answer the research questions in Table 1.1. Chapter 2 considers the literature on management and organization. Chapter 3 considers the unorthodox streams in economics: Austrian/Schumpeterian and the resource–competence view. Chapter 4 considers evolutionary theory. Chapter 5 analyses the structure of institutions. Chapters 6 and 7 turn to cognitive science.

There are strong connections between Schumpeterian and evolutionary economics and innovation systems, because of their shared interest in innovation. There is also a link between evolutionary and institutional economics, because institutions form part of the selection environment in economic evolution, and the evolution of institutions themselves is an important issue. In institutional economics there is a substantial difference between 'neo-institutionalism', which harks back to the 'old' American institutionalists, and the 'new' institutional economics, which focuses on transaction-cost economics. The differences are discussed in Chapter 5.

In sociology, industrial dynamics and inertia or adaptiveness of firms have been studied in population ecology. Sociologists have of course been engaged in institutional issues much longer and more extensively than economists. It sometimes seems that in their study of institutions economists are naïve and simplistic about social interaction, and are reinventing sociology, rather than making use of it. On the other hand, sociologists are naïve and simplistic about the working of markets and competition, rather than making use of economics.

In the literature on innovation systems, innovation has often been seen as something that is produced in interaction between firms and other organizations. This yields a link with the literature on networks, in both economics and sociology.

Cognitive science has emerged as a combination of cognitive psychology, artificial intelligence, linguistics, and semiotics. It has as yet had only limited impact on the other streams. Of course it is connected with social psychology, and through that it is connected to organization theory, with notions of 'framing', 'mental models', 'schemata', 'action learning'. But there is scope for further development of foundations from cognitive science. This is to be expected not only in issues of cognition, but also in issues of language, meaning, and communication, in order further to strengthen the foundations of the role of language and the use of symbols in organizational learning. This is taken up in Chapters 6 and 7.

Relevant also is the literature on systems dynamics, complexity, adaptation, self-organization—a well-known centre in this area is the Santa Fé Institute. In the present book that literature is incorporated only to a very limited extent, simply because I am familiar only with a small part of it (Khalil 1998). I suspect that the heuristic of learning that is offered in Chapter 9 is in fact a theory of self-organization. A brief discussion on this is given in Chapter 11. One reservation, probably just a prejudice that I have, is the suspicion that models derived from physics and biology may not satisfy the specific conditions of systems of intelligent, sense-making, socially interacting people. Interesting methods have been developed for computational modelling, as opposed to analytical models of dynamic processes, in cognitive science (especially in its branch of artificial intelligence). They have also been used in evolutionary economics. More recently, they have emerged also in the area of organization theory.[7]

If all these streams of literature have a contribution to make to the theory of learning and innovation, how can we bring them together in a reasonably coherent fashion? I propose that the 'resource–competence' view, going back to the work of Penrose (1959), occupies a central position. It serves to connect and integrate the other streams. This is discussed in Chapter 3, which looks at organizations as bundles of competencies, at learning as the development of competencies, partly on the basis of interorganizational interaction, supported by institutions, exploitation as their utilization, exploration as their development, and markets as their discovery and selection.

1.3.5   Towards a New Discipline?

We are facing a dilemma. On the one hand, it is clear that connections should be crafted between the different fields of literature. On the other hand, there is the danger of eclecticism: we may get lost in syncretism. The price of leaving a disciplinary fold and gathering eclectic pickings from a variety of disciplines is lack of coherence and lack of cumulative development. As will be argued later, the movement towards more or less stable dominant designs, in technology as well as science, is generally required not only for efficient exploitation and diffusion, but also for discovering the limits of a paradigm and indications for how to transform it. In fact, this notion forms the basis for the general heuristic of learning developed in Chapter 9. If that is true, the

[7] See the journal and the society for 'Computational and Mathematical Organization Theory (CMOT)'.

principle might apply to our own science. And indeed this is the customary argument for a scientific discipline: impose limits of inquiry in order to provide the basis for rigorous and cumulative argumentation and testing. We run the risk that in a flight from established discipline we end up in an indeterminate chaos of loose ideas flying off in all directions without means to test their consistency and coherence.

Indeed that is what we encounter in the literature on management and organization, in Chapter 2. This has set up a stage for the gurus. We see an accumulation of different terms for seemingly identical concepts, and testing or even argument becomes very difficult when it remains unclear whether people are talking about the same things or not, and, if not, what the differences are. In the organization literature we often hear about the approach of 'grounded theory': stylized facts are interpreted as indicating more general principles, which at some point in the future will develop into real theory, i.e. a more coherent set of premises and implications. This allows us to explain a wide range of phenomena, on the basis of hypotheses specified in terms of limited ambiguity and clear operationalization, in which we can build upon each other's results. This is not unreasonable: what it says is that in the absence of relevant theory we should work inductively. But if everyone thus grounds his own theory differently, on different sets of phenomena, yielding different terms for possibly identical concepts, theory indeed remains grounded and will not take off.

We should also learn from the failure, in economics, of the 'behavioural theory of the firm' (Cyert & March 1963) to develop into a dominant paradigm. The intuition of bounded rationality, with the notions of 'satisficing' and 'procedural' as opposed to 'substantive' rationality were no doubt correct, but the framework was not developed to the point of yielding sharp, falsifiable predictions and a basis for the accumulation of insights and experience. Mainstream economists, to ward off criticism, often use this failure: mainstream economics may be unrealistic and inadequate to explain phenomena of innovation and learning, but at least it is analytically coherent, and forms a basis for accumulation. Of course, this yields an argument much like that of the drunk who justifies looking for his lost keys where the street lantern sheds light rather than in the dark where he lost them. I will argue, in Chapter 3, that mainstream economics is suffering from dogmatism to such an extent that we have no choice but to cross disciplines. We should no longer be deterred from making novel combinations, but we should be aware of the risks of syncretism and lack of coherence.

Thus, I am not saying that interdisciplinary research is easy or without risk. But for the purpose of this book it is needed. I also believe that the time is right for a synthesis between economics, sociology, and cognitive science, in a unified science of behaviour.

1.3.6   *Fixity and Flux*[8]

It is a sobering thought, frustrating to some but perhaps delightful to others, that some of the fundamental issues that are advertised as new, in the literature on innovation

---

[8] An earlier version of this section appeared in Nooteboom 1989.

and learning, are associated with philosophical issues that have been around for a long time, and sometimes go back to the dawn of thought. Philosophy is relevant. According to a well-known maxim, good practice requires good theory, and I add that good theory requires good philosophy. Theory of innovation and learning requires theory of knowledge, thought, language, motivation, and an underlying view of reality (metaphysics). Such metaphysics is always there, if not explicitly then implicitly, and it is better to bring it into the open so that it can be subjected to debate. Philosophy lifts discourse to higher levels of abstraction. That entails the danger of losing contact with reality. But it is needed to create some conceptual order and coherence. This is necessary in particular in the management and organization literature, because, as will be shown in Chapter 2, that yields a cornucopia of fascinating but ill-connected ideas that are sorely in need of a higher level of abstraction to achieve more coherence. Thus, I will use philosophy unabashedly. But if the reader wishes, he can skip these reflections without loss of continuity.

The central issue in this book, concerning the paradox of stability and change, of fixity and flux, goes back to preSocratic philosophy. The paradox of fixity and flux and connected paradoxes of identity and change and of unity and diversity have occupied humankind since early antiquity (in particular, the ancient Greeks). For the following, the main source is Copleston (1962).

According to some Greek philosophers (notably Heraclites) permanence (fixity) and unity form an illusion, and only change and diversity exist, while according to others (notably Parmenides) it is the other way around. A typical attempt at reconciliation was 'decomposition' or 'atomism' (Leucippus, Democritus): reconstruct reality as a variety of combinations of basic elements (such as earth, air, fire, and water), or more basic elementary atoms. This saves the appearance of variety while maintaining underlying fixity. As argued in Chapter 6, we still find this as a fundamental paradigm in cognitive science.

While the preSocratic philosophers were preoccupied only with nature, later philosophy (from the sophists on) turned to man and his culture. Plato attempted to reconcile the flux and uncertainty of phenomena with the certainty of the pure, abstract ideas of which material phenomena are merely reflections. The pure idea was certain, eternal, unchangeable, and could in principle be conceived as such by human beings through a kind of vision. This also can be recognized in mainstream cognitive science.

Aristotle explained change from a more organic perspective as the realization of a potential which is internally already present and which can reveal itself under certain enabling conditions. Our word 'dynamics' is derived from this concept of potential. Aristotle's ideas dominated in the Middle Ages, but subsequently the research strategy of decomposition and atomism re-emerged (Hodgson 1993). It has persisted to this day: the diversity of phenomena is reconstructed from combinations of elementary entities with forces or computations performed on them. This basic intuition is applied not only in natural science but also in economics and cognitive science. One is reminded of this when reading about attempts to model dynamics (in the usual sense of structural change) in terms of relatively stable 'deep structures' that are able to generate a variety of surface phenomena (Gersick 1991). The temptation to utilize this ploy is irresistible, and I will also succumb to it in parts of this book.

The notion of a 'paradigm' derives from Socrates' philosophy: it is an idea or image that serves as an exemplar from which individual manifestations can be derived through some form of emulation. This, however, raises the question of how exactly the process of emulation is to be understood. This was already a subject of discussion in Plato's *Parmenides*. Is it a question of participation in the example (*'methexis'*) or imitation of it (*'mimesis'*). If it is the first (*methexis*), then what is the difference between the fundamental concept and what is made of it in concrete manifestations? If it is the second, it entails an unpacking into differentiated concrete manifestations, and how then can the original be said to be fundamental? This issue reappears, in a new garb, in the literature on management and organization (Chapter 2), the notion of 'competencies' (Chapter 3), cognitive science (Chapter 6), and organizational learning (Chapter 13). The above account almost reads as an issue in human-resource management: How can management guide an organization to realize its mission by cultural means such as role models and guiding symbols rather than command and control.

For Aristotle, in contrast to Plato, only individual things exist, and the idea of a class of things is an immanent essence that does not lead a separate existence. We still observe a similar issue in debates on language and knowledge: To what extent can we say that in cognition we operate on symbols that somehow have an independent exist-ence in the mind, or should we accept that such a notion is misleading, and meaning is irreducibly context-dependent? Nevertheless, Aristotle agreed that there are fixed essences, which can as such be known by a subject, even if they do not lead a separate existence. The question of whether a subject can in fact know an independent reality as it is in itself was only raised after the Middle Ages (by Hume and in the Kantian revolution). Kant's philosophy was revolutionary in that it argued that perception does not follow reality, but reality is perceived and constructed according to inevitable cognitive categories that are part of the subject (in his view not the individual subject but the generalized human subject).

Similar issues arise in economics and organization. Does a product have an iden-tifiable utility as such, which can be taken up in calculation, in combination and com-parison with utilities of other products, which satisfy the axioms of choice (such as the axiom of transitivity), or is utility defined only in a specific-use context? Kant's prob-lem of knowledge clearly anticipates later notions in the organization literature on sense making and 'enactment' (Weick 1979) and the 'social construction of reality' (Berger & Luckman 1967).

None of this gives a direct answer to my research questions, but it helps to put them in perspective. In the recent movement of 'post-modernization' we see some of the classical themes reappearing, in a shift towards a Heraclitean perspective. This entails a shift of focus from identity to change; from unity to diversity; from order to chaos; from regulation to anarchism; from the universal to the individual; from consensus to dissensus; from clarity to ambiguity; from structure to process. One may wonder if reconciliation with a more Parmenidean perspective is possible. That is what, on a deeper philosophical level, the paradox of exploitation and exploration is about.

1.4   METHODOLOGY

This book combines a constructivist theory of knowledge with a realist methodology. That sounds paradoxical: How can this be justified? Further, this book seeks to combine elements from different disciplines, and this yields a dilemma. Methodology seldom helps discovery but is sometimes needed for justification, and can prevent mistakes. The reader who is not interested in methodology can skip this paragraph without much loss.

1.4.1   Realism?[9]

The notion of 'realism' has many and various connotations, as reflected in the following questions (cf. Vromen 1995):

1. Should our theoretical assumptions reflect our beliefs about how the world works?
2. Should our theory aim to provide a basis for application to economic or business policy?
3. How much wealth of detail should theory include?
4. Can we have objective knowledge of the world?
5. Do facts represent objective knowledge?
6. Is there a reality that can help us to detect our errors of thought?
7. What items exist in reality?

   My answers to these questions are as follows:

1: Yes.
2: Yes.
3: As much as needed for the practical purpose, in a trade-off between richness of detail and simplicity of analysis.
4: No; at least we can never know whether we do.
5: No; again we cannot know whether they do.
6: Yes.
7: Next to the physical furniture of the world, and people, there exist organizations, institutions, cultural products, and social structure, in the sense that they exert causal influences.

---

[9] Part of this section appeared in Nooteboom 1986.

The function of theory is to provide abstraction, and theory cannot and should not reflect all that we observe. Yet I adopt a realist philosophy of behavioural science, as follows. Economic theory should be plausible in the sense of being based on behavioural assumptions that are realistic, i.e. that can be seen to apply. There are two arguments for this. The first argument, following Nooteboom (1986), is that it is not enough to yield correct predictions at the level of markets and industries. As Popper argued, falsifiability is a necessary condition. It is widely recognized that in economics predictions are shrouded in *ceteris paribus* assumptions that cannot themselves be tested, so that the empirical grip of falsification on theory is weak. Especially under these conditions we should recall the implication of the Duhem–Quine thesis: Theory is underdetermined by its predictions and implications. When a theory makes correct predictions, there can be an infinity of alternative theories that predict equally well. Thus, we need an additional selection criterion to select among empirically equivalent theories. Such a criterion used to be simplicity. However, that is no longer self-evident, given the increased computational power that we now have. Another criterion, then, is plausibility, i.e. realism of behavioural assumptions, in the light of direct evidence and insights from psychology and sociology into the motivation and causality of behaviour. This criterion still carries some of the notion of simplicity in the sense that it increases coherence in behavioural science (Nooteboom 1986). That is still important in spite of increased computational power. Note that the implications are that methodology is not the same for economics and natural science. In the latter, there are fewer *ceteris paribus* assumptions and there is more scope for testing under controlled conditions. Furthermore, explanatory assumptions typically cannot themselves be tested directly, and we can only test them by their implications for what we *can* observe. By contrast, in behavioural science the assumptions pertain to observable behaviour and can be tested directly. The only question is how much detail from observed behaviour they should include.

The second argument for plausibility is that for practical reasons theory should contribute insight into causal processes that produce outcomes at the level of markets and industries. In other words, explanation, in the sense of reproducing observed phenomena from the deductive structure of theory, in the behavioural sciences should include understanding of how causal processes work to produce the outcomes. What use are predictions at the level of markets and industries if they yield no basis for the analysis of action, for policy? Policy makers do not intervene in outcomes but in the processes that yield outcomes. If they could interfere in equilibrium outcomes, those would not be outcomes. Often they do not interfere directly or even intentionally, but policy will in principle have direct and indirect effects, and one needs insight into causal processes to have any chance of assessing and anticipating the effects. Agents, playing roles in social structures of organizations, form the direct, efficient cause that produces outcomes at the industry or market level, and therefore, in order to contribute insight into causal process, theory should yield empirically testable and tested assumptions concerning behaviour.

For example, it will not do to retain the 'as-if' assumption that firms maximize profit, while granting that they are not in fact capable of achieving that, as mainstream economists have been admitting for a long time (Friedman, Machlup, Alchian). Their argument for maintaining the assumption is that it yields valid predictions at the level of markets and industries. Their explanation of this is evolutionary: selective pressures of competition eliminate suboptimal profits. Even if we simulated non-maximizing behaviour, we would, under certain conditions concerning competition, arrive at profit-maximizing outcomes, as Nelson and Winter (1982) have demonstrated with their simulation models. It will be argued in Chapter 4 that the conditions concerning competition often do not apply and that in general the evolutionary argument is not correct, as shown by Winter (1964). But apart from that I reject the argument for two reasons. The first reason is that we are interested not only in population-level phenomena in markets and industries but also in phenomena at the organizational level. We are interested in the latter for themselves, but also as part of the causal process that yields outcomes at the industry level. At the organizational level the assumption of rational choice is a bad predictor. In the present context of innovation and learning, two salient features of behaviour are radical uncertainty and bounded rationality. They are salient because they have implications for transaction costs, and thereby affect our understanding of markets. They also have implications for innovation policy, concerning the diffusion of knowledge, for example, and that is relevant in studies of innovation systems. We cannot accept that those conditions prevail and have implications for our interpretation of results and yet refuse to accept the consequences in our theorizing. By this criterion, Nelson and Winter's models were better than mainstream economics in their explanation of market and industry phenomena, even if they did yield the same predictions at that level.

Rational-choice explanations of industry phenomena invite the policy conclusion that there should be no government intervention concerning firm behaviour. That is not valid, because the behavioural assumptions are admitted not to be valid at that level. But what then is the use of that theory, if it is not valid for drawing conclusions for policy?

1.4.2   Objections

There are two possible objections to my realist methodology. One is that, as we learned from the philosopher Kant, we cannot observe the world 'as it is in itself'; we cannot descend from our mind to inspect how theory is hooked on to the world. As a result, even facts do not reflect reality, and are to a greater or lesser extent 'theory-laden': based on theoretical notions underlying observation and our making sense of it. That view is accepted here. However, it does not deny that reality exists, just acknowledges that we know it only imperfectly. This view is implemented in the constructivist theory of knowledge used in this book, as indicated before. That yields a methodology of 'constructive realism', to be developed below.

A second objection to realism is that it defeats the purpose of theory. The purpose of theory is to employ as few and as simple principles as possible so that with subsidiary assumptions we can by deduction reconstruct as many diverse facts as possible. Such economy of thought has brought us a long way. One part of this objection to realism is that if we require explanatory principles to reflect all the observed detail of phenomena we defeat the purpose of simplicity. But the answer to that is that principles can be sufficiently simple and yet be sufficiently realistic. Note that I made the qualification that theory should be consistent with 'salient' facts: facts that are relevant to the issues studied, and that are of central rather than peripheral importance. In the present book the issues are innovation and learning, and for these we cannot ignore bounded rationality and radical uncertainty. I do take into account the trade-off that is involved here: more detail increases realism but reduces simplicity. However, as noted above, with the increase in computing power that we have witnessed in the last decades this trade-off is bound to shift: we can analyse much more complex models than we could before. If we cannot solve a problem analytically, we are increasingly able to compute it. Hence the emergence of computational methods.

1.4.3   Constructive Realism

People perceive, interpret, and evaluate the world according to forms or categories of thought that they have developed in interaction with their physical and social environment. This view is not new: up to a point it employs ideas from the symbolic interactionism of G. H. Mead (1934, 1982) and the developmental psychology of Piaget and Vygotsky. Cognitive construction builds on our bodily and neural make-up, as developed in biological evolution: cognition is rooted in the body (Merleau-Ponty 1964, Lakoff & Johnson 1999). Neural structures develop as tentative entities, selected and reinforced on the basis of success in the physical and social environment (Edelman 1987, 1992). This connects with the pragmatic (or 'pragmaticist') view of knowledge (Peirce 1957), that truth and meaning are based on what works, rather than on untestable claims of coherence with objective reality. It also links with Wittgenstein's idea that meaning and correct reference are based on viable use, reflected in 'rules of the game'.

This epistemological view underpins the competence view of the firm, discussed in Chapter 3: It is because of such idiosyncrasy and path dependence of thought that the competencies of firms cannot immediately be copied and firms can enjoy a temporary, partial monopoly. It also underpins the notion of 'absorptive capacity' (Cohen & Levinthal 1990): people, and firms, can understand only what fits into their idiosyncratic, path-dependent categories. This is developed in Chapter 8.

So, how can this be reconciled with a realist methodology? Doesn't a social-constructivist theory of knowledge inevitably lead to relativism, in which any theory is as good as any other, and the surrender of any debate in terms of 'truth'? The answer is that it does yield a brand of relativism. But it is not the radical relativism of most postmodernism. Since cognition is constructed in interaction with the world it is not arbitrary, and is constrained and enabled by reality, at least as a material cause. In that sense it 'embodies' reality (Lakoff & Johnson 1999). Lakoff and Johnson (1999) gave the argument that since our cognitive construction is rooted in the body, and people share bodily processes as an inheritance from evolution, their cognitive processes and constructions are bound to be similar to some extent. This is reflected in the fact that basic metaphors in thought are shared across widely different cultures. Another argument is that the physical environment, which is part of the environment in interaction with which we construct cognition, is also shared and subject to universal laws of nature. However, that does not detract from the fact that categories are constructed and that we are unable to descend from our mind to inspect how our ideas are hooked on to the world. Constructed categories enable but at the same time constrain cognition. Cognition is to some extent idiosyncratic and path-dependent: to the extent that people have evolved separately and in different environments their cognition varies (Nooteboom 1992a). 'Higher-level' cognitive constructs are built largely on social interaction, and the environment for that varies greatly. Thus, within constraints there is variety of cognition. Note that it is precisely because we cannot climb down from our minds to see how our knowledge is hooked on to the world, and because other people perceive and interpret the world differently, that we must listen to other people in our search for truth, or the best approximation to it that we can achieve. Short of the long-term selection effects that reflect reality, at any point in time other people are the only source we have for finding out about our prejudices and errors. Critical debate is more important than ever.

The answer to the problem of how I can reconcile a realist methodology with a constructivist epistemology is this: in the same way that Karl Popper made his falsificationist methodology consistent with the fact that, as he granted, observation statements that form the basis for falsification are theory-laden. To the extent that we can agree about observation statements, in spite of differences in theoretical view, we can agree about the falsifiers, so that the procedure of falsification can work. Popper underplayed the possibility that differences in theoretical perspective are so fundamental that no such agreement about 'the facts' can be reached, in claiming that we can 'at any time' step out of the prison of our categories. Consider the following quotation (Popper 1976: 56):

I do admit that at any moment we are prisoners caught in the framework of our theories; our expectations; our language. But we are prisoners in a Pickwickian sense: if we try, we can break out of our framework at any time. Admittedly, we shall find ourselves again in a framework, but it will be a better and roomier one; and we can at any moment break out of it again

But Kuhn overplayed his thesis of 'incommensurability' between different paradigms. Not just in spite of the constructivist view, but indeed following from it, people will agree on the facts to the extent that they have constructed their categories in a common physical and cultural environment. Thus, a theory can be realistic in the sense that it takes into account the facts as we construct them intersubjectively. As Popper indicated, this does not give us any 'rock-bottom' foundation, since we may be mistaken in our facts, but, nonetheless, they are generally more stable and more reliable than theoretical hypotheses. Note that all this is not intended to imply that I accept Popper's falsificationist methodology; just that I accept his notion of socially constructed facts.

1.4.4 Structure and Agency

How far does realism go? What do I include in my ontology? Are there social entities with a causal influence? Here, I take a position close to that of Archer (1995). People as agents constitute the only direct, efficient cause there is. However, present social and cultural structures have been produced by past agents in their actions; they now condition (constrain and enable) action and are susceptible to reproduction or transformation by the effects of present actions. People are born into a social position and a corresponding endowment of resources and opportunities, which induce their interests, and this renders them into agents, seeking to fulfil roles on the basis of their interests and opportunities, and in those roles become actors. Typically, they play roles in the context of collective actors, such as organizations and other interest groups. Especially, the actions of these collective actors have direct and indirect, largely unforeseeable and unintended, results, at several levels: of the agents involved, of groups and collective actors, and social and cultural structure. Social structure is associated with material resources, and cultural structure with ideas and knowledge, embodied in cultural products such as books, works of art, etc.

In this book, I flesh out the causal architecture of efficient cause and conditions from social and cultural structure with the multiple causality of Aristotle. This includes efficient causes (people) who employ material inputs (material cause) according to knowledge and technology (formal cause) in order to achieve goals (final cause), under conditions of law, social position, infrastructure, language (conditional cause). Material cause and material infrastructure appear to approximate Archer's social structure, and formal cause and immaterial parts of conditional causes appear to be close to her cultural structure. Final causality is added to deal explicitly with incentives, because that offers an indispensable dimension for economic policy. In Chapter 5, this Aristotelian causality is used to structure the notion of 'institutions'.

Part I

BUILDING-BLOCKS

Part I

BUILDING BLOCKS

2
Management and Organization

This Chapter gives a critical review of some of the theoretical perspectives on learning and innovation from the organization literature. First, a review is given of a number of relevant themes. Next, three recent books are discussed that attempt to yield a coherent account of knowledge and learning in organizations: Nonaka and Takeuchi (1995), Choo (1998), and Volberda (1998).

2.1 THEMES

First, a number of themes are reviewed that are relevant to learning and innovation. They are: 'sense making' and knowledge, in particular the role of tacit knowledge; the 'multilevel' issue of learning by people and organizational learning; co-ordination mechanisms needed for efficient exploitation; the inertia that can result from 'dominant designs and logics'; evolution and 'punctuation'; different levels of learning; the central paradox of exploitation and exploration.

2.1.1 *Knowledge and Meaning*

Herbert Simon made fundamental contributions to the field of organizational cognition, especially with his notion of bounded rationality and its implications for satisficing, routinization, and procedural versus substantive rationality.

Another important perspective in the organizational literature also is the social-constructivist view, which is based, among other things, on the 'symbolic interactionism' of G. H. Mead, and was introduced to the organizational literature by Weick (1979, 1995), with his notions of enactment and sense-making. According to this view: '[People] construct, arrange, single out and demolish many "objective" features . . . unrandomize variables, insert vestiges of orderliness, and literally create their own constructs' (Weick 1979, quoted by Choo 1998: 6). Mental construction occurs by means of 'mental models, frames or schemata'. The basic notion that people structure their observation and understanding according to 'categories' of perception and interpretation was first proposed by the philosopher Kant, so, in an attempt to create some unity of terminology, I suggest we use the term 'categories'.

A central task of organizations is to create shared categories, in order to enable shared perception, interpretation, and evaluation, for the sake of goal attainment, coherence, effectiveness, and efficiency. Organizations are seen as 'sensemaking systems' (Weick 1979, 1995), 'systems of shared meaning' (Smircich 1983), 'focusing devices' (Nooteboom 1992*a*, 1996*b*), or interpretation systems (Choo 1998). I propose that this yields a more fundamental reason for organizations to exist than transaction costs. However, I do grant that transaction costs are part of the story, as will be discussed in later chapters. In Chapter 10 this notion of organization as a focusing device is related to the concept of self-organization from the theory of system dynamics.

The categories of perception, interpretation, and evaluation, lying at the basis of shared meanings, are closely associated with the notion of 'culture'. Schein (1985) defined culture as basic assumptions and beliefs, which form the basis for values, which produce overt behaviour and artefacts (including symbols of status). Others prefer to define culture as including the surface phenomena of symbols, rituals, myths, but then we can say that underlying categories of perception, understanding, and evaluation form culture's 'deep structure'. This notion of a deep structure of categories that underlie a surface structure of visible forms will also be applied to an analysis of institutions, in Chapter 5.

According to Schein (1985: 14, 88–110) the basic categories that constitute organizational culture concern the following:

- The relationship to the environment: Does one dominate it or is one subjugated? Is the primary focus technological, economic, political, or socio-cultural? The domination/subjugation distinction is similar to the notion of 'locus of control': Does control lie in oneself or outside?
- The nature of physical and social reality and truth: Is one pragmatic or does one seek validation in a general philosophy, moral system, or tradition? Does one avoid uncertainty or does one have tolerance for ambiguity? How does one perceive time and space? For example, does one move towards the future or does that move towards one, or is time past duration (cf. Lakoff & Johnson's (1980) analysis of 'metaphors we live by')? Is truth universal or context-dependent; absolute or relative; subjective or objective?
- The nature of human nature: Is it good, evil, or both? Are people active or passive, perfectible or not? What are sources of motivation?
- The nature of human activity: Is it oriented towards being or towards accomplishment? Is it self- or other-directed.
- The nature of human relationships: views on power, influence, hierarchy; on intimacy, love, peer relationships; coercive, utilitarian, aimed at goal consensus; degree and source of authority. Here, Schein also adds dimensions proposed by Parsons: dimensions of relationships, such as universalistic (equal rights) or particularistic, achievement-oriented or based on ascription (family membership, class), oriented to self or collective.

Similar categories will be used as the basis for institutions more generally, in Chapter 5. Cultural paradigms consist of shared, coherent patterns of such categories, applied to and reproduced in interaction between people. Schein defines leadership (contrasted with management and administration) as the building, mobilization, maintenance, and change of culture as defined above. This aligns with Schumpeter's notion of the entrepreneur as a charismatic figure.

Mental categories enable but also constrain perception, interpretation, and evaluation, and shared categories have that effect in organizations: they create but also limit absorptive capacity (Cohen & Levinthal 1990).

This social-constructivist perspective is related to the perspective of communitarianism in political philosophy, as opposed to the liberalist view of Rawls. The communitarian view is that people do not choose their values but are constituted by them. People develop their identity in interaction with their social environment. Liberalists take an unacceptable, solipsistic view of individuals, while communitarians tend towards an authoritarian subjection of individuals to the dictates of the dominant opinion. But there is a middle way between those views. This has been developed, for example, by Habermas (1982). One can very well maintain that people 'make sense' and construct categories, and thereby develop their identity, in interaction with others in a social community, and yet allow for that identity to become individualized, so that the individual can exercise a more or less independent view, choice, and ethical judgement. One reason to delve into cognitive science, in Chapter 6, is to find further foundations for this view (they will be found in the situated-action theory of knowledge and language).

The fact that firms exist and survive is proof of the fact that radical liberalism (in the sense of autonomous agents such as economists tend to perceive) is economically dysfunctional. But we should remember that the collapse of totalitarian, centrally planned economies was primarily the result of the lack of innovation consequent upon a lack of variety of personal ideas and initiatives. The point here is that there is a potential tension between individuality and community, in organizations as well as societies more generally. The view of organizations as 'interpretation systems' highlights the communitarian side. They are needed to achieve a common understanding and purpose, which are needed to achieve goals—in other words, for exploitation. But we need the variety of individual perspectives and ideas as a source of innovation—in other words, for exploration. Thus, the tension between community and individuality is closely connected with the tension between exploitation and exploration.

It is not so strange to look at organizations from a political perspective too. In the organizational literature 'resource-dependence theory' (Pfeffer & Salancik 1978), which goes back to the work of J. D. Thompson (1967), takes a political view of organizations: Firms strive for maximization of resources, minimization of their own dependence, and maximization of the dependence of others. Within organizations, those groups are most powerful which control the resources that are most scarce and crucial for the firm's survival and independence. But if others, inside or outside the firm, control resources that one needs, one may need to surrender independence in order to gain access to them.

2.1.2   Tacit Knowledge

Categories and absorptive capacity are based on previous experience, which contains much tacit knowledge. Thus, culture, or its deep structure of underlying categories, is typically tacit. Tacit knowledge is closely related to knowledge in the form of skill or 'knowledge in action':

> The famous example is riding a bicycle. One can do it, but it is difficult to explain to one's child how to do it. One can only demonstrate it and let the child imitate, and then support it to find its balance, show it again, and catch it from falling when it halts, until it can stop and descend properly and on its own.

The notion of tacit knowledge has become quite popular in theories of organizational knowledge and learning (see, e.g. Nonaka & Takeuchi 1995). The origins of the notion have been ascribed to Polanyi (1962, 1966, 1969). However, it can also be found in the work of Hayek, and can even be traced back to a fifth-century Indian sage Bhartrhari (Ayer 1965: 46): 'The expert's knowledge of the genuineness of precious stones and coins, incommunicable to others, is born of practice and not of reasoning.'

Tacit knowledge is generally characterized as knowledge which cannot be 'coded'. Cohen and Bacdayan (1996) introduced from cognitive science the useful notion of procedural as opposed to declarative memory. In the first we store knowledge that constitutes a cognitive or motor or other practical skill, including, for example, the skill to ride a bicycle or to speak a language. In the second we store knowledge of facts, events, formulas, etc. This distinction is not so new either. The ancient Greeks already made a distinction between practical knowledge, called '*techne*', and knowledge about things, called '*episteme*'.

Procedural knowledge is more difficult to access than declarative knowledge, and it is more durable. Clearly, procedural and tacit knowledge are closely related, if not identical. The interesting consequence is that one may no longer know why one does the things one is expert at.

> One may know whether a sentence in some language is wrongly constructed without being able to tell why, since one has forgotten the underlying grammatical rules (or perhaps never knew them).
>
> The same goes for social procedures. An amusing example is the analysis of artillery teams. When their activity was examined and coded systematically, it was detected that just prior to firing, one or two artillerists stepped back and held still for a moment, for no apparent reason, even to the artillerists themselves. It turned out that this was left over from the time when guns were horse-drawn, and the horses had to be held during firing to prevent them from bolting. Another example is the following: During the Cuban missile crisis Russian soldiers landed at different times and in civilian clothes to conceal their military presence from the Americans, but then waited for each other and were marched off in a trim military line.

These phenomena are relevant here, because on the one hand they provide a basis for efficient exploitation while on the other hand they can yield powerful obstacles to adaptation and change. For change, implicit, tacit, procedural knowledge may first have to be made explicit before it can rationally be criticized. In other words Tacit knowledge is involuntary, like a reflex, and to be subject to change by conscious design it must first be seen as voluntary, for which it must be made explicit.

> An example from personal experience is the following: During a stay in Lisbon I tried to draw money from an automatic teller machine, using my bank card and PIN (personal identity number), to be typed on the keyboard. The machine refused, with the announcement that 'communication was disturbed'. That fitted in with my prejudices concerning the state of technology in a less developed country, so I tried again half an hour later. The same message appeared, and I became suspicious: Might I be doing something wrong? Was I using the correct PIN number? Surely, I could not be mistaken about that! I was not sure of it declaratively, as a number, so I could not check whether the number I was typing was correct, but I knew that I knew it procedurally, as a pattern of finger movement on the keyboard. There was no doubt about that. It happened without a thought, and my body resisted the mere trial of any other pattern. I didn't know, but my hand did. So I tried again. Then it hit me: the keyboard was arranged differently: in the Netherlands it counted from the top to the bottom row, while in Lisbon it counted from the bottom to the top. So I had to mentally reconstruct my number from my hand movement on the Dutch keyboard. Then I knew the number for sure, declaratively, and could type it correctly on the Portuguese keyboard. By that time my card was blocked, as is the rule after three mistrials.

In organizations, good practice, with all its inveterately tacit elements, its rich experience with specializations for different contexts, with corresponding 'work-arounds', cannot be completely canonized into written 'standard operating procedures', manuals, or training programmes, without any unspecified residual (Brown & Duguid 1996). It is one of the pitfalls of management to think that it can be. The inadequacy of that view is illustrated when processes break down because people 'work to rule'. It is also illustrated in the insight that for diffusion of knowledge in a firm it may be better to rotate staff than to issue written rules or procedures (Cohen & Bacdayan 1996).

2.1.3   The Multilevel Issue

The literature has of course recognized the multilevel problem: What is the relation between knowledge and learning at the level of people and on the level of an organization, and how does the latter concept make sense (Cohen 1991, Cook & Yanow 1996)? There are two approaches to this issue: from the theory of knowledge and from the pragmatics of organization. The two are related if one adopts a pragmatic theory of knowledge.

Knowledge and learning at the organizational level are difficult to understand if one takes the dominant computational–representational view from cognitive science, because knowledge is then defined only in terms of the autonomous individual. The issue is easier to deal with from the interactionist, social-constructivist view of knowledge and motivation espoused in this book. Then, knowledge even at the level of the individual is seen as constituted socially, on the basis of interaction in a given community, and the organization can then be seen as that community, as a framework for shared perceptions, interpretations, and evaluations. This ties in with the discussion above of the organization as a system of shared meanings. Such sharing and joint, interactive production of cognition might then be seen as organizational knowledge and learning. This issue requires more systematic attention, and is picked up again in Chapter 6.

Primary processes of production in firms require co-ordination as soon as production moves beyond the individual craftsman. Exploitation, to a greater or lesser extent, requires co-ordination, in rule-based procedures, which have been called performance programs (March & Simon 1958) and organizational routines (Cyert & March 1963, Nelson & Winter 1982). Cyert and March (1963) classified four types of rule-based procedure: task performance, maintaining organizational records, information–handling procedures, planning rules (quoted in Choo 1998: 112).

Later, in Chapter 10, the notion of 'scripts' will be employed to model such processes. That notion has been used to model cognitive frames for rule-based activities in individual cognition by Abelson (1976) and Shank and Abelson (1977). For example, the notion of a restaurant corresponds with a sequence of activities to be performed in certain ways: entering, sitting down, ordering, eating, paying. An organizational process can be modelled in a similar way. The organizational script then represents knowledge at an organizational level in the way that the script for a concept represents knowledge at the level of a person. The total organizational script may not be part of the knowledge of any single member of the organization: it is an organization-level constellation into which individuals fit their actions and interpretations. In the connectionist view in cognitive science knowledge is embedded in neural nets, and if organizational cognitive identity in terms of nets of activities is problematic, then individual identity in terms of neural nets is equally problematic (Nooteboom 1997).

As indicated by Smith Ring and van de Ven (1994), the connection between the level of people and that of organizations can be made in terms of the organizational roles that people play, and the relation between these roles and personal behaviour ('*qua* persona'). This connects with Archer's (1995) distinction between people, agents, and actors. People develop agency on the basis of their position and endowments and become actors in organizational roles, and then 'personify' those roles. A crucial question is how much scope for choice and individual creativity people have when they play their roles in organizational script-like procedures, and how this can provide a source of exploration. This is picked up in Chapters 5, 10, and 13.

2.1.4   *Dominant Designs and Logics*

Abernathy & Utterback (1978) recognized that innovation gravitates towards a dominant design. This may yield 'industry recipes' (Spender 1989) or a 'dominant logic' (Bettis & Prahalad 1995). These are partly embodied in rule-based procedures, such as the performance programmes, routines, or scripts indicated in the previous Section.

It is recognized that this yields the need to 'unlearn' (Hedberg 1981), for the purpose of exploration. This can be difficult, for several reasons. Dominant designs can be defeated by their success: one becomes imprisoned in cumulative efficiency along the 'experience curve' (Yelle 1979). Dominant logic can become part of the cognitive constitution of organizational members, absorbed into tacit knowledge. Novelty may be obstructed by the uncertainties about its success or failure and about the organizational repercussions of such novelty (March 1991). All this can result in inertia. However, some coherence and continuity is always needed: this was the argument for 'community' and coherence. As Weick put it: 'The trouble with total flexibility is that the organization can't over time retain a sense of identity or continuity . . . chronic flexibility destroys identity . . . is dysfunctional because more economical ways of responding might never be discovered; this in turn would mean that new environmental features would never be noticed' (Weick 1979: 215; quoted in Volberda 1998: 209).

2.1.5 Exploitation and Exploration

This brings us back to the central issue of exploitation and exploration (Holland 1975, March 1991). As discussed in Chapter 1, this is related to notions of 'first- and second-order learning' (Hedberg, Nystrom, & Starbuck 1976, Fiol & Lyles 1985), single- and double-loop learning (Argyris & Schön 1978), lower-level and higher-level architectural change (Henderson & Clark 1990). Since this is the central issue of the book it will not be discussed in any further detail at this point. But it seems clear that the solution of the paradox will need to be based on an analysis of how people operate in organizational structures that develop to yield a basis for exploitation, and how individual and organizational knowledge interact.

2.1.6 Evolution

The notion of evolution, inspired by Darwinian evolution in biology, has had much impact on theory in sociology, economics, game theory, organization science, and psychology. The term 'evolution' has been used in the loose sense of 'development', and in the sense of the development of an individual, given his genetic heritage ('ontogeny'), but here I refer to the more specific meaning of 'phylogenetic' evolution of populations. Is evolution a biological metaphor, or a general principle that may apply more widely? According to Metcalfe (1998) it is the latter: it entails a general principle of population thinking; populations may change in their composition of a variety of life forms, as a result of differential selection and multiplication, even if individual life forms do not adapt in any way. Thus, the crucial features are a variety of forms with different characteristics, a selection environment that yields different durations of existence for different (combinations) of characteristics, transmission of characteristics at a rate that depends in some way on duration of existence. When we pursue the biological metaphor, in Darwinian evolution, this suggests, in addition, that characteristics derive from the genome, i.e. a set of genes (or their analogues). It is the genes and not characteristics acquired during the lifespan of a form that are transmitted, transmission is based on sexual procreation, there is no procreation across different species, and variety is generated by random combinations and mutations of genes.

Perhaps in one form or another this perspective can help to solve the paradox of exploitation and exploration. An evolutionary view is attractive, in principle, for several reasons. Above all, it explains how populations adapt to environments other than by creation, design, or instruction. Interesting for the project of this book is that it explicitly tries to deal with the core problem of how transformation and continuity may be reconciled and connected: genes provide continuity; differential expressions and combinations of genes and differential survival provide transformation at the population level. Thus, it offers one way in which novelty may arise (exploration) from forms of life as they function in their environment (exploitation)—which is the central theme of this book. However, as will be discussed in Chapter 4, there are major pitfalls in using the biological metaphor in socio-economic contexts. What is the equivalent of a gene here, and of a species? Is the change of the analogue of genes random? Characteristics acquired during life are transmitted (if we can speak of evolution it is Lamarckian rather than Darwinian). Transmission is non-sexual and occurs by means of language. How is the selection environment made up, and how stable is it? However, a judicious use of the notion of evolution, which keeps its distance from the biological metaphor, may serve us well.

In organization theory there is a notion that strategy is not so much a matter of rational design by some central planning authority as a process of 'emergence' (Quinn 1982). In this process ideas of strategic import arise from practice, from different parts of an organization, and are subjected to a process of internal selection that is partly rational, partly 'political', and partly fortuitous. In some cases the process can be quite chaotic and random, in what is known as the 'garbage-can' view of decision making (Burgelman 1996). However, the question arises, here also, as to how stable the internal selection environment is. The whole point of organizational transformation, in second-order (or second-loop) learning, is to change the internal selection environment: to give novel ideas, which do not satisfy current requirements of co-ordination, a chance. In organization science and economics selection is related to institutions, and a core question is how we can deal with institutional innovation.

In the organizational literature we also encounter the notion of punctuated equilibria (derived from the work of Gould 1989). As indicated before, in Chapter 1, Tushman and Romanelli (1985), Gersick (1991), and Romanelli and Tushman (1994) utilized the idea of punctuated equilibria in the development of organizations. Related to the issue of exploitation and exploration, the central question is how we can reconstruct 'punctuation': Where does it come from; on what is it based? While the literature has produced fascinating cases, it has not answered this question.

The notion of endogenously created paradigm breaks may suggest a link with the literature on self-organization, auto-poiesis, and 'complexity'. In this book I will not investigate this perspective at any great length. That may be a subject for future work. I will, however, try to develop a theory of self-organization, in Chapter 9, on the basis of insights derived from cognitive science to be discussed in Chapters 6 and 7. As will be argued in more detail in Chapter 4, metaphors taken from cognition and language appear to yield a better basis for explaining innovation and organizational change than biological metaphors of evolution.

2.1.7   Strategic Fit

An old but persistent theme is that of 'contingency' or 'strategic fit', and this connects with the theme of exploitation and exploration. Several researchers (Burns & Stalker 1961, Lawrence & Lorsch 1967, Thompson 1967) have argued that flexible, loosely integrated, organic structures and styles are appropriate (successful) in turbulent (complex and volatile) environments, and more co-ordinated, integrated, mechanistic structures and styles are appropriate in stable, predictable environments. The relation with the theme of exploitation and exploration is that the first is likely to be associated with a more stable situation and the latter with a more turbulent situation, so that this literature may inform us about organizational structures and styles appropriate for exploitation and exploration. These notions will be picked up, in particular, in Chapter 11.

2.2   ORGANIZATIONAL LEARNING

In this paragraph three books are discussed that make an attempt at a systematic conceptual framework for processes of organizational learning. The first (Nonaka & Takeuchi 1995) focuses on the role of conversions between tacit and explicit knowledge in innovation, the second (Choo 1998) on processes of sense making and the management of information, and the third (Volberda 1998) on transitions between different degrees of organizational flexibility.

2.2.1   Knowledge Conversion

Nonaka and Takeuchi (1995) offered a view on how novelty emerges from different stages in the conversion and combination of knowledge. Explicit knowledge is combined with other explicit knowledge ('combination') for efficient and systematic utilization. In the context of the present book I would say: for the sake of efficient exploitation. As a practice spreads, explicit knowledge is 'internalized' into tacit knowledge. Tacit knowledge, ripened with accumulating experience, is passed on between people, in 'socialization', in what Brown and Duguid (1996) called 'communities of practice'. Tacit knowledge is also taken from outside practices encountered on the way.

Nonaka and Takeuchi give the example of how a cook's expertise in kneading dough is absorbed to improve the design of a bread-baking machine. For this purpose, this tacit knowledge had to be 'externalized' into explicit knowledge.

This serves as a paradigm for the generation of ideas for new products. According to Nonaka and Takeuchi such externalization of tacit knowledge yields explicit ideas for approval by top management.

One implication for strategy and structure that Nonaka and Takeuchi offer is that management should be conducted 'middle-up-down'. It is a job of middle management to facilitate the externalization of tacit, experiential knowledge from below, for proposals to be put to management, and to facilitate the combination of different areas of explicit knowledge at lower levels, where internalization and socialization then take place. From this perspective, the currently fashionable 'downsizing' and 'flattening' of organizations, by cutting out middle management, could have disastrous consequences for this indispensable process of knowledge conversion. For exploring innovative, novel combinations, Nonaka and Takeuchi recommend a 'hypertext' organization, by analogy to windows processing on computers. This is somewhat like a flexible form of matrix organization: cross-functional and cross-departmental groups are formed, but this is done *ad hoc*, according to the opportunity at hand, like opening windows on the computer.

This work is interesting. It recognizes the great significance of tacit knowledge for processes of innovation and learning, but also the need to employ explicit knowledge. It yields the first attempt, as far as I know, to bring them together in a systematic framework in which the relations between the two are made explicit. It also yields some indication of how the multilevel problem might be tackled; how interaction between people in the organization might yield learning and innovation at the level of the organization.

There is also ground for criticism. Many crucial questions are not asked, let alone answered. There is no theory of knowledge underlying the process of knowledge conversion, other than the distinction between tacit and explicit knowledge. For example: What is the basis for internalizing tacit knowledge? Are there limitations to the absorptive capacity of people, and what would the implications be? Nothing is said about any selection process, either internal or external to the firm. Neither competition nor collaboration with customers, suppliers, or others, in alliances or otherwise, is in evidence. This yields a solipsistic view of the firm that begs questions concerning conditions for survival. Internally there is supposed to be selection of proposals, derived from 'externalization', by top management, presumably without opposition, conflict, or failure of vision or understanding, with unlimited absorption capacity. It is simply assumed that the paradox of exploitation and exploration is solved somehow. Nonaka and Takeuchi focus on exploration while neglecting exploitation, and the relation between the two. The problem of trading off efficiency of current production against uncertain yields of innovation and uncertain implications for change of organizational structure, and its feasibility, does not arise, while this seems perhaps the most central task of management. Apparently there is no problem of disrupting exploitation in the formation of cross-functional and cross-departmental task groups for exploration. It is not clear whether there are any restrictions imposed on 'combination', and on who socializes with whom. There is no discussion of problems of organizational transformation or the 'punctuation' of equilibria.

2.2.2   The Knowing Organization

Choo (1998) tried to develop a 'holistic view' of how organizations use information, from the perspective of the management of information and the design of information systems. His book is very comprehensive: rich in useful ideas and attempts to unify themes from the wide-ranging organizational literature. Here, the purpose is not to give a full review: I pick out what is relevant to the present project, and will be taken up in later analysis.

The main basis of the book is formed by Weick's (1979, 1995) views of 'sense making' and 'enactment', with organizations as 'interpretation systems', and Simon's (1983) notion of organizations not controlling decisions but controlling premises upon which decisions are made. The relation between the organization and its members, in learning, is characterized as follows: While most of the organization's knowledge is rooted in the expertise and experience of its individual members, the organization provides a physical, social, and cultural context so that the experience and growth of this knowledge takes on meaning and purpose (p. 105).

The implications for the limitation of absorptive capacity are identified. Choo was fully aware of what in Chapter 1 was called the paradox of identity and change, which includes both the paradox of exploitation and exploration and the related paradox of individuality and community. Although the entire process (of sense making, enactment) operates to reduce equivocality, some equivocal features must remain if the organization is to be able to survive in a new and different future. Indeed, organizations can only continue to exist if they maintain a balance between flexibility and stability (Choo 1998: 6).

Thus, a basic task of management is the 'management of ambiguity'. The basic mode of sense making is 'discourse', on the basis of shared mental frameworks in a 'social order', while maintaining sufficient 'residual ambiguity'.

The basic scheme that Choo proposes for understanding organizations and managing information is a 'knowing cycle' of sense making, decision making, and knowledge creating. Sense making and decision making are connected by 'premise control'. Sense making must tap into the mental models and experiences of individual members of the organization. The resultant shared interpretations provide a framework for organizational action.

Acquisition of knowledge is formulated in terms of information search for the solution of a problem, with stages of initiation, selection, exploration, formulation, collection, and presentation, which leads to the resolution of the problem, in a movement from uncertainty and vagueness to confidence and clarity. Different types of emotion at different stages drive or inhibit the process. One aspect of this is that too much redundant information causes boredom, and too much 'unique' information causes anxiety. The analysis takes into account different 'situational dimensions', which include the sets of people involved, the type of problem, work settings, and shared premises. It also takes into account several 'information seeking and use behaviours'.

Choo refers to Vygotsky's 'activity theory' as an underlying theory of knowledge and language (p. 224), and the idea that activity systems are mediated (in language, technology, collaboration), situated in particular contexts, provisional (forever subject to development), pragmatic (purposive and object oriented), and contested. This perspective is similar to the one I take, in Chapter 6.

The main limitation of the book is that while it recognizes the paradox of exploitation and exploration, and discusses it from multiple angles, it does not yield a solution for it:

An organization can break loose from the success trap . . . by raising aspirations to levels that induce exploration . . . or by feedback that exaggerates the . . . value of exploration . . . Symmetrically, an organization can break out of a failure cycle of repeated explorations and failures by lowering aspirations . . . To strengthen exploration, organizations may provide safety nets for exploratory failures, celebrate the lessons learned from failures, and slow down the process of socialization and acculturation (pp. 253–4) . . . [Under outside pressures of selection] the organization uses its structural context of administrative rules and routines, as well as cultural preferences and norms, to induce, design and direct new initiatives so that they build on past successes and existing capabilities. The structural context from time to time needs to be revised to respond to the selective pressures of the external environment (p. 259)

This begs the most fundamental questions. How is change reconciled with continuity? Which 'existing capabilities' should we retain and which should we change, and how do we find out? What 'aspirations' should be raised, and how does one determine that? How do we 'celebrate the lessons from failures'? What if the change requires a change of the 'structural context', so that it can no longer be used to effect the change? Which parts of that context can we still use, and how do we know? A clue is given: Search is serial rather than parallel . . . alternatives in the neighbourhood of the problem symptom are searched first.

2.2.3   The Flexibility Paradox

Volberda (1998) puts the paradox of exploitation and exploration, which he calls the 'flexibility paradox', squarely in the centre of attention. The goal is to find:

organizational forms that are able to explore new opportunities effectively as well as exploit those opportunities effectively, that allow firms to change their strategic focus easily even while developing and maintaining some strategic direction, and which can change their dominating norms and values as well as correct deviations from essential norms and values (p. 5)

Several ways are identified to lift the paradox. One is separation in place: one part of an organization engages in exploitation (typically in production departments), another in exploration (typically in R & D departments). Another is separation in time: exploitation occurs at one time, and exploration at another. This yields the 'oscillating' (Burns & Stalker 1961), or 'ambidexterous' (Duncan 1976), or 'two-state' (Shepard 1967) mode, with a to and fro between loose and open to tight and homogeneous, and back again. A third way is to transcend the paradox by showing how exploitation and exploration can be combined at the same time and place. Tools for this may be joint ventures, 'skunk works' (3M Company), internal corporate venturing, and Nonaka and Takeuchi's (1995) 'hypertext' organization. Volberda mentions the 'punctuated equilibrium' view, indicated above, and with reference to van de Ven and Garud (1988) notes:

the punctuation process itself remains underdeveloped. When does preservation stop and change begin? Most attempts at temporal resolution (of the paradox) have glossed over the issue of transition points and focused instead on the periods of relatively pure action of either preservation or exchange (p. 78)

I will need to take this comment to heart, because I will later, in a proposal for a heuristic of learning, in Chapter 9, come up with a 'temporal resolution' of the paradox, among other solutions. The main challenge is indeed to account for the transitions between stability and change.

A useful distinction is made (p. 117) between different types of flexibility: steady state, operational, structural, and strategic flexibility, defined by their location in a two-by-two matrix that crosses variety of capabilities and speed of response. Operational flexibility entails low variety and fast response; structural flexibility high variety and slow response; strategic flexibility high variety and fast response. In the steady state, of course, both are low.

Volberda specifies the following obstacles to change: technology, means of transformation, mode of production, physical layout, breadth of skill and knowledge, organizational form (functional, divisional, matrix, etc.), planning and control procedures, invisible decision-making procedures, process regulators, types of interdependence (Thompson 1967), forms of delegation and participation, cultural barriers (shared values, etc.), identity formation, leadership style, and external orientation (pp. 122–84). This reads like a detailed account of the more general notions of 'dominant design', 'dominant logic', and 'organizational interpretation systems' from the literature.

The 'basic assumptions of the framework' (p. 204) are as follows:

1. Management's 'flexibility mix' (repertoire of capabilities) must match the degree of environmental turbulence.
2. To activate a sufficient flexibility mix, the design of organizational conditions must provide adequate potential for flexibility.
3. The two must be continuously matched with the degree of environmental turbulence.

Competitive forces are analysed in terms of the following 'dimensions of environmental turbulence': the familiar dichotomies of static/dynamic, complex/simple, predictable unpredictable. Under 'low competition', which is identified with 'static, simple and predictable (non-competitive) environment', the optimal form is the 'rigid' one: limited flexibility mix, routine technology, mechanistic structure, and a conservative culture. Under 'moderate competition' (dynamic and/or complex but largely predictable) there should be a more comprehensive flexibility mix, dominated by operational flexibility, a less routine technology, a relatively mechanistic structure, a conservative culture, attempts to establish oligopolies, entry and mobility barriers. Under 'hypercompetition' (unpredictable, dynamic, and complex environment) there should be a broad flexibility mix, dominated by structural and strategic flexibility, non-routine technology, organic structure, and an innovative culture. However, on page 210 it is acknowledged that:

The previous model ignores the process of variation in the composition of the flexibility mix and organizational design over time. In other words: how does management cope with change? Shifts may occur in the level of competition . . . the composition of the flexibility mix and organizational design must vary correspondingly. An ongoing process of variation is needed. In this process the organization has to prevent itself from overshooting and becoming extremely rigid or chaotic

The book then yields another typology of alternative flexible forms: rigid, planned, flexible, chaotic. Examples of the flexible form are the social-network firm and the 'cluster organization', and 'regional cluster organizations' (presumably what in the economic literature is called 'industrial districts', going back to the work of Marshall). In the chaotic firm: 'innumerable initiatives are impossible to implement . . . [there is] no distinct technology, stable administrative structure, or basic shared values [so that] the organization is controlled by the environment' (p. 214).

It is proposed that there is a process of 'routinization' of entrepreneurial firms at 'decreasing levels of competition'. First, 'flexibility . . . is created from . . . chaotic international expansion activities . . . As the level of competition decreases, the flexible organization faces a crisis. It must become more efficient in its operations to extract greater benefit from the changes that it introduced previously, and to exploit its existing knowledge and opportunities' (pp. 217–18). Here, the organization has to go from flexible to planned. Then there is a danger of becoming rigid.

A problem with the characterization of the environment in terms of turbulence is that it says nothing about specific processes of competition, co-operation, and strategic interaction. It is misleading if not false to associate turbulence with intensity of competition. As already indicated in Chapter 1, when novelty settles down, competition will, contrary to what Volberda states, increase. Temporary monopolies from innovation wear out, knowledge is diffused, new competitors enter, and price competition increases. It is because of that *increased* competition, with pressure on price, that firms need to utilize opportunities for increased efficiency, among others by increase of scale, which entails specialization and the ensuing need for co-ordination and hence a certain amount of formalization.

At the end of the book Volberda returns to the different ways to solve the paradox: spatial or temporal separation, or the 'balanced corporation'. Spatial separation, leading to what is now called the 'dual corporation', allows for separation by level (top vs. middle, central vs. front line), function (e.g. rigid or planned production and flexible R & D), or location (mature and new divisions; skunk works, corporate ventures, new venture departments). Temporal separation (the oscillating organization) is said to be a speciality of small entrepreneurial firms. In the balanced corporation, mechanistic structure is compensated by 'encouraging and promoting cultural heterogeneity' (p. 274). The hypertext organization (Sharp is an example) combines the steady-state flexibility of the functional form with the strategic flexibility of a flat, cross-functional task force (Nonaka & Takeuchi 1995). Even more complicated is Olivetti's 'platform corporation' in which there is coexistence of a multiplicity of organizational forms (Ciborra 1996) '. . . but [which] retains the underlying bedrock of the collective cognitive schemas of participating managers' (p. 275).

All this is certainly interesting and valuable, but it does not answer the basic questions. We are back at the problem that Volberda himself identified earlier: If we postulate different modes of organization at different stages, how do we account for the transitions between them? Where and how, and on what basis, is there transition from stability to flexibility? And if we solve the paradox by spatial separation, in different parts of the firm, how do we account for the interfaces between them? How, and on what basis, do stable and flexible parts of an organization connect, and what are the conditions for the success of it? And in the balanced organization, how is the balance achieved? How do flexibility and stability interact and build upon each other? Like Nonaka and Takeuchi, Volberda suggests that it is the task of management to see to this. But that begs the question how this is to be done. However, to maintain perspective, the present book will certainly not come up with any final answers either.

2.3 CONCLUSION

What has the management and organization literature offered? What are the limitations and problems? How can we proceed?

The literature has produced a wealth of interesting cases, of which some were discussed in this and the preceding Chapter. It has tried to tackle the central issues, in accepting that rationality is bounded and that uncertainty is fundamental. It has demonstrated the importance of 'sense making', the role of organizations in this, the richness and relevance of the notion of 'enactment', and the way in which this may contribute to a solution of the multilevel problem of people and organizations (Weick). It has contributed to the description and analysis of issues underlying the paradox of exploitation and exploration. The central problem has been sharpened in terms of 'punctuation' (Tushman & Romanelli, Gersick). Many authors have demonstrated the variety of forms in which the paradox manifests itself. It has demonstrated the importance of 'conversion' between tacit and explicit knowledge (Nonaka & Takeuchi). It has shown how, in detail, processes of 'sense making' and 'knowledge production' are connected with information sources, information management, and decision making (Choo). It has explored the logically possible ways of resolving the paradox (spatial or temporal separation or balance), and has indicated different forms of organization associated with them (Volberda).

The array of ideas, terms, and propositions that the literature offers is fascinating but also bewildering. Repeatedly, different terms refer to concepts that seem similar if not identical. What is the difference between tacit knowledge, knowledge in action, procedural knowledge; between documented, explicit, coded, and declarative knowledge? What is the difference between exploitation, single-loop, first-order, and parametric learning; between exploration, double-loop, second-order, architectural learning, and the punctuation of equilibria? What is the difference, or the relation, between dominant design, industry recipe, dominant logic, mental models, frameworks, schemata, and inertia? What is the difference between organizations as interpretation systems, shared meanings, and focusing devices? It seems that inspired by experience from practice different scholars more or less independently rediscover the same ideas, give them new names, and develop their own 'grounded theory'. If the different terms do not refer to the same concept, what is their difference, and how are they related? If we do not find out, both replication and criticism of research are difficult and we will continue to proceed in a fragmented, haphazard, non-cumulative fashion.

As suggested in Chapter 1, the criticism I offer seems to have an ironic parallel with the very problem we are investigating. To use Volberda's terms concerning degrees of flexibility: Fleeing from the rigidities of economics the organizational field seems to have entered a state of chaos. The need now is for more coherence, for some consolidation in a dominant design, to better exploit the potential of the theory, provide a basis for division of labour and co-operation, and for the more systematic operationalization and testing of theory. To achieve this, perhaps we need to raise the analysis to a higher level of abstraction; to ground the notions we use on a more fundamental level. This is what I try to achieve in the following Chapters.

The most important point is that the literature has not yet explained how, and on what basis, exploitation and exploration are connected. How does the one lead up to the other? How do they build on each other? One clear element here, that has been around for quite a while, is that novelty emerges in chaotic beginnings, and is at first indeterminate, and then needs some consolidation in a dominant design, in order to utilize its potential.

A final point of criticism is that in much management and organization literature the 'environment' is treated in terms such as 'turbulence versus placidness or stability' and 'complexity versus simplicity'. These terms are far too general, unstructured, vague, and unspecified to connect with decision variables in relations between a firm and its environment. Furthermore, such global views of the environment as some homogeneous, anonymous field hamper the understanding of a firm's identity and development as the result of interaction not only between people within the firm but also between firms. 'The environment' consists of specific other firms, institutions, consumers, etc. 'Turbulence' is not some global, undifferentiated property, but a phenomenon of specific exits and new entries to a market and specific competitors producing innovations, especially Schumpeterian creative destruction. In addition to competition there can be co-operation between specific firms offering complementary assets, competencies, or knowledge. 'Complexity' entails specific systemic relations of substitution or complementarity between parts of technology, elements of consumer demand, and participants in a supply chain.

Partly as a result of the influence of transaction-cost economics, organization scholars have increasingly looked at the environment in more specific terms of decisions of 'make or buy', interfirm interactions, and forms of organization 'between market and hierarchy', in buyer–supplier relations, alliances, networks. This connects with the interaction view of knowledge and learning taken in this book. It also connects with the view, taken in studies of innovation systems, of innovation as arising from interaction between organizations. This is taken up in Chapters 8 and 11.

The fact that economics tends to ignore or misrepresent issues of learning, sense making, and radical uncertainty does not imply that there is nothing useful left. A range of concepts from industrial-organization economics remains useful. Examples are the following: entry barriers, sunk costs of market entry, economies of scale, scope and experience, substitutes and complements in consumption and production, opportunity costs, price elasticity, types and intensity of competition, spillovers of information, transaction-specific assets, asymmetric information, adverse selection, moral hazard, externalities, non-exclusiveness of information use, the revelation problem concerning the value of information (Arrow's paradox), etc. In the next Chapter I therefore turn to a review of useful elements from economic theory.

3

Innovation, Entrepreneurship, and Competence

The economics literature has mostly treated learning only in a very limited sense of increasing efficiency on the basis of experience or obtaining information from others. Here, we are primarily interested in learning in the sense of innovation and discovery. Most of mainstream economics is unfit to deal with those issues, but we should not discard it completely. More useful, however, are non-mainstream or non-standard branches of economics: Austrian/Schumpeterian economics, the resource–competence view of firms, evolutionary economics, and institutional economics. This Chapter focuses on the first two. Chapter 4 discusses evolution, and Chapter 5 discusses institutions.

3.1 LEARNING?

The economics literature has dealt mostly with first-order rather than second-order learning, in the sense discussed in Chapters 1 and 2. In other words, it has dealt with exploitation rather than exploration. It has focused mostly on increase of efficiency in production. And part of what was ascribed to the 'learning' curve was in fact purely the result of effects of scale. Where it has turned to quality improvement of products, and product differentiation (Malerba 1992), it has come closer to exploration, but there also it does not approach issues of discovery.

3.1.1 *Productivity*

Productivity studies have identified the 80 per cent rule: a doubling of turnover yields a reduction of average cost to 80 per cent of its original level. This has sometimes been ascribed to the 'learning curve' (Yelle 1979). However, this rule can be explained fully by an effect of scale that has nothing whatsoever to do with learning in any sense.

> This effect of scale obtains in industries whose production is based on a container. Containers are used for chemical reactions or physical processes in the oil, chemical, and food industries. Containers, in the form of vehicles, are also used for transport: cars, trucks, and aeroplanes. For containers, costs tend to be proportional to the surface of the container: cost of the material from which the container is built, weight and hence transportation costs, cost of heat loss through

radiation, costs of cleaning. On the other hand turnover, i.e. capacity, equals content. Now, if for convenience we take the container to be a sphere, surface and hence cost (c) is proportional to the square of the radius (r), while content and hence turnover (q) is proportional to its cube. As a result, average cost (costs/turnover c/q) is proportional to one over the radius (1/r), that equals one over the cube root of turnover ($q^{-1/3}$). This by itself yields the 80 per cent rule ($0.5^{-1/3} = 0.8$). Thus, if you go to twice as big a container (chemical reactor, plane), average costs fall to 80 per cent. Learning is nowhere in sight.

Another effect of scale that has nothing to do with learning, and which occurs especially in service industries, is the result of fixed set-up or threshold costs: the minimal capacity of one person at a service point for the duration of its opening time (Nooteboom 1987). Beyond that threshold, additional capacity can be variable, to suit patterns of arrival of customers and optimize capacity utilization, by means of part-time labour.

Under widely applicable assumptions, costs (c) are linear in turnover (q) from that threshold (d) onwards: $c = d + e.q$ (Nooteboom 1982). The effect of scale results from the fact that at a greater turnover threshold cost is less in relative terms. The threshold phenomenon includes an attendant at a counter (in a shop, café, restaurant, and hotel) or at a call centre or emergency station (hospital, police, fire station), but it also includes the driver of a vehicle and a teacher before a class. Thus, transport entails two types of scale effect: the effect regarding the size of the vehicle, discussed above, and the threshold cost of the driver. Transaction costs include set-up costs, such as the costs of setting up contact, contract, and control in transactions, and these cause a scale effect (Nooteboom 1993*a*). They have a structure similar to threshold costs.

3.1.2 Experience

Other effects of scale do have to do with skills, and thereby come closer to the notion of learning. One effect, going back to Adam Smith's renowned pin factory, is that with larger volume one can achieve division of labour, which enables specialization, through which skills can be more focused. Specialization is accompanied by standardization, which enables mechanization and automation, which also increase efficiency without learning. There is, moreover, 'learning by doing' along the 'learning curve', which to prevent misunderstanding should preferably be referred to by its other name: the 'experience curve'. Here, cumulative experience yields a further elimination of redundancies of movement, planning, control, materials, repair, in a further honing down of skills, mutual adjustment, material flows, stocks. That does have to do with learning, but only in the sense of first-order learning, in exploitation. It is essentially a process of reduction rather than opening up to novelty.

3.1.3 Knowledge Transfer

Next, the economic literature deals with transfer of knowledge, mistakenly construed as the transfer of information, as if knowledge could be taken as a commodity, to be taken from the shelf like rolls of bread at the bakery. That this is indeed a mistake will be argued in much more detail in Chapters 6 and 7, which give a systematic analysis of issues of cognition and language. Here, let it suffice to say that the intake of information to construct knowledge requires absorptive capacity (Cohen & Levinthal 1990). Understanding requires the right cognitive structure to make sense of a particular piece of information. As will be argued later in this Chapter, the value of information depends on the 'cognitive distance' between the receiver and the source of the information (Nooteboom 1992*a*, 1999*a*).

In knowledge transfer knowledge can take several forms. One form is disembedded, explicit knowledge, documented in publications, blueprints, formulae, algorithms, and software. This may be public, to be obtained from public research institutes, or it may be private, more or less protected property of firms. Transfer of the latter is part of what in the literature is called 'spillover'. Another form is knowledge that is largely tacit, embedded in people, organizational structures, routines, or cultures. This includes ways of thinking, seeing, and sense making. Knowledge may also be embedded in machinery, instruments, and other tools. These forms of knowledge may be transferred by flows of machinery, tools, etc., flow of people, and the takeover of parts or wholes of firms. However, here also we should be aware that 'adoption' of innovations, whether they are embedded or not, will in general require a form of reinvention by the adopter, who needs to transform his cognitive structures, including organizational structures, routines, and modes of perception, to absorb the information. In principle, knowledge is never simply absorbed but is reproduced. Adoption is to be seen as the development of competencies of absorption.[1]

3.1.4   *Discovery*

Finally, we approach the issue of exploration and discovery: not the transfer but the production of new knowledge. This has rarely been approached in the economics literature. It does appear on the agenda where attention is paid to quality change in products, as in horizontal and vertical product differentiation (Malerba 1992). As will be argued at length later, in Chapter 9, differentiation is part of a discovery procedure; of the way in which exploitation proceeds into exploration.

3.2   MAINSTREAM ECONOMICS

Unorthodox branches of economics, i.e. evolutionary, Austrian/Schumpeterian, institutional economics and the resource–competence view, are useful for the purpose of

---

[1] Chapter 6 will indicate that according to a branch of cognitive science (Edelman 1987, 1992, Rose 1992, 1997) even individual memory is not a matter of retrieving some bit of information stored somewhere, as in a computer. It is re-enactment of paths in a field of neurons that is modulated by the context in which recall takes place.

this book. Mainstream neoclassical or neoWalrasian economics (Weintraub 1988) is less useful, even misleading. In unorthodox branches of economics scholars by and large try to salvage what they can from mainstream economics. The literature on management and organization tends to jettison it lock, stock, and barrel. This is understandable, but runs the risk of throwing out the baby with the bathwater. Below, I indicate what seems relevant and what irrelevant in mainstream economics. Subsequently I discuss Austrian/Schumpeterian economics and the resource–competence perspective.

3.2.1 The Irrelevance of Mainstream Economics

According to Weintraub (1988) the 'hard core' (in the sense of Lakatos 1970, 1978) of the 'neo-Walrasian research program' consists of the following principles: Economists (should) study (1) equilibrium outcomes in (2) connected markets, based on (3) rational choice by (4) autonomous agents. The underlying perspective is that of methodological individualism. In studies of innovation and learning we are interested in its virtual antithesis: (1) out-of-equilibrium processes in (2) markets and organizations with significant transaction costs, under (3) conditions of radical uncertainty (in the sense of Knight 1921) and bounded rationality, with (4) meaning and knowledge arising from interaction between people. The underlying perspective is neither methodological individualism nor methodological collectivism but what might be called methodological interactionism.

> For an illustration of the shortcomings of mainstream economics in the way it deals with uncertainty I turn to recent economic theory and models of innovation. Models have been developed of R & D decision making (Dasgupta & Stiglitz 1980, Loury 1979, Lee & Wilde 1980), on the basis of an R & D 'production function', which entails a 'hazard rate' for the incidence of success: you do not know how long it will take for results to appear. But this rate can be increased, at a cost, with a higher intensity of R & D. It is also assumed that outcomes, when success appears, can be various, and are subject to a probability distribution. Revenues depend on the level of R & D spending. A further uncertainty is that there are x number of firms competing in the same process, and this is modelled as a 'patent race' in which the winner takes all (the latter restriction can easily be taken away). Thus, there is threefold uncertainty: Who will win the race? If one wins, how long it will take to achieve success? What will the revenue of that success be? Nooteboom (1991), Nooteboom and Vossen (1995), and Vossen and Nooteboom (1996) extended these models with scale effects, and used them for empirical studies of the participation and spending in R & D of small firms compared with large firms. The econometric results were significant, and hypotheses concerning effects of scale could be nicely tested. Yet these models lack credibility.

Most, if not all, economic models of innovation dodge the fundamental problem that in R & D there is radical uncertainty, which cannot be modelled with a range of possible outcomes subject to a probability distribution. Even the use of a hazard rate of success still derives from an existing set of possible outcomes that is assumed to be known to decision makers. In fact, one often does not know what could come out, whether it will fit to user requirements and wider systems of production and distribution. (See the issues of fit and the 'Leonardo' and 'King Saul' effects noted in Chapter 1). In fact, one often has to first decide and take action before the options for rational choice become clear, precisely to find out what the options are.

As noted in the methodological discussion in Chapter 1, while economics tends to focus on equilibrium outcomes, management scholars must pay attention to processes, because it is their task to provide a basis for intervention, and you can only intervene in processes, not outcomes. Economists are not concerned with intervention; indeed they mostly aim to show that intervention is undesirable. In firms, equilibrium is likely to entail inertia, which may well be the death of the firm. The essential problem of management is radical uncertainty, and the central point of organizations is that people are not autonomous in sense making, understanding, and action. Problems of rationality cannot be left implicit or unspoken, but require an explicit link with cognitive science, which economists largely choose to ignore, and interaction between people requires a link to sociology, which economists tend to abhor.

3.2.2   Knowledge and Learning

It is absurd that, while we are full of talk about the 'knowledge society', 'learning economy, region, and firm', economics does not have an explicit, let alone an adequate, theory of knowledge and learning. Its implicit 'theory in use' can be characterized as naïve realism: We can know the world as it is, information entails such knowledge, we can acquire and transmit that information, and when different people have the information they have the same knowledge. That theory is not tenable. People perceive, interpret, and evaluate the world according to categories (or 'schemata, frames, or mental models') which they develop in interaction with their physical and social world. They make sense and gain understanding by fitting experience into such categories, and are able, in some ways and only up to a point, to adapt the categories when experience does not fit. For further analysis, Chapter 6 will argue for a cognitive theory of situated action, according to which knowledge is internalized action, supported by the context of the action. Knowledge is jointly produced with others. That lends a dimension to interpersonal relations in and between firms that is absent in traditional transaction-cost theory and in conventional treatments of spillover.

As a result, people will see and interpret the world differently to the extent that they have developed in different physical and social conditions and have not interacted. The consequences of this simple premise for economic theory are pervasive. As will be discussed later it has crucial implications for our view of the purpose of firms, competition, and the working of markets, with important implications for government competition—and innovation policy.

From the perspective of sense making and understanding as a result of interaction between people, some of the economist's preoccupation with incentives to deal with self-seeking opportunism and problems of 'adverse selection and moral hazard' is exaggerated. Social programming on the basis of shared norms and routinization, or preferences for trust-based dealings built on personal bonds, may foreclose the awareness of 'opportunities for opportunism', or the desire to utilize such opportunities, and thus provide a basis for trust (Nooteboom 1996, 1999c). That is part of the function of organizations.[2]

3.2.3   Economics of Organization

Economics has become much more useful for scholars of organization in the modern economics of organization, with its acceptance of bounded rationality and asymmetric information, in principal-agent theory, theory of incomplete contracts and transaction costs, and their extensions and refinements (Milgrom & Roberts 1992). The great strength of these approaches is the usual virtue, in economics, of clarity and analytical rigour. There is much of use here, which organization and business scholars should employ as much as is warranted. However, uncertainty still tends to be reduced to risk. An exception is transaction-cost economics, which accepts that contingent contracts may be impossible because of radical uncertainty concerning intentions (degree of opportunism) and concerning events that are unforeseeable and generate 'opportunities for opportunism' (Nooteboom 1996a). Furthermore, it is recognized that even if all relevant contingencies were known, there would still be incompleteness of contracts because of the 'bounded writing and communication skills' (Hart 1990: 699) and the fact that 'language would not be rich and precise enough to describe all the eventualities' (Milgrom & Roberts 1992: 129).

However, in spite of this recognition of the imperfections of language and the presence of radical uncertainty, a peculiar twist is made. Williamson, in particular, assumes that people can rationally, calculatively deal with conditions of bounded rationality, in a way which preserves the rational-choice perspective. Recognition of bounded rationality paradoxically leads on to an assumption of super-rationality. The idea is that given the awareness of bounded rationality and radical uncertainty, people rationally design governance structures to deal with those conditions. But surely, if rationality is bounded, that is bounded as well. To rationally calculate economizing on bounded rationality one would need to know the marginal (opportunity) costs and benefits of seeking further information and of further calculation, but for that one would need to decide upon the marginal costs and benefits of the efforts to find that out. This yields an infinite regress (Hodgson 1998, Pagano 1999).

When confronted with arguments against rationality, mainstream economists usually concede that assumptions of full rationality are counterfactual, and then sidestep the argument by resorting to the 'as-if' argument of economic selection. Only the most efficient forms of governance will survive, as selected by the pressures of competition. This argument is still trotted out in spite of the fact that it was already shown in the sixties, by Sidney Winter, that it is false and based on an erroneous use of the theory of evolution, as indicated in Chapter 1.

---

[2] Even so, this does not eliminate the possibility of opportunism, and trust should never be blind, as Williamson (1993) and others have argued.

Worst of all, the implicit view of knowledge is still the erroneous view that objective knowledge is packaged in information, which is in principle accessible to all, and will yield shared objective knowledge that is the same for all takers. Personal knowledge is reduced to 'private information', which yields 'information asymmetries' (Milgrom & Roberts 1992: 140). This ignores issues of sense making and interpretation. It maintains what Quine (1960) called the 'museum' metaphor of meaning, according to which words are labels attached to some context-, speaker-, and hearer-independent package of meaning, as exhibits in a museum, and the 'conduit' metaphor of commun-ication, according to which the packages are transportable like objects. The implicit theory is that of the representational–computational theory of knowledge which is indeed the dominant view in cognitive science. I will criticize that, in Chapter 6, to arrive at the alternative theory of situated action, which supports the interactionist perspective.

With its erroneous view of knowledge, present economic science cannot access the idea that opportunism may be constrained (but not necessarily eliminated) by the fact that in social interaction people not only construct their partially idiosyncratic knowledge, but also internalize norms and values of conduct which limit oppor-tunism. Together with the routinization of behaviour this provides a basis for trust (Nooteboom 1996a, Nooteboom, Berger, & Noorderhaven 1997). Being based on an erroneous theory of knowledge and motivation, economics cannot appreciate how interaction produces learning and collaboration, and therefore it cannot appreciate the most fundamental reasons for interfirm collaboration and for communication within the firm.

The conclusion is not that we should ignore the progress that has been made in eco-nomics, but that we must seek out and where necessary transform the elements that remain valid from the interactionist perspective advocated in this book.

3.2.4 The Relevance of Economics

In spite of all the criticism, we pay a price for shedding mainstream economics entirely. Some elementary concepts from economics, especially industrial-organization economics, make sense and are useful to the purpose of this book. For example, decreasing marginal returns, economies of scale and scope, opportunity costs, entry barriers, sunk costs, transaction-specific investments, and their implications for the 'hold-up' problem.

I adopt the competence view of organizations, going back to Penrose (1959). That entails that the essence of competition lies in firms trying to be different, with differ-entiated products in different market segments, to evade pure price competition. They often succeed in achieving this, on the basis of firm-specific competencies, and thereby achieve economic rents. Even so, the old idea of pure price competition between close substitutes, on the basis of a stable, diffused technology, can still be useful as a bench-mark to contrast reality with. In some cases reality approaches that 'ideal', which is the entrepreneur's nightmare, in some markets for agricultural products, and raw materials, and financial markets. However, we see that where in view of close substitutes and stable, accessible, and diffused technology markets might approach the ideal, it is not achieved for other reasons. The ideal is not achieved because of protection of farmers in agricultural markets, or because of market concentration related to economies of scale, for example in process industries, or as a result of qualms about the destabilizing effects of efficient financial markets, which might lead to some form of regulation.

From the perspective of industrial-organization economics, with its 'structure–conduct–performance' perspective, market structure determines profit opportunities for firms. Porter (1980, 1985) brought this perspective into the management literature, in what has become known as the 'positioning view'. Strategy of firms entails that they find a proper place in a field of competitive forces, where they need to choose among 'generic strategies' of scale, differentiation, or 'focus' on some special market segment. His view has been justly criticized on the basis of the resource–competence argument that opportunities are not quite exogenous, but can be created by firms on the basis of firm-specific competencies, and this yielded the perspective of 'strategic choice' or 'strategic stretch', as opposed to 'strategic fit'. Rather than opportunities determining the allocation of resources, the allocation of resources to develop competencies determines opportunities. But the contrast between the positioning view and the view of strategic choice has been exaggerated. Porter's differentiation strategy makes sense only if obstacles to imitation protect differentiation. One basis for this is that the underlying competencies are more or less firm-specific, i.e. protected from 'spillover', which implicitly connects this view with the competence–resource view. Another basis might be collusion through some agreement not to imitate and to stay out of each other's markets. And the perspective of 'strategic choice' seems to be going overboard in a neglect of markets and competition. Thus, otherwise very valuable recent studies on organizational knowledge and learning (Nonaka & Takeuchi 1995, Choo 1998, Volberda 1998, see Chapter 2) tend to neglect markets and competition. Surely, we should combine both perspectives—of the creation of resources and competition. Why would organizational rigidity ever be a problem if there is no external threat of competition?

> For example, as discussed in Chapter 2, Nonaka and Takeuchi (1995) give interesting examples of how ideas for new products arise from taking tacit knowledge from some outside source, fitting it into inside tacit knowledge (in a process they call 'socialization'), and then transforming it into explicit knowledge (in 'externalization'). According to Nonaka and Takeuchi, ideas of such origin are put forward for decision by top management. The question is: From where does management obtain the wisdom to choose? There is no selection process in evidence, either internally or in markets. Another example is Volberda's interesting (1998) account of types of organizational flexibility. Here, the contingency driving the organizational form needed is 'turbulence', which is associated with 'hypercompetition': innovations and market changes tumble over each other at great speed. Here, one needs the highest level of organizational flexibility, with a danger of sliding into uncontrollable and counterproductive 'chaotic' forms of organization. That is a very

reasonable account. Next, as turbulence lessens (and technology settles into a dominant design), there is an opportunity to make the transition to a more stable, efficient, co-ordinated structure and process (for the usual reasons of scale and scope). Now, because the degree of turbulence is associated with degree of competition, the story is told as if the transition from chaos to system goes together with decreased competition. From a perspective of industrial-organization economics the opposite is the case. As the rate of innovative change reduces, technology settles into a dominant design, and patents start wearing out, it will tend to become less proprietary, and will spill over and diffuse. This raises the level of (price) competition, and thus creates a need to utilize opportunities for economy of scale, enabled by the growth of demand as new products diffuse. And how does the dominant design come about? This may be the result of internal selection, on the basis of testing prototypes technically and in trials with potential users, but often it is also market selection which will settle which design becomes dominant. Think, for example, of the case of the video recorder discussed in Chapter 1.

Summing up: We should combine processes of learning with market processes, and economics can still serve us to some extent, even if we reject the hard core of its research programme. What non-orthodox economists are in fact doing deviates substantially from that hard core. Even mainstream economists deviate from it, in their use of game theory, as I will indicate below. Scientific ideology is belied by the truth of actual practice. In this way, in some of its branches economics is losing its coherence and inertia, so that it may contribute to a new synthesis.

3.2.5   Game Theory?

If we are prepared to retain, quite opportunistically, whatever may be useful from economics, a thorny question concerns the relevance of game theory to the present project. In principle, game theory is not a theory but a method. But explicitly or implicitly theoretical assumptions need to be made for its application. In my view, prospects are dim for using it to construct models of specific, single-firm conditions, with the claim that they capture the situation sufficiently realistically to be used for prediction. One reason for this is that the outcomes of a game (in terms of Nash equilibria) are notoriously sensitive to the conditions assumed for the game. These include the identification and definition of strategies, the pay-offs, the assumption of rationality and the predominance of self-interest (absence of altruism or feelings of obligation), and the availability of information about all this to the players. Above all, the assumptions ignore the radical uncertainty that is characteristic of innovation and learning. In fact, strategies are often not identifiable prior to action, but evolve from it.

Nevertheless, game theory may be useful for analytical, taxonomic, and illustrative purposes. One definition of strategy, in the business literature, is that it concerns issues of long-term survival of the firm, which in turn entail issues concerning the firm's basic purpose and identity ('mission'), core competencies, or positioning in markets. Another meaning of 'strategy' derives from military thinking, and entails that one has to deal with intelligent opponents, in 'strategic' interaction. Game theory gives the only tool for the systematic analysis of such interaction that we have. How do we decide when and where the play of move and countermove stops? The notion of a Nash equilibrium yields a not unreasonable answer: It stops when for each player it is the case that given the current strategies chosen by the other players he cannot improve his position by changing his strategy. This begs a number of questions: How are such equilibria arrived at (trial and error, thought experiments?), and, if it is by trial and error, how stable are the game parameters in the process of search? In view of the restrictions we may be inclined to reject game theory, but what alternative do we have? How acceptable could it still be as a tool? Canonical game-theoretic models, such as prisoner dilemmas, co-ordination, and hawk–dove games serve to illustrate aspects of real phenomena, and to classify types of behaviour.

For example, the famous models of the prisoner's dilemma serve to illustrate a wide class of problems of co-operation. It is especially enlightening in its form of a repeated game, which illustrates the trade-off between defection now and the 'shadow of the future' in terms of the benefits of continued co-operation in the future. The game of 'chicken' may illustrate the problem of competitive collision in competition through simultaneous entry to a market. Games of co-ordination may illustrate the need for institutions to regulate behaviour on the basis of shared technical standards or rules.

> An example of the use of game theory for exploratory analysis is the following: In Nooteboom (1998) game theory was used to analyse when 'Japanese' forms of co-operative supplier–buyer relations are viable from a perspective of strategic interaction, in the sense that it can be construed as a stable outcome, in the form of a Nash equilibrium. No conditions could be found in which this is the case, and this raised some doubts as to whether perhaps the story of 'Japanese relationships' is a myth.

Game theory may function as a Trojan horse in economics: its enthusiastic reception in the neoclassical citadel is leading to the infiltration of forces of destruction. Game theory has thrown up the pervasiveness of multiple equilibria, not just in co-ordination games but in the generality of repeated games, and has thereby raised the spectre of indeterminacy. Equilibrium selection is often resolved by means such as 'focal points' (Schelling 1963), conventions, or other institutions that select an equilibrium in non-rational and non-individualistic ways, through socially inculcated habits or routines. This yields transgression of the limitations imposed by the 'hard core' of mainstream economics to rational choice and methodological individualism. Equilibrium selection in evolutionary game theory, in terms of evolutionary stable strategies, yields analytically tractable solutions only under very restrictive assumptions. This calls forth the need to actually model the evolutionary process of selection, by simulation perhaps. And if in the passage of time there is entry and exit, death and survival, why not also allow for learning and innovation, with changing pay-offs, preferences, and strategies? Along this path evolutionary game theory may call attention away from equilibria to dynamic, evolutionary processes of generation and selection of alternatives.

3.3   AUSTRIAN AND SCHUMPETERIAN ECONOMICS

Core features of Austrian and Schumpeterian economics are a process view of markets, subjectivity of knowledge, and entrepreneurship. Hayek, for example, argued
that the main concern of economics should be how 'knowledge is acquired and communicated'. The relevance to the project of this book is clear. Below, I discuss some
of the elements of Austrian economics and the views of Schumpeter, with a focus on
theories of entrepreneurship.

3.3.1   *Market Process*

When the only issue in markets is price determination, and we have the Walrasian
auctioneer of economic theory, there is no role for an entrepreneur. One might try to
save the concept of the auctioneer by saying that it constitutes a metaphor for the
totality of microlevel actions of arbitrage by entrepreneurs, which yield '*tâtonnement*'
towards equilibrium. But when equilibrium is claimed to arise instantaneously there
is no time for entrepreneurial action. According to the Austrian view of markets, the
determination of a market-clearing price is far from trivial. In a field of dispersed
knowledge, producers and consumers have to identify opportunities, recognize them
as relevant, match them with preferences, technological feasibilities, and their own
competencies. According to Austrian thought, this is done on a subjective basis:
different people not only have different preferences but also different perceptions,
interpretations, and understandings of utilities and feasibilities, which they adapt in
mutual interaction and communication. 'Different minds think different things'
(Lachmann 1978). This is highly attractive compared to mainstream economics,
which operates with notions such as the 'representative firm', and 'production functions', which assume that knowledge lies on the shelf, packaged in 'information' which
is equally accessible to all. It may entail 'search costs', but, when that expense is made,
different people have the same, objective knowledge.

   Austrians generally expect that interaction between these different minds thinking
different things sooner or later will yield an equilibrium of common understanding.
But I propose that interaction produces new perceptions, interpretations, meanings,
and technical possibilities. Products are adapted to a variety of tastes, and preferences
change. There is hardly a perspective for equilibrium ever to arise. The Austrians do
not tell us how that would work. This is because they put the individual on a pedestal,
to be respected and revered but not investigated. In the Austrian preservation of
methodological individualism the individual remains a black box, and there is no
analysis of the formation of preferences, perceptions, meaning, or knowledge. But this
position is very odd. If there is radical subjectivism, with different minds thinking different things, how can there be equilibrium through diffusion or growth of knowledge
without individuals changing their knowledge in interaction with others? We will

remain ignorant of the market process as long as we refuse to analyse how those minds work and how learning takes place. But if one performed such analysis, one would discover that perception, interpretation, and evaluation develop in interaction with other people, and this would constitute a threat to methodological individualism. This analysis is performed in Chapter 6.

3.3.2 Schumpeter

It is debatable whether Schumpeter is properly to be seen as an Austrian economist. He came from Austria, also took a process view of markets, and was interested in entrepreneurship. However, as Witt (1993*a*) has pointed out, he did not subscribe so much to the idea that knowledge is widely dispersed. According to Witt, Schumpeter viewed entrepreneurs as an élite, while according to (other) Austrian theorists (especially von Mises), entrepreneurship is widely dispersed.

The entrepreneur according to Schumpeter has variously been characterized as being non-adaptive, causing disequilibrium, generating innovation in the form of novel combinations, giving rise to creative destruction, and increasing uncertainty (Cheah & Robertson 1992). The entrepreneur according to (other) Austrians (Menger, Hayek, and, more recently, Kirzner) is adaptive, reacting to exogenous shocks of change, and draws the economy towards equilibrium, even if such equilibrium will never be achieved, because of changes of conditions along the way. There is an important difference, also, in the more modern Austrian theory of Kirzner. Consider the following quote (Kirzner 1973: 127, quoted in Foster 1998: 14): 'For Schumpeter the entrepreneur is the disruptive, disequilibrating force that dislodges the market from the somnolence of equilibrium; for us the entrepreneur is the equilibrating force whose activity responds to the existing tensions and provides those corrections for which the unexploited opportunities have been crying out'.

While Kirzner's entrepreneur is more 'alert' to new possibilities than other people, this is 'not really a theory about how agents create new data, but how they react to new data' (Foss 1994: 111). The question is how entrepreneurial action can also yield 'new data': how entrepreneurs can break through existing categorical imperatives. That does not necessarily mean that Schumpeterian entrepreneurship is inconsistent with other Austrian thought. It can mean simply that he focused on a feature that others did not. This fits with the endeavour of the present book: There is an overall process of discovery, in which different perspectives on entrepreneurship fit and are complementary. But note that Schumpeter also was unable to endogenize creation in the form of invention (cf. Witt 1993*a*): innovation was the realization of potential offered by invention. In the present book the ambition is to endogenize not only the realization but also the creation of potential, and thereby bring diverse notions of entrepreneurship together in a unifying theory.

Schumpeter made a well-known distinction between two different sources of innovation. The first, often called Schumpeter's 'mark I' notion of entrepreneurship, is the independent small entrepreneur, who acts by intuition, in bounded rationality, and survives or succumbs in trial and error. The second, or 'mark II', source of innovation is the large, rationalized Weberian firm, with innovation by planning on the basis of specialized teams. Usually, these 'first' and 'second' notions of entrepreneurship are interpreted as Schumpeter changing his mind. On the basis of quotes from Schumpeter's older and later work Langlois (1998) shows that the mark II notion was already present in his earlier work. The two notions are sequential not in the sense that Schumpeter changed his mind but in the sense that in the development of capitalism both the early (1909, English translation 1934) and late (1943) Schumpeter expected mark I to be replaced by mark II, in an ongoing Weberian process of rationalization. But this yields a puzzle: Can one have radically novel combinations, and the associated creative destruction of technology, while preserving the organizational integrity of a large firm? In this book it will be argued that one cannot, and that while there are good reasons for Chandlerian integration of activities in a large firm, disintegration is needed for ongoing innovation. It will be argued that mark I and mark II follow each other, in an ongoing cycle of discovery. There is no end to history.

In his later work Kirzner (1985) recognized the linkage and complementarity between Schumpeterian innovation and Austrian arbitrage. Cheah and Robertson (1992) made a further attempt to demonstrate the complementarity and interdependence of Schumpeterian and Austrian entrepreneurship, by proposing that along the product life cycle shifts occur between the two types of entrepreneurship. I will extend and partly modify their argument.

3.3.3   *Entrepreneurship*

While the subject of entrepreneurship is characteristic of Austrian economics, other economists of course have also considered it (cf. Hébert & Link 1982, van Dijk & Thurik 1998). There is a range of notions of entrepreneurship, emphasizing different things, in different combinations. This may include innovation (Bentham, Thünen, Schumpeter, and perhaps Say), the identification and utilization of possibilities for consumption and production (Cantillon, Smith, Menger, Mises, Hayek, Kirzner), the configuration and management of production factors for efficient production (Say, Marshall, Mises), and the provision of capital (Marshall). Some theorists emphasize the acceptance of risks (Cantillon, Say, Knight), and the role of fundamental, unpredictable uncertainty (Cantillon, Knight, Menger).

Associated with different roles of entrepreneurs different characteristics, resources, or competencies have been identified: imagination, alertness, perceptiveness, open-mindedness; judgement, sense of realism; risk acceptance, risk reduction; perseverance, ambition or need for achievement, independence, charisma, strength of personality; capability of leadership, managerial capability. This book will propose, in Chapter 13, that rather than any single notion or characteristic of entrepreneurship being universally 'true', regardless of context and conditions, different notions fit different stages in an overall development process.

There are cases of entrepreneurship that cannot without serious distortion be assigned exclusively to the Schumpeterian or the Kirznerian type, because they contain elements of both.

> Consider the example of railroads discussed by Schumpeter himself (1939, quoted in Andersen 1992). Uncertainty is reduced as railroads diffuse, and entrepreneurship in this area becomes increasingly routine. But now consider the 'ice-station' innovation of beer brewer Annheuser Bush (AB). By combining railroad transportation with the cooling of beer by means of 'ice stations', AB greatly extended the feasible distance between market and production, thereby realizing great economies of scale in brewing. An innovation which seems Schumpeterian was produced as a combination of well-diffused, settled technologies of railroads and cooling, in an identification of possibilities from existing technology and practice which might as well be seen as Kirznerian.

Schumpeterian entrepreneurs build on inventions that are already there, and in that sense also 'merely' utilize existing potential. And there are different levels of innovativeness: basic innovations, which have pervasive effects for many production sectors and markets, and cumulative innovations in the form of diverse applications and modifications of such basic technology in different fields or contexts. Without such innovations of application, creative destruction would not take place, and the basic innovation would remain a mere potentiality. Is this secondary innovation Schumpeterian or Kirznerian? It is Schumpeterian in that it creates forms that did not exist before, upsets the allocation of resources previously established, and exerts creative destruction. It is Kirznerian in that in the process of diffusion along the technical trajectory (cf. Dosi, 1984) uncertainty is reduced, and gaps between actual and possible use are reduced. Thus, along the trajectory we find a combination of the two types, with the emphasis shifting from Schumpeterian to Kirznerian, as pointed out by Cheah and Robertson (1992). Conceptually the distinction may be maintained, but mixes or intermediate cases appear.

Note that diffusion does not consist in a simple mechanical 'working out' of a single innovation. Generally, new contexts or new applications require adjustment or 'reinvention'. Often, novel combinations are achieved in a mix of complementary innovations in technology, marketing, organization, and institutional conditions. Different firms have different constellations of resources, partly firm-specific, partly embedded in teams, organizational structure, and culture, where adoption of innovation is seldom a mere slotting in and typically requires a reconstruction of existing structure, procedure, and culture. What is established at an industry level may require quite fundamental shifts at the firm level. That is why in the innovation literature a distinction is made between processes new for the world, for an industry, and for a firm. In short, diffusion requires innovation on the part of users.

In this book entrepreneurship is seen in both the creation and the realization of potential. A Schumpeterian entrepreneur creates potential in the form of a new product or process, which is subsequently diffused, but realizes potential in that existing knowledge (invention) is transformed into commercially viable products and processes. An inventor creates potential for Schumpeterian entrepreneurs, but realizes potential from pre-existing knowledge. So, we retain the conceptual difference between Schumpeterian and Kirznerian entrepreneurship, as the production and realization of potential, but in a framework which allows for intermediate cases and recognizes that entrepreneurship will have more or less of the one or the other. We no longer have a Schumpeterian Shiva of creative destruction, far above the uniform grey masses of routine conduct, but a spectrum of innovation and diffusion, of creation and realization of potential.

The point now is that in order to satisfy the Schumpeterian challenge, not only innovation but also the formation of perception, knowledge, meaning, and preference must be endogenized (cf. Rosenberg 1992). Furthermore, as will be shown in later Chapters, the creation and realization of potential are mutually dependent, not only because realization requires prior creation, but also because realization provides the basis for a next round of creation. We need a theory that gives an account of the process of realization and creation of potential, which shows how creation arises from realization endogenously. How can we conceptualize an ongoing and open-ended process (Vaughn 1994: 169)? What conceptual framework can we devise to reconcile permanence, coherence, and flexibility (Vaughn 1994: 157)?

If innovation is creative destruction, what are the sources and process of creation? Does it strike at random? Is it like mutation in biological evolution? Does economic structure evolve from chance hits of entrepreneurial success, and evolutionary pressures eliminating maladapted firms? The evolutionary perspective will be discussed in a separate chapter (Chapter 4).

3.4   THE RESOURCE–COMPETENCE VIEW

The resource–competence view is of central importance in this book. I propose that in combination with an interactionist, social-constructivist theory of knowledge and meaning it can provide the basis for a theoretical synthesis. That development will be presented in Part II of the book. Here, the basic principles are set out. Finally, the differences between resources and competencies are considered.

3.4.1   *The Basics*

The resource- or competence-based view goes back to the work of Penrose (1959). (For an introduction and survey see Foss and Knudsen (1996).) The central point is that firms are seen as bundles of resources or competencies which to a greater or lesser extent are specific to the firm. They cannot be instantly copied by other firms because they are to some extent inscrutable or subject to 'causal ambiguity' (Lippman & Rumelt 1982), and difficult to imitate. This is so because the knowledge involved is to a greater or lesser extent tacit and embodied in the heads and hands of people, in teams, organizational structure and procedures, and organizational culture. It is particularly such unique capabilities of firms, in addition to market structure (concentration, price elasticity, and other entry barriers), that yield a profit.

The interest of economists in the revival of Penrose's ideas is somewhat surprising to the business scholar, who looks on in amazement at how economists are surprised at the revelation that the distinctive property of firms is to build and exploit firm-specific competencies. In the business literature, this is a resounding triviality.

This view has implications that are equally unsurprising to the business scholar, but nevertheless of great importance to economics. In particular, it affects our view of what competition entails and how markets operate. It abolishes the notion of the 'representative firm': firms try to be different, and generally succeed, and this difference is crucial for our understanding of competition and markets. Firms compete not by striving to do the same thing most efficiently, but by trying to be different; to offer differentiated products on the basis of firm-specific competencies. Whereas former notions of markets and firms as production functions saw market opportunity driving the utilization of resources, here it is rather the other way around: resources determine market opportunities.

3.4.2   Tacit Knowledge

The notion of tacit knowledge was discussed in Chapter 2. Here, the discussion is extended in the context of the operation and generation of competencies. Tacitness of knowledge, next to the embedding of knowledge in teams, organizational structure, and culture, forms an important part of the reason that competence does not spill over easily, and firms can protect their distinctive competencies from imitation for at least some time.

With this I do not want to suggest that explicit and implicit knowledge are separated in the mind. They are intertwined, and externalization into documented knowledge will always involve some loss of tacit knowledge. Organizational 'routines' (Nelson & Winter 1982) generally include both documented, implicit non-documented but documentable, and implicit, tacit, and hard-to-document knowledge. Probably there are also degrees of tacitness: knowledge that has sunk more or less deeply into non-voluntary, automatic-reflexive and less reflective reaches of the mind–body constellation (Merleau-Ponty 1964, Lakoff & Johnson 1999).

Thus, there is a difference between knowledge which is documentable, with more or less effort, because once it was explicit and part of declarative knowledge, and knowledge which is very hard to document, because it was never part of declarative memory and has always been only procedural, obtained in learning by doing rather than in formal instruction.

As indicated in Chapter 1, tacit knowledge may present an obstacle for change, by blocking absorptive capacity. But it is also useful, and in any case inevitable. It is useful for the same reasons that Herbert Simon adduced for the rationality of routines. In fact, routines, in the sense that he used the term, as implicit, non-reflective practices, and tacit knowledge are closely related, and probably overlapping, concepts. Simon's argument followed from his notion of bounded rationality: If our capacity for rational evaluation is limited, it is rational to limit rationality in the sense of leaving some behaviour up to an 'automatic pilot', in the form of a subconscious or semi-conscious routine. The practice that it involves may once have been based on explicit, declarative knowledge, but it was effective ('satisficing') so consistently that one could permit it to become tacit, and thereby reserve capacity for explicit, rational evaluation for novel conditions that demand priority of attention. Routines form a mechanism for survival. The relegation of conduct to routines is itself not reflective but a routine: we do it automatically. But of course routines entail a danger: If conditions change to make the routine inappropriate, we may not notice it in time, or we may not be able to change it. This also indicates the rationality of emotion: triggered by exceptional danger or opportunity it shifts the agenda to the reconsideration or break-up of routines (Simon 1983), unless they have sunk too deep for that into our mind–body constellation.

Routines are efficient not only in human thought, but also in organizations. They allow for co-ordinated behaviour between different, complementary activities, for the sake of efficient exploitation. They eliminate the need to specify and discuss at each moment what precisely has to be done and how. People acquire such routines when they join an organization by a process of socialization, in a community of practice (Brown & Duguid 1996). Since routines are efficient, it is irritating to the community of practice to question them, and such questioning may turn one into an outcast. It is precisely the efficiency of all this that turns it into such an obstacle to change.

Summing up: tacit knowledge neatly reflects the core issue of this book—how to combine efficient exploitation, which requires routinization in tacit knowledge, with exploration, which requires deroutinization. As a result, organizational learning is to a large extent a problem of dealing with tacit knowledge, as Nonaka and Takeuchi (1995) understood so well.

3.4.3   Firm-Size Effects

It was noted how tacitness of knowledge may seriously inhibit adaptation and absorption capacity. This tends to be a bigger problem in smaller firms, because knowledge tends to be more tacit there. Here lies the deeper significance of the notion of 'craft industries'. In 'communities of practice', competence is often acquired not by formal instruction but by learning by doing. The apprentice imitates the master, his role model and exemplary cause (remember that this was the root meaning of 'paradigm'), and builds up his tacit cognitive repertoire on the basis of this. The same thing happens to a greater or lesser extent in large firms, but it is typical of the crafts that tend to prevail in smaller firms. It is also part of being a 'professional'. In large firms communities of practice have to submit, to a greater or lesser extent, to an encompassing regime of co-ordination and control, which requires legitimization and communication on the basis of explicit, documented knowledge.

This explains the familiar phenomenon that often in small business it is difficult to get novel technology adopted. This provides a problem in government technology policy. That sensibly seeks to stimulate not only innovation but also its diffusion, especially among small firms.[3] The customary explanation of the problem of diffusion is that small businessmen typically have too low a level of education and abstraction to grasp novel technology. While that is often true, a better explanation is that in small firms there is a greater share of tacit, procedural knowledge, which has the property indicated above. For transfer of new knowledge to small business, it is not very useful to just drop off a blueprint or manual, or even to try and explain what the new knowledge entails and how it is to be used. In view of the predominance of tacit knowledge, one needs first to create awareness of existing practices and make them explicit. The consultant has to operate like Socrates, and cull out awareness of existing knowledge and prejudice by letting the entrepreneur find out for himself, by intellectual midwifery ('*maieutics*') (Nooteboom 1994). This typically takes the form of sitting around a table with entrepreneurs who are sufficiently similar to make sense to each other and sufficiently different not to be direct competitors, and by comparing their practices to make them explicit. Here, metaphor can be effective, as is demonstrated in Plato's dialogues.

Another way to circumvent the problem of knowledge transfer to small business is to transfer it embodied in people rather than programmes. Then one has to go through a lengthy process of absorbing novelty by socialization, which requires actually working and interacting with people in the small firm, to demonstrate how the novelty would work in practice. That is why one effective method of technology transfer to small firms is to station people in the firm who are skilled in the new technology, for a sufficient length of time. For small firms the proof of the pudding often is not in the recipe but in the eating.[4]

It should be noted that there are good reasons for knowledge being more tacit in smaller firms. It is feasible because there is less division of labour and more direct supervision because of the small scale of operation and proximity between workers and the entrepreneur. This limits the need for documentation that would otherwise be required for co-ordination and control across many people and greater distances. It is desirable for greater flexibility, speed of adjustment, and custom-made products: when there are no formal rules one can more easily improvise. Such customized production has been a traditional strength of the smaller firm. It is also desirable because it allows for more integrated task performance, which tends to yield more job satisfaction and motivation.[5]

---

[3] Even in developed economies they constitute more than 90 per cent of all firms, and some 60 per cent of total employment in the market sector. Diffusion of technology to them is needed because it is not so much in the generation as in the use of novelty that economic growth emerges.

[4] This explains the success of a programme, in the Netherlands, called 'Knowledge Bearers in Small- and Medium-sized Enterprise'. It was instituted to transfer technology by subsidizing the trial employment in small business of graduates from universities and polytechnics.

[5] This does not imply that in smaller firms work is more attractive in all respects. There are fewer career prospects because there are fewer hierarchical levels. The firm's risk of discontinuity, and hence risk of layoffs, is greater because there is a smaller spread of risks across different markets and products. Small firms can more easily dodge labour laws and regulations because they are expensive to monitor for control agencies. It can be less attractive for small firms to offer internal training because then staff are tempted to leave sooner because of the limited career prospects available.

A greater share of tacit knowledge is also desirable for limiting spillover, since tacit competencies spill over less easily than documented ones. This is important because for small firms patent protection is less feasible because of the higher set-up costs of a patent, higher cost of monitoring patent infringement, and lesser credibility of the threat of legal action in case of infringement. This is because of more limited abilities for monitoring and the relatively greater costs and risks of legal action.

A greater share of tacit knowledge also carries disadvantages. The limitation of absorptive capacity provides an obstacle for change, which is a problem in itself, as discussed, but it also raises transaction costs for the small firm's partners (Nooteboom 1993*a*). Since knowledge is less documented, knowledge about the firm's knowledge requires relatively intimate and time-consuming contact (e.g. to conduct the '*maieutics*' mentioned before). This has already been mentioned as a problem for a consultant who aims to help the firm adopt novel technology. However, it is a problem for transaction partners more generally: the supplier who needs to find out what the firm needs, the buyer who wants to assess the competencies and reliability of the firm.

A further problem of tacit knowledge in the hands or heads of people is that when the people leave the knowledge leaves also. The firm is more vulnerable to the loss of people. This applies also to the entrepreneur himself: much of the knowledge of the firm is stored in his head, and gets lost when he drops out in illness or in death.

3.4.4   *Resources and Competencies*

Finally, we need to face the question of what the differences are between 'resources' and 'competencies'. One view is that competencies are a special kind of resource. In this view, resources are made up of those things to which one can lay a claim of property rights, called assets, abilities to which one cannot lay such a claim, called competencies, and 'positional advantages' of market position, location, or network position (Stoelhorst 1997).

Another view sees competencies as abilities to utilize resources. Yet another view sees competencies as the basis for developing resources. As discussed in Chapter 2, Schein (1985) distinguished between the deep structure of culture, in the form of fundamental categories of perceiving the organization, its relation with the environment, and people and their relations, and the surface structure of organizational symbols, heroes, rituals, myths, and the like which it produces. Similarly, competencies might be seen as underlying categories of perception and knowledge that yield a surface structure of knowledge, skills, and other resources.

Perhaps the latter two views can be combined, as follows. Foss (1996: 1) defines competencies as 'a typically idiosyncratic knowledge capital that allows the holders to perform activities . . . in certain ways, and typically to do this more efficiently than others'. That seems a very reasonable definition, close to our common understanding of the notion of competence. If we allow for a wide meaning of efficiency, to include dynamic efficiency and learning, the efficient performance of an activity entails both the efficient use of resources and the development of such resources. Here, we are back at the basic theme of this book: the theme of combining exploitation and exploration. Then competencies can be understood to entail both the efficient use and the development of resources.

If we accept that activities arise at different levels, with higher levels of activity utilizing resources that in turn entail activities using lower-level resources, we arrive at a multilevel, relative conceptualization. Then a competence is a resource in a higher-level activity, and the resource used in any one competence will often entail lower-level competencies. Later, in Chapter 10, I will develop this notion of different levels of nested activities in terms of multilevel scripts.

The attraction of this view of different levels of competencies and resources is that it may contribute to an answer to one of the research questions, concerning the multilevel issue: How can we link the levels of people, organizations, and industries.

3.5 COMPETENCE, KNOWLEDGE, AND LEARNING

The competence view of the firm calls forth the need for an explicit theory of knowledge and learning. As indicated before, I employ a constructivist, interactionist theory. The underlying theory of knowledge and language is developed more fully later, in Chapters 6 and 7. Here, I summarize the main implications for the theory of the firm.

3.5.1 *The Firm as a Focusing Device*

As a result of construction by interaction, cognition is cumulative, and to a greater or lesser extent idiosyncratic and path-dependent (Nooteboom 1992*a*): past experience determines absorptive capacity (Cohen & Levinthal 1990). People and firms have different knowledge to the extent that they have different experiences and little interaction.

Consequently, as discussed in Chapter 2, the primary function of the firm may be cognitive, as a focusing device (Nooteboom 1996*b*): in order to achieve anything at all, a firm must direct and align perception, understanding, and evaluation by the people connected with it.

This connects with the Schumpeterian idea of the entrepreneur as a charismatic figure who not only combines resources but also aligns people in their cognition and purpose (cf. Witt 1998*b*). It also fits with Weick's (1995) view that 'the process of decision making must embrace the process of sensemaking . . . shared assumptions and experiences . . . constrain the ways that people in an organization perceive the world . . . [this forms] aspects of premise control . . . which joins sensemaking with decision making' (quoted in Choo 1998: 16).

But this solution to the problem of cognition and action raises another problem: By focusing in one direction one runs the risk of missing out on perception of opportunities

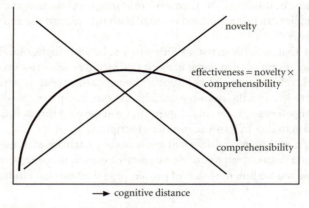

FIGURE 3.1   *Cognitive distance*

and threats from other directions. The need for such focusing as well as the problem
of myopia that it involves are greater to the extent that the environment is more
complex and variable, and to the extent that firms must strive to differentiate their
products. For several reasons there is such a tendency towards 'radical product differentiation' (Nooteboom 1999*a*). The causes of it are analysed in Chapter 8.

3.5.2   *External Economy of Cognitive Scope*

To hedge the risk of myopia, one needs complementary, outside sources of cognition:
cognition by others, which is relevant but also different. I have called this the principle of 'external economy of cognitive scope' (Nooteboom 1992*a*). Such outside
sources of complementary cognition require a 'cognitive distance' which is sufficiently small to allow for understanding but sufficiently large to yield non-redundant,
novel knowledge.[6] For the external source to maintain novelty it is crucial to maintain
distance. This is illustrated in Figure 3.1.

A large cognitive distance has the merit of novelty but the problem of limited comprehensibility. Effectiveness of learning by interaction can be construed as the product of the two, which yields an optimal cognitive distance (Nooteboom 1999*a*/*b*). The
argument indicates that in order to co-operate one may have to invest in sufficient
knowledge to understand the partner and achieve sufficient absorptive capacity. If
knowledge is codifiable, maintaining R & D in the areas of the partner's activity can do
this. This explains the empirical phenomenon that when firms outsource activities
their R & D does not necessarily go down (Granstrand, Patel, & Pavitt 1997). In other

---

[6] The analysis links up with the notion from evolutionary economics that innovation requires a source
of variety to generate novel experiments that are subjected to the selection mechanism of markets. When
cognition is firm-specific, novelty requires a collection of different firms with different perceptions based
on different experiences.

words, firms may invest in R & D outside their areas of core competence. Of course, one may at the same time find that there is less R & D in the case of co-operation than in its absence, because one now utilizes the complementary competence and R & D of the partner. When we look at total R & D, the two effects may cancel out. This explains why in some studies one finds a positive effect between R & D collaboration and internal R & D, in some cases no effect and in some cases a reverse effect, as discussed in Chapter 1. But Pavitt (1998) is no doubt correct in concluding that when we talk of 'core competence' and the need to engage in outside collaboration, we need to distinguish between competence in product development, production, marketing, and distribution, and technological competence. The latter may need to remain wide ('distributed') in order to maintain outside collaboration.

However, when knowledge is tacit one will need prolonged intensive interaction to achieve mutual understanding. Thus, we arrive at two measures of absorptive capacity: R & D in the case of codifiable knowledge and interaction in the case of tacit knowledge.

The argument also indicates that a low absorptive capacity entails a downward shift of the line indicating comprehension, yielding a shift to the left of optimal cognitive distance. In other words, firms with low absorptive capacity, such as, typically, small, technologically not very advanced firms, will need to utilize sources with limited cognitive distance—not so much universities and technological institutes as customers, suppliers, banks, colleagues. This is what has repeatedly been found in empirical research, as indicated in Chapter 1.

A sharp test of the hypothesis of cognitive distance can be made. In the estimate of the effect of distance on the effectiveness of information from partners (effect on innovation, productivity, or profit), add a quadratic term. If it has a significant negative effect, it would confirm the hypothesis of an inverted U shape (Figure 3.1).

Later, in Chapter 8, the notions of cognitive distance, absorptive capacity, and learning by interaction will be developed in more detail.

3.6 CONCLUSION

Can economics help us in resolving the paradox of exploitation and exploration? In Schumpeterian economics, innovation seems associated with exploration and diffusion with exploitation, but the connections have not yet been clarified. In particular, the origin of creative destruction has not been clarified, other than that it yields novel combinations. How do these novel combinations arise? Why should they have any chance of success? As discussed before, this is the fundamental problem of abduction, and no solution has been given.

Austrian economics yields the needed process view of markets, and considers competition as a discovery procedure. However, it deserts us when it comes to the clinch of understanding how knowledge shifts in interaction between 'different minds thinking different things', because the black boxes of the minds of individuals and the knowledge in firms remain closed.

However, it seems that on the basis of the competence view of firms we can arrive at a reasonably coherent theoretical framework, in which we can build bridges between the literatures on management and organization and (mostly non-mainstream) economics. Such a synthesis has not been achieved yet. One might have the intuition that evolutionary theory might offer solutions. That is the subject for the next Chapter.

4

Evolution[1]

This Chapter examines the usefulness of an evolutionary perspective. That perspective is useful, in some respects, but entails many pitfalls when applied in socio-economic contexts. There, institutions form at least part of the selection environment. However, they not only select but also enable and constitute behaviour, and they are themselves shaped by the behaviour that they select. Furthermore, by focusing on population effects, evolutionary theory tends to neglect adaptation and innovation by learning, the generation of novelty in behaviour. This is especially serious since the generation of novelty is embedded in the selection process. I conclude that the biological metaphor of evolution may have reached the point of being more misleading than useful. At this stage of development, I prefer to employ metaphors or models from knowledge and language to arrive at a theory of self-organization. After all, organizations and innovation systems are not so much biological organisms as learning systems based on symbols, communication, and thought.

4.1   EVOLUTIONARY THEORY

Evolutionary economics goes back to the nineteenth century, in the work of Malthus and Veblen, and has enjoyed a revival since the seventies (see in particular Nelson & Winter 1982, and, for more recent views, Witt 1993*b*, Hodgson 1993, Vromen 1995, and Metcalfe 1998). This paragraph gives a summary of evolutionary theory and reviews the reasons why it may be of interest. It has had an important effect in drawing the attention of economists to dynamic processes of change, and to the diversity of firms.

4.1.1   Evolution

By 'evolution' I do not mean development in any loose sense but 'phylogenetic' evolution of populations. This can be characterized as follows (derived from Rose 1997: 181):

[1] I thank Richard Nelson and Geoffrey Hodgson for comments on a draft of this Chapter. Of course the usual disclaimer applies.

1. A population ('species') is characterized by a gene pool ('genome'). Like breeds with like, i.e. within the species, and breeding yields inheritance of genes.
2. Inherited genes enable development ('ontogenetic development') of a variety of individual life forms ('phenotypes').
3. Some of these varieties fit their environment better than others.
4. All life forms together produce more offspring than can survive to breed in their turn.
5. The better-fitting varieties are more likely to survive long enough to breed ('selection').
6. Hence there will be differential birth and death, with a greater share of the fitting varieties in the next generation ('sorting'), and in this way the species will evolve over time ('phylogenetic development').

Step 4 is necessary in the syllogism: if resources are unlimited and can support both fit and unfit individuals, selection and sorting need not occur. This first escaped Darwin, until he adopted it from Malthus.

According to one view (Metcalfe 1998), evolution entails a general principle of population thinking that may apply to any population, not just in biology. A population of different forms may change its composition because of differential selection and multiplication, even if individual forms do not adapt in any way. This yields the basis for formal analysis that may apply in a number of fields.

That may deviate considerably from Darwinian evolution. There, characteristics derive from a set of genes (or their analogues); it is the genes and not characteristics acquired during the lifespan of a form that are transmitted; transmission is based on sexual procreation; there is no procreation across different species; variety is generated by random mutations of genes. Novel combinations of genes, in Mendelian processes, with dominant and recessive properties, yield a variety of life forms.

Classical Darwinism was non-hierarchical, i.e. focused on evolution at a single level of life forms. There, selection and sorting go together. Eldredge and Gould (1972) recognized that there may be a hierarchy of several levels (genes within the organism; species of organism), and then selection and sorting may separate and take place at different levels: sorting at one level may be the result of selection at another. Species sorting may be the result of selection on its individuals, and then is thoroughly Darwinian. It may also be the result of species selection, on the basis of group characteristics affecting the fitness of the species, which is controversial in biology. Such characteristics may, or may not, take the form of emergent characteristics that arise by non-additivity and interaction among lower-level traits, affecting differential birth rate, for example (Gould 1989).

Punctuated-equilibrium theory, initiated by Eldredge and Gould (1972), seeks to explain the stylized fact that in the development of many species there have been prolonged periods of stasis, punctuated by change that is abrupt in terms of geological time. The explanation of stasis is not yet satisfactory, but some indications are given. It is attributed to external constraints on variety, such as inherent limitations of geometry, physics, and chemistry, and to internal factors, such as the elimination of deviants in the population. Punctuation is attributed to 'allopatric speciation': small populations isolated at peripheries of parental ranges develop into separate species.

> An example of geometric constraint on forms of life lies in the geometry of spheres and circles. In Chapter 3 I discussed the economy of scale involved. Costs are associated with surface, which for a sphere is proportional to the square of the radius, and turnover is associated with the content of the sphere, which is proportional to the cube of the radius, so that the ratio between turnover and costs is proportional to the radius. The same principle applies to the ratio between the surface and periphery of a circle. However, in life forms increase of scale can be a liability—for example, if metabolism (consumption of nutrients and waste production) is proportional to content and assimilation of food and excretion of waste are proportional to surface, as in a cell. Then, beyond a certain size the life form will starve or poison itself. In animals, heat exchange with the environment also operates through the surface, while heat production is proportional to content. Therefore, when there is a large difference between internal and external temperature, as in the case of warm-blooded animals in polar climates, or not so warm-blooded animals in hot climates, animals need to be large and bulbous, or to have thick fur or skin. Consider whales, polar bears, walruses, elephants, and hippopotami. However, animals that in their strenuous exertion produce a lot of heat in hot climates, such as panthers, cougars, and the like, need to be thin and slim.

For the project of this book, an evolutionary view is attractive, at first glance, for several reasons. It tries to deal with the core problem of how transformation (at the population level) and continuity (of genes) may be reconciled and connected; how novelty may arise from forms of life as they function in their environment. Perhaps the functioning of life forms in their selection environment can be interpreted as exploitation, and the emergence of novel population structures as exploration. Evolution operates without any preceding design, which is what we need, in view of radical uncertainty. In other words, it may give us a handle on the problem of abduction. The evolutionary perspective emphasizes differences between firms: variety is needed for the evolutionary process to yield change at the population level. This connects with the resource–competence perspective, discussed in Chapter 3, which also emphasizes interfirm differences as the basis of competition.

4.1.2   Metaphoric Shift

In economics, the metaphor of evolution is fairly straightforward and it is useful for several reasons. It is straightforward as an analogue of Adam Smith's struggle for profit to survive in markets. In fact, rather than economics following evolutionary theory, it was Smith's vision that 'provided Darwin's immediate inspiration for the fully articulated theory of natural selection' (Gould 1989: 126).

Evolutionary theory is useful to break down the notion that firms are homogeneous —represented by the 'representative firm'—and to show that the diversity of firms is crucial for the development of industries or innovation systems, and that diversity of opinion is crucial for learning in organizations. It is also useful to draw attention away from the equilibrium outcomes that preoccupy mainstream economics towards the dynamic of processes which generally will not lead to equilibria, to emphasize the irreversibility of time, and to emphasize that 'development' does not necessarily yield improvement (Hodgson 1993). As such it illustrates one of the themes in this book: the role of metaphor in discovery.

Paradoxically, however, as mentioned in the methodological discussion in Chapter 1, economists use the evolutionary metaphor to justify rather than reject equilibrium analysis, through the argument that market selection produces efficient equilibrium outcomes. This goes back to the celebrated 'Friedman debate'. Milton Friedman (1953) argued the 'instrumentalist' position that realism of explanatory principles is irrelevant: all that counts is that they yield correct predictions. Of course people do not make full rational calculations in choice, but somehow, if we 'do as if', and make the assumption, we arrive at predictions that are valid. Alchian (1950) and Friedman also gave a more substantive defence of rational choice, on the basis of an evolutionary argument. If firms do not choose and implement the most efficient possible solutions they will not survive in competition: the market will select them out.

> Suppose that at some moment a thousand motorists depart from Chicago in random directions, but there are petrol stations only along one route. Then, a thousand miles out we will see cars moving only along the route with stations, and it is as if that route has been consciously and rationally chosen by those motorists.

I will not repeat the arguments for realistic assumptions, given in Chapter 1. The point here is that the evolutionary defence of the rational-choice assumption does not hold water, as shown by Winter (1964). First, even if competition is as stringent as indicated, it is not the best possible (absolute fitness) that survives, but the best that happens to be available in the population at the outset (relative fitness). Second, if there is economy of scale, large firms may survive at the expense of small firms even if they are inefficient for their size. Moreover, large firms arise according to Gibrat's law: if percentage growth is allocated randomly, then firms that happen to get a large growth rate will tend to increase their lead (Ijiri & Simon 1977). Third, competition may not in fact be so stringent as to yield the 'situational determinism' of maximum efficiency as the 'single exit' of survival in the selection environment (Latsis 1980). There may be other 'exits', as the result of economy of scale, as already mentioned, collusion, and entry barriers or product differentiation. Above all, if we allow for the passage of time in an evolutionary process, we should allow for learning, innovation, change of preferences, and change of institutions in the selection environment. In spite of these refutations of evolutionary arguments for maximum efficiency, recent economists such as North (1990) and Williamson (1975, 1985) have maintained the notion.

Finally, as Koopmans (1957) indicated, if the argument is that selection allows only the single exit of maximal profits, then the theory should say precisely that, and not hide in a counterfactual behavioural assumption. If the argument is evolutionary, then let us be consistent and develop theory in explicitly evolutionary terms, and study evolutionary processes.

Product differentiation is especially important, because it is pervasive, if we accept the resource–competence view that firms manage to be different, yielding different advantages in different market segments, and can protect at least some of their advantage for at least some of the time. As a result of product differentiation they can make a profit. This allows for some slack: suboptimal efficiency in the static sense. This may not be bad from the perspective of dynamic efficiency: such slack allows for the learning and experimentation that yield innovation, as I investigate in this book.

4.1.3 Population Ecology

Population ecology (Hannan and Freeman 1977) takes an evolutionary approach. Especially in its earlier versions, change occurs not at the firm level but only at the population level, as a result of the selection process. Firms are taken as inert, or, in more sophisticated formulations, as 'relatively inert': in the long run their capacity for ongoing adaptation will lag behind environmental change (Hannan & Freeman 1984). But this is difficult to square with the stylized fact that regularly organizations manage to perform drastic and repeated transformations and to survive in the long run. It is also theoretically implausible, and seems to derive from an exaggerated analogy with biology. The behaviour of the phenotype (a firm) is not entirely 'hard-wired', like instinctual behaviour in animals, but is amenable to a certain amount of 'reprogramming', called learning. Thereby it has an ability to adapt to the selection environment (Levinthal 1996), or even to modify or construct that environment by innovation. A lesser complication is that if we take the firm as the phenotype on which selection exerts its grip, we run into problems: When does a firm die, and how should we deal with mergers and acquisitions? How do we define the identity of a firm, and how do we trace its existence through time? How do we establish the identity of populations? A bigger problem is what constitutes the analogue of genes: What is the source of the characteristics of a firm or part of a firm (such as a business unit), how do they mutate, is this mutation random, and how are characteristics transmitted? How do new species evolve? These questions apply to population ecology as they do to evolutionary economics.

4.1.4 Evolutionary Economics

According to Hodgson (1993), evolutionary theory in economics, in the specific, phylogenetic sense indicated above, in terms of the evolutionary trinity of variety, selection, and transmission, goes back to Malthus and Veblen. While other major economists, such as Marshall and Hayek, employed notions of 'evolution' and made analogies to biology, this did not consistently include selection processes. It referred to evolution in a looser sense of 'development' (Marshall), or was combined with the maintenance of an equilibrium of 'spontaneous order' (Hayek), which is in conflict with the ongoing change, not necessarily for the better, that evolution entails. Hodgson also argues that contrary to the common opinion that Schumpeter is the evolutionary economist *par excellence*, he expressed himself against biological meta-phors as not useful, or even misleading. Schumpeter was also ambivalent in the sense that he persistently maintained the ambition to reconcile innovation with Walrasian equilibrium. Schumpeter was interested in discontinuities; in saltations of innovation that upset equilibrium, after which forces of diffusion again tend towards equilibrium.

Veblen, still according to Hodgson's account, from the beginning maintained a consistent, selectionist evolutionary view, in which he showed awareness of some of the crucial differences from biological evolution. In particular, he accepted that not only phenotypes were 'units of selection', i.e. subject to selection and evolutionary change, but also institutions, which he defined as 'settled habits of thought that apply to the generality of people'. In his view the process is Lamarckian: institutions are adapted before they are passed on to subsequent generations. At the same time he re-cognized 'institutional inertia' and saw institutions also as 'factors of selection', i.e. they are part of the environment that selects individual behaviour. It remained unclear, however, what constitutes the environment for selection of institutions, how such selection takes place, and how institutional adaptation and inertia are combined. As we will see later in this Chapter, that is still a central issue.

The subject is important, because it is close to the central issue in this book: How can established ways of thinking and of doing things operate as selection devices for behaviour, for the sake of exploitation, and yet be somehow changed and replaced, in exploration? How can we reconcile continuity and change?

In modern evolutionary economics, what is the analogue of the genome? Usually it is some configuration of technology and organization, in the form of routines (Nelson & Winter 1982), or business units (Metcalfe 1998). We may interpret entrepreneur-ship as the source of variety, yielding novel combinations of 'genes', and perhaps also novel 'genes'. Markets and other institutions form the selection environment. And we may interpret the growth of firms, creation of subsidiaries, spillovers, teaching, and training as parts of a transmission mechanism.

Evolutionary economics makes more allowance for organizational change than population ecology did (until recently at least). Nelson and Winter (1982) allowed for adaptation of organizational routines. Here, adaptation is not random, but based on search induced by failure, and consists of novel combinations of elements from old routines. However, adaptation remains separate from selection: generation of variety and selection are separate processes, and occur in succession (Vromen 1995). While this is understandable for practical reasons of tractability, for the purpose of model building it is ultimately unsatisfactory. I will return to this crucial issue later.

The question now is this: If the 'genes' adapt, what remains of selection as a deter-minant of population structure? That depends on how fast and efficient adaptation is, relative to selection. With Nelson and Winter, the emphasis is still on market selec-tion, on the basis of realized profits, so that an equilibrium outcome is still possible (Vromen 1995). Metcalfe (1998) focused entirely on selection.

Thus, Metcalfe proceeds as follows: 'without saying anything of substance about the origins of innovation, . . . as a first step . . . take the set of different behaviours as given' (p. 7); and: 'The population perspective does not require a theory of how variety is generated. It is sufficient to take variety as given and work through the consequences' (p. 24). It is admitted, however, 'that selection environment and unit of selection are not always so easily separated' (p. 37).

That sounds reasonable, if we want to focus on population phenomena. But I will argue below that it is in fact seriously misleading.

4.1.5 Neural Selectionism

In cognitive science (Edelman 1987, 1992), the development of perception and knowledge has been reconstructed in evolutionary terms: neuronal groups compete for fit with experience and in so doing provide a model of how knowledge might develop as 'internalized action'. This will not be discussed in the present Chapter, but in Chapter 6. There, I conclude that the evolutionary perspective is useful to understand issues of knowledge and meaning. The criticism of the evolutionary perspective when applied to systems of people, on the ground that people employ thought and thereby escape from the randomness of variety creation, does not obtain at the neuronal level. Neuronal groups do not themselves think but provide the building-blocks of thought.

4.2 PITFALLS

There are two kinds of pitfall in the use of the metaphor of evolution in socio-economic contexts. The first kind relates to the interpretation of evolutionary theory itself, the second to differences between biological and socio-economic evolution.

4.2.1 The Intricacies of Evolution

The first pitfall is that the notion of evolution tends to deteriorate into a simplistic, stereotyped 'folk version' of the evolutionary perspective that does not satisfy the intricacies that the theory actually entails (Hodgson 1993). Some of them are listed in Table 4.1.

> For an example of frequency dependence I modify the example given by Hodgson (1993: 208). Suppose we have two forms, x and y, whose survival depends on their relative productive yields, which are determined as follows:
> $px = a + bY; py = cY;$ where:
> px = production by x's, py = production by y's, Y is the number of y's in the population.
> This models the situation that, for example, the y's co-operate with each other to produce, and the x's prey on them.

TABLE 4.1   *Subtleties of evolution*

1. Genes express themselves through the production of enzymes, which enable the production of proteins, in a process that is dependent on the cellular and metabolic environment, and genes do not express themselves independently but in mutual interaction. Genes are inhibited or activated as a function of their environment and the stage of ontogenetic development. Not all characteristics are determined by genes: quite a number are bounded by structural, physical, and mathematical constraints. Thus, there is no simple relation between genes and characteristics (Rose 1997).
2. It is not absolute but relative fitness that counts: it is not the best fit possible that survives but the best that happens to be around. This implies the possibility of surviving not by increasing one's fitness but by reducing that of one's competitors.
3. Characteristics may survive not because they contribute to fitness but because they are irrelevant to it.
4. It is not only fitness that counts but also the rate of reproduction: less fit but very rapidly reproducing phenotypes may compensate for lesser survival with larger progeny, yielding a net increase of their share in the population.
5. It is not only fitness and reproduction that count, but also ease of entry into the population: characteristics that make for easy entry do not necessarily make for high fitness or reproduction.
6. Fitness is not equal to goodness or efficiency. It is defined by the requirements of the environment. This may promote characteristics that are in fact 'bad', in terms of efficiency or moral quality, or may lead into a 'blind alley', selecting characteristics that do not contribute to survival in future environments.
7. Path dependence: initial 'accidents' may create a lock-in to suboptimal paths of development.
8. Frequency dependence: fitness of a form depends on the number of its representatives or its share in the population, so that it attains differential advantage only beyond some 'critical' mass. Suboptimal forms may prevail in a population if they prey on optimal forms; i.e. appropriate some of their fitness.
9. Depletion: the form that is most fit to profit from environmental resources, and procreates most, may also be the form that most depletes non-renewable resources and thereby eliminates the basis for survival.
10. Symbiosis: different forms, of more and less fitness, may coexist in a stable pattern of shares, in a dual structure, because the more fit forms leave niches which are not worthwhile to them, allowing a continued existence for the less fit forms.

Then in a population consisting of only x's, single y entrants do not have a chance, because the productive yield of each x (a) exceeds what a y could achieve (b.0 = 0). Now suppose we have a population consisting only of y's, with $a/c < Y < a/(c - b)$. Then average production is larger than it would be in a population consisting only of x's: $py = cY > a$. But it is less than the yield for an entrant x ($cY < a + bY$ because $Y < a/(c - b)$). Thus, all y's will be pushed out and replaced by x's, yielding a less productive population. It is only when $Y > a/(c - b)$ that incumbent y's are more productive than entrant x's, so that they can prevail.

4.2.2   Socio-economic Evolution

The second pitfall in using the evolutionary metaphor is that variety, selection, and retention in socio-economic evolution are fundamentally different from biological evolution (de Bresson 1987, Hodgson 1993, Foster 1997). There are at least thirteen important differences between biological and socio-economic evolution, as indicated in Table 4.2.

TABLE 4.2   *Characteristics of socio-economic evolution*

1. It is not clear what the analogues of genes and species are: firms, products, technologies, organizational routines, competencies, cognitive categories such as ways of viewing and interpreting the world, and values, norms, or rules of conduct.
2. There is cultural in addition to biological parenthood: teachers, friends, role models, and mythical figures influence behaviour, by setting examples and transferring knowledge, norms, and values.
3. Inheritance is 'Lamarckian': determinants of behaviour are acquired during life and transmitted to others. In the process they are absorbed, in individual, idiosyncratic interpretations.
4. Transmission occurs through imitation and communication, and thereby does not yield integral and faithful replication, as for genes (for which copying errors are rare). It is subject to deformation and drift, as a result of imperfect communication and understanding. The reproductive power of some form thus depends on the ease of imitation and communication of its features. For example, documented knowledge will replicate more easily than tacit knowledge, because it is more easily transmitted.
5. There are group characteristics, such as culturally embedded, shared, tacit categories of perception and thought and norms of conduct.
6. More plausibly than in biological evolution there is the possibility of group next to individual selection. The problem of free riding that emerges when characteristics are transmitted through the individual, as in the case for genes, is solved if people are forced to conform, perhaps through a reputation mechanism, or when characteristics are group characteristics; i.e. when group norms are tacitly inculcated in individuals.
7. It is not clear what death is. If the phenotype is a firm, does it die only when it goes bankrupt or also when it is taken over? If the latter, how about a merger between two firms? Or would that be marriage?
8. There is 'cross-species breeding': whereas a camel and a horse cannot mate, according to Schumpeter innovation arises as 'novel combinations' of sometimes radically different technologies. Examples are: information and communication technologies; optics and robotics; physics and chemistry in the development of new materials. In thought we have metaphors that produce novel combinations.
9. There is re-emergence of 'defunct species': old technologies or practices can be revived. An example is the design of new sailing ships during the oil crises in the seventies (with aluminium, computer-controlled sails), which were shelved when the oil price sank again.

TABLE 4.2   *(cont'd)*

10. The generation of variety, associated with Schumpeterian entrepreneurship, is intentional and, though it is subject to a high rate of failure, it is not entirely random.
11. Life forms (whether firms, technologies, or competencies) are not inert and passively subject to selection, but adapt though learning, the creation of tools and instruments outside the body, and the organizing of groups to compensate for individual limitations.
12. The selection environment, consisting of markets and institutions, or internal selection procedures in a firm, is not exogenous. In fact, it consists of routines as much as the firm does: routines of users of products, routines in industry supply chains, routines in labour markets, legal systems, etc. Those are themselves subject to both population change and individual change, and they can be affected by collusion and political action or created by (radical) innovation. This yields much more scope for path dependence than in biological evolution: some accidental event may create its own survival conditions.
13. In biological evolution, new forms are built layer by layer upon old forms, which have each had to be viable in the environment at the time of their emergence. New forms have somehow to deal with that ineradicable, embodied history, by revising or inhibiting the function of the substrate within a limited scope of possibilities. In socio-economic evolution, one can eliminate, replace, or redesign the substrate, short of 'deeper' levels that are irredeemably tacit and involuntary. Certain basic perceptual and cognitive categories or deeply ingrained 'metaphors we live by' (Lakoff and Johnson 1980) belong to that category (see Chapter 5).

A famous example of socio-economic path dependence is the emergence of the oil-fuelled engine for cars. Initially, an electric engine or an engine based on the conversion of hydrogen into water was equally viable. However, these were no longer options after the oil-based technology had created its installed base of knowledge and technology for finding and extracting oil, refineries for processing it, chemical industry using some of its output, pipelines and petrol stations distributing products, and the resulting vested interests of oil companies. However, the pressures of pollution may revitalize such species as did not evolve.

4.2.3   *Units of Selection*

In evolutionary theory, the question lingers as to what we should take as the unit of selection in markets. According to Nelson and Winter (1982) it is organizational routines; according to Metcalfe (1998) it is business units. In the organizational literature, next to a market-selection mechanism outside the firm, a selection mechanism within the firm has been postulated: internally generated ideas are subjected to a sometimes erratic mechanism of selection in organizational bureaucracies (Burgelman 1996). Recall that Veblen characterized institutions as 'settled habits of thought that apply to the generality of people'. This seems similar to units of selection in the form of ideas or routines in firms and industries. Again, the question arises as to how to distinguish between the units of selection (what is selected) and the factors of selection (what does the selecting). There may not be any single type of unit of selection: ideas, routines, teams, divisions, business units, and entire firms may all qualify. They may all be units of selection at one level of aggregation and factors of selection at another. They all select while at the same time being subject to selection. But, as will be argued below, the whole notion of selection, by analogy to biological evolution, may no longer be very useful. I am tempted to see the indeterminacy of the unit of selection as another indication that in human affairs evolutionary theory is simply not adequate. What would be the unit of selection in language, in speech, scientific articles, and story-telling? And in learning; in applying ideas and changing them in the process? The question does not seem to make sense.

In both biological and economic evolution, group selection is controversial. The problem is that any trait that is conducive to group survival is transmitted through the individual, who is better off to free ride or prey on other people's commitment to the group, and this would favour the proliferation of genes of opportunism. Only commitment to next of kin might survive the logic of selection, because the genes of the individual and his next of kin are sufficiently close.

> Consider the following example of group characteristics and group selection. Hill (1990) proposed that if trust building on the basis of a culturally inculcated ethic of conduct reduces transaction costs, then societies with such an ethic have a competitive advantage among nations, so that in the long run trust and trustworthiness will prevail. It is not certain that this will work. Such a country is an attractive target for invasion by opportunists from countries without such an ethic, preying on the trust that prevails. As a result, the basis for trust may unravel. The institutional basis for trust may be protected by entry barriers, but then the country is likely to be ostracized and barred from world trade, as a sanction against not opening up to competition. The case of Japan comes to mind. The question then is whether this penalty may not outweigh the advantages of low transaction costs. In this particular case group selection may not work. But the point of the example is that it shows how it might.

In socio-economics, transmission is social rather than individual, in communication, and in communication the transmission of some characteristics may be barred. The interests of the individual may be tied to the interests of the group. This may be the case for cognitive reasons: because of the focusing and creation of shared meanings and categories that I proposed as the crux of the firm. In fact, this is part of the reason why this *is* the crucial function of the firm. Here, opportunism may be limited by default, on the basis of routines: certain 'opportunities for opportunism' are not perceived. This is how trustworthiness may go beyond calculative self-interest (Nooteboom 1996a, 1999a). Alternatively, the inclination to utilize opportunities for opportunism may be contained by ethical categories of norms and values, or reputation mechanisms. And to the extent that people still seek and attempt to utilize such opportunities, we try to contain them through the incentive mechanisms with which the economic literature abounds, or through legal or social procedures of monitoring and control.

In the literatures on innovation and organization there is a persistent trend to associate disintegrated organizational structures with innovation: they allow for novel combinations. That will be discussed extensively in Chapter 11. In the present context we can interpret that as the loosening of group cohesion in order to escape the constraints of group selection and establish selection at a lower level of units of selection, such as divisions, teams, and ideas.

4.2.4   Selection and Firm Strategy

How independent is the selection environment from the behaviour it is supposed to select? What if behaviour in turn creates and selects the institutions? And what else would create and select them? To ask this question one does not have to be a proponent of methodological individualism (which I am not). This issue has already been raised in Chapter 2. The point is this: If the selection environment is in turn determined by the units it is supposed to select, what is left of the notion of a selection environment? The very notion might become meaningless. Of course in biological evolution also life forms affect the environment in which they are selected, by foraging, creating refuse, etc., and they may to some extent select their niche by migration. There is the notion of co-evolution: two species co-evolve if they exert selection pressures upon each other. We find this when species prey on each other or live in symbiosis.

> Zeleny (1998: 141) gives the following examples: 'A bird must undoubtedly adapt to a mountain. A society (network) of birds can make the mountain adapt to them. By overconsuming particular berries, the new brush growth is controlled, the mountain's erosion enhanced, and the production of both berries and birds thus limited until a temporary balance or harmony is restored. Colours of flowers have co-evolved with the trichromatic vision of bees; shapes of flowers with the structural traits of insects and animals; modern breeders with the changing tastes and preferences of man'.

Zeleny goes on to quote Lewontin (1983), as follows:

The environment is not a structure imposed on living beings from the outside but is in fact a creation of those beings. The environment is not an autonomous process, but a reflection of the biology of the species. Just as there is no organism without an environment, so there is no environment without an organism.

The notion of co-evolution from biology is useful, up to a point, but in the context of human systems it is also seriously misleading. Perhaps it does make sense to say that the selection environment of markets and (other) institutions co-evolves with firms or routines or competencies. However, in socio-economic evolution the influence of firms on selection by competition is of an entirely different, non-biological, cognitive and linguistic order. Here, we are dealing with cognition, communicative interaction, social construction of selection conditions, alliance formation, mergers and acquisitions, political manoeuvring. To put it more precisely, in biological co-evolution the environment sets the selection conditions for the species, and the species affects the selection conditions for its environment. In human systems, however, the species (a form of organization or routine or competence) not only affects the selection conditions for the institutions in its environment, but by cognitive and communicative ingenuity may dodge or directly affect the selection conditions that the environment sets for it. That is a fundamental difference, and it makes biological analogies suspect.

In this book I will argue at length that the way in which variety works out, which is associated with exploitation, should not be separated from the generation of new variety, which is associated with exploration. I will argue that it is in the process of 'working out' that both the motive and the material for new variety are accumulated, in a process of incremental innovation which leads up to a next round of radical innovation. For this I will develop a heuristic of discovery, in Chapter 9. It is an open question whether, or under what conditions, this yields an escape from selection and whether (relative) inertia prevails or not. In a clever balancing of exploitation and exploration firms may escape from selection.

From this perspective Schumpeter may have been quite right, and perspicacious, not to commit himself to biological metaphors of selection. If the selection environment is changed by the behaviour that is supposedly selected, i.e. not by population effects but by the actions of individual phenotypes, we can envisage that the supposed equilibrating tendencies of a selection process are continually being upset by disequilibration as a result of endogenous shifts of selection criteria. This leads to notions of self-organization rather than evolution, in the realm of 'complexity theory', as suggested by Foster (1998). This will be taken up later, in Chapter 10.

As Foster noted, from this perspective Schumpeter can perhaps be seen as an exemplary evolutionary *economist* in that he may have been the only one who grasped the notion of an endogenous selection environment that is so characteristic of socio-economic as opposed to biological evolution. This would make sense of his talking of evolution while rejecting biological analogies and his use of such a non-evolutionary term as 'creative destruction'.

This brings us back to the discussion, in Chapter 3, on the positioning view versus the view of strategic choice, in the management and organization literature. The issue is relevant here. While generally we tend to think that economics can inform the management and organization literature, perhaps here it is the other way around. The positioning view derives from the structure–conduct–performance perspective: market structure determines conduct, and conduct determines performance. The underlying assumption, as generally in mainstream economics, is that technology and demand are given and that firms find themselves in an established field of competitive forces, in which they should find an appropriate niche. This assumption has been criticized from the competence perspective for its neglect of strategic choice and entrepreneurial abilities to transcend competition for existing scarce resources through the creation of novel resources and to distinguish a firm from its competitors by means of firm-specific competencies. As indicated in Chapter 3, the difference between these perspectives is sometimes exaggerated. Of course a firm cannot create any environment and any competencies it likes. It will need to make entrepreneurial use of technological and institutional opportunities, and will need to overcome internal and external obstacles to change. Nevertheless, the notion of strategic intent and the scope for entrepreneurial shifts of technology and preferences to alter the field of competitive forces yields a useful shift of perspective on the nature of the selection environment in evolutionary economics.

The bias towards exogenous market and industry structure, in studies that explain conduct and performance as a result of industrial structure and properties of technology, still prevails in much neo-Schumpeterian and evolutionary innovation research. Such researchers typically devise sector taxonomies and derive conditions for conduct and performance from them (Pavitt 1984, Malerba & Orsenigo 1995).

There are more than innovations changing objective possibilities for products and production, and political action influencing the making of laws. We should recognize that many of the institutions that govern technological development are not objectively given but are to a greater or lesser extent socially constructed; they form a 'negotiated order' (Bijker *et al*. 1987, Latour 1987, Latour & Woolgar 1979). Technology and its evaluation have a common cognitive basis.

> An illustration of this is given in the study by Garud and Rappa (1996) of the development of hearing aids by implants in the cochlea, in the inner ear. There were two rival systems: a single-channel and a multiple-channel device. The first carried less risk than the second did, but the second yielded a greater and less cumbersome improvement of hearing. The problem was that objective, independent measures of these dimensions of performance were not available, and the balancing between them is subjective. The same ideas that informed the choice of device also informed the methodologies for selecting between them, so that there were rival evaluation methods. The rival methods were championed by rival commercial interest groups, and the stakes were high. The single-channel group argued that the obvious choice was to begin with the low-risk device, and step up to the other once its risks were clearer and could be reduced. The multiple-channel group argued that this would not reduce risk but add to it in the process of taking out one device and replacing it with the other. No objective experience was available to back up either claim.

We need to achieve a synthesis of entrepreneurial action that creates new conditions and competencies, and conditions from the environment in terms of other firms and institutions, which enable and constrain such actions, in patterns of co-operation, competition, and negotiation. Such analysis of strategic 'action in context' requires the recognition of different kinds of cause, of action and context that complement each other.[2]

> Nooteboom and Constandse (1995) provide an illustration of the combination of strategic choice and positioning in the emergence of the Dutch United East India Company (VOC) in the seventeenth century. Entrepreneurial daring utilized largely fortuitous opportunities of location and political conditions to initiate a dynamic of trade. This was supported by many mutually reinforcing technical innovations in the building of ships, windmills, and dikes, and institutional innovations,

---

[2] For this, in an analysis of institutions, in Chapter 5, I will employ the multiple causality of Aristotle.

such as the first limited liability company with shares traded on a stock market. These transformed competitive conditions, which created the platform for further, global expansion, again aided by historical coincidences in the wider political arena, and sheer luck. While the notion of a selection environment may make some sense here, this does not look like Darwinian evolution at all.

4.3   CONCLUSION

I started with the idea that selection processes in firms and markets, inspired by the evolutionary metaphor, might help us to understand how exploitation and exploration are related. Perhaps internal selection within the firm and external selection of firms in markets can be combined along the following lines: Organizational interpretation systems and routines constitute a selection environment, in the form of the organization's dominant logic, for ideas and competencies as internal units of selection. Organizations, as coherent systems of interpretation governing organization-specific sets of routines or competencies, are units of selection in a higher-level selection process of markets. But note that this dual selection process has to be tailored to the specific characteristics of socio-economic, as distinct from biological, evolution, as indicated in Table 4.2. Among many other things, we need to deal with the fuzzy identity of firms, with a proliferation of forms of organization 'between market and hierarchy'.

But I am struggling with the notion of evolution. On the one hand, the idea that institutions, which include both organizational 'institutional arrangements' and 'institutional environments', yield selection environments, at different levels, is attractive. On the other hand, the biological metaphor of evolution tends to be misleading. We are, in particular, faced with the question of how institutions themselves develop and are selected, how strategic behaviour and innovation may contribute to the formation of selection environments, and what sense the notion of a selection environment then still makes. It was shown that this issue is connected with the debate in the management and organization literature, with the issue of the positioning view versus strategic intent. I argued that although entrepreneurial behaviour can shift the institutions that govern selection, this is not magic and is still subject to constraints and opportunities offered by the environment. Thus, something like a selection environment, extended with the notion of co-evolution of firms and markets, may still make sense. However, we should then note that this entails a notion of co-evolution that is of a fundamentally different order than that in biology.

Perhaps the most fundamental problem with an evolutionist perspective is the lack of attention to adaptation of forms during their lives, in processes of learning. As a result, one cannot separate the process by which variety 'works out' in selection and the process by which variety is created. It is in the working out of variety that incentives and indications for new variety are obtained. That is what learning entails. As a result, the generation of new variety is subject to the problem of abduction, as discussed before. However, learning from experience yields a basis for abduction, and while new variety is subject to much error of insight it is not random. The idea that the selection environment is created by the behaviour that it selects leads on to notions of 'self-organization', as proposed by Foster (1998).

It is generally recognized, from Veblen's work onwards, that in economics evolution is Lamarckian, because experience acquired during life is transmitted to later 'generations'.[3] But this acquisition entails learning, and the transmission entails communication and language.

Summing up, in contrast with biological organisms in their selection environment, people and organizations adapt and learn. What is more, this process of adaptation by learning is mixed up with the selection process. That is what the fundamental issues of this book, the issues of abduction and of exploitation and exploration, entail. It is from our errors that become apparent in the selection process that we learn, and thereby we can often escape selection by changing either our survival capabilities or the selection environment.

One of Hodgson's (1993) criticisms of Hayek's use of evolutionary concepts was that he committed the functionalist fallacy: the existence of a rule of behaviour is accepted on the argument that it contributes to (individual or group) survival. This will not do. We need to examine 'the procedures and mechanisms involved in its adoption by each individual. Clearly, such an explanation would have to delve into psychology, habit formation and the nature of individual choice, among other factors' (Hodgson 1993: 169).

So, we should develop an explicit theory of learning and language. Therefore, I will turn away from the metaphor of evolution and turn to theories of cognition and language. Such theory seems more apt for innovation and learning. Organizations and innovation systems are not just systems of selection but also systems of innovation and learning. I propose that from this perspective we can develop an interactionist perspective, as an alternative to both the methodological individualism of economics and the methodological collectivism of sociology. Perhaps that will help us further to understand the relation between exploitation and exploration. However, first we need a discussion of institutions and institutional economics, given in Chapter 5.

---

[3] I employ the following definition of Lamarckianism: the thesis that experience during the life of the phenotype can be absorbed in his genes.

5

Institutions[1]

As proposed already by Veblen, and reiterated by Nelson and Winter (1982), North (1990), and many others, and as discussed in the previous Chapter, in socio-economic evolution the selection environment includes institutions. In the previous Chapter the question arose how institutions relate to the conduct that they enable and select. In an attempt to understand that, this Chapter delves more deeply into the concept of institutions: What are they, how do they function, what is their role in economics, how do they develop? It recognizes different strands of institutional theory, and tries to build bridges between them. It yields criticism and a transformation of transaction-cost economics.

5.1   INSTITUTIONS AND ORGANIZATIONS

What is the relation between institutions and organizations?

5.1.1   *What Are Institutions?*

Institutions are related to culture, but without further qualification 'culture' is too broad and vague a term. Following Kohnstamm (1998), I distinguish the following notions of culture. The broadest concept of culture is that of culture as opposed to nature: everything made by man. This includes art, law, customs, ethics, but also science, technology. It also includes pollution, persecution, and warfare. A second concept is culture as heritage: the stock of documented or otherwise embodied achievements from the history of civilization: arts, artefacts, and documents.[2] The anthropological concept of culture denotes the totality of norms and values developed in a certain group. This is the idea when we talk of 'multicultural communities'. The sociological concept of culture denotes the habits and lifestyles that distinguish a group. Here, one can talk, for example, of 'youth culture'. And finally there is culture as art. When someone says that the young lack culture, he can mean that the young have insufficient knowledge of our heritage, that they lack the norms and values he is accustomed to, that he objects to their lifestyle, or that the young are insufficiently interested in what he considers art (or that he does not like their art). Institutions are related to the anthropological and sociological notions of culture: norms and values of conduct,

[1] I thank Richard Nelson and Geoffrey Hodgson for comments on a draft of this Chapter. Of course the usual disclaimer applies.   [2] This is akin perhaps to Popper's 'third world'.

habits, and lifestyles. When people talk of the need for immigrants to acculturate, they can mean that immigrants must accept prevailing norms, adopt domestic lifestyles, or must come to appreciate our art.

North (1990) defined institutions as the 'rules of the game' that constrain behaviour, and thereby reduce transaction costs. In his view organizations are not institutions but players confronted with institutions. Sociologists have a wider notion of institutions, as not only regulating but also constituting behaviour, as not only constraining but also enabling it. Institutions are associated with rules that relate to roles, relative to social contexts, and thereby shape expectations, and make behaviour predictable. Institutionalization also entails a degree of permanence.

The term 'rule' may emphasize constraints too much. As Nelson and Sampat (2000) put it, it is odd to see a road across a swamp as a constraint. Rules seem to indicate sanctions in the form of physical punishment or financial penalty. What I have in mind is a much broader notion of 'enabling constraints' in social interaction. Enablers always entail limitations in some respect. To help and guide behaviour in one direction directs attention away from alternatives. It involves focus, and to look in one direction entails not looking in other directions. The notion of enabling will receive further theoretical development in the discussion of thought and language in Chapter 6, with the notion of 'scaffolding' (Shanon 1993) as a support for shared meanings and cognition. From that it follows that 'penalties' for deviance from 'rules' may also be social (lack of recognition, legitimization, acceptance), psychological (loneliness), cognitive (lack of learning by interaction), or, more generally, loss of identity.

For a paradigm example of an institution I propose language. It demonstrates very well how an institution enables and constrains behaviour, while it is also subject to shifts on the basis of that behaviour. For this, in Chapter 7 I employ de Saussure's distinction between the intersubjective order ('langue') and personal creative language use ('parole').[3] That allows for rigorous rules of scientific meaning as well as poetic licence. The issue of exploitation and exploration is closely connected with this tension between individual and community. Exploitation requires co-ordination (langue), which ties individuals down to a greater or lesser extent; exploration arises from individual deviance (parole) as a source of innovation. An attempt to employ these Saussurian concepts for an improved understanding of market processes was made in Nooteboom (1992b).

Since institutions include language and shared categories of perception and thought, a further elucidation of institutions requires a theory of knowledge and language. This is taken up in Chapters 6 and 7. A crucial question is how the socially constitutive and regulative can be combined with personal idiosyncrasy and variety of interpretation, and freedom of choice. The fact that institutions are internalized from social interaction does allow for differentiation between individuals and for a certain amount of autonomy and free will. This is relevant, because the issue has been raised

---

[3] Note that de Saussure himself focused on the intersubjective order of 'langue', almost to the exclusion of 'parole', while this book focuses at least as much on the latter.

(Hodgson 1993) as to whether social selectionism can be consistent with intentionality and free will. This connects with the tension between liberalism and communitarianism mentioned in Chapter 2. As indicated in that Chapter, one can very well
maintain that people develop their identity in interaction with others in a social community, and yet allow for that identity to become individualized, so that the individual can exercise a more or less independent view, choice, and ethical judgement.
One reason to adopt the situated-action theory of knowledge and meaning, discussed
in Chapters 6 and 7, is that it further supports this view.

The analysis of categories of knowledge as partly idiosyncratic constructions from
social interaction provides a connection with the doctrine of subjectivism in Austrian
economics: different minds think different things. But, unlike Austrian economics, I
will open up the black box of the agent to consider the origins of thought, and I propose that categories arise from interaction. This is my view on how competition, or
markets more generally, constitute a Hayekian discovery process.

5.1.2   Institutionalizing

Consonant with Austrian economics, Nelson and Sampat (2000) proposed that institutions are 'social technologies that have come to be regarded by the relevant social
group as standard in the context'. However, Nelson and Sampat also allow for institutions as underlying rules, conditions, or enablers of such practices. This is related to
the distinction made by North and Thomas (1973) between the institutional environment and institutional arrangements. The former supports, conditions, constrains,
and enables the latter. This seems to correspond to the distinction between culture
in the sociological sense (habits, lifestyles) and culture in the anthropological sense
(underlying norms and values). The former seems descriptive (how people behave)
and the latter normative (how people are guided or constrained to behave). However,
the two are intertwined: established practice serves as a norm, in routinized behaviour.
The notion that institutions are rule-like, in the sense that they are established and that
they govern conduct, remains appropriate.

The institutional environment includes a lot: laws and regulations, police and the
judiciary, professional, educational, scientific, and financial structures, physical infrastructure, technical standards, but also language, basic categories of thought, and
norms and values. Institutional arrangements include organizations and a wide variety of established social practices. The latter arise at many levels: in communities, fam-
ilies, firms, teams, or any community of practice. Arrangements are often set out in a
hierarchy: an industry supply chain embraces firms, which embrace divisions, teams,
which embrace people. How can we come to analytical grips with this vast ontology of
institutions?

Perhaps we should treat the concept of 'institution' not so much as a noun but as an
adjective, not as an entity but as an activity of institutionalizing, i.e. offering or imposing
enabling constraints. Then practices or social entities can be more or less institutionalized, i.e. more or less subject to guidance and constraint.

Perhaps we should see a road not as an institution but as more or less institutionalized, i.e. subjected to institutions in the form of rules of traffic. Institutionalization of roads has increased. We now have: rules for right of way and parking, differentiated limits for car and truck traffic, different lanes for different modes of traffic, time differentiation of limits and lanes, safety belts (first only on front seats, then also in the back), helmets for motorcyclists, approved baby seats, electronic payment for road use, rules of 'zipping' for efficient merging of traffic streams. Science is institutionalized to the extent that it is subject to standards of legitimacy (accreditation) and excellence, procedures of evaluation, peer review, rating by publication record, quality rating of scientific journals, criteria for allocation of subsidies, gender policies for hiring, criteria for PhD theses. The labour market in the Netherlands, say, is more institutionalized than in the US. Methodology institutionalizes, if we see methodology as regulative and constitutive of science, since it consists of a set of rules how to conduct and legitimize science. However, methodology is also itself institutionalized by categories of truth and knowledge.

This move from institutions as entities to institutionalization as an activity has two great advantages. First, it eliminates the need to give a complete inventory of institutions. We can specify the process of institutionalization and leave it at that: specific institutions emerge when the activity of institutionalization is applied, depending on the context. The second advantage is that we can account for a hierarchy of institutions: specific activities are institutionalized by enabling constraints in the environment, and themselves form enabling conditions for more detailed, 'lower-level' activities.

Legal frameworks (property rights, liability, safety, antipollution), physical infrastructure (roads, transport systems, telecommunication), and markets (suppliers, customers, competitors) institutionalize industry supply chains. Those in turn enable and constrain the activities of firms in the industry. Firms enable and constrain activities within their purview.

Note that the 'institutional environment' is now no longer some fixed class of entities, but has become a relative concept: more encompassing structures form the institutional environment for less encompassing ones. Thus, whether we see an entity as an institution or as an institutional arrangement depends on the level from which we look at it. Linking back to Chapter 4, on evolution, we can see more fundamental institutions forming the selection environment for less fundamental ones. Multiple institutional environments yield multiple levels of evolution. Thus, we can have evolution of action patterns in the interaction between people in communities of practice, evolution of ideas and proposals for products and processes in a firm, and evolution of firms in industries. Then, we have a hierarchy of selection environments, and corresponding institutional environments. In Chapter 10 I model this hierarchy in terms of a hierarchy of scripts. This helps to solve the multilevel problem of explaining the linkages between the levels of people, firms, industries, and economies that was identified in Chapter 1 as one of the key research questions.

Also, recall the brief discussion, in Chapter 1, on complex adaptive systems. In the relevant literature self-organizing systems are seen to consist of levels or hierarchies, with 'higher' levels constraining lower levels to maintain structure, while allowing for more or less autonomy at lower levels. This discussion is picked up in Chapter 10.

We can still talk of an institution as an entity. When we call something an institution, we mean that it provides enabling constraints at some 'lower' level, while it may itself be subjected to 'higher-level' institutions. A firm is an institutional arrangement in the context of national innovation systems, but an institutional environment in the context of intra-organizational processes.

5.1.3 Organizations

Organizations develop their own specialized semiotic systems: language, symbols, metaphors, myths, and rituals, which institutionalize firm behaviour. This is what we call organizational culture. These are similar for different firms to the extent that they share an institutional environment. However, within that environment they offer specializations, and those differ between organizations to the extent that they have accumulated different experiences, in different industries, technologies, and markets. As discussed in Chapter 2, one way to look at organizations is to see them as a set of rules to regulate and constitute behaviour, as a 'focusing device' for perceptions, interpretations, and evaluations, and then we see them as institutions. By that we mean that they form the institutional environment for activities in the firm.

Organizations are also themselves institutionalized in the sense that they are subject to rules, and embedded in industry structures, in their institutional environment, in regions or nations. Organization embraces arrangements both within and between firms, and thereby includes the governance of interfirm relations. Thus, we speak of 'organization between market and hierarchy'. In this way, we obtain a spectrum of organization from tight, centralized organizations through decentralized organizations, joint ventures, non-equity alliances, networks, industrial districts.

This duality of levels, of organization and its institutional environment, is reflected also in trust. Trust prior to exchange is based on the 'infrastructure of trust' that is part of the institutional environment. Trust can be further developed and deepened in the institutional arrangement of a relation. To the extent that the institutional environment lacks a shared basis for trust, trust takes more effort and time to build up in specific relations.

5.1.4 Institutions and Competencies

Chapter 3 discussed the notions of competencies and resources, and proposed, there also, a multilevel, relative concept. Competencies entail the efficient use as well as development of underlying resources. I proposed that this is related to the issue of exploitation and exploration. Competencies are typically embedded in higher-level activities, in which they appear as resources. Resources typically entail activities, making use of lower-level resources. Then a resource can be seen as a competence.

Thus, there appears to be a connection between competencies and institutions. Competencies are institutions, in the sense that they institutionalize, i.e. enable and constrain, the resources used in the activity. This aligns with the notion, proposed above, that an organization institutionalizes the activities in its purview, and that an organization is a bundle of competencies. These competencies are more or less idiosyncratic, and thereby the organization distinguishes itself from others. The reverse does not necessarily apply: there may be institutions that are not competencies.

5.2   HOW DO THEY WORK?

How do institutions function, what is their role in economics, and how do they arise?

5.2.1   *Causality of Action*

There is a literature on 'varieties of capitalism' (e.g. Hollingsworth & Boyer 1997, Whitley 1998) which proposes that institutional differences between different countries are pervasive and durable, and that this will prevent convergence even under pressures of globalized capital markets. In order to determine in what respects institutional environments in different countries differ and how durable these differences are, we need to further structure the institutional environment. As indicated, rather than providing a complete taxonomy of institutions, I approach taxonomy in terms of institutionalization: How do enabling constraints arise, and how are they imposed?

If institutions are 'enabling constraints', what precisely does that mean? I propose that it means that institutions affect the causality of action. They enhance or restrict whatever is required for social interaction to take place. Are all enabling constraints institutions? Absorptive capacity enables and constrains cognition. Is it thereby an institution? At the level of personal cognition perhaps not. Institutions are social: they regulate social interaction and they are socially accepted.

To proceed we now need a theory of the causality of action. I propose a causality of action inspired by the multiple causality of Aristotle: final causes (goals that people have), efficient cause (agency), material causes (inputs used), formal or exemplary causes (knowledge, skill, methods, models), and conditional causes that constrain or enable the operation of the other causes. The paradigmatic example is the carpenter (efficient cause) who uses wood (material cause) to make furniture, according to professional know-how (formal cause) or some guiding model (exemplary cause), in order to earn a living (final cause), subject to conditions of law and market structure (conditional cause). Final causality is a conjunction of man's intentionality and external motivating conditions. I proposed that an organization is an institutional arrangement, as a focusing device to align perceptions, interpretations, and evaluations. This is to say that it brings together actors (efficient cause), with certain common goals

TABLE 5.1   *A taxonomy of institutionalization*

Aristotelian cause	Institutional effects	Institutions
Final	Incentives for entrepreneurship	*Surface:* Ownership and decision rights Tax and social security Financial markets and rules of corporate control Market entry and exit conditions *Deep:* Categories concerning virtue, risk Responsibility, independence and 'locus of control'
Efficient	Labour	*Surface:* Wage and labour conditions *Deep:* Work ethic, voice/exit
Material	Material inputs	*Surface:* Import conditions, capital markets
Formal	Knowledge/ technology	*Surface:* Education, training, science Dissemination/transfer *Deep:* Categories concerning cognition, skill
Conditional	Time and space Industry structure	*Surface:* Physical and communication-infrastructure Supply chain, entry/exit barriers, and market concentration

(final cause), and perceptions and knowledge of how to do things (formal cause), and/or exemplars to imitate (exemplary cause).

Table 5.1 shows how this can yield a taxonomy of institutionalization: how institutions affect (enable and constrain) different causes of action.

Thus, the constellation of property rights, market entry and exit conditions, tax and social security affect the incentives to become an entrepreneur. When social security is low, people may be pushed into self-employment under adverse labour-market conditions (unemployment, discrimination). This is the 'refuge hypothesis' of entrepreneurship. Laws of bankruptcy affect exit conditions, and thereby affect the incentive for entry: If the venture fails, with how little damage can one get out? There are also motivators at a deeper level of categories of perception, interpretation, and evaluation, such as sense of responsibility, independence, and 'locus of control'. The latter concept is familiar in the small-business literature. It indicates whether people attribute outcomes of actions to their efforts and initiative or to outside conditions. Note that the conditions interact. If there is little internal locus of control, people may not move into entrepreneurship even

under adverse labour-market conditions and low social security. Other institutions affect other
conditions of entrepreneurship. Thus, there may be lack of finance (seen here as a material cause)
because of lack of venture-capital institutions. Level of education and training affect how an
entrepreneur and his firm will work, and affect transaction costs.

Note the distinction in Table 5.1 between 'surface' and 'deep' structure of institutions. The first consists of specific institutional structures that enable and constrain
activities of firms. The latter consists of underlying, fundamental categories of perception, interpretation, and evaluation that are part of culture (in the anthropological
sense). This brings in the Veblenian notion of 'settled habits of thought that apply to
the generality of people'.[4]

The notion of deep structure is also inspired by Schein's (1985) proposal, discussed
in Chapter 2, that organizational culture has a deep structure of categories of thought
concerning the relation between organization and its environment, reality, truth, the
nature of people, and their interaction. These generate a surface structure of symbols,
rituals, heroes, and role models that constitute a more proximate cause of organizational behaviour.

In the hierarchy of institutional environments and arrangements the deep structure
of categories of thought forms the institutional environment for the formation of the
surface structure of institutions that form part of the institutional environment of
firms. A deep structure of shared categories of perception, understanding, and evaluation generates the rules attached to a surface structure of laws, regulations, habits of
commerce, labour unions, employers' and industry associations, labour markets,
financial markets, educational and scientific systems, and the like. This approach
offers the advantage of being able to reconcile change at the surface level with a more
enduring deep structure.

> For example, in the Netherlands there is a certain shift in corporate governance towards the
> Anglo-Saxon emphasis on shareholder value. Whatever comes out will reflect a more enduring
> deep structure of categories concerning the nature and purpose of organizations, their stake-
> holders, and the Dutch need for deliberation and consensus.

It is not clear at this stage what precisely belongs to deep structure and what does
not. There are intermediate structures. How about risk taking/aversion, power distance
(between authorities and subordinates) (Hofstede 1980), individualism/collectivism
(Hofstede 1980), exit/voice (Hirschman 1970) (see below, Subsection 5.3.3), élitism/
egalitarianism? I am inclined to see them as deep, but cannot be sure. Power distance
may be more changeable than the others. These are empirical matters that require
study in cognitive science.

---

[4] A somewhat awkward mix of metaphors now obtains. On the one hand, I speak of 'higher levels' of
institutions offering enabling constraints for 'lower levels', and, on the other hand, I now add the distinction between 'deep' and 'surface' structure. In fact, the 'deep' structure of basic categories corresponds with
the 'highest' level of institutions. It is not customary to combine the deep with the high, but such is the awk-
wardness of metaphorical expressions. Or should we distinguish two dimensions, one dimension of levels
in a hierarchy and another dimension of depth of categorization? I leave that question unanswered here.

For example, under pressures of competitive and technological conditions managers might become more attentive and responsive to subordinates even while maintaining a sense of élitism or an orientation towards exit rather than voice. This might be reflected in detailed performance measurement and reward systems. Equally, under pressures for flexibility and the utilization of complementary competencies, the governance of interfirm relations might shift from legal to 'relational' contracting (Nooteboom 1999a), even while an orientation towards exit and rivalry is maintained. This might be reflected in instruments of governance, with a focus on safeguards in the form of carefully balanced mutual dependence or exchange of hostages (see below, Sub-section 5.3.6) rather than trust.

One might object that all this is too rich and lacking in parsimony. What are the causes of Aristotelian causality? Can they be reduced to fewer underlying causes? Clearly, formal causes, such as knowledge and technology, are cultural products of people in interaction with nature and each other. The same applies to the artefacts, rules, and structures that constitute material, final, and conditional causes. Thus, the multiple causes can be reduced to the efficient causality of man, his intentionality that is part of final causality, and material and formal conditions of nature. Beyond that, material, efficient, and formal causes are reducible to mathematics and natural science. In Chapter 6 I investigate how thought and language may be rooted in neural mechanisms. Thus, final causes, the categories of thought that are part of formal causes, and further categories that constitute the deep structure of institutions are ultimately reducible to neural mechanisms. These are in turn rooted in physics and chemistry. Thus, in one way or another natural science yields the ultimate causes, but this detracts nothing from the multiplicity of derived causality at the level of human behaviour.

5.2.2 Structure and Agency

How does the analysis compare to Archer's (1995) rendering of structures that condition agency? She distinguished between social structure, which is 'primarily dependent on material resources, both physical and human' (Archer 1995: 175), and a cultural, ideational structure, characterized by logical rather than causal relations, in terms of ideas, theories: 'all intelligibilia . . . a propositional register, embodied in books and other cultural productions, comparable to Popper's "third world"' (Archer 1995: 179–80). The latter seems close to the notion of culture as heritage, indicated above, but this also includes artefacts as the embodiment of ideas and theories, and these are also material resources. Conversely, social structure is imbued with, and rooted in, cognitive and normative 'ideas and theories'. In other words, social structure includes culture in the anthropological sense. Thus, the cleavage between social and cultural structure is problematic: they overlap and pervade each other. My 'deep structure' of basic categories of perception, interpretation, and evaluation (including morality) is clearly cultural in the sense that they form part of our heritage, and in the anthropological sense that they regulate our ideas, norms, and values. The deep structure does not include our entire cultural heritage: not theories, artefacts. It does not include culture in the sociological sense of lifestyles: that I would assign to 'intermediate levels'.

5.2.3   The Economic Role of Institutions

Institutions are needed to make behaviour predictable and to limit transaction costs. By guiding and constraining behaviour they reduce opportunism, which, according to transaction-cost economics, is one of the causes of transaction costs. Trustworthiness has extrinsic value: to reduce the need for detailed regulation to reduce opportunism. Trust also has intrinsic value: people may prefer to deal with each other on the basis of trust, as part of their preferences. People will balance material gain against social approval and the demands or attractions of solidarity, and which is salient will vary between individuals, their social positions, and institutional conditions. But I believe that beyond rational choice institutions include internalized ethics of proper conduct, which go beyond calculative self-interest. Norms become part of habitual, routinized, non-reflective behaviour, in tacit knowledge, in procedural memory (Nooteboom 1996a, 1999c).

The fact that institutions are needed to limit transaction costs does not mean that in fact they always do so. They may increase transaction costs. One reason for this is that institutions constitute selection environments, for ideas within organizations and for products in markets. Since they form selection environments there are incentives for people within organizations and for organizations in markets to influence them in order to enhance survival, by innovation, rhetoric, or political action. Thus, they are open to interest seeking, which may raise transaction costs. It is not always easy to determine whether existing institutions limit or create transaction costs.

> Here is an example. I have been involved, in an advisory capacity, in the revision of legal regula-
> tion concerning the establishment of enterprises in the Netherlands. For entry as an entrepreneur,
> the rules required general knowledge of laws and regulations (on property, employment, environ-
> ment, etc.), and specific technical knowledge and skills concerning the trade or craft involved.
> Some saw these as entry barriers that limit competition. Others saw them as needed to limit trans-
> action costs and other hazards to customers and employees. Swayed by fashionable market
> rhetoric, civil servants wanted complete liberalization. Trade and craft associations were in favour
> of complete maintenance of regulation. They were accused of protecting vested interests. To some
> extent that was certainly the case. They tried to protect their members, and they themselves had
> an interest in preserving regulation because they offered trade- and craft-specific training. There
> were Schumpeterian arguments against trade- or craft-specific conditions of entry: innovation
> often comes from novel combinations, crossing the boundaries between trades and crafts. On the
> other hand, on the basis of transaction cost considerations there are good reasons to maintain
> conditions of a minimum general knowledge on laws and regulations. So, a compromise was
> reached: to abolish the specific and to maintain the general conditions.

5.2.4   *Institutional Change*

Chapter 4 indicated that institutions both conduct selection and are subject to selection, i.e. are both units and factors of selection. This puzzle can be resolved by recognizing that while institutional conditions are more or less durable, more or less objective, and more or less negotiated, some are more durable, objective, and negotiable than others. If we revert to the survey of institutions and institutionalized conditions, in Table 5.1, it is clear that some are more subject to entrepreneurial or political action than others. Physical infrastructure and markets for products, labour, finance, and other inputs are more easily changed by innovation, negotiation, and rhetoric than laws of property and contract, while basic cultural categories of perception, understanding, and morality are most difficult to change. The categories, norms, and values that form the institutions that select behaviour are acquired, i.e. internalized by the people who exhibit the behaviour, and in discourse they can employ rhetoric to try and shift or shape categories, norms, and values. Such attempts mostly fail to catch on, and when they do this tends to be a slow process, but it can be accelerated by crises that create a general awareness of the need for change.

This aligns with Archer's (1995) argument, offered in criticism of Giddens's structuration theory, that institutions are to a large extent shaped not contemporaneously with the behaviour they condition, but by previous generations, and yield the conditions which present agents inherit, in terms of an endowment of resources and a position in social structures. Depending on positions of power and influence, exerted by role-playing in 'corporate agents', people can shift institutions, but hardly wholesale.

This also aligns with my proposal of language as an exemplary case of an institution. There is intersubjective order (Saussurian *'langue'*) that conditions individual, idiosyncratic, and creative language use (*'parole'*), and the latter can shift the intersubjective order, but only bit by bit. For this process, in Chapter 7 I use the hermeneutic circle, according to which meanings may be shifted by means of metaphor, inspired by novel combinations encountered or created in specific new contexts of discourse.

5.3   INSTITUTIONAL ECONOMICS

Institutional economics has two quite different branches: old and new institutionalism. This paragraph explains the difference and attempts to build bridges between the two.

5.3.1   *Neo- and New*

One type of institutionalism goes back to the 'older' American institutionalists, such as Veblen, Commons, Mitchell, and Clark. As indicated in the paragraph on

evolutionary economics, in the discussion of Veblen, this branch of institutional economics, with its acceptance of the irreversibility of time and the path dependency of
institutions, has a much greater sense of history than is usual among mainstream
economists. It is much closer to sociology than economists tend to be, and does not
cling to methodological individualism. It accepts that people are to some extent 'pro-
grammed' by norms, values, and habits, embedded in culture, which limit and direct
their perception, interpretation, and evaluation of the world. It accepts the notion of
trust, supported by institutions in the form of norms and values of conduct. Here, I
will not discuss further that branch of institutional economics, and I proceed to present attempts to incorporate important elements from it in a new synthesis, which
might be called 'neo-institutional economics'. This combines elements from the old
institutional economics with insights from sociology and elements from the other
branch of institutional economics, called the 'new institutional economics'. The 'neo-'
indicates a link with the old; the 'new' indicates something which claims to succeed it.

The 'new-institutional' brand focuses on transaction costs, mostly according to the
theory set out by Williamson (1975, 1985), and stays much closer to mainstream economics. It is static, i.e. it does not include innovation and learning, it seeks equilibrium
outcomes, supposedly arising from the market selection of the most efficient practice,
it maintains the doctrine of calculative self-interest of opportunistic agents, and it
negates the relevance of trust (Williamson 1993).

One of my ambitions has been to combine what is useful in new institutional economics with a perspective of social exchange adopted from sociology, and to integrate
this into neo-institutional economics. This has been attempted in earlier work (for a
survey, see Nooteboom 1999*a*), to which I turn in the following Sections. Such an
attempt at a synthesis between old and new institutional economics may be a hopeless
affair, or so I have often been told, because in their foundations the differences are too
deep. Indeed, at a fundamental, conceptual level what I preserve from the new institutional branch is quite limited. However, it is still substantial at a more practical,
instrumental level. I accept the basic notion of transaction costs. While I accept the
notion of trust, I preserve the possibility of opportunism, and I agree with Williamson
(1993) that trust should not be blind. I accept that dependence in relationships may
yield problems of hold-up, and that some governance is needed to deal with relational
risk. I accept as still useful a number of instruments for such governance.

A summary of differences between new institutional economics and the neo-
institutionalism that I arrive at is given in Table 5.2.

5.3.2   *Transaction-Cost Economics*

In interfirm relations there are transaction costs, which include costs of contact
(search), contract, and control. These include various problems of co-ordination.
There are problems of co-ordination in a technical sense: how to align resources to
make a complex project work. That is related to competence, i.e. ability to perform.
Other problems relate to agency; to intentions to perform to the best of one's ability.

TABLE 5.2   *Differences between old and new institutionalism**

Neo-institutionalism	New institutionalism
Dynamics: change of institutional environments	Comparative statics: alternative institutional arrangements
Out-of-equilibrium process	Efficient equilibrium outcomes
Dynamic efficiency	Static efficiency
Heuristics, learning	Rational coping with bounded rationality
Habitual, routine behaviour	Rational choice
Social embeddedness; *homo socialis*	Methodological individualism; *homo economicus*
Market as discovery	Market as selection
Positive feedback: lock-in	Negative feedback: error correction
Preference formation	Given preferences
Transaction relations	Transactional events
Trust is basic	Opportunism is basic
Dependence as bonding	Dependence as threat
Knowledge as intersubjective construction	Objective knowledge

* adapted from Nooteboom (1993c).

The question is how to motivate people to take others' interests to heart. This is the central problem of governance. Here, the focus is on such problems of agency. Agency problems arise especially when relations entail dependence and power. Here, I employ the well-known definition of power as the ability to influence another's choices, by affecting either his choice set or his selection from the set. Note that in this sense power can be not only constraining but also benevolent: it allows for the generation of new opportunities of choice.

As will be discussed in more detail later (Chapter 8), differentiated products yield a higher profit margin than standardized products. However, they often require investments that are specific to the product. This entails problems of dependence and hold-up, as discussed in transaction-cost economics. Examples of specific investments are: specific instruments, machinery, tools, training, and buildings. The problem does not arise when technology is flexible: when a variety of products can be made with a generic technology.

In this book, use is made of a theory that combines a perspective of social exchange with elements taken from transaction-cost economics, to incorporate a dynamic view of innovation and learning, and trust next to opportunism (Nooteboom 1992a, 1996a/b, 1999a/c). Thereby, transaction-cost theory gets much closer to the old institutionalism. Prominent in social theory are the notions of reciprocity, mutual forbearance, and trust. Transaction-cost economics, on the other hand, emphasizes opportunism, the monitoring of performance and sanctions by legal punishment or other penalties. I claim that we can fruitfully employ a wider theory, which combines elements from both traditions. There are valid and fundamental objections to transaction-cost economics, but this should not make us throw out the baby with the bathwater. Useful elements can be salvaged from the theory, particularly for the design of forms of governance. There is no space here to set out the complete theory. I assume knowledge of social-exchange theory and focus on two things. First, I summarize the criticism of transaction-cost economics and salvage elements from it that are still valid and relevant. In the following paragraph I summarize some crucial features of the slippery notion of trust.

A fundamental shortcoming of transaction-cost economics is that it is static (offering comparative statics at best), and does not include innovation in its classical formulations (Williamson 1975, 1985), while in this book innovation and learning are central. The transformed theory used here includes the notion of 'external economy of cognitive scope', discussed in Chapter 3: people, and firms, require outside sources of complementary cognition to complement their own biased and myopic cognition. This adds a crucial dimension of the utility to outside, interorganizational relations, which was not included in 'classical' transaction-cost economics. Among other things, this yields a prediction that is opposite to a prediction from such transaction-cost economics. When uncertainty is large, the outcome is not more integration under 'hierarchy', as predicted by transaction-cost economics, but more 'outsourcing' of activities, in intensive, more or less durable, relations, because the need for outside, complementary cognition increases.

> This explains the stylized fact that, especially in industries facing the uncertainty of rapid change in technologies and markets, firms engage more in intensive relations with other firms, even while that entails 'specific investments'. These cannot be recouped in alternative relationships, whereby partners become dependent on each other and susceptible to hold-up risk, as explained in transaction-cost economics. Firms accept this problem in view of the need for complementary capacities of cognition. They solve the problem by sophisticated means of governance, including trust.

Transaction-cost economics focuses on the risks of opportunistic exploitation of dependence. The preoccupation with opportunism, and the neglect or even rejection of the notion of trust, is misguided and theoretically inconsistent (Nooteboom 1996a, 1999a). The passage of time is critical in transaction-cost economics. The point of specific investments is that they have to be made prior to transactions and can be recouped only in a subsequent sequence of transactions. At the same time, opportunism is assumed to be important not because everyone is opportunistic, but because prior to a relationship one does not know how opportunistic the partner is. Therefore, to control risk it is safe to act on the assumption of opportunism. There are two inconsistencies here, and one perverse effect. First, the argument negates reputation effects, while elsewhere those are part of the theory. More importantly, it ignores the possibility of learning more about the degree of one's partner's opportunism as the relation unfolds in time. The perverse effect is that by assuming opportunism one is signalling mistrust, which may cause a vicious circle of mutual constraint and may actually stimulate opportunism. I will return to this in the later discussion of forms of governance.

Finally, like economics more generally, transaction-cost theory commits the functionalist fallacy. This argues that organizations must yield optimal efficiency since they exist. If they were not optimal they would not have survived. As discussed in Chapter 4 this evolutionary argument of optimality has been refuted long ago, starting with Winter (1964), but it is still being used as an excuse for reasoning in terms of ideal, optimal, equilibrium outcomes rather than processes operating in reality.

Nevertheless, in spite of these fundamental shortcomings, transaction-cost economics yields elements that are worth salvaging, in a wider theory that encompasses a social-exchange perspective. One piece of salvage is the notion of specific investments as a cause of dependence. They have to be made 'up front', while they can be fully recouped only in subsequent transactions with the same partner. This yields what is called the problem of 'hold-up': the partner can misuse one's dependence to expropriate value (shift the division of added value to his advantage). If the partner defects to an alternative relation one is left with assets that have become useless, and with a gap in production. I propose that this notion of specific investments is worth keeping. The theory also yields useful instruments of governance. One is the notion of 'hostages'. (An example will be given below.) Another form is the redistribution of the ownership of specific investments to eliminate one-sided risk of hold-up. A third is the balance of mutual dependence to ensure mutual threat of retaliation in case of opportunistic behaviour. A fourth is the reputation mechanism: one behaves decently in order not to lose reputation and forego fruitful relations in the future. These instruments will be taken up in the later discussion of forms of governance in learning by interaction, in Chapter 8.

5.3.3   Trust

In his earlier work Williamson (1975) recognized the importance of 'atmosphere' in relations, but in his later work (Williamson 1985) this concept seems to drop out. Later, Williamson (1993) subjected the notion of trust to explicit and detailed scrutiny and finally rejected it as superfluous and misleading. Williamson asked the question whether trust goes beyond calculative self-interest. If it does not, it does not add anything to existing economic approaches, and is therefore superfluous. If it does, it yields blind trust, which is unwise and will not survive in markets, and should be discarded for that reason. So, whichever way one looks at it, it should be discarded. Nooteboom (1996a) countered the argument as follows: Trust can go beyond calculative self-interest without being blind (in the intended sense of being unconditional and without rational basis). There are two ways for this. One is ethical behaviour on the basis of tacit, socially inculcated norms in a society. The other is the build-up of routine perception, interpretation, and behaviour in specific relations, by which conformity of behaviour is taken for granted, and awareness of opportunities of opportunism becomes 'subsidiary' (Polanyi 1962). This was supported by subsequent empirical research (Nooteboom *et al.* 1997).

People will forego even major opportunities for opportunism, if they are aware of them, until the limit of their resistance to temptation is reached. All this goes beyond calculativeness but is not blind in the sense of being without rational foundation and being unconditional. Norms and routines have a rational foundation in the sense that they are based on successful performance in the past. They are not unconditional: when observed behaviour exceeds certain tolerance levels suspicion will be triggered, to yield some action of redress. This need not bring about immediate exit from the relation. It could yield 'voice' (Hirschman 1970): the signalling of discrepancies between expectations and realization, and debate as to how they arose and how to redress them.

However, trust is a slippery notion: different people may mean different things by it, and this may cause dangerous misunderstandings. What precisely does it mean? What is its basis? What are its limitations? First of all, we should distinguish between trust in competence, trust in intentions, and confidence in external conditions.[5] Are partners able to follow through on a deal, do they intend to do so to the best of their ability, and will their endeavour not be thwarted by unforeseen and uncontrollable conditions? It is important to distinguish between competence trust and intentional trust, since their breakdown calls for different action. If competence fails, one may give support to improve it. If intentions fail, one may improve incentives or give threats. The problem of course is that when the real reason for lack of performance is lack of intention, such as opportunism, the culprit will claim failure of conditions or shortcomings of capability as an excuse. The most complicated type of trust is intentional trust, and I focus on that.

As indicated by Williams (1988), we can classify sources of collaboration in a two-by-two matrix. Sources can be macro, applying to a community as a whole, or micro, applying to individual relations. They can be based on self-interest or on concern for others. A macro egocentric source is the law, with its threat of punishment. An other-directed macro source is norms and values of decent conduct. Micro egocentric sources constitute the realm of the forms of governance proposed by transaction-cost economics: power on the basis of dependence, distribution of ownership, monitoring, hostages, and reputation. Micro other-directed sources are bonding by emotions or kinship and habituation or routinization in specific relations.

I propose that the same sources apply to intentional trust. Nooteboom (1996*a*) gives a narrow and a wide definition of intentional trust. The wide definition is: the expectation that someone will not intentionally damage one's interests, or the neglect of that possibility, whatever the basis for such expectation or neglect. It may be based on a tight contract, or the conviction that it would not be in a partner's material

---

[5] Luhmann (1988) distinguished between trust and confidence. Trust applies to things one can choose and later regret; confidence applies to things beyond one's control or choice, such as laws of nature, God, the legal system, government, natural disasters, accidents.

interest to cause damage. In the narrow definition, the expectation is that damage will not be caused even if there is both an opportunity and an incentive for the partner to cause such damage. The latter definition approaches the common-sense notion of trust. According to that notion there is no trust if it is based on legal coercion or self-interest. Note the danger of misunderstanding involved. When someone says he can be trusted he can mean that he is contractually bound, or he can mean that he will not act opportunistically even when he has the opportunity and the interest to do so. It is important to know which of the two is in play.

Prior to a relation, there can be initial trust, based either on previous experience with the partner or on underlying institutions in the form of categories or habits concerning people and their interaction. Trust can be deepened in the course of a relation, in what Zucker (1986) called 'process based trust', but it can also break down. This may be because of misunderstanding. One source of misunderstanding derives from the difference between trust in competence and trust in intentions. If something goes wrong in a relation, this may be because of incompetence, accident, or opportunism. The problem is that opportunists will claim that accidents or incompetence are the cause of disappointing results, and the question is whether this can be verified.

5.3.4 Modes of Governance

Particularly in innovation and learning, it can be highly counter-productive to utilize formal instruments of control, in the form of detailed, legal contracts, procedures for monitoring, and credible threats of litigation (Nooteboom 1996a, 1999a). It is not only difficult and costly, especially for small firms, to handle this legal instrument. It also threatens to stifle the relations between participants and block rather than support the required exploration through trial and error. If you do not yet know precisely what co-operation will yield, because you engage in co-operation to develop novelty, you cannot specify precisely the obligations that participants should fulfil. Furthermore, too detailed and formal contracts may seriously inhibit the growth of trust.

Thus, particularly in innovation, one must seek recourse to alternative, more informal mechanisms of control: reputation mechanisms, exchange of hostages, and trust. These yield more flexibility and economize on the costs of governance (Nooteboom 1996a). In these forms of governance small firms have less of a disadvantage, and in some respects even an advantage, compared to large firms. Trust is also important when there is risk of spillover in knowledge exchange.

The relation between trust and contracts is not simple either. Trust economizes on contracts, but is also needed for contracts (Klein Woolthuis 1999). Setting up contracts is costly, and one needs prior trust that the effort will be worth it. Contracts, and even the legal language used for them, cannot achieve closure against risk, and trust is needed to cover the gaps. Thus, some trust is needed for contracts, but contracts may remain limited when trust is large.

There is talk of the 'death of distance': because of advanced information and communication technology distance no longer matters. But, for the forms of governance indicated here, distance does matter: reputation, trust, and bonding are best achieved at short spatial, cognitive, and cultural distance. As discussed, trust is either based on *ex ante* shared norms and values, embedded in national or local culture, or on bonds of friendship or kinship, or is built up in a relation. The first requires shared culture, the second clan or family membership (Ouchi 1980), and the third is greatly enhanced by local, face-to-face interaction. It is not only that proximity and shared culture provide an easier basis for trust and intensive, frequent interaction, in each individual relation, but also that they provide a basis for swift and flexible set-up of relations. Otherwise, it would entail not only higher costs but also more time to set up a new relation, which would reduce relational flexibility.

A more detailed analysis of governance in the context of learning by interaction will be given in Chapter 8.

5.3.5   Boundaries of the Firm

I proposed that firms need to engage in relations with each other and this entails organizational entanglement, in order to govern risks of mutual dependence and hold-up, in forms of organization between market and hierarchy. In view of this, do boundaries of the firm and the very notion of a 'theory of the firm' still make sense? Perhaps we should rather speak of a general theory of organization, with tightly integrated firms at one extreme and spot markets of 'arm's-length' transactions at the other, with many intermediate forms, with greater or lesser integration of operations or ownership. One might object that firms' boundaries still serve as boundaries of ownership. But ownership also can be distributed. Employing concepts from the literature on incomplete contracts, one might arrange organizational forms according to their degree of integration along two dimensions: residual claims to profit and residual claims to decision making, as is done in Nooteboom (1999*a*). 'Residual' means after allowance for contractual obligations. The result is reproduced in Figure 5.1.[6]

Recall, however, the central idea in classical transaction-cost economics, that under certain conditions a central authority is needed. This position can be reformulated as follows. Suppose that close co-operation, with dedicated investments and risks of spill-over, is needed. Suppose that uncertainty precludes complete contracts and asymmetry of information precludes close monitoring. Suppose further that this problem cannot be solved by relegating ownership of assets to those who can dodge monitoring, so that we might fall back on spot-market contracting between independent operators. Suppose, finally, that the basis for other forms of governance, with balanced mutual dependence, reputation mechanisms, and trust, is also lacking. Then the need arises for some degree or form of authority that can demand information and can impose decisions that could not be imposed on independent operators, in a court of law. This basic idea from transaction cost economics remains for such cases.

---

[6] In fact, one can distinguish more dimensions. In Nooteboom (1999*a*) nine dimensions are found behind the two dimensions in Figure 5.1.

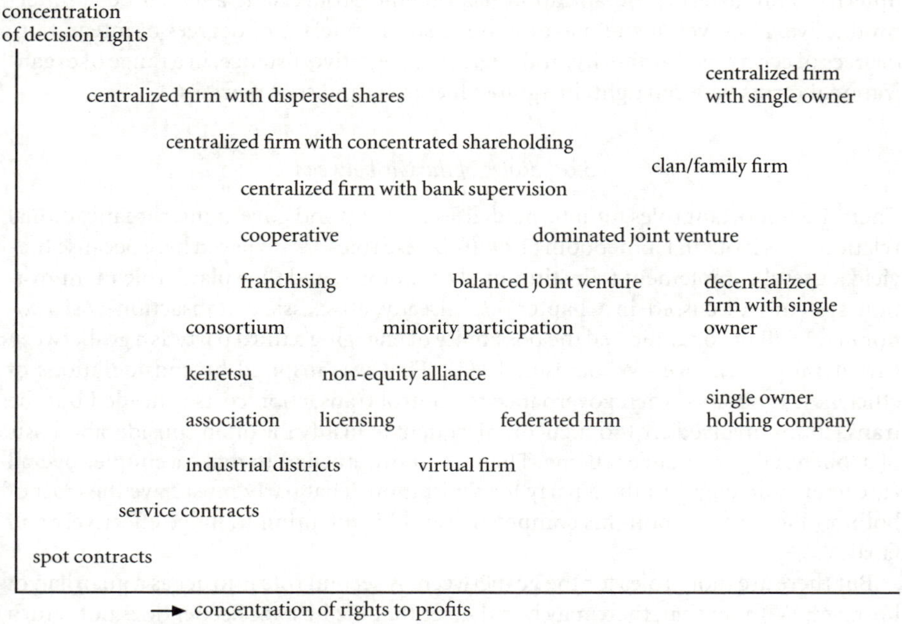

concentration
of decision rights

                                                                        centralized firm
            centralized firm with dispersed shares   with single owner

                    centralized firm with concentrated shareholding
                                                                  clan/family firm
                        centralized firm with bank supervision

                        cooperative   dominated joint venture

                    franchising   balanced joint venture   decentralized
                                                                      firm with single
                consortium   minority participation   owner

            keiretsu   non-equity alliance
                                                                single owner
            association   licensing   federated firm   holding company

            industrial districts   virtual firm

        service contracts

spot contracts

⟶ concentration of rights to profits

FIGURE 5.1   *Degree of integration*
Source: Nooteboom (1999*a*).

While the notion of clear boundaries of the firm evaporates, we can still see varying degrees of centralized authority. For example, in an equity joint venture authority is delegated for a certain range of joint activities to the board of the venture, on which the parents are represented. This may be an appropriate form of organization to control hold-up and spillover risks. For further details of the analysis and design of interfirm alliances, see Nooteboom (1999*a*).

Recall that according to the perspective set out in this book the primary function of the firm is not the reduction of transaction costs but the focusing of perception, interpretation, and evaluation, in order to achieve joint, co-ordinated action. This requires a certain amount of coherence, in which boundaries of the firm still make some sense. However, to obtain the needed complementary cognition from outside sources, linkages of sense making and cognition should extend across the borders of the firm. At the same time, for mutual understanding, cognitive distance should not be too large. Therefore, along these lines also, next to considerations of governance, the boundaries of firms become permeable and fuzzy. But that does not mean that boundaries disappear altogether. They just become fuzzy.

Summing up: Increasingly, the boundaries of the firm have become fuzzy and permeable, and the distinction, in the field of management and organization, between 'internal' and 'external' organization has become problematic and can be counter-productive. However, it still makes sense to speak in terms of degrees of integration, degrees of centralized authority, and degrees of cognitive distance, in a range of organizational forms between tight, integrated hierarchy and spot markets.

5.3.6   Roles of the Go-between

There are important roles for intermediaries to set up and govern interorganizational relations, as set out in Nooteboom (1999*b*). These roles are reviewed here because they yield a useful complement to institutional economics, and they play a role in innovation systems, discussed in Chapter 12. Already, in classical transaction-cost economics, Williamson indicated the possibility of engaging a third party as a go-between ('trilateral governance', Williamson 1985). That was inspired by considerations of efficiency. It obtains when governance to control transaction costs is needed but the transactions involved are too small or infrequent to justify the often considerable costs of a 'bilateral' governance scheme. Then it is more efficient to make a simpler overall agreement and engage a third party for arbitration. That party must have the trust of both protagonists, in both his competence and his intention to judge effectively and fairly.

But there are more roles for the go-between. A second role is to act as a guardian of hostages. Without that, there may be a danger that the hostage keeper does not return the hostage even if the partner sticks to the agreement. The third party has an interest in maintaining symmetric trust and acceptance by both protagonists. He can be trusted more to sacrifice the hostage without hesitation if the giver does not stick to the agreement, and not to keep the hostage longer than agreed. This solution is antique, and was practised in the Middle Ages, in the exchange of hostages between kings (de Laat 1999), with an emperor as the third party.

A third role for the go-between is to act as a filter against spillover. This is important when change is not so fast as to render information useless by the time it is imitated. Especially at the beginning of a relation between parties that do not know each other, there is the problem that one does not want to make specific investments before one has sufficient trust in the competence and intentions of the partner. But in the giving of information there is the paradox of Arrow, yielding the 'revelation problem': to judge the value of information one must already have it, but then there is nothing left to bargain about, and the damage of spillover may have already occurred. The third party already knows both sides well enough reliably to inform them on the competence and intentions of each other, without surrendering much information on content.

A fourth role, connected to the third, is to act as an intermediary in the building of trust. Trust relations are often entered with partners who are trusted partners of someone else one trusts. Intermediation in the first, small and gingerly, steps of co-operation, to ensure that they are successful, can be very important in the building of a trust relation. As noted above, things may go wrong in a relation either because of mistakes or because of opportunism, but in practice these are difficult to distinguish because an opportunist will claim mistakes or mishaps as the cause of disappointing results. The intermediary may solve misunderstandings that turn mistakes into perceived indications of opportunism.

A fifth role is to act as a lookout, a sieve, a channel, and an amplifier in reputation mechanisms. For a reputation mechanism to work, infringement of agreements must be observable, its report must be credible, and it must reach potential future partners of the culprit. The go-between can help in all respects: to monitor infringement, to sift true reports from gossip, to connect with future potential partners of the culprit and bridge the distances involved.

Finally, go-betweens may help in the timely and least destructive disentanglement of relations. That is desirable to enhance flexibility of novel combinations for radical innovation, as indicated above (cf. Nooteboom 1996*b*, 1999*a*).

The third and fourth roles are especially important in innovation, because there exchange of knowledge or information is crucial, with corresponding risks of spillover, and specific investments need to be made to set up mutual understanding and co-operation. There are corresponding risks of hold-up, while, especially in innovation, the competencies and intentions of strangers are difficult to judge. Particularly in innovation, detailed contracts tend to have the adverse effect of a straightjacket, constraining the variety of actions and initiatives that innovation requires. Third-party arbitration then yields a less constraining alternative.

Note that in all roles it is crucial that the go-between command trust in both his competence and his intentions. He should be known to be impartial and incorruptible. He should have an interest to act scrupulously, with a view to maintaining his reputation as a go-between. In the parlance of social-network theory, he needs a great deal of 'social capital'; in particular the position to bridge 'structural holes' in networks (Burt 1992).

5.4 CONCLUSION

Institutions not only constrain but also enable behaviour in markets. To grapple with the complexity of institutions I propose to approach them in terms of the activity of institutionalizing rather than in terms of a fixed inventory of institutional entities. That activity consists of the provision of enabling constraints that affect the causality of action. A social structure forms the institutional environment for another structure if it affects the causality of its actions. For the causality of action I employ the multiple causality of Aristotle.

This approach yields multiple levels of institutions. There are variable products of institutionalization, at the surface level of organizational forms. There is an intermediate level of institutions such as laws, physical infrastructure, technical standards, educational and research system, professional organizations, etc., which form part of the institutional environment of firms. There are also highly invariable institutions, at the deep level of categories of thought and values and norms of conduct. Changes on the surface are guided by the deep structure. The institutional environment of firms consists of both the surface level of laws, etc. and the deep structure of cognitive categories. On the basis of the deep structure of categories, organizations develop specialized categories and symbol systems to serve their function as 'focusing device'. Thereby they form institutional environments, called oganizational cultures, for activities in the firm. There is a connection between institutions and competencies: competencies are institutions in the sense of enabling and constraining resources and their use in activities. The fact that both organizations and competencies can be seen as institutions aligns with the notion of the firm as a set of competencies.

In contrast with old institutional economics, the new institutional economics of transaction-cost economics lacks the dynamics of learning and innovation and lacks institutions in the form of norms and values of conduct and basic categories of thought. As a result, it is preoccupied with opportunism and finds it difficult to deal with the concept of trust. However, transaction-cost theory still yields useful elements. It is possible to build bridges between old and new institutional theory, to arrive at a wider and useful neo-institutional theory of interaction in organizations and economies.

6

Knowledge[1]

This Chapter begins with a review of the reasons for delving into cognitive science. It next considers two rival views of knowledge: the mainstream computational–representational view and the emerging situated-action view. The latter underpins the interactionist, constructivist view of knowledge adopted in this book. However, I retain mental representations in some sense. For this I employ Edelman's 'neural Darwinism'. For a further exploration of cognitive structure, this Chapter considers the concept of scripts, and the criticism of it.

6.1 MOTIVATION

It is a major effort to delve into cognitive science, which is a combination of cognitive psychology, artificial intelligence, linguistics, and semiotics (the science of signs). As in economics and sociology, in cognitive science too we encounter different schools of thought, and we have to make up our minds which to choose, or how to combine different perspectives, if that is possible. Such incursion into a discipline of which one is not a master is hazardous: one runs the risk of dilettantism. Thus, we must have good reasons to engage in the effort.

Several reasons were given in previous Chapters. First, and most generally, it seems obvious that, since our discourse is full of terms such as the 'knowledge economy', the 'learning organization', and the 'learning region', we should employ a theory of knowledge and learning. Indeed, it seems quite odd that systematic efforts in this direction have not been made before. As indicated in previous Chapters, use is made, in various literatures, of the notions of 'bounded rationality', 'tacit versus codified knowledge', 'absorptive capacity', 'procedural versus declarative memory', 'sense making', and 'enactment'. The question is how these notions are related, in a coherent theory of knowledge, learning, and language.

In Chapter 3 it was noted that new institutional economics, in particular transaction-cost economics, accepts bounded rationality but then paradoxically proceeds to deal with that in the mode of rational choice. The rationality involved in coping with bounded rationality is itself bounded. It is high time to stop dodging the issue and find out how bounded rationality works. A theory of knowledge and learning is needed to

[1] I thank Benny Shanon and René Jorna for comments on earlier versions of this chapter. Of course, once again, the usual disclaimer applies.

open up the black box of the agent, in contrast with economics, including Austrian economics, in order to understand the Hayekian 'discovery process' of markets.

A theory of knowledge and language is also needed to solve the 'multilevel' issue identified in Chapter 2: How can we make sense of learning at the organizational level, and how does that connect with learning at the level of individuals?

As discussed in Chapter 2, Nonaka and Takeuchi proposed that processes of 'knowledge conversion', with transformations and combinations of tacit and codified knowledge, form the basis of innovation in firms, but how this works has not been clarified.

In earlier Chapters I employed the constructivist view that knowledge arises from categories that people construct in interaction with their physical and social environment. The question is whether this can be substantiated by theory of knowledge and language. I proposed that there is a perspective of methodological interactionism, replacing both the methodological individualism of economics and the methodological collectivism of (some) sociology. We need a theory of knowledge and language as a basis for it. We need that to explain the nexus between structure and agency, as discussed in Chapters 1 and 5. We need it to understand the relation between selection processes and changes in the selection environment, as discussed in Chapter 4. In particular, we need to know what the role of context is in knowledge and meaning.

Theories of knowledge and language are intimately related, through issues of meaning, but I try to discuss them separately. The present Chapter discusses knowledge, and the following Chapter discusses language.

6.2   THE REPRESENTATIONAL–COMPUTATIONAL VIEW

While the so-called 'representational–computational' (RC) view of knowledge (cf. Newell and Simon 1972) has been increasingly subjected to criticism, it still appears to be the dominant perspective in cognitive science. I give a critical review of the main tenets. In my criticism I make use of the work of scholars who criticize the RC view to a greater or lesser extent (Shanon, Rose, Hendriks-Jansen, Lakoff and Johnson), while trying to remain critical of that as well.

6.2.1   *Content and Motivation*

The RC view assumes that knowledge is constituted from symbolic mental representations and that cognitive activity consists of the manipulation of (the symbols in) these representations, called computations (Shanon 1988: 70). A crucial implicit assumption is that the representational elements are well-defined, i.e. are part of a given lexicon, and their structure is well-formed, i.e. accords with rules that together comprise a syntax. The implication is that representations are exhaustive, i.e. all that is known is specified in the representations, and is determinate, i.e. each representation specifies a particular, single interpretation, and fixed, i.e. novel manifestations of knowledge are composed from a fixed set of elementary representations.

Shanon (1993) claims that the representations according to the RC view are:

1. *symbolic*: signs are used, which entail a separation of a medium and the content conveyed in it
2. *canonical*: a given, predetermined code is assumed, which is complete, exhaustive, and determinate
3. *structured/decomposable*: it is assumed that well-defined atomic constituents yield well-formed composites
4. *static*: mind is the totality of its representations; structure and process are well demarcated; learning is occasional modification of given structure
5. *abstract*: the medium is immaterial; the material realization (physiology) is of no relevance

Summing up: Semantic representations are well-formed structures of well-defined, abstract, static, symbolic entities constituting a complete, determinate, and exhaustive canonical code (Shanon 1993: 12).

The basic intuition is that behaviour is based on beliefs, desires, and goals, and representations are postulated as entities that specify them (Shanon 1993: 9). The reconstruction of variety as variable, combinatorial operations on fixed elements is an ancient ploy: the ploy of decomposition. In formal grammar it yields the 'standard principle of logic . . . hardly ever discussed there, and almost always adhered to' (Janssen 1997: 419), that the meaning of a compound expression is a function (provided by rules of syntax) of the meanings of its parts. It was adopted by Frege, in his later work (Geach & Black 1977, Thiel 1965, Janssen 1997).[2]

The motivation for this view is in a respectable scientific tradition of yielding a parsimonious reconstruction, in terms of stable entities and procedures of composition of those entities into a variety of structures, to account for orderly and regular human behaviour across a large variety of contexts. It goes back to the ancient search for identity and fixity underlying observed variety and change, discussed in Chapter 1. It is a principle of reduction for the sake of mental economy. It also explains how people can understand sentences they have never heard before. A subsidiary motivation is that by interposing the cognitive as an intermediate level between psychological

---

[2] According to Janssen compositionality entails the following assumptions:

1. the distinction between syntax and semantics
2. output of the syntax is input for meaning assessment
3. the rules specify how to combine parts
4. the grammar determines what the parts of the expression are
5. all expressions that arise as parts have meaning
6. meaning is determined not only by the parts but also by the compositional rules ('John loves Mary' versus 'Mary loves John')
7. for each syntactic rule there is a semantic rule that describes its effect on meaning
8. there is no other input; if the context of discourse should contribute to meaning, the notion of meaning has to be enriched to capture this

phenomenology and physiology we can circumvent the need for a full reconstruction in terms of physiology, and we can thereby evade reductionism.

However, there are empirical and theoretical objections to such a symbolic, semantic, representational view (Shanon 1988, Hendriks-Jansen 1996).

6.2.2   *Empirical Objections*

If meanings of words are based on representations, it should be easy to retrieve them and give explicit definitions, but in fact that is often very difficult. This criticism may be countered by arguing that one can maintain the availability of representations while granting that they may not be accessible.[3] However, that opens the door to sub-conscious cognition, and how could that be reconciled with the notion of thought as computation? A further point of criticism is that people are able to recategorize observed objects or phenomena, so that representations vary, if they exist, and then they are no longer determinate. Words generally have more than one meaning, and meanings vary across contexts. Closed, i.e. exhaustive and universal, definitions, that capture all possible contexts, are often either unfeasible or extremely cumbersome. For most definitions one can find a counter example that defeats it.

> For example, what is the definition of 'chair'? Should it have legs? No, some chairs have a solid base. Not all chairs have arm rests or back rests. Neither has a stool, but we distinguish it from a chair. A child seat on a bike has a backrest, but is not called a chair. At least in some languages, a seat in a car is called a chair. A chair is used for sitting, but so is a horse. A cow is not a chair, but years ago I saw a newspaper item 'Watch Him Sitting in his Cow', with a picture of someone who used a stuffed cow for a chair. If it were customary for people living along a beach to collect flotsam to use for chairs, it would make sense, when walking along a beach, to point to a piece of flotsam and say 'Look! What an attractive chair.' Not to mention professorial chairs.
>
> One may think that this example is too easy, because it concerns an 'artificial kind': an object made for a purpose, which thereby has variability and indeterminacy built into it, because different people might have different purposes. But indeterminacy applies also to natural kinds, such as 'gold' and 'water', as will be discussed later, in the chapter on language and meaning (Chapter 7).

The point, recognized by many (e.g. Putnam 1957, Winograd 1980), is that meanings are unbounded, and open-ended with respect to context. Novel contexts not only select from a given range of potential meanings, but also evoke novel meanings. Of course this does not imply that meanings are without any restriction. The core issue of this book is to discover the relation between change and its constraints, in meaning change and discovery. I will return to this in the chapter on language (Chapter 7).

Opportunities for and mechanisms of meaning change are crucial to the purpose of this book, which is to find out how novelty comes about. What the above suggests is that novelty is produced in contextual variation. This is one of the cornerstones of the

---

[3] Personal communication from René Jorna.

heuristic of discovery that will be proposed in Chapter 9. The role and workings of contextual variation will be further investigated in the present Chapter. It is the opening towards change across contexts that constitutes the main attraction of the situated-action theory of knowledge and meaning, discussed in the next paragraph.

Summing up: Representations cannot be exhaustive, or determinate, or single-valued, or fixed. As Wittgenstein (1976) proposed in his *Philosophical Investigations*, in his notion of 'meaning as use', words are like tools: their use is adapted to the context, in the way that a screwdriver might be used as a hammer.

6.2.3   THEORETICAL OBJECTIONS

One of the theoretical problems, recognized by Fodor (1975), who is a proponent of the RC view, is the following: If cognitive activity is executed through computation on mental representations, the initial state must also be specified in terms of those representations, so that all knowledge must be innate. That is preposterous, and certainly will not help to develop a theory of learning and innovation.[4]

Another theoretical objection is that if one admits that meaning is somehow context-dependent, as most cognitive scientists do, also if they are adherents of the RC view, then according to the RC view context should be brought into the realm of representations and computations. Shanon (1993: 159) characterizes this as the opening of a 'disastrous Pandora's box'. To bring in all relevant contexts would defeat the purpose of reducing the multiplicity of cognitive and verbal behaviour to a limited set of elements that generate variety in the operations performed on them. Furthermore, we would get stuck in an infinite regress: How would we settle the context dependence of representations of contexts? Note that contexts in their turn are not objectively given, somehow, but subject to interpretation. As Shanon (1993: 160) puts it: 'If the representational characterization of single words is problematic, that of everything that encompasses them is hopeless.'

> Janssen (1997) specifies several examples of ambiguities that can only be resolved through reference to the context, and thereby appear to militate against compositionality. One is the ambiguity of 'unless':
>
> > Every person will eat steak unless he eats lobster. (They eat either steak or lobster.)
> >
> > No person will eat steak unless he eats lobster. (They eat both steak and lobster.)
>
> One can save compositionality by recognizing two different meanings:
>
> > disjunction (either . . . or . . .), which applies for 'positive subject' (every person)
> >
> > conjunction (. . . and . . .), which applies for 'negative subject' (no person)

---

[4] Fodor made rescue attempts in later work, by introducing a mechanism (a 'transducer') to import the richness and variability of experience, in order to allow for cognitive change. But that still assumes absorption in the repertoire of some prior, internal language.

Chris can win any match. (universal statement)

Jean does not believe Chris can win any match. (existential statement)

The solution to preserve compositionality here would be, again, to have two meanings of 'any', with one eliminated 'if it is incompatible with the context'. Janssen's view is that it is always possible to preserve compositionality by introducing new meanings, new basic parts, or new constructions. But he admits (p. 440) that these new elements should apply throughout, not to be thoroughly *ad hoc*, and 'other expressions may then be produced in new ways, and new ambiguities may arise'. This illustrates the 'Pandora's box' mentioned by Shanon.

In recent developments in the logic of language, the notion has come up of 'discourse-representation theory'. In the words of van Eijck and Kamp (1997: 181): 'Each new sentence S of a discourse is interpreted in the context provided by the sentences preceding it . . . The result of this interpretation is that the context is updated with the contribution made by S.' The merit of this theory is that it yields a dynamic perspective on semantics: truth conditions are defined in terms of context change. This theory can even be formalized so as to preserve compositionality (Janssen 1997).

However, I propose that the dynamic of interpretation and context is more creatively destructive than is modelled in discourse-representation theory: the interpretation of a novel sentence can rearrange the perception of context and transform interpretations of past sentences. That is the process of exploration that I am after in this book.

Summing up: Compositionality is problematic because of context dependence and the fact that contexts themselves are subject to interpretation and reinterpretation. Or, to put it differently: The meaning of the whole is not only determined by the meaning of the parts, but feeds back to produce shifts in meaning of the parts. To understand this, in Chapter 7 I will employ the notion of the 'hermeneutic circle'.

6.2.4   A Reflection on Criticism

The criticism of the RC view seems to be based on the wish for realistic theory: theory, which reflects what we believe, actually happens in the mind. We can believe that people have representations in the mind, but not that these satisfy the axioms of the RC view. The defence of the RC view seems to be based not on what we believe happens in the mind, but on a different, instrumentalist principle; the principle of the Turing test: A mechanism yields an adequate model of the behaviour, if the behaviour it reproduces cannot be distinguished from real behaviour.

This is reminiscent of the debate on criticism in economics, discussed in the methodological section of Chapter 1 and in Chapter 4. In economics the instrumentalist view is that at the aggregate level of economic phenomena one need not employ a realistic theory of cognition. The relevant question is whether theory can reproduce observed phenomena, not whether it represents underlying processes in reality.

Here, as in Chapters 1 and 4, I prefer realism of theory. The question then is whether this entails reductionism. Does theory of phenomena at higher levels of aggregation have to be built from theory at lower levels? Does economic theory have to be based on a theory of cognition? Does cognitive theory have to be based on a theory of neural processes? The problem with economics is that it maintains the reductionist principle of methodological individualism, and at the same time sees no obligation to use a theory of how people think and act, and even accepts explanatory principles that contradict such theory.

In cognitive science, it seems to me that many adherents of the RC view will reject the strong condition of abstraction: that material realization (physiology) is irrelevant. I think that most cognitive scientists accept that cognitive theory must not be untenable in the light of what we know of neural processes. They do claim, however, that neural processes do not by themselves specify higher-level processes. I accept this, but it does seem to me that it would be nice if our knowledge of neural processes could inform theory of cognition, and that ultimately this is a goal we should try to achieve.

Lakoff and Johnson (1999) offer an evolutionary argument to take into account how cognition is 'embodied in the flesh'. Contrary to the opinion of Descartes, cognition is not separate from the body but is embodied. In evolution, it has been tacked on to bodily processes thrown up by previous stages of evolution. It is rooted in proprioceptive perceptions and mechanisms, reflexes, emotions (see also Damasio 1995). This bodily embedding has implications for how cognition works. Thus, Lakoff and Johnson build on their previous work (Lakoff and Johnson 1980), in which they proposed that to conceptualize abstract notions, such as happiness, goodness, etc., we can only fall back on more primary bodily perceptions, so that even the most basic categories we use are in the nature of metaphors rather than literal descriptions. For example, goodness, happiness, health, achievement, control, are 'up': thus we speak of performance 'going up', people 'going up' in society, having 'high standing', feeling 'up to something', the 'upper classes', etc. This is related to the primary experience of standing up when healthy and lying down when ill or dead. The core point is that since cognition is rooted in the flesh, to understand it we cannot ignore how it is embodied.

Therefore, I use insights from the neural Darwnism proposed by Edelman (1987, 1992), because I believe that it indicates how we might resolve some problems of meaning and knowledge. Additionally, apart from neural processes, I don't see how the RC perspective can help to develop a theory of learning and innovation, since it does not give an account of how change of meanings, bits of cognition, and their composition in mental structures can occur from experience that varies across different contexts.

6.2.5   What Else?

I don't see how we can account for learning and innovation on the basis of representations that satisfy any, let alone all, of the assumptions of the RC view: separation of medium and content; a predetermined, complete, exhaustive, and determinate code; well-defined and static constituents of composites. However, this does not mean that we need to throw out the notion of mental representations altogether. If we do not internalize experience (context) by means of representations, and relegate it only to the outside world, how would cognition relate to that world? How can we conceptualize rational thought other than as playing around with mental models, i.e. representations that we make of the world?

Despite his radical criticism of the RC view, of course even Shanon (1993: 162) recognized this: 'On the one hand, context cannot be accounted for in terms of internal, mental representations . . . on the other hand, context cannot be accounted for in terms of external states of affairs out there in the world'. For a solution, he suggests (1993: 163) that: 'Rather, context should be defined by means of a terminology that, by its very nature, is interactional. In other words, the basic terminology of context should be neither external nor internal, but rather one that pertains to the interface between the two and that brings them together.' Similar criticism and conclusions were offered by Hendriks-Jansen (1996), who concluded that we should take a view of 'interactive emergence', and Rose (1992), who proposed the view of 'activity dependent self-organization'. This leads to the situated-action perspective. Of course, in the context of this book this sounds very promising: it seems to connect directly with the constructivist, interactionist view that I use, in the search for 'methodological interactionism'.

If there is an interface between the external and the internal, which 'brings the two together', then by implication there is something 'internal'. What is that if it is not a representation in some sense, i.e. something that has arisen in the mind, on the basis of some physiological process in the brain, on the occasion of experience with action in specific contexts? We can and need to accept mental representations in that sense, without having to go along with the RC view and accept that they are 'well-formed structures of well-defined abstract, static, symbolic entities constituting a complete, exhaustive and determinate canonical system' (Shanon 1993).

6.3　SITUATED ACTION

This paragraph first indicates the roots and the promise of the situated-action perspective. Then it proceeds to develop it, mainly on the basis of the work of Piaget and Vygotsky. At the end, it returns to the question in what sense we can still speak of internal representations.

6.3.1　Cognitive Structure and Action

One could say that up to a point the situated-action view goes back to early associationist theories of cognition. That was proposed, in various forms, by Berkeley, Hume, William James, and the later behaviourist school of thought (Dellarosa 1988: 28, Jorna 1990). However, a crucial difference with behaviourism (notably the work of Skinner and his followers) is that here there is explicit concern with internal representation and mental processing, even though that does not satisfy the axioms of the RC view.

Nevertheless, in some important respects the situated-action view seems opposite to the RC view. It proposes that action is not so much based on cognitive structure as the other way around: cognitive structure is based on action. However, the cognitive structuring that arises as a function of action provides the basis for further action. Thus, both are true: action yields cognitive structuring, which provides a new basis for action. Rather than taking one or the other position I take both, in a cycle of development. Knowledge and meaning constitute repertoires from which we select combinations in specific contexts, which yield novel combinations that may shift repertoires of knowledge and meaning. Such shifts of knowledge and meaning occur in interaction with the physical world, in technological tinkering, and in social interaction, on the basis of discourse (cf. Habermas's (1982, 1984) notion of 'communicative action').

This perspective has the great merit of providing a basis for solving the multilevel problem of organizational learning and innovation, discussed in Chapter 2. Organizations provide structures, shared meanings, and contexts for action and communication in which people learn, and this individual learning contributes to new organizational structures and meanings, which constitutes organizational learning. Institutions provide structures and contexts for the actions of people in organizational roles, which yield organizational learning, which yields innovation, which contributes to the shift of institutions.

6.3.2 Internalized Action

According to some psychologists (Piaget, Vygotsky) intelligence is internalized action. Through interaction with the physical and social environment, the epistemological subject constructs mental entities that form the basis for virtual, internalized action and speech, which somehow form the basis for further action in the world. This internalized action is embodied in neural structures that can be seen as representations, in some sense, but not necessarily in the semantic, canonical, decomposable, static sense of mainstream cognitive science. In contrast with Piaget, Vygotsky (1962) recognized not only the objective, physical world as a platform for cognitive construction, but also the social world with its affective loading. While according to Piaget a child moves outward from his cognitive constructs to recognition of the social other, according to Vygotsky the social other is the source of the acquisition of knowledge and language.

In language acquisition by children, a phenomenon on which Piaget and Vygotsky agreed was that at some point children engage in egocentric speech, oriented towards the self rather than social others, and that this subsequently declines. Piaget interpreted this decline as an outward movement *from* the self to the social other; a 'decentration' from the self. Vygotsky ascribed it to a continued movement *into* the self, in an ongoing process of formation and identification of the self and development of independent thought. The reason that egocentric speech declines is that overt speech is partly replaced by 'inner speech'.

Before that stage, however, speech is preceded by and based on sensori-motor actions of looking, gesturing, and pointing, aimed at satisfying a want.

Werner and Kaplan (1963) demonstrated 'that reference is an outgrowth of motor-gestural behaviour. Reaching evolves into pointing, and calling-for into denoting'. They note that 'it is in the course of being shared with other people that symbols gain the denotative function'. Anglin 'showed that the order in which the terms of reference are acquired by children is associated with the actions that the children can perform with the objects named' (Shanon 1993: 351). 'Piaget [observed] that a child's utterance of "dog" signified a request to get any object from a particular balcony. In other words, the term indicated not a particular referent, but rather a particular context of action defined by the child's perspective' (Shanon 1988: 79). A similar observation, quoted by Shanon (1988: 79), was 'an early use of the term "kitty" . . . [with which] the child would demand the return of a toy cat she had thrown from her crib; the child used the same word to demand the return of other thrown objects as well'.

Both Shanon and Hendriks-Jansen use the interesting notion of the 'scaffolding' that the context yields. It yields leverage, especially when it is based on intentional support in a social context. A scaffold is used in the building of an arch: stones are aligned along a wooden scaffold until they support each other and the scaffold can be removed. The paradigmatic case in cognitive development of children is the support provided to the infant by its mother. According to the account given by Hendriks-Jansen (1996), infants do not have an innate language capability as claimed by Chomsky.

They have innate repertoires of activity sequences, such as facial 'expressions', eye movements, and myopic focusing, kicking movements, randomly intermittent bursts of sucking when feeding, random gropings. At the beginning these movements do not signify anything nor do they seek to achieve anything , and they certainly do not express any internal representations of anything. The mother, however, instinctively assigns meanings and intentions where there are none, and this sets a dynamic of interaction going in which meanings and intentions get assigned to action sequences selected from existing repertoires on the occasion of specific contexts of interaction. Thus, the random pauses in sucking are falsely picked up by the mother as indications of a need to jiggle the baby back into feeding action. In fact, it is not the jiggling but, on the contrary, the stopping of it that prods the baby to resume the action. The taking turns in stops and jiggles does not serve any purpose of feeding, as the mother falsely thinks, but a quite different purpose, for which evolution has 'hijacked' what was thrown up by previous evolution. It is 'used' to ready the child for the 'turn taking' that is basic for communication: in communication one speaks and then stops to let the other speak. Here, the child acts, stops, and triggers the mother to action, who jiggles and then stops and thereby triggers the baby to action.

At first, the infant can focus vision only myopically, which serves to concentrate on the mother and her scaffolding, so that it is not swamped by impressions from afar. Later, the scope of focusing vision enlarges, and the infant randomly fixes its gaze on objects around it. The mother falsely interprets this as interest and hands the object to the infant, and thereby generates interest. The child is then inclined to prod the mother's hand into picking up objects, first without and later with looking at the mother.

Groping and prodding develop into pointing, which forms the basis for reference that is the basis for meaning and language. While the child points and utters sounds, the mother responds with the correct words, and so language develops. In egocentric speech the child starts to provide its own scaffolding, which further contributes to the development of its own identity. Along these lines, meaning and intentionality do not form the basis for action but arise from it, with the aid of scaffolds from the context.

As indicated, according to Vygotsky overt speech is next internalized, to yield virtual speech, and cognitive constructs serve as a basis for virtual action: to explore potential actions mentally, through the construction of mental models, deduction, mental experiments. While cognition is not necessarily achieved in terms of language, and can to some extent develop without it, its development is tremendously enhanced by language, in the development of internal speech.

This process of embedding knowledge and language in the body, and the resulting interaction between body and mind, align with the philosophy of Merleau-Ponty (1964), according to whom the light of reason is rooted in the obscurity of the body. This perspective, and the awareness that cognitive functions build on non-cognitive bodily and emotional functions 'thrown up' by evolution also plays an important role in Lakoff and Johnson's recent (1999) book on 'philosophy in the flesh'. We will encounter this view also later, in Chapter 7, in a discussion of metaphor, which builds on the earlier work of Lakoff and Johnson (1980).

6.3.3   Representations?

As indicated, the situated-action view contests the idea of *semantic* representations as a necessary and universal basis for all knowledge, but it allows for representations in some sense as the basis for at least some behaviour. For example, it might be consistent with connectionism: the view that cognition is based on neural nets, which can generate systematic regularity without the explicit specification of generative rules in underlying representations. Such nets are representations in some sense, generated, by some mechanism, from experience in the world (cf. Smolensky 1988).

In parallel-distributed processing (PDP, cf. Rumelhart & McClelland 1987) two radical steps are taken. One is to no longer accept the computer metaphor of sequential processing according to some algorithm, but to approach knowledge and learning in terms of parallel processes that interact with each other. The second is to recognize that knowledge is not stored in units, to be retrieved from these, but in patterns of activation in connections between units. Knowledge is implicit in this pattern of connections rather than in the units themselves (Rumelhart, Hinton, & McClelland 1987: 75). What is stored is the connection strengths between the units that allow the patterns to be recreated (McClelland, Rumelhart, & Hinton 1987: 9).

Edelman's (1987, 1992) neural Darwinism seems to yield a viable perspective for understanding how situated action might work in terms of neural networks (or 'neuronal groups', as he calls them). These are selected and reinforced according to operative success. According to Edelman, memory, both short- and long-term, is not the 'retrieval' of some entity, but a process of recategorization; of reactivating, and in the process possibly shifting, the process of selection among neuronal groups. This implies, in particular, that memory also is context-dependent, and that the process of recall may affect the template of future recall. The difference between connectionist models of PDP and neural selectionism is that the former aims to operate at some notional, abstract level between symbols and neural networks (Smolensky 1988) whereas the latter operates directly at the level of neuronal groups. PDP retains symbols as some higher-level, aggregate, emergent outcome of lower-level processing.

The central point is that a mechanism of selection among neuronal structures shows in what way performance may precede competence; how meanings may be constructed from discourse (sense making) and knowledge from action (intelligence as internalized action), and provide the basis for ongoing action. This account seems consistent with Johnson-Laird's account of mental models and Hendriks-Jansen's account of how children learn language. This approach indicates how mental structures might emerge from experience in a way that allows for openness and variability across contexts. It offers an evolutionary perspective rather than a perspective of rational design. The programmatic significance of evolutionary theory is that it forces us to explain development not as the result of conscious, goal-directed, top-down, rational design by decomposition of functions, but as selection from among a repertoire of activity sequences, on the occasion of the demands and opportunities of specific contexts.

Summing up: As a basis for situated-action theory, and the interactionist, constructivist view of knowledge and meaning that it supports, I employ an evolutionary, connectionist theory of cognitive development. On the occasion of experience, selections and recombinations are made from partly overlapping and competing patterns of neural connections (Rumelhart & McClelland 1987, Edelman 1987, 1992, Rose 1992). According to these theories, performance, in interaction with and with support from the context, yields competence as much as competence yields the basis for performance. This underpins methodological interactionism.

6.3.4   Stages of Learning

According to Piaget (1970, 1974), development in children proceeds in stages, yielding successively 'higher' levels of cognitive competence.

> Thus, an infant needs to form the notion, at about eighteen months of age, that objects exist independently from their observation. This happens in a relatively short period of time. Evidence for this is that in contrast with earlier behaviour it snatches away a handkerchief in the expectation of retrieving an object that was hidden under it. When a ball is pitched behind a sofa it turns its head in the expectation of seeing it reappear at the other side. Later, at the age of around seven, the child needs to master the laws of conservation of number, mass, and volume. Before that, it may think that when water is poured from a narrow, tall glass into a wide, low glass the volume changes, or that when a row of objects is spaced out its number increases. Rather suddenly, it grasps that changing the spatial configuration of some coins on a table does not change their number, and that the volume of water remains the same when it is poured from a tall, slim glass

to a long, low one. Often, the new vision is not directly stable, and in a transition period there are relapses to the old practice (*'decalage'*).

The precise content of those stages, the ages corresponding with them, the necessity and consistency of their sequence, the sharpness of transitions, and absence of overlap are contested in the literature (Flavell 1967, Boden 1979). There is evidence which conflicts with the uniform and universal march of reason suggested by Piaget. The social context and conditions of support matter for the moments and the speed at which steps of development take place. There are prodigies who acquire abilities at an astonishingly low age. Children have a much better ability at eidetic ('photographic') memory than adults. However, it is striking that several authors (Gardner, for example) first castigate Piaget for ascribing the acquisition of competence too rigidly to specific stages at specific ages, and then proceed themselves to talk in those terms.

Another point of criticism is that Piaget attends only to the development of logico-mathematical thought, and there are other areas of intelligence. According to Gardner (1983) we can add: spatial/pictorial, linguistic, musical, kinaesthetic/movement, intra- and interpersonal intelligence. In a previous section I already noted the criticism that Piaget underestimates, and in fact largely ignores, the social and emotional sources and conditions of experience and cognition (Flavell 1967, Hamlyn 1978, Vuyk 1981) and the scaffolding role of context. In view of this criticism, Vygotsky's view is much more acceptable.

What I want to pick up here, however, is Piaget's notion of 'functional invariants': principles of application and transformation that recur at subsequent levels of development. These are more important than the precise content or order of stages (Vuyk 1981: 58). Adjusting Piaget's account a little: Experience is 'assimilated' in existing cognitive structures, in steps which lead to a transformation ('accommodation') of such structures to 'higher-level' structures at the next stage of development. This process is assumed to be caused by an inherent drive of existing structures to assimilate the widest possible range of experience. When fit is not complete, the first attempt is to reduce experience to make it fit. But persistent lack of fit will drive the structure to 'accommodate'. Assimilation proceeds in steps. First is 'generalization', in which existing competence is applied in wider contexts, next 'differentiation' to adjust it to differences between contexts, and 'reciprocation' to synthesize elements from different practices encountered in novel contexts. That suggests something like a process of exploitation leading up to exploration, and is therefore of great interest to the purpose of this book. Piaget's notions form a central source of inspiration for the heuristic of discovery developed in Chapter 9.

6.4 SCRIPTS

Abelson (1976) and Shank and Abelson (1977) used the notion of a script to model cognitive representations of stereotyped, rule-guided, recurrent, more or less routine

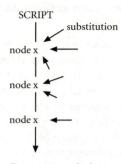

FIGURE 6.1   *Script*

activities. This is an interesting concept, which I later use as a tool to model competencies and routines more generally, also at the level of organizations and industries.

6.4.1   Definition

As illustrated in Figure 6.1, a script consists of a sequence of nodes, which act as 'components' or 'chunks'. With these nodes correspond sets of events or actions, which are
'substituted' into the node (like values into a mathematical variable). The node produces outcomes, which are substituted into other (subsequent) nodes in the script, or
into nodes of outside scripts. Substitution into a node allows for a range of different
'permissible alternatives' or 'functional equivalents', that satisfy conditions corresponding with the node and its place in the script. These constraints can be more or less
restrictive. The sequence of the script may be logical or causal and in the latter case is
also temporal.

> Consider this example, taken from Shank & Abelson (1977). In a restaurant script, the nodes rep-
> resent successive activities of entering, sitting down, ordering, eating, paying, and leaving. Each
> of these can be done in different ways. For example, paying by cash, by cheque, bank card, credit
> card, or chip card.

For observations to make sense they need to be assimilated into mental structures,
which is modelled here as substitution into nodes in the script. Scripts make up one's
cognitive, categorical framework or absorptive capacity. It can yield errors of attribution. When observations can be fitted into a script, we tend to infer that the script
applies, and we attribute other nodes of the script to the activity in hand, even if we do
not observe them. This is efficient but can be a source of prejudice and error.

The notion of scripts can help us to deal with the multilevel issue. This is taken up
in Chapter 10, but it is useful to summarize the argument here. If cognitive scripts
exist, at the individual level, then interpretation is a process of fitting perceptions into
the nodes of cognitive scripts, and learning is a process of changing scripts, in novel
substitutions into nodes, or, in more radical change, novel arrangements of nodes, in
novel script architectures. The actions of people, in turn, based on their cognition, are

substituted into nodes of organizational scripts, where the nodes represent tasks and organizational scripts represent 'routines' or 'performance programs'. Organizational learning can then be rendered as finding novel substitutions into nodes, or more radically, novel architectures of nodes. Firms, in their turn, provide substitutions into user scripts, or novel architectures of such scripts, and they substitute activities or products into industrial-supply-chain scripts. Innovation can be rendered as novel substitutions or architectures in production or consumption scripts, and industrial dynamics as novel substitutions or novel architectures in supply chains. In this way we could establish connections between different levels of change, with a nesting of scripts with subscripts and superscripts.

6.4.2 Criticism

The notion of scripts has been criticized, in cognitive science, for being too stereotyped, rule-based and rigid for most everyday contexts of life (see, e.g., Johnson-Laird 1983). It seems to allow only tightly prescribed actions, and to brook no surprises. This is an important issue: we must preserve ambiguity, because that provides the holes into which novelty can creep and break the system open. Exploitation must allow for the variety that is needed for exploration.

> In the restaurant script, what happens if a dog enters? There is no prescribed behaviour. But in some restaurants it will be allowed if the dog is accompanied and lies under the table. Some people may sneak food to it. In the US some restaurants provide 'doggy bags' to take home remaining scraps of food. Such eventualities are not provided for, but neither do they have to be taken as excluded. What happens if a goat walks in? That will probably be forbidden. What is not prescribed is left to the discretion of the management, and will vary with whoever is in charge.

Thus, the notion of a script appears to entail at least some of the problems identified in the criticism of the RC view of knowledge and language. Especially, it seems to claim exhaustiveness, and not to leave enough room for novelty in novel contexts. As formulated by McClelland, Rumelhart, & Hinton (1987: 9), scripts ('frames' and 'schemata') are useful structures (for storing knowledge):

but . . . only approximations . . . any theory . . . will have to allow them to interact with each other to capture the generative capacity of human understanding in novel situations. Achieving such interactions has been one of the greatest difficulties associated with implementing models that really think generatively

Here, 'thinking generatively' is clearly akin to our 'exploration' and 'second-order' learning. Nevertheless, the notion of a script is extremely attractive, to use as a model of, in particular, organizational processes and industrial supply chains, as I will argue in more detail in Chapter 10. So, can the concept be made sufficiently flexible and malleable, and tolerant of ambiguity, to be retained? The scripts that people have in their repertoires of action vary because their experiences vary. Shank and Abelson (1995) described this as follows:

Scripts serve as a kind of storehouse of old experiences of a certain type . . . When something new happens to us in a restaurant that tells us more about restaurants, we must have some place to put that new information so that we will be wiser next time . . . My restaurant script won't be exactly the same as yours, but they will both include information such as 'one can expect forks to be available without asking, unless the restaurant is Chinese'.

We must allow for different variants of the script for different contexts. Perhaps we can interpret a script as a set of 'default rules': they apply until challenged, and then if in context the challenge 'works', the script is changed. Novel situations require the merging of different scripts that cannot be specified in advance for all contingencies. This can only be left to the discretion and skill of the people involved. Shank (1980) described the following case:

> Suppose that in a restaurant you get a headache. Your usual script would be to walk to the medicine cabinet, at home. Here, without hesitation, you ask the waitress for an aspirin, which was not foreseen in the restaurant script.

Furthermore, the variability of scripts must be such that allowance is made for novel combinations.

> Take, for example, a self-service restaurant as opposed to a service restaurant. The sequence of nodes is different: in contrast with the service restaurant, one generally pays before sitting down and eating.

Summing up: Although it is clear that a single, deterministic script does not suffice as a full model of competence, it can form an important building-block. Perhaps actual practices should be seen not as single scripts but as collections of different variations upon a script for different conditions (Holland *et al.* 1989).

6.4.3 Stories

There are many situations in ordinary, daily life, beyond the regimentation of logical argument or production processes in firms, that do not seem to be governed so strictly, and are less stereotyped and less determinate than scripts. For this reason, Shank and Abelson later (1995) reverted to stories alongside scripts, to account for knowledge and language more generally: 'Obviously, we can understand some novel experiences even if no scripts seem to apply. We do this by seeing new experiences in terms of old experiences' (p. 6). This does not mean that Shank and Abelson now reject scripts:

A script is a set of expectations about what will happen next in a well-understood situation. In a sense, many situations in life have the participants seemingly reading their roles in a kind of play . . . Scripts are useful for a variety of reasons. They make clear what is supposed to happen and what various acts on the part of others are supposed to indicate. They make mental processing easier, by allowing us, in a sense, to think less. You don't have to figure out every time you enter a restaurant how to convince someone to feed you. All you really have to know is the restaurant script and your part in it. Scripts are helpful in understanding the actions of others as long as we know the script they are following (p. 5). [However:] Situations that one person sees as a script may seem quite open-ended to another person

Note that exactly the same efficiency argument that here is adduced for scripts, in the organizational literature was used for routines (Nelson & Winter 1982) or performance programmes (March & Simon 1958). This aligns with my proposal of a multilevel script theory, in which such routines or programmes are the organizational equivalents of mental scripts.

Hearing stories, people build up their repertoire of stories, and when they next hear a story they try to fit it into a story already in their repertoire. Again, this yields attribution: When a story one hears fits sufficiently into an existing story in one's repertoire, the rest of the latter is attributed to the former. In this way one reads one's own stories in those of others. As in the case of scripts, this is efficient, because a few words suffice to recognize a plot, but it is also a source of prejudice. Different experiences yield different story-based understanding. Interpretations are made to fit experiences that one has had oneself, and thus depend on the role that one has played in similar stories, e.g. the role of victim or the role of perpetrator. Interpretations are tailored to fit purposes, exercise of control or power, moral justification of one's own past roles, support for one's sense of self-worth. There is a tendency towards dramatic polarization to either negative or positive extremes: myths of fulfilment or romantic failure, depravity and evil, heroic virtue (Baumeister & Newman 1995: 105). This helps to catch attention. It helps memory when we tell a story about experience, but in the telling we add and subtract, and what we remember is, in a sense, a lie. As we retell it, details are lost and embellishments added.

This is reminiscent of Johnson-Laird's (1983) proposal that people construct a mental model on the basis of their experience, from the clues given in the discursive context, in order to capture the significance of what is said, and thereby go beyond what is actually said. It is also reminiscent of the neural Darwinism that we discussed: stories in the mind may have partly overlapping versions, from which context-bound stimuli select, and which are enhanced or weakened by this selection.

Read and Miller (1995: 142) note the fundamentally social nature of storytelling, and point out that it has normative in addition to cognitive functions: it enables people to gossip, which can be used to enhance group cohesiveness.

According to Shank and Abelson, to handle stories in memory, they must be 'indexed' or labelled for 'retrieval'. The richer a story is the more indexes it contains, and the more opportunity we have to hook it on to past experience. The context helps us to select and to assign a relevant index. Thus, indexing, storytelling, and story interpretation are path-dependent. Indexes are often in themselves condensed stories or 'skeletons'. Understanding means mapping stories heard into stories held. Intelligence depends on the ability to translate descriptions of new events into indexes that help in the retrieval of prior events (Shank & Abelson 1995: 10). Experts should be modelled as users of case-based reasoning on stores of relevant examples rather than as processors employing rule-based reasoning. This confirms the importance of para-digms as exemplars, noted previously.

The neural-selectionist view suggests that there is not any single story in the mind, with several indexes, but a population of versions, to be selected, enhanced, and recombined by cues from the context. In time, stories may reduce to mere events, but event memory may also be prior to storytelling. Shank and Abelson distinguish event-based memory from story-based memory. In the first the coherence of a story plot is lost; in the second it is retained.

The relevance of all this to the project of this book is this: Scripts clearly pertain to exploitation, but have to be loosened in exploration, where perhaps we can be said to revert to storytelling. Apparently, scripts are not radically different from story-based memory, because in the latter also the connectivity between events or actions is important. One wonders how event-based memory and story-based memory relate to the distinction between declarative and procedural memory indicated before (Chap-ter 1). Perhaps indexes and skeletons of stories might be associated with organiza-tional myths and symbols, employed to guide memory and the selection and telling of stories.

Scott (1995) reminds us that even scripts plus storytelling do not exhaust mental activity: there is also musical ability, imagery, gestures, spatial conceptualization, sensori-motor co-ordination. This corresponds with Gardner's (1983) view that there are multiple kinds of intelligence.

6.5 CONCLUSION

The non-standard, situated-action view of 'interactive emergence' (Hendriks-Jansen 1996) or 'activity dependent self-organization' (Rose 1992) of knowledge and lan-guage provides a theoretical basis for the perspective of methodological interaction-ism. Theory and empirical evidence show how it can be that action in contexts yields meaning, knowledge, and competence, rather than action being based on knowledge and meaning that inhere somehow, independently from context and action. However, internalized action and speech yield knowledge on the basis of which one can think: infer, reason, and perform 'virtual action' in the brain to simulate novel possibilities for real action.

Partly, Dupuy (1998: 73) arrived at a similar conclusion from the theory of complex adaptive systems. He claimed that the notion of an autonomous (adaptive, self-organizing) system:

Entails a criticism of the representationalist paradigm which dominates the cognitive sciences. According to this paradigm, there exists a homomorphism between the state of the environ-ment and a given being's knowledge of it. In the new paradigm, however, to know is not to recog-nize, but to bring forth a world according to the forms that are allowed by one's own internal organization.

The excursion into cognitive science shows that intuitions of interaction as a basis for innovation and learning, in the economic-innovation literature and the literature on organizational learning, are not just loose hunches or metaphors. They are supported in an admittedly heterodox, but emerging, perspective of situated-action theory, in the field of cognitive science. The view of knowledge as internalized action and the situated-action perspective show how knowledge is constructed according to present cognitive structure, but also how that structure is adapted on the basis of experience. The environment in which action takes place, whether this is an organizational environment for ideas or a market environment for firms, does not only constitute an evolutionary selection environment, with the negative function of selecting out what has the least fitness to that environment. It also has a positive function of scaffolding, of selecting from cognitive repertoires to fit the context and strengthening what is successful. Thereby it contributes to cognitive development.

According to Piaget cognitive development is based on cycles of assimilation, in which experience is fitted into existing ways of doing things, and accommodation, in which those ways are adapted. This view is adopted in an attempt at a general theory of exploitation and exploration, in Chapter 9.

Scripts serve as a model for cognitive structures associated with rule-governed behaviour. A condition for this is that they allow for sufficient variability across contexts. To understand how this might be, I seek insight from an analysis of meaning variance in language, in Chapter 7. Scripts represent absorptive capacity: people make sense of phenomena by trying to substitute them into nodes of scripts. In connection with less rule-governed behaviour we should consider stories rather than scripts. I propose that stories precede scripts, and may develop into scripts for rule-based behaviour. When scripts systematically fail to function, they break down and people resort to stories, which may develop into new scripts.

In Chapter 10, at the level of firms, I use scripts to represent organizational processes, as a further development of the notion of an organizational routine (Nelson & Winter 1982) or performance programs (March & Simon 1958). Or, in other words, I use it to model 'social technologies' (Nelson & Sampat 2000). At the level of firms, industries, and economies, I use it to model institutions. A script acts as a selection environment, or institutional environment, for the nodes in it. I propose that scripts are nested, or have a 'fractal' nature: when we apply a magnifying glass to a substitution into a script we see 'subscripts'. A script substitutes outcomes into one or more nodes of a higher-level 'superscript'. This models the multilevel nature of institutions proposed in Chapter 5. I use it to solve the multilevel problem of connecting different levels of learning and innovation: the individual level, the level of teams or divisions in firms, interfirm networks, industries, innovation systems or economies.

7

Language[1]

We need insight, in particular, into the variability of meaning and processes of meaning change. Among other things, I turn to the 'hermeneutic circle'. Together with the theory of knowledge and cognitive development set out in Chapter 6, this theory of meaning and meaning change provides the inspiration and the basis for a general theory of discovery, to be developed in Chapter 9.

7.1   MOTIVATION

Like theory of knowledge, theory of language and meaning yields multiple schools of thought, which need to be disentangled to arrive at a choice, and again the question arises whether it is really necessary to make that effort.

In the most general terms, a theory of language is needed because in the interactionist perspective knowledge is supposed to arise from interaction between people, and it is through communication, in language use, that people interact with each other and thereby learn. More specifically, in Chapter 2, following the views of Weick, firms were seen as systems of shared meaning, engines of sense making or enactment, or as focusing devices. To understand what we are talking about here we need a theory of meaning, sense making, and language.

A second reason is that in Chapter 3 it was recognized that even if there were no uncertainty, complete contracts would be impossible because of limited skills in language and limitations to the precision that language can offer. This suggests that we should investigate what, more precisely, the possibilities and limitations of language are.

A third reason is that in Chapter 5 I proposed that language yields a paradigm (in the root sense of an exemplary case) of institutions. Language provides a basis for discursive action, but living speech, storytelling, and poetry create novelty and shifts of meaning. Understanding of this may help us to understand more generally how institutions enable behaviour and are shifted by it. The process of language use and language change may provide a metaphor, or a model, of innovation that brings us further than the metaphor of evolution.

We need a theory of identity under variability. In the literature on management and organization, discussed in Chapter 2, it has been recognized that organizational

[1] I thank René Jorna for his comments on an earlier version of this Chapter. Of course the usual disclaimer again applies.

routines (Nelson & Winter 1982) or performance programmes (March & Simon 1958) need to allow for flexibility and variability, while maintaining sufficient coherence to fulfil their function. That function is to provide coherence, with sufficient clarity of tasks and connections between them, and stability, for the sake of efficient production; in other words, for exploitation. For the sake of exploration, however, a certain amount of variability is needed. This issue is crucial for the central theme of this book: how to combine exploitation and exploration. I expect to find insight into this from language because, after all, there we see variability and stability of meaning combined. In fact, that was one of the reasons that I proposed language as a paradigm example of an institution.

7.2   THEORY OF LANGUAGE

With a basis in the theory of knowledge, in Chapter 6, I now delve a little more deeply into issues of meaning and communication. Analysis of language is usually classified in four categories: phonetics (sounds), syntax (sentence structure), semantics (meaning, in the sense of reference), and pragmatics (actual language use). Perhaps we should add semiotics. Here, phonetics and syntax will not be considered, and I focus first on semantics. Then I turn to pragmatics. I will conclude that there is no useful semantics aside from pragmatics.

7.2.1   *Sense, Reference, and Truth*

Semantics aims to deal with meaning in terms of truth conditions. Frege (1892) made a famous distinction between reference ('*Bedeutung*': 'extension') and sense ('*Sinn*': 'intension'). Reference is that which a term refers to, such as an individual or a class of objects, or in the case of a proposition its truth value. Frege characterized sense as 'the way in which extension is given': how we establish reference. How do we identify an individual, determine whether an object belongs to a certain class, whether a proposition is true? This gives rise to the notion that the meaning (intension) of an expression is the method of its verification.

One issue now is whether intension is a mental category, i.e. an idea, which yields 'psychologism', or constitutes some outside reality, which yields 'realism'. According to Frege it is separate from individual, subjective ideas: truth conditions are to be kept separate from the mental processes by which one may become conscious of them. If intension truthfully establishes extension, then it cannot be a subjective idea, because then all people would have perfect and identical knowledge. We would all be one in God. Thus, to allow for human failure and preserve the idea that intension is in the mind, intension would no longer represent objective truth conditions but ways in which people determine class membership and seek truth, often erroneously. If intension represents personal knowledge, it is in fact a belief that can be false. If, on the other hand, we maintain that intension constitutes objective reality, we are back at the problem, indicated before, of how we can establish the way in which our knowledge is hooked on to that reality, since we cannot descend from our minds. If it is external and objective, how do people grasp it and how does it guide their judgement?

A related issue is whether intension provides necessary and sufficient conditions for class membership and truth. An attractive ploy is to assume that there is some essence that constitutes such necessary and sufficient conditions, and this is what the Fregean tradition in semantics has picked up. It brings us all the way back to Aristotle, who held that a concept has an immanent essence, which has no separate existence but can be grasped. According to the later philosopher Locke such an essence can be arrived at through abstraction: by reducing characteristics of members of a class until we arrive at essential, common characteristics. Later, it was operationalized in the notion that there is a lexicon of all primitive terms, with appended to them 'selection restrictions' which limit their use to 'proper' use (Linsky 1971).

Putnam (1957) proposed that there is a 'linguistic division of labour': specialists know the 'real' intension, such as the chemical formula and resulting properties of water (H_2O), and this ultimately establishes true class membership. Ordinary people can refer to it in case of doubt, but for day-to-day action employ a 'stereotype', such as water being clear, drinkable, boiling at 100 degrees Celsius, freezing at 0 degrees, and expanding when it freezes. This does not entail necessary and sufficient conditions, and is not always correct: when under pressure water boils at a higher temperature than 100 degrees, and freezes at a lower temperature than 0 degrees.

> This may even be important in ordinary life. It makes skating possible, which is important for some. The high pressure of the thin iron of the skate melts the ice and yields a film of water on which one can glide. When it gets too cold this stops and you can no longer glide.

In fact, the stereotype can be false, and in conflict with what the specialist knows. An example Putnam uses is gold. The general idea of gold that prevails in the community includes yellowness, while in fact there is also white gold.

This idea is interesting and useful, but the trouble with it is that new scientific discoveries may shift or even revolutionize the specialist's knowledge, and at any point in time we don't know whether this will happen or not, so that objectivity evaporates again.

7.2.2   Family Resemblance, Defaults and Prototypes

Wittgenstein, in his later work *Philosophical Investigations* (1976), achieved a revolution. According to him there are no necessary and sufficient conditions, and the criteria for judging a proposition to be true, or proper, or adequate, are pragmatic and conventional: something is true if it achieves its operational purpose. In communication and joint action what determines meaning is whether it aligns with common practice and satisfies established rules of the game. This is the notion of 'meaning as use', in which a concept is seen as an instrument. For an instrument we would not ask if it is true or what the necessary and sufficient conditions for proper use are a priori. Its adequacy appears in its specific use in a specific context. This is open-ended, and allows for unorthodox but nevertheless adequate use: we may in some conditions use a screwdriver as a hammer, with adequate results.

Johnson-Laird (1983: 189) employed Minsky's (1975) notion of 'default values' to elucidate how conventional criteria of meaning might work. Characteristics are assumed unless there is evidence to the contrary. They are assumed on the basis of established practice, i.e. on the basis of what it is possible to think, until contested by new practice, which shifts what we can think. This is a crucial idea in the context of this book.

Wittgenstein offered the idea of 'typical cases' that represent a norm, and one deals with borderline cases by reference to the norm. Different occurrences, in different contexts, do not always share common features, let alone necessary and sufficient features, but sometimes at best only 'family resemblances'. Proximate members of a family may have shared characteristics, but distant members often do not. Members of a class form a chain, with common characteristics at each link, but no characteristic shared by all members of the class. X is in the same class as Y not because they have common characteristics but because they both share characteristics, but different ones, with a third member Z.

Others have subsequently proposed similar ideas. Well known is Rosch's (1977) idea of a 'prototype', which represents an exemplar of a class that connects others in the class. Class membership is decided on the basis of resemblance to a salient case, or a typical case, which serves as a prototype. This allows for family resemblance: there may be no single trait shared by all members of the class.

Note that this idea goes back to the ancient notion of paradigm, discussed by Socrates, in the sense of an exemplar to be emulated, as discussed in Chapter 1. I noted that this is a method of reduction, to spare limited cognitive capacity, that may serve as an alternative to the equally ancient reductive principle of decomposition.[2] This is what occurs in management. Co-ordination typically takes place not by analysis into elementary activities and rules of combination, in 'performance programs', but by setting exemplars for emulation. That indicates the role of culture. Of course activities sometimes can be and are analysed, codified, and prescribed in a scheme of action, such as a script. But this is the exception rather than the rule for the totality of organizational processes.

Johnson-Laird (1983: 196) noted, reasonably, that we should keep in sight the differences that occur in the tightness (my term, not his) and character of intension. Technical terms often do satisfy necessary and sufficient conditions, as in mathematical or legal terms. In fact, those terms have been designed for it. Natural-kind terms (water, gold, roses, and the like) do satisfy something like Putnam's stereotypes plus specialist criteria we may refer to in case of doubt. By contrast, 'constructive' terms,

---

[2] This is how we might reconstruct the development of Wittgenstein's thought: the switch from the reductive principle of decomposition, in his earlier, analytic philosophy (of the *Tractatus*), to the reductive principle of an exemplar, in his later philosophy (of the *Philosophical Investigations*).

such as chair, do not possess an underlying structure that determines membership; no appeal to experts.

Ferdinand de Saussure (1979) was perhaps the first to recognize that meanings of concepts do not stand alone but are related to the meanings of other concepts. The signs of words ('signifiers') are arbitrary: a rose could be called by any other name, and in other languages than English it is. The concept indicated by the word ('signified') has a meaning that is related to the meanings of other words: 'a word means what other words do not'. Meaning is not an autonomous entity but a systemic effect. A concept carries associations with other concepts, by which meaning becomes a field of connected meanings rather than a set of isolated meanings. In English we speak of the 'war of the roses', which to people not familiar with the rose as a symbol of British royalty might seem like the title of a new Disney film.

If we thus allow for differences between languages, and subcultures within languages, why not for individual people, and for different contexts for a given person? What keeps us from falling into radical, postmodern relativism?

7.2.3   Embodied Realism

Lakoff and Johnson (1999) argue that our cognition is constituted by neural structures that are rooted in bodily, physiological processes that we have inherited from evolution. This notion of the light of reason being embodied in the darkness of the body goes back to Merleau-Ponty (1964). Our cognition is realistic in the sense that our cognitive structures are constructed in interaction with reality. In the absorption of phenomena we construct our understanding of them. Thus, the idea of realism as a connection between separate worlds of reality and cognition is fundamentally mistaken. Our cognition is not separate from reality but constructed from it, and in that sense it is realistic. This construction is shared between people, and not arbitrary, because we conduct our cognitive constructions on the same biological basis, 'thrown up' by a shared evolution. A second reason why our cognition is to a large extent shared, and not arbitrary, is that we construct it from a shared physical environment, governed by universal laws of nature. In that nature we have to survive, and only those cognitive constructions will survive that yield adequate performance in the world. Note that this is consonant with the Wittgensteinian notion of meaning as use.

This is why, especially, 'middle-range' concepts are most likely to be realistic. An example is the notion of a chair, rather than its components, and rather than the more general notion of 'furniture'. Realism of middle-range concepts, relating to objects we deal with, is crucial for survival. If we did not categorize things like threatening animals, people, stones, rivers, trees, tools, houses, cars, roads, and the like reasonably correctly, our chances for survival would have been dim. This applies much less to the lower- and higher-level concepts. We can survive if our characterization of the biological make-up of a sabre-toothed tiger is wrong, and if we attribute it to the wrong species, but much less if we misjudge its speed and the danger of its fangs and claws.

However, our cognition does remain a construction, and thereby it is not objective, and in that sense relativism is inevitable, even though it is not radical in a postmodern sense that any view is as good as any other. Especially, judgements outside the middle range are subject to error. Emotions and abstract notions are less easy to grasp directly than physical experience, and therefore we seek determination of the former in terms of the latter. Since there are systematic correlations between our emotions and our sensori-motor experiences, such as touching, grasping, pulling, pushing, lifting, dropping, breaking objects, these form the basis for metaphor. We experience ourselves as entities, containers, made of substances, and with sight and touch we experience boundaries. Time is understood as movement, causation in terms of manipulating objects, labour in terms of material resources, and argument may be perceived as battle (Lakoff & Johnson 1999: 56–71). Higher-level concepts are built on these basic metaphors, to yield higher-level metaphors. Thus, we conceive of abstract notions in terms of containers, location, movement, and the like. For example, we conceive of life as a voyage, and meaning (reference) in terms of containers (extension). This yields what I would call an object bias regarding abstract concepts. The notion of the fuzzy boundaries of a concept may be instinctively scary because it triggers emotion-laden associations with a leaking roof that admits the rain and cold, or cracks in walls that might admit the sabre-toothed tiger.

However, while basic metaphors tend to be shared across cultures, since they derive from survival in interaction with a shared natural environment, higher-level metaphors tend to vary. In present-day society social interaction has come to equal or even dominate interaction with the physical world as a basis for cognitive construction, and since in contrast with physical nature social environments vary, cognition may vary across cultures. Thus, I come round to my earlier proposal that to the extent that people have developed in different physical and social environments they entertain different categories or forms of thought, in other words, different absorptive capacities. Recall that this was the basis for my claim, in Chapters 2 and 3, that the fundamental purpose of firms is to create alignment in cognitive categories in order to achieve a common purpose. To Lakoff and Johnson I grant that variety of cognition operates on a substrate of shared, object-oriented cognitive constructions.

7.2.4   Neural Embodiment

In Chapter 6 I argued that while it is not methodologically necessary to explain all cognitive theory in terms of neural processes, theory should not contradict neural facts, and it would be nice if explanation could be supported by a theory of neural processes. If Lakoff and Johnson speak of 'embodied realism', can we find out how this embodiment actually works in terms of neural processes? For this I turn again to the work of Edelman.

While Edelman (1987) is hard to grasp, even for insiders, perhaps the following summary is correct: Wittgenstein's notion of categorization by family resemblance is reflected in neuronal groups that partly overlap, in their 'arbors' of 'dendrites' (neuronal inputs) and 'axons' (neuronal outputs), thus giving a physical representation of 'members of the family' sharing some features but not others. These groups compete in the sense that selection among them is made by stimuli from the specific context, thus evoking 'members' that best fit the context. Successful selections are reinforced by adjustments in the synaptic thresholds that determine the patterns of neuronal 'firing' that define a group. In this way shifts in categorization and dominant exemplars can arise as experience shifts between contexts. As Edelman (1987: 317) noted: 'while certain general principles may underlie such categorization, its instantiations are always special purpose'.

7.3 MEANING CHANGE

How does meaning change? What is the relation between stability and change in language? What is the role of the context? What is the role of individuals in their community?

7.3.1 Stability and Change

Now we get what I hoped to get from the analysis of language: a model for the combination of stability and change, of identity and its variation. This model derives from the notions of prototype and default. We can look at institutional arrangements, including routines or 'social technologies', and scripts as a model of them, in terms of such prototypes and defaults.

At some stage of development, a prototype script emerges, and further practice takes place on the basis of more or less similarity to that prototype. Similarity here may be a shared architecture, in the form of sequences of nodes, shared nodes, or shared substitutions into nodes. This in fact yields a hierarchy of similarity. One stays closest to the prototype when architecture and nodes are the same, and only some substitutions in some nodes vary. The prototype may serve only as a default, so that when deviations from the prototype are increasingly needed, an alternative or adapted prototype is adopted. This may yield different prototypes for different contexts. In script terms, there may be different branches, which may share some but not all nodes, possibly in different sequences. Substitutions into a given node may not coincide (although they are likely to overlap). This is illustrated in Figure 7.1. Note that scripts are not necessarily like trees: branches may turn back to the trunk.

> An example would be the difference between a service and a self-service restaurant. The nodes are similar: entering, selecting, sitting down, eating, and paying. But the sequence is different: in service one pays after eating, and in self-service prior to it. Substitutions into nodes also differ. In service the waiter gets the food, in self-service the customer.

Note that the notion of a prototype, allowing for a variety of family resemblance, eliminates the greatest objection to the notion of a script, discussed in Chapter 6: the objection that it seemed too rigid and does not allow for the variety that we observe and that we need, to allow for flexibility and change.

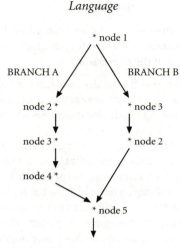

FIGURE 7.1 *Script variety*

7.3.2 *Context, Exploitation, and Exploration*

What I am after in this book is an understanding of the process of exploration; of discovery and the change of meaning. In particular, I want to understand how we can combine exploitation and exploration. I propose that the context dependence of meaning provides a key. We exploit existing meanings and knowledge by employing them in different contexts, and in the process we produce new knowledge and create new meanings.

Johnson-Laird (1983: 245–65) proposed that in interpreting discourse people go beyond what is actually said and heard, and this is needed to progress from understanding what is said to understanding the significance of what is said, i.e. the utterer's communicative intention. This is done by constructing a mental model 'on the basis of inferences from the general knowledge triggered by the discourse'. In other words, from clues given in the specific context of discourse, and employing the knowledge and experience that the hearer has, significance is inferred. Here, we encounter again the notion of default; the model is a proposal to oneself, so to speak, that is maintained until contradicted by further evidence from the context. This line of thinking allows for transformations of the interpretation of the context, and for reinterpretations of previous sentences in a discourse.

Along the lines indicated, meaning is no longer a logical construct, as it was in semantics, but a pragmatic, psychological, and social concept, in terms of linguistic community, linguistic division of labour, stereotype, and specialist criteria.

In a specific context one of the possible meanings of a word is picked out. This brings us back to the notion of scaffolding, which arose in the situated-action theory of knowledge. As proposed by Johnson-Laird (1983: 233), the context helps to solve problems of meaning by indicating what the referent of an expression is, which guides us to pick the apposite meaning of parts of an expression. In other words, the reference of one part of an expression, or the context in which it is uttered, helps to determine the sense of other parts of the expression.

> If we say 'he went into the house', the presupposition is that 'he' went through the door, and we pick out the feature that a house has one or more doors. However, if 'he' is a burglar, he might have gone through a window. But if the context in which the sentence is embedded does not indicate burglary, that possible interpretation remains latent.
>
> Johnson-Laird employed the following illustration. Consider the sentence: 'The ham sandwich at table 5 is getting impatient.' If we were to disambiguate this sentence *ex ante*, through a complete set of 'selection restrictions' on the proper use of linguistic entities, which we could then tick off, it would make nonsense of the very notion of a selection restriction, because it would exclude practically nothing. The sentence is disambiguated by the context: the customer who ordered a ham sandwich is indicated by the latter, in metonymy: using a characteristic to refer to its carrier. The connection between characteristic and carrier is often present only in context.

If the use of an expression is governed by an exemplar, prototype, or stereotype, that may be in focus when entering a context. However, it carries along a trail of accumulated, subsidiary possible features with traces of past contexts in which they have 'worked', which may be elicited by the actual context, and these may have no more than Wittgensteinian family resemblances. Let us call this a 'paradigmatic repertoire'.

It has already been noted, in Chapter 1, that a paradigm, in the sense of an exemplar to be emulated, is a reductive device that helps us deal with complexity in spite of limited cognitive capacity, which may serve as an alternative to the reductive principle of composition. However, it works as such, with family resemblance driving emulation of the exemplar, resulting in a proliferation of family members as experience accrues, only if there is some scaffold to help us pick out the appropriate member of the family. This is what the context provides.

Most important of all is that the movement across contexts can produce novelty: in the process of exploitation we explore. With the apparatus set out above, how can such 'novelty' be reconstructed? It goes beyond the 'picking out' of features from an established repertoire. Thus, one form of novelty is that novel contexts add to the repertoire some feature not previously associated with the term attached to it. This may happen through family resemblance or, as we shall see later, through metaphor. A more radical novelty could perhaps usefully be associated with an 'intensional rupture': a break of intensional lines connecting meanings of words across different sentences. Features or references are redistributed over words: features that were formerly seen to belong to different words are now combined under a single word; features seen to belong to one word are now assigned to another. If again we associate intension with 'sense', this literally entails 'sense making'. Things that seemed the same are now seen as different, and things that seemed different are now seen as the same. To effect such a break is, I propose, the function of metaphor, which carries over a feature from one word to another and thereby sheds a different light, which might cause us to form a novel concept by a redistribution of features. That, I will propose later, in a heuristic of discovery, in Chapter 9, is the deeper meaning of Schumpeterian novel combinations.

7.3.3 *Community, Individual, and Meaning Change*

I proposed before, in Chapters 2 and 5, that there is a middle ground between communitarianism and liberalism. We can escape from the choice between methodological individualism and methodological collectivism, and opt for methodological interactionism. In firms, community is needed to achieve a common understanding and purpose, in view of the need for co-ordination and coherence, and to reduce the incentive problems that mesmerize economists. This is needed to achieve goals, effectiveness, and efficiency of scale and scope by division of labour. In other words, it is needed for exploitation. But we need the variety of individual perspectives and ideas as a source of innovation; in other words, for exploration. This may be obtained in the firm, to the extent that it can be reconciled with the need for co-ordination for the sake of exploitation. In so far as this is not possible, one needs linkages with outside sources of cognition, based on different experience. That is the notion of 'external economy of cognitive scope'. The point here is that the tension between community and individuality is closely connected with the tension between exploitation and exploration.

As previously noted, Saussure (1979) recognized that language has an individual side (*parole*) and a social side (*langue*), and that we cannot conceive of the one without the other. Every moment the system is at the same time established and in evolution (Saussure 1979: 24). *Langue* provides the intersubjective order, in the form of established conventions, that 'synchronically' enables mutual understanding and hence individual parlance (*parole*), but is at the same time its product in time ('diachronically') (p. 37).

According to Saussure language develops by force of idiosyncratic language use (*parole*). However, he proceeded to elaborate *langue*, to the neglect of *parole*. When he does look at change rather than structure, attention goes to phonetic change rather than change of meaning. Interestingly, in the present context, he talks about 'waves of innovation' (p. 275) and their 'propagation' by 'contagion', but does not elaborate. This parlance reminds one of studies of the diffusion of innovations, in marketing and sociology, in which contagion produces the characteristic logistic diffusion curve.

This predilection for the structure rather than the process of change makes Saussure a structuralist *par excellence*. He says that *langue* transforms itself without individuals being able to transform it, and that 'the principle of change founds itself on the principle of continuity' (p. 108). This is obscure: Saussure was struggling with the linguistic equivalent of the problem of exploitation and exploration. The relation between sign and signified is arbitrary,[3] and this makes language vulnerable: it is 'radically powerless to defend itself against factors which shift from one moment to the next the relation between signified and signifier'. In contrast with other human institutions—customs, laws, etc.—which 'are founded, to different degrees, on natural relations of

[3] Symbols are not arbitrary: they picture the concept they represent. Thus, justice is symbolized by a scale, to represent the careful weighing of evidence and interest, or a blindfolded lady, to represent disregard for identity, to ensure equality under the law—or the combination: blindfolded lady, 'Justice', holding the scales.

things; there is in them a necessary conjoining between the means used and the goals pursued' (p. 110). It is likely that this perceived need to save linguistic order from chaos created Saussure's predilection towards *langue* rather than *parole*. But if we follow the reasoning of Merleau-Ponty, Shanon, Hendriks-Jansen, Rose, Piaget, Vygotsky, and Lakoff and Johnson, then Saussure is mistaken when he says that meaning is not grounded in 'natural relations of things'. Meaning is grounded in bodily, sensori-motor experience, and coheres in contexts of experience.

The study of 'diachronic' change is characterized as the study of 'the relations connecting successive terms not perceived by a similar collective consciousness (as in langue), and which substitute for each other without forming a system between them'. That is very unclear. Let us explore processes of meaning change. For this I turn to the notion of the 'hermeneutic circle'.

7.4   HERMENEUTIC CIRCLE

'Hermeneutics' originally referred to the interpretation of religious texts, but the term now applies more generally to interpretation and explanation of speech and writing. The term derives from 'Hermes', the messenger of the gods. The hermeneutic circle refers to the way in which we use existing meanings to express ourselves and understand others, but in the process shift those meanings. I propose that this is akin to the central issue of exploitation and exploration, and provides a metaphor, if not a model, for it.

7.4.1   *The Basic Notion*

Gadamer (1977) is the recognized 'father' of hermeneutics. The basic notion, according to him, is that, like an institution more generally, language provides an 'enabling constraint' (my term, not Gadamer's). It enables us to interpret and understand but thereby also constitutes a prejudice, an interpretation that we construct and impose rather than an objective meaning that we find. This interpretation is not purely subjective, but largely intersubjective, embedded in the history of the speaker in his speech community. As Gadamer (1977) put it:

Prejudices are biases of our openness to the world. They are . . . conditions whereby we experience something . . . But . . . Is not our expectation and our readiness to hear the new also necessarily determined by the old that has already taken possession of us? (p. 9). [There is] always a world already interpreted . . . into which experience steps as something new, upsetting what has led our expectations and undergoing re-organization itself in the upheaval . . . Only the support of the familiar and common understanding makes possible the venture into the alien, the lifting up of something out of the alien (p. 15)

word meaning

sentence meaning

FIGURE 7.2   *Hermeneutic circle 1*

This constitutes the hermeneutic circle: we interpret according to perspectives built on the past and in so doing may change those perspectives to some extent. The context of interpretation is not objectively given but is itself already constructed. However, it is not thereby subjective, but embedded in a history we share with others. This notion is close to the purpose of this book: in exploitation we somehow provide the basis for exploration. Language and categories of understanding are rooted in the past, enable and constrain our actions now, and are subject to shift as a result of our actions. This corresponds with my view of institutions as enabling constraints that are subject to change under the impact of our actions, as discussed in Chapters 4 and 5. This is also consistent with the view of the origins, effects, and change of social and cultural structure proposed by Margaret Archer (1995).

One issue, in particular, in hermeneutics is the relation between the meaning of parts (words) and wholes (sentences, discourse). On the one hand, sentence meaning is somehow composed from prior word meaning. On the other hand, word meanings develop from the use of words in sentences, or more widely, in discourse, in specific contexts. According to the notion of the 'hermeneutic circle' both are true. At a given moment a word offers a range of possible meanings, the meaning can become determinate only in the use of a word in a specific context, and the meaning of a sentence somehow depends on the ranges of possible meanings of constituent words plus grammar and syntax. But as a word is used in different contexts, its meaning stretches and shifts; novel interpretations and connotations accrue. This is illustrated in Figure 7.2.

This is interesting, because I am looking for a similar process to solve the paradox of exploitation and exploration: here, new meanings of words are explored while their current meaning is exploited. This indicates that further exploration of cognitive science may be fruitful: it may yield useful conceptual tools. In other words, I expect that there is a more general principle at work, according to which competence develops from performance, and then provides the basis for further practice at a 'higher' level of development.

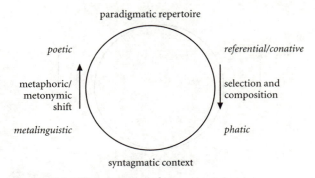

FIGURE 7.3   *Hermeneutic circle 2*

7.4.2   *The Syntagmatic and the Paradigmatic*

In his attempt at a reconstruction of poetics, Roman Jacobson (1987) employed the notion of the syntagmatic axis and the paradigmatic axis. The syntagmatic axis represents the sentence, the linear flow of text, or the 'axis of combination'. Paradigmatic axes represent repertoires of word meanings, or 'axes of selection' (from them meanings are selected in sentence construction). 'Paradigm' here does not mean exemplar to be followed (i.e. a prototype), as elsewhere in this book, but a repertoire of possible connotations of a word. The two concepts of paradigm are connected in that some exemplar guides selection from the repertoire.

In sentence construction we select from the paradigmatic axes to substitute into the syntagmatic axis of a sentence. Jacobson indicated that such use of language has a number of dimensions. In the *referential* dimension words refer. In the *conative* dimension they express an orientation towards the addressee, for evocation or direction. There is also a *phatic* dimension: words serve to maintain the flow of conversation, with interjections such as 'listen' or 'let me tell you'. There is a *metalinguistic* dimension where we want to clarify the use of language itself, with interjections such as 'I mean', 'What are we talking about?', etc. Finally, there is a *poetic* dimension, which is defined as 'projecting the principle of equivalence (the similarities involved in a paradigm) into the axis of combination (the syntax)' (Jakobson 1987: 72). What this means is that surprising connections between words with different meanings, i.e. from different paradigms, arise from their juxtaposition in a line of text or from similarity of sound in the sentence. This can make the referential function of words ambiguous and thereby yield an exploration of novel meaning. This elaboration of the hermeneutic circle is illustrated in Figure 7.3.

Summing up: Sentences, or more generally contexts, determine word meaning in two ways. By settling reference they help us to pick out appropriate meanings from a paradigmatic repertoire. They can also cause a paradigmatic shift, interpreted as an intensional rupture, with a redistribution of features across words.

Could this yield a model of learning and innovation, I wonder, which is perhaps more apt than a biological metaphor of evolution? Later, in Chapter 9, I will generalize the hermeneutic circle into a general heuristic of discovery.

7.4.3 *Metaphor*

As indicated by Jacobson, in his theory of poetics, and discussed by Ricoeur (1975), metaphor plays an important role in the shift of paradigmatic repertoires along the hermeneutic circle. As words are combined in sentences, in specific contexts of discourse, yielding novel combinations of meanings selected from existing paradigmatic repertoires, meanings may undergo metaphoric shifts of repertoire. In metaphor, we consider one thing in terms of another. A metaphor provides a link between two previously unconnected fields of meaning (Miall 1982, Neisser 1987). In metaphor, a given subject ('principal subject', 'tenor', or 'target') is talked about in terms ordinarily used to describe a subject of another type ('secondary subject', 'vehicle', 'base'). The tenor is represented in a new light, in terms of the vehicle. Or, in other words, a concept (vehicle) is applied to something (target) outside its ordinary domain. Metaphor highlights certain features and thereby also hides others. Metaphor also plays an important role in reducing cognitive distance, in making something intelligible from one cognitive framework to another, by expressing something from one framework in terms of the other. As shown by Nonaka and Takeuchi (1995), metaphor plays an important role in innovation.

Lakoff and Johnson (1980) demonstrated how important and pervasive metaphors are in guiding our thought and action. In my criticism of mainstream economics, in Chapter 3, I pointed out the powerful influence of the 'conduit' metaphor of language, according to which knowledge is packaged in information which can be transported. This object bias towards concepts and meaning probably derives from the Piagetian process of conceptual development in which the manipulation of objects forms cognitive structures that in turn form the basis for conceptualization. Lakoff and Johnson point out the basis of metaphor in sensori-motor experience. Metaphor serves as a vehicle for understanding a concept only by virtue of its experiential basis, and 'cannot be comprehended or even adequately represented independently of its experiential basis' (Lakoff & Johnson 1980: 18, 19). Thus, it is thoroughly pragmatic. Metaphor works when it serves a purpose.

> In Chapter 6 I noted how, according to Lakoff and Johnson, the metaphor of good, happy, life, wakefulness, power being 'up' probably derives from the fact that when we are healthy, alive, awake, and in charge we are erect and when we are ill, dead, asleep, or forced into submission we lie down. These facts are part of what Lakoff and Johnson call 'orientational' metaphor. Metaphors are not isolated but systematic. Thus, virtue and rationality are 'up' because good is, and the powerful and prestigious are 'up' because power is. However, uncertainty is also 'up' because things we cannot 'grasp' tend to be 'up in the air'. Lakoff and Johnson propose that this is why questions, expressing uncertainty, end in an 'upwards' intonation.

There is a culturally bound coherence between fundamental concepts and fundamental values.

> More, bigger, and future are better and therefore 'up'. In our western culture more as 'up' has
> priority over good as 'up', so that we can say 'the crime rate is up'. In some cultures balance plays
> a greater role than more, and in some cultures active is up while in others passive is up (Lakoff &
> Johnson 1980: 24).

Ontological metaphors are used to turn abstract concepts, such as anger, peace,
happiness, love, health, fame, the mind, into objects which can then be referred to, be
quantified, be seen as having identifiable aspects, act as cause, be set as goal, act as a
container, have boundaries. Personification metaphors turn objects into people.
Thus, the mind can be seen as a machine, which can break down, or as a brittle object,
cracking up. We can 'seek' fame, do things 'out of' anger, encounter a 'lot' of trouble,
'have' emotional health, and be 'in' love. Love can be seen as a physical force (mag-
netism), patient (sick relationship), magic, war (conquest), hidden object. Ideas can
be seen as food, resources, money, cutting instruments, fashions, light sources. Theories and ideas can 'explain' or 'hide', a fact can 'argue', life can 'cheat' (pp. 26–32, 47–9).

In metonymy we use one entity to refer to another. Examples are 'the House of
Lords', an organization for the people in it; a place for an institution: 'the White
House'. In synecdoche a part stands for a whole: motor or wheels for a car. However,
these are not the same as metaphor: they do not conceive one thing in terms of
another, but use one thing to refer to another.

Lakoff and Johnson propose that most of our normal conceptual system is meta-
phorically structured, and one can wonder whether there are any concepts at all that
are understood without metaphor. 'Literal' as opposed to metaphorical meaning is in
fact mostly conventional metaphor. This carries only some features from one domain
to another, and leaves other features of the vehicle unused. Every true statement is a
lie by omission. When the unused parts are used this is perceived as 'figurative'.

> One can say 'I feel like a million dollars' without causing surprise, until one adds 'all crumpled and
> green'.

While in the computational–representational view, discussed in Chapter 6, categorization purports to be complete and closed with respect to circumstance, metaphor
is downright partial, picking out only salient aspects from experience, as the context
suggests or requires. Here, we find the notion of 'scaffolding' again: the context helps
us to pick out what is salient. This connects with the prototype theory of meaning discussed before (Rosch 1977): we categorize with open ends and possible shifts, according to family resemblances to some paradigmatic example. This allows for 'hedges':
calling an object a member *par excellence*, or a 'regular' or 'veritable' example, or an
example only 'to some extent', or 'not strictly speaking', or 'technically' (Lakoff &
Johnson 1980: 123). Summing up: Metaphor is an engine of abduction.

For the present book the creative role of metaphor is of great importance. Effective
metaphor serves to cause a shift of focus, to highlight aspects hitherto ignored or

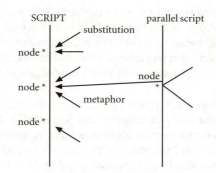

FIGURE 7.4 *Metaphorical transfer in a script*

neglected, and to hide aspects that were dominant before, to set new goals. Perhaps Schumpeterian novel combinations can be seen as brought about by metaphor or its logical equivalent. The discussion of metaphor also helps us to understand the workings of 'enactment' and 'focusing' in organizations, and the way in which management can direct action, and change direction, with effective metaphor. It helps us to understand how people can reduce cognitive distance.

7.4.4 Metaphor and scripts

In language use we might associate the syntagmatic axis (a sentence, say) with a script, and the paradigmatic repertoire with the range of substitution into a node. This range is developed from previous substitutions in different scripts or different applications of a script. Note that 'permissibility' or 'equivalence' is open-ended and governed by default rules. Across scripts some activity, constituting a substitution into some node, might be performed differently, and which way is chosen is determined by the context in which the script operates. The context yields scaffolding by giving clues for substitutions.

Metaphor could now be associated with substitution across scripts: a substitution into a node in one script is substituted into a node of another script. This is illustrated in Figure 7.4.

7.5 CONCLUSION

Categorization is open-ended, with family resemblances (Wittgenstein) to some paradigmatic example, prototype (Rosch), or stereotype (Putnam), which allows for partial and doubtful, or 'hedged' categorization, on the basis of defaults (Johnson-Laird). Categories are typically based on metaphors, grounded in bodily, sensori-motor experiences. They are open and subject to metaphoric shift, with figurative extensions of conventional metaphors. Metaphor works when it serves a purpose. This fits Wittgenstein's notion of 'meaning as use'. The importance of metaphor confirms the pragmatic, situated-action view: metaphor cannot work when divorced from context. Metaphor is the mechanism by which shifts of knowledge and meaning across contexts work.

In view of the discussion, I take a thoroughly pragmatic approach to knowledge and learning. Pragmatics is the study of language use. Semantics is the study of meaning apart from peculiarities of use. Semantics is reduced to pragmatics to the extent that truth can be determined only in context; to the extent that truth lies in adequacy or effectiveness of use, as proposed by Wittgenstein and Quine. If even memory is not a state but a process of recategorization, as Edelman (1987) proposed, perhaps the very notion of knowledge as a state is misguided, and we should argue always in terms of processes of categorization and recategorization; of learning and shifts of meaning. The discussion of language confirms the criticism of the computational–representational view, discussed in Chapter 6: the entities from which we compose mental representations are not static, determinate, complete, or exhaustive.

The analysis shows that with the issue of exploitation and exploration we seem to be dealing with a much more general issue of structure change on the basis of structure function. It applies not only in organizations but also in individual learning, in Piagetian cycles of development, and in language use and language change, along the hermeneutic circle. It shows that the solution to the paradox probably lies in the variety that is generated across novel contexts of use, and the use of metaphor in shifting focus of attention and generating novel combinations, with individual, idiosyncratic use and interpretation as its source.

In Chapter 9 I proceed to use all this in the development of a heuristic of discovery at the level of individuals, organizations, and industries. I expect it to be something like a hermeneutic circle.

Part II
CONSTRUCTION

8

A Theory of Interactive Learning

This Chapter further develops and clarifies the notions of absorptive capacity and cognitive distance discussed in Chapter 3. This includes the consideration of issues of governance: how to deal with relational risk in learning. That builds on a theory of exchange which was developed in earlier work, and which includes elements from transaction-cost economics and a perspective of social exchange. The need for interorganizational learning has intensified because of the emergence of radical product differentiation, and rapid change of technology and products. This is discussed first.

8.1   PRODUCT DIFFERENTIATION

One well-known reason for increased attention to the exchange and production of knowledge between firms (in the 'network economy') derives from the conditions of increased competition ('globalization'), increased product differentiation, and increased speed of change in products and technologies. It is useful to review the arguments for increased product differentiation, because that has implications for specific investments and hence for problems of hold-up.

8.1.1   Background

Several technological developments, especially in information and communication technology, enable an increased variety and differentiation of products. They offer rapid design and testing of virtual rather than physical prototypes of products, flexible production, and the use of just-in-time supply to reduce stocks that would otherwise expand explosively with an increase of product variety. In consumer markets there is a paradoxical development. On the one hand, across nations tastes and lifestyles are becoming more similar, because of the ubiquitous sharing of information and recreation on television, radio, film, and Internet. On the other hand, within nations there has been a movement of ongoing individualization. This provides market opportunities and hence a motivating cause ('pull') for product differentiation. As a result of globalization of markets, one can achieve large sales in large markets, and hence large-scale production, and corresponding lower costs, in spite of such differentiation.

Individualization is related to the increase of prosperity, which raises consumers to higher levels in a Maslovian 'hierarchy of needs'.[1] At lower levels of this hierarchy, needs, such as the physical needs of food, warmth, shelter, are similar between different consumers and therefore less amenable to differentiation. At higher levels, of social distinction by 'lifestyle', and 'self-realization' on the basis of spiritual values, preferences are more idiosyncratic. Furthermore, at higher levels differentiation can more easily be achieved, because utility assumes a more abstract, immaterial form (image, atmosphere) or a superficial form (packaging, appearance) that can be differentiated by comparatively cheap means (design, packaging, and advertising). Thus, more product dimensions arise (more levels in the hierarchy), the new dimensions are more idiosyncratic, and they can be differentiated more cheaply.

A further motivating cause of what Zuscovitch (1994) called 'radical' product differentiation is provided by increased competition. Firms are pushed into product differentiation by increasing competitive pressures arising from globalization, from the opening up of markets to competing producers from diverse parts of the world. Product differentiation is sought in an attempt to escape from pure price competition. Differentiated products have a higher profit margin than standardized products. The reason for this is that different products target different market niches, and since in a niche the dedicated product is closer than alternative products to what customers want, the products are incomplete substitutes for each other. In other words, (different) products have higher quality in the sense that they satisfy (different) requirements more closely. Customers are more captive, price elasticity between products is less, and this yields a higher profit margin.

> During a trade fair in Turin in 1993 Fiat tested computer programs with which a buyer could choose colour, upholstery, and configuration of add-ons, after which the order was sent directly to the factory.

The argument can be made more precise with a spatial model. A product (which includes both goods and services) can be conceptualized as a bundle of characteristics (Lancaster 1966), and we can model this as a point in a multidimensional characteristics space (Eaton & Lipsey 1989). Product dimensions include more than just basic functional characteristics: design, style and image, ease of use, training, installation, maintenance, repair, and availability (distribution). Product differentiation then entails that different products occupy different points in such characteristics space. Competition takes the form of seeking out where demand is located in characteristics space, offering products in regions of high demand, adding product dimensions, and being the first to invade the newly extended space (Péli & Nooteboom 1999).

The profit advantage of product differentiation can now be specified as follows. In terms of the spatial model of Lancasterian product characteristics, the consumer's ideal product is a point in space and the distance to the point representing the product determines the cost of compromise, or opportunity cost. A 'nearby' product can

---

[1] Maslow's hierarchy of needs is usually presented as universal. However, as the German historian Mommsen observed (in a personal communication), in the Middle Ages virtue, in view of contemporary belief in the afterlife, was more basic than worldly goods or even protection, shelter, and food.

add a profit to its cost, related to the extra distance a consumer would have to accept for the best substitute, i.e. the nearest alternative product.

8.1.2   Implications for Learning

Increased product differentiation and speed of change in products and technology turn competition into a race to markets, and to have a chance of winning such races one should limit oneself to one's core competencies. This implies that complementary competencies for the creation of complex, differentiated, fast-changing products must be obtained from elsewhere. One does not have the time to build up all the required competencies oneself, and one must maintain flexibility in making novel combinations. As already recognized in the early beginnings of the 'competence view' of firms (Penrose 1959), knowledge creation is a central feature of core competence. Later work (Prahalad & Hamel 1990) also recognized that core competence does not constitute one's ability regarding any specific product or technology, but one's ability to develop new products and technologies, or new applications or combinations of technology.

Flexibility of Schumpeterian novel combinations is larger in loosely connected, network-type structures than in centralized hierarchies. It is easier to reconfigure networks of firms than to integrate and disintegrate parts of firms, unless firms become extremely loose and volatile themselves, and in fact turn into loose networks. However, networks also require a certain amount of durability and stability, for reasons to be analysed later. Thus, an important challenge is to find an adequate balance between stability and flexibility of network connections.

However, beyond the argument for flexibility there are deeper, cognitive reasons for interfirm connections. These are based on the theory of knowledge and learning developed in previous Chapters. As indicated in Chapter 3, I espouse the view of the 'firm as a focusing device'. This implies the need for outside, complementary cognitive competence, according to the principle of external economy of cognitive scope. A trade-off needs to be made between cognitive distance, for the sake of novelty, and cognitive proximity, for the sake of efficient absorption. Information is useless if it is not new, but it is also useless if it is so new that it cannot be understood.

The virtue of firms, with cognitive proximity within them, engendered by corporate culture, is a detailed and close understanding needed for efficient production (exploitation). The virtue of interfirm relations lies in cognitive distance, for variety of cognition to create novelty (exploration).

8.2   A LOGIC OF LEARNING BY INTERACTION

It would be nice if we could be more precise about the notions of absorptive capacity and cognitive distance. This leads to a more abstract and somewhat technical account, and readers who dislike that can skip this paragraph without much loss of continuity.

8.2.1   A Cognitive Function

It is fairly straightforward to conceive of *cognition* as a function in the mathematical sense, which maps a cognitive *domain*, consisting of observed phenomena (including linguistic expressions of others), into a cognitive *range* of categorizations (which include inferences). The mapping is conducted on the basis of categories or mental forms of thought, i.e. of perception, interpretation, and evaluation. In short, this mapping is *thinking*, and the forms of thought constitute one's *cognitive repertoire*. It may or may not be useful to consider forms of thought and the categorizations they produce as mental representations. If we did that, we would have to conceive a second, linguistic function, which maps categorizations into linguistic expressions. At this stage of the analysis, in order not to complicate matters unduly, I limit myself to one cognitive function, whose range also includes linguistic (and other, non-verbal) expressions. Later this might be interpreted as the product of two functions: representation and expression. This also saves us the trouble of having to indicate to what extent and how knowledge and language are separated and connected. As discussed in Chapters 6 and 7 there has been a long debate in philosophy and cognitive science as to whether thought precedes language or vice versa. The conclusion is that thought and language enable or stimulate each other, but it would take too much trouble to sort out the connections in the present analysis.

We might now interpret *absorptive capacity* as the domain of cognition: the phenomena one can *make sense of*, i.e. which one can perceive, interpret, evaluate. *Learning* entails extension of cognitive function. As indicated in Chapter 1, in the literature on organizational learning a distinction is made between first- and second-order learning (Hedberg, Nystrom, & Starbuck 1976, Fiol & Lyles 1985) or, equivalently, between 'single loop and double loop' learning (Argyris & Schön 1978). Here, first-order learning may be interpreted as an extension of domain or range for given forms of thought, and second-order learning as change of forms of thought; i.e. of the way in which the domain is mapped into the range, i.e. an extension of cognitive repertoire. A change of forms of thought is likely to engender a change of domain and range, but the reverse need not be the case.

Note that parts of the range can also be part of the domain: we are able to make sense of many of our categorizations. Also forms of thought, which map the domain into the range, may be part of the domain: one is able to categorize one's categories of cognition; one is able to understand, up to a point, how one thinks.

My constructivist, interactionist theory of knowledge implies that forms of thought develop in their use, in interaction with one's physical and social environment. Let us explore how this works.

8.2.2   Cognitive Distance

Cognitive distance now is difference in cognitive function. This can be a difference in domain, range, or the mapping between them. People could have a shared domain but a difference of mapping: two people can make sense of the same phenomena, but do so differently. It is also logically possible that they share both domain and range but differ in their mapping function: different forms of thought may yield the same categorizations. Cognitive distance can also entail a difference of domain: the people involved make sense of different phenomena.

There is a difference between *reducing* cognitive distance and *bridging* it. Bridging cognitive distance is *communication*, which entails a mapping from one's own cognitive range to another's cognitive domain, i.e. insertion into the latter's absorptive capacity, or making someone else make sense of the sense one makes of the world. Perhaps we can indicate this loosely by saying that communication yields overlap between ranges and domains. This is the leverage created in learning by interaction: by communication one taps into another's absorptive capacity. Note that this does not necessarily entail reduction of cognitive distance. That would entail overlap between ranges, overlap between domains, and overlap between forms of thought. The mapping of communication employs a language. People *make sense* of each other to the extent that this mapping from range to domains is possible. *Understanding* goes further: it entails that a person can make sense of the mapping from domain to range (categorization) that another performs. In other words, forms of thought of the one are mapped into the other's cognitive domain. Thus, people can understand each other at a cognitive distance: they can make sense of each other's mental mappings without having the same ones. *Explanation* helps understanding: it maps one's forms of thought into another's domain. Agreement may mean that between two people there are phenomena they make the same sense of. In other words, they have domain overlap mapped into range overlap. It may mean that they share forms of thought. They may agree in the first sense without agreeing in the second sense.

- *thought*: mapping from domain to (one's own) range
- *communication*: mapping from range to (someone else's) domain
- *understanding*: bringing (someone else's) forms of thought into one's domain
- *explanation*: bringing one's forms of thought into someone else's domain

Sense making, understanding, and agreement are more or less limited. People can collaborate without agreeing, it is more difficult to collaborate without understanding, and it is impossible to collaborate if they do not make sense to each other. Partial sense making may not be enough for a given purpose of interaction, and then one needs to stretch one's domain (absorptive capacity) in order to have a better chance of making sense of what others say. Alternatively, one may stretch one's range, to yield a better chance of finding items that can be transferred to the other's domain, or to improve the mapping (the language used). Perhaps language, domain, and range are not independent. Perhaps change of domain or range goes together with change of language. That would agree with the idea that meaning is context-dependent.

Previously, I claimed that we need to accomplish a trade-off between cognitive distance for the sake of novelty and cognitive proximity for understanding. Now that can be made more precise. One needs to maintain cognitive distance in the sense of evading overlap of domains, i.e. absorptive capacities, i.e. ability to make sense of the same phenomena. On the other hand, for the sake of communication there must be at least a sufficient mapping from ranges to domains. Loosely speaking, there must be sufficient overlap between range and domain. So, for optimal learning by interaction one should seek limited domain overlap and sufficient overlap between ranges and domains.

8.2.3   *Elaboration*

Collaboration is much enhanced by understanding, supported by explanation: a mapping from forms of thought to domains. In interaction, people conduct first-order learning by extending cognitive domain or range, enabled and necessitated by communication. Communication may require first-order learning, to achieve sufficient mapping between range and domain. It generates first-order learning by injecting novel items into one's domain. Second-order learning, i.e. the change of one's forms of thought, can occur in several ways. It can arise of one's own accord, by experimenting with different mappings from one's domain to range, and seeing how they perform, i.e. yield successful results in action and communication. If new mappings consistently perform well, they develop into more or less stable forms of thought: they enter one's cognitive repertoire. Learning is leveraged greatly by absorbing other people's forms of thought. That offers mappings for trial that have already been proved useful by others, in their contexts of action.

It was proposed before that categories, or forms of thought, develop in interaction with one's physical and social environment. The analysis clarifies why social interaction creates much more leverage for learning than interaction with non-intelligent physical nature. This goes back to Wittgenstein's (1976) idea of the impossibility of a private language. The idea is that if one makes mistakes in language (reference) or thought (inference) one needs others to point it out: one can hardly be an independent judge of one's own thoughts and reference. One cannot climb down from one's mind to inspect how thought is hooked on to the world. Wittgenstein's thesis is perhaps debatable. One cannot exclude the possibility of correcting one's errors and developing stable meanings on one's own, in interaction only with one's physical surroundings. But since non-intelligent surroundings do not adapt their response to one's conduct, the scope for correction is severely restricted. Leverage for adapting one's ideas and understanding is hugely greater in social interaction.[2]

Tacit knowledge can now be interpreted as hidden mappings, i.e. mappings that cannot be specified, and thereby cannot be mapped into a cognitive domain. The hidden mapping can be a cognitive mapping from domain to range: some forms of thought cannot be mapped into a domain. Note that one's knowledge may be tacit to oneself but not to another: one's forms of thought may be part of another's domain

---

[2]   Thus, mutual interaction not only yields problems of co-ordination, as studied in game theory, but also opportunities for learning.

and not of one's own. In this way a psychiatrist can know how we think, while we ourselves don't know. The hidden mapping can also be the mapping from range to domain, i.e. language use. In fact, much of language is tacit: we employ meanings without being able to explain them. If knowledge, i.e. the mapping from domain to range, is tacit to oneself, one cannot explain it; that is, one cannot help to map it into another's domain. This constrains understanding and hence collaboration. Tacit knowledge may once have been part of one's domain, but then has slipped from it, as knowledge subsides into 'subsidiary awareness' (Polanyi 1962). In that case, perhaps it can be 'recalled' into the domain. This is not the case if knowledge has 'sunk into the body' to such an extent that it has become part of our basic physiology, instinct, or basic metaphors (cf. Lakoff and Johnson 1999). Then forms of thought constitute a black box. One may observe items in a domain and items in the range, and try to infer the mapping: how the one leads to the other. This is the process of *externalization*: making tacit knowledge explicit. An important point here is that communication may yield a significant aid in externalization. By inspecting behaviour and asking questions about inputs in domains and outputs in ranges, one may elicit the forms by which the mapping takes place, or at least hypotheses about them. This is the process of *maieutics*, or 'intellectual midwifery', mentioned in Chapter 3. Thus, tacit knowledge can often be communicated or demonstrated only in direct interaction, with hands-on participation by the intended recipient or co-worker, corrected in mutual adjustment between them, in communities of practice (Brown and Duguid 1996).

Note that in learning from relations there is a first-order effect in the width of one's domain (absorptive capacity), but also a second-order effect in the width of one's range. The latter improves opportunities for understanding by the partner, and this gives him a chance to help one to learn from him.

8.2.4   Convergence

As people interact closely, and share experiences, in due course cognitive distance will be reduced. First, mutual sense making is increased by mapping ranges into domains, then understanding is increased by mapping forms of thought into domains. As people interact more closely and share experiences over longer periods of time, cognitive distance will decrease, with an increase of range overlap, domain overlap, and overlap of forms. This entails agreement, in different forms. Efficiency of collaboration increases as cognitive distance is reduced, but learning potential declines. At its limit, efficiency is perfect when there is no cognitive distance: domains, ranges, and forms of thought coincide. This will never happen between people, for two reasons. The first reason is that cognitive forms in their development are somehow connected to one's genotype, which is never identical to another's. The second reason is that people do not have exactly identical environments and experiences, and therefore develop different cognitive constructions of domain, range, and forms of thought. This is a source of misunderstanding and disagreement, but also of learning. The potential for learning decreases as cognitive distance declines.

The problem of exploitation and exploration can now be rephrased as follows: For exploitation one needs cognitive proximity, for exploration cognitive distance. They can be combined by having a group of people with cognitive proximity, typically within an organizational unit, as well as communication with groups at a cognitive distance, typically between different organizational units. These organizational units can be firms or more or less autonomous divisions within a firm. One form of entrepreneurship is the creation of cognitive proximity, through shared domains, ranges, and forms of thought. Another form is to bridge cognitive distance. The greatest challenge for management is to balance the two, and thereby balance exploitation and exploration.

Note that in learning from relations there is a first-order effect in the width of one's domain (absorptive capacity), but also a second-order effect in the width of one's range. The latter improves opportunities for understanding by the partner, and this gives him a chance to help one to learn from him. Here, altruism, in the sense of helping the other to understand, may be beneficial, in improving the learning potential of the relation.

8.2.5   Scripts and Learning

Of course the range of cognitive output is structured: elements are connected. In Chapter 6 I adopted the notion of a script for rule-based behaviour, and storytelling for less rule-based behaviour. These yield models of mental forms; of how cognitive inputs from the domain are transformed into cognitive outputs in the range. Scripts and stories entail attribution: if observed and salient parts fit, complementary elements are attributed even if not observed. This is efficient but also a source of prejudice and error.

To make sense, a person tries to fit observations of someone's range into his scripts. One cannot make sense of another to the extent that this fails. The overlap between range and domain that is needed for communication thus entails that elements of a range can be fitted into scripts that define a domain of understanding. In other words, cognitive scripts constitute absorptive capacity.

In firms, cognitive distance between people working in it is reduced as far as is needed for efficient production (exploitation). This entails script overlap, or script fit: the range of individual cognition must satisfy conditions imposed on substitutions into nodes, in scripts, that represent the individual's contribution to the organization. Cognitive proximity, in that sense, must be greater to the extent that conditions on node substitution are stricter. The nodes one is involved in demarcate one's organizational role.

The organizational scripts into which individual activities and cognitions are fitted constitute the absorptive capacity of the firm. Organizational learning is the change of organizational scripts. First-order learning entails greater efficiency of substitution into scripts, and thereby enhances exploitation. This can be achieved by pruning redundant nodes or redundant or suboptimal substitutions into nodes. Second-order learning entails change of script architecture, in processes of exploration. How this works is the subject of Chapter 9, in which I develop a general heuristic of learning.

8.3   GOVERNANCE

As discussed in Chapter 5, in interfirm relations there are transaction costs, which include costs of contact (search), contract, and control. These include various problems of co-ordination. Here, the analysis of governance is deepened from the perspective of learning by interaction.

8.3.1   Hold-up and Spillover

As explained in transaction-cost economics, and discussed in Chapter 5, specific investments create dependence, which yields a risk of hold-up. In learning by interaction such specific investments arise in several ways. Search and knowledge exchange often require that one become familiar with intra-firm networks, in order to select the right mix of people for the purpose involved, and to ensure effective co-ordination, and that constitutes a specific investment. Another example of specific investments is the build-up of trust to be able to collaborate without extensive and constraining contracts. This is related to the organization-specific investment involved in getting to know who is who in partner firms, in becoming familiar with the partner firm's internal networks. In view of the present analysis, there are specific investments arising from cognitive considerations.

An important question is to what extent the investment in making sense of someone, and understanding him, by extending one's domain, and extending one's range to help him understand, is specific, in the sense analysed in transaction-cost economics. Bridging cognitive distance in one direction does not entail bridging distance in another direction. Investment in bridging distance has alternative uses only for alternative partners who are cognitively close to each other. The degree to which the investment in communication is specific depends on the availability of a shared language, the tacitness of knowledge, and the degree to which range or domain extension is specific. Tacit knowledge cannot be expressed in language, and requires close interaction, in a community of practice, to elicit understanding. Then, perhaps it can be externalized, with the aid perhaps of new language. If a new language has to be developed, it is at first likely to be specific to the relation. It may be used for communication with others in the future, but that requires others to absorb it first. Note that language entails network externalities: its usefulness is limited until it is adopted by a larger number of potential discussion partners. Specialized language that is operative only in specific relations is discouraged. However, it may be used to block spillover.

Investment is not specific to the extent that one's language, or repertoire of languages, has a wide scope, i.e. covers a wide range of potential partners, and one has a wide cognitive range and domain. All these features are enhanced as a function of experience in bridging cognitive distance. The odd thing, compared with bridging distance in geographical space, is that here 'travel' (bridging distance) decreases its own cost: experience in bridging cognitive distance makes it easier to bridge distances in future, since it extends one's domain, range, and linguistic scope. There are cumulative returns to scale. Experience in understanding diverse people makes it easier to understand new acquaintances.

Another problem in learning by interaction is that of spillover.[3] Mutual advantage lies in novel combinations of knowledge from different partners, and in joint production of knowledge. This requires a certain amount of openness. However, one may fear that information which is competitively sensitive, i.e. close to one's core competence, will be copied by ('spills over' to) competitors. This may be accidental or on purpose, to harm the partner. Indeed, information may be used as a hostage, with a threat to harm the interest of a partner by leaking information to his competitor.

Spillover risk depends on a number of factors. Risk of spillover increases with cognitive proximity. Here is another reason for keeping cognitive distance, next to the reason of maintaining novelty of sources. Another contingency is the degree to which the knowledge involved is tacit. Obviously, tacit knowledge flows less easily than documented knowledge. But this does not mean that it does not spill over at all. If it is embodied in individual people or teams these may be poached. If people have more allegiance to their profession than to their firm, their knowledge may spill over when they are stationed at other firms, or when they do joint research, or when they meet at conferences. If knowledge is embodied in the structure and culture of a division it can still be expropriated by takeover. However, then the question is how quickly and effectively that culture can be integrated into the acquiring firm, i.e. how cognitive distance can be sufficiently reduced to yield efficient exploitation. Apart from the tacitness of knowledge there may be several other reasons why there is no significant risk. One possibility is that the knowledge spilled over is too far from core competence to cause damage. Another is that competitors would not be able to employ the knowledge for effective competition usefully and efficiently, because cognitive distance is too large, and their absorptive capacity is limited. Another is that the speed of one's knowledge change is so high that by the time it has reached a competitor and he is able effectively to absorb it, it will have changed. Finally, communication may be based on idiosyncratic language and difficult to translate to language used in other relations.

When the problem of spillover does arise, it entails problems of agency. To what extent are network members motivated not to steal competitive advantage from their partners and to guard against spillover to the partner's competitors? Information and knowledge can play the role of 'hostages'. Yielding sensitive knowledge whose appropriability one wishes to retain makes one dependent on the ability and effort of the partner to maintain confidentiality. It gives the recipient power: he may threaten to

---

[3] In view of the previous analysis, spillover turns out to be a misnomer. It suggests that there is no problem of absorption; that everybody's domain covers everybody's range. That may apply in some extreme form of equilibrium, but it is not the case to the extent that there is variety and change. Nevertheless, to maintain continuity with established discourse I will employ the term.

divulge it to your competitors. He may use this, for example, to keep you away from contacts with his competitors. Conversely, the information you receive from a partner may limit access to other parties that are potential competitors to the focal partner.

Recall that the risk of spillover requires a trade-off. What is the potential loss as a result of spillover, compared with the acquisition of knowledge, and the beneficial role that the surrender of knowledge may play in gaining allegiance or reputation, to improve network position?

> For an illustration, see the study of patenting by Smith-Doerr *et al*. (1999). They showed, on the basis of an empirical study of patenting in biotechnology, that the most important role of patents might not be the potential for own production or licensing fees but the increase of attractiveness as a network partner for others. In terms of the present analysis, patenting extends one's cognitive range.

In fear of spillover there is a danger of being too protective of knowledge, of myopically attaching too much weight to appropriability, while neglecting the dynamic of new knowledge creation in the network, and the development of communicative and learning capacity. But of course this does not imply that appropriability no longer plays any role at all.

Openness can yield a problem also for bargaining position. For fruitful collaboration a supplier needs to provide information on his competencies in design and production ('open-book contracting'), but this reveals production costs, which jeopardizes his bargaining position, if bargaining focuses on price. One solution, learned from Japanese practice, is 'price minus costing'. Here, the buyer guarantees a profit margin to the supplier, which is deducted from the maximum price the buyer can pay, which yields the cost price for which the supplier has to supply, but this is seen as a joint effort, with pooled resources. The openness needed for pooling is possible because in view of the guaranteed margin there is no need for the supplier to be secretive. Game-theoretic analysis has cast some doubt on the viability of this solution (Nooteboom 1998). Once information has been exchanged, the buyer is tempted to renege on his guarantee of the supplier's margin. However, reputation effects may keep him from doing that.

The issues of spillover and hold-up need to be analysed together, because there are connections between them. For example, it has already been indicated that openness has implications for both spillover and bargaining position. Another example is that one can reduce dependence and hold-up risk by engaging multiple partners for a given activity, but this can increase the spillover risk that one causes for the partners. Multiple partners for a given activity increase the variety of knowledge sources, which enhances innovative potential, but again it may also multiply both spillover risks and the volume of specific investments.

Another problem of agency is that of free riding. There may be a temptation for partners not to develop new knowledge (in R & D co-operation, say) to their full ability, and to free ride on partners' efforts. This may yield a prisoner's dilemma, resulting in mutual non-compliance. Note that this problem is reinforced by the problem of spillover. Giving knowledge is discouraged both by spillover risk and the temptation to free ride on partners. Contractual solutions depend on the measurability and predictability of performance and efforts, and these are typically limited. Mutual monitoring of efforts may require that partners enter each other's firms, and this may be shunned for fear of spillover: information leaking to competitors. A solution might then be to involve a third party as a go-between, who does not constitute a spillover threat, as indicated in Chapter 3 (Nooteboom 1999*b*). Another classic solution arises if the effort one is expected to put in is required to achieve the absorptive capacity needed to utilize the outcome of partner's efforts. Other familiar solutions for such prisoner's dilemmas are a tit-for-tat strategy and a reputation mechanism.

8.3.2   *Asymmetry*

Cognitive distance does not represent the same obstacle or cost for different agents (people, firms). A problem of asymmetric advantage arises if one side's absorptive capacity is greater than another's. If A can more easily understand B than vice versa, this may create a hold-up problem: B has to make more investments than A, and thereby becomes dependent on A. This often happens in the interaction between large and small firms: large firms typically have a larger absorptive capacity. This problem is greater to the extent that those investments are more specific (because of lack of language, tacit knowledge). The generation of understanding of A, and practice in exchange of knowledge with him, will increase B's ability to bridge cognitive distance to others in future, but here and now he is the more dependent party. Those who have more practice in bridging cognitive distance will gain an advantage. Their communicative capacity increases relative to others, yielding lower specific investments, whereby they become less dependent on durable relations, and thus become more footloose. If environmental complexity no longer increases, then in due course the laggards may catch up.

One can help others to absorb one's own knowledge, and lower their specific investment in understanding. Thereby one may forego an 'opportunity for opportunism' (Nooteboom 1996), but it makes one even more attractive as a partner. This increases one's opportunities for interaction, which enhances one's communicative capacity. Again, altruism in the form of helping others to understand can pay. However, that is likely to entail an extension of one's cognitive range, and that may constitute a specific investment. If that is the case, A may be willing to help B to develop his understanding only if the relation is expected to endure sufficiently long to recoup the investment. If the environment is not conducive to sufficiently durable relations, this may stimulate opportunistic exploitation of asymmetric absorption capacity, which widens the asymmetry, resulting in increasing inequality of knowledge.

8.3.3   *Location*

Let us consider issues of location. Locational patterns of industry and agglomeration effects have been ascribed to geological factors (natural resources), geographical factors (e.g. population characteristics, infrastructure), cultural factors (e.g. religion), climate, and economic factors (e.g. size of market, transaction costs). As early as 1920, Marshall distinguished three economic factors: concentration of related firms offers a 'pooled' market for specialized labour, facilitates the development of specialized products and services, and allows firms to profit from externalities in the form of spillovers.

The notion of 'external economy of cognitive scope' seems similar to the third factor from Marshall: spillovers between firms. But there is a fundamental difference. Marshall's notion refers to spillover, i.e. the speed and efficiency of the acquisition of 'information', as some cognitive commodity that one could have obtained otherwise, but then more slowly or expensively. By contrast, external economy of cognitive scope refers to the filling of gaps that, because of the path dependence and ensuing idiosyncrasy of one's cognitive apparatus, one could not have filled. It is not a matter of receiving information but of extending one's cognitive scope.

Cognitive distance is correlated with spatial distance, depending on the nature of the knowledge involved. Information and communication technology (ICT) enables rapid and cheap collection, dissemination, and access to massive amounts of data. Later, it will be argued that in the 'process of discovery' innovation passes from tacit to documented knowledge. With ICT, documented knowledge can spread quickly across the world. Detailed data on consumer purchases are obtained from bar-code scanning at shop checkouts, and from remote electronic shopping. Movement of orders, products, and payments can be monitored continuously and in minute detail. This enables firms to reduce stocks through tight control of logistics ('just-in-time' supply). When knowledge is tacit, spatial distance matters more than when knowledge is documented, to the extent that for the transfer of tacit knowledge one needs close, face-to-face interaction. However, it may be that increasingly such interaction can be provided also at a distance, with multimedia and virtual interaction. Will distance ever become totally irrelevant; will there be 'death of distance'?

In communication at a distance the question is not only how knowledge can be transferred, but also what knowledge and to whom. In exploration of new knowledge, chance encounters play a role, and for this one needs more or less frequent and unstructured interaction of people meeting each other pell-mell in a context of roughly shared interest (like scientists at a conference, or firms in an industrial district). While this seems to require at least occasional physical proximity, so that spatial distance matters, perhaps Internet begins to provide such a facility at a distance.

A further reason why distance may still matter is that exchange of knowledge also requires trust, which may be enhanced by frequent face-to face meetings.

8.3.4 Forms of Governance

The problems of hold-up and spillover can be avoided or solved by a number of forms of governance, as follows:

- *evasion*: i.e. not yielding sensitive information and not engaging in specific investments
- *integration* under unified administrative control, i.e. by merger or acquisition

- formal *contracting* to control hold-up, and patenting to control spillover
- mutual *self-interest*
- *trust*[4]
- *network structure*, and one's position in it

All these forms have their advantages and disadvantages.

One way to avoid relational risks is of course *evasion*: i.e. not yielding sensitive knowledge and not engaging in specific investments for the set-up of knowledge exchange. One tradition in organizational science is to design and explain organizations on the basis of the avoidance of dependence (e.g. Thompson 1967). Dependence entails subjection to power, which is seen as risky and hence to be avoided.

However, from the perspective of social capital, and especially learning, the avoidance of dependence can be highly detrimental: the price of social capital is dependence, and while that in itself tends to be a liability, there may be a positive net advantage. Power can also be beneficial: partners can open up new opportunities. As discussed above, the advantage lies in the creation and utilization of complementary competencies, by means of specific investments and knowledge sharing, for differentiated products, learning, and innovation. Thus, rather than evading dependence, as a goal in itself, the challenge is to maximize the returns and minimize the risks of dependence.

The advantage of *integration* is that different parties are brought under 'unified governance' (as it is called in transaction-cost economics): there is an overarching authority that can establish monitoring backed up by enforceable demands for information, and can impose resolution of conflict, by administrative fiat. Of course even within an organization there are limitations to this, but the scope for resolution by authority is larger than between independent firms, where the last resort is a legal court. However, as argued in transaction-cost economics, integration in the firm involves the surrender of the 'high-powered incentives' that apply to an independent producer who has his own responsibility for survival, and it may involve the renunciation of economy of scale in specialized outside production. It can be hazardous to try and integrate different cultures. Integration reduces flexibility in the configuration of activities, unless firms are easy to break up. Integration improves the control of spillover, but can cause cognitive inbreeding: the loss of variety of experience and learning on the basis of cognitive distance.

The advantage of *contracting* between firms is that it constrains opportunities for opportunism (Nooteboom 1996a). It should be noted that most of the time there will be a contract of some form. The question is not so much whether there is a contract but what its content is and how elaborate it is. As shown by Klein Woolthuis (1999), a contract has several functions: not only is it a legal document to constrain opportunism, but also a mere record of agreements, as a basis for technical co-ordination,

---

[4] Here, the word 'trust' is used in the narrow, strong sense discussed in Chapter 5. That entails the expectation that, within constraints, the partner will not utilize opportunities for opportunism even if they are to his advantage, or will neglect such possibilities, because of habituation.

to prevent misunderstanding, or as a 'ritual of agreement' to seal the intention to collaborate. Here, the focus is on the first function: How far does one go to foreclose opportunism? One problem with contracting is that it is not always possible, because of uncertainty concerning future contingencies, and because of the imperfections of language. Secondly, formal contracting and patenting make sense only if compliance and the lack of it can be observed, and sanctions are credible. The set-up costs of contracts and monitoring systems can be significant, which makes the cost relatively high for smaller firms. A third problem is that contracts may form a straightjacket that prevents the utilization of unforeseen opportunities that arise, especially in innovation. It is paradoxical to aim to specify in detail all tasks, rights, and obligations for something that is new and unpredictable. Furthermore, detailed contracting to prevent opportunism sets a relation off on a basis of mistrust, and may frustrate the building of trust. Patents may not be possible or effective, for small firms the costs of monitoring infringement are high and the threat of litigation may not be credible, and patent information may reveal too much.

Management by *self-interest* has the advantage that it is cheaper than contracts, is more flexible, and it is in the players' own interest to be seen to comply with agreements. It requires a judicious mix of mutual interest, shared ownership of specific investments, hostages, and reputation, to achieve a balance of mutual dependence. There is need not for balance in every form separately, but for balance in the mix. Thus, one-sided ownership of specific assets may be balanced by one-sided hostages going the other way, or by a rigorous reputation mechanism. The main problem of this form of governance is that it is not self-policing. Again there is a need for observation, measurement, and monitoring. How does one measure and monitor degree of dependence, spillover, specificity of investments?

For example, if a player claims that his investment in the relation is highly specific, and that he needs compensation for this, can he be believed, or is there a need to demand sight of his books to check that the investment is indeed not used for anyone else? Reputation works only if breach can be observed, and can be credibly communicated to potential future partners of the culprit. If the culprit can move out to an unknown destination this may be impossible. The culprit may claim that the accusation is unjust and that there are ulterior motives to harm him.

Self-interest in the form of agreements of secrecy, and the use of bilateral exchange of information as a hostage, makes sense only if spillover can be monitored. The breach of agreement to guard against spillover of knowledge cannot be observed if flows of knowledge cannot be observed. Such monitoring is more difficult to the extent that the knowledge involved is tacit. In contrast, when the knowledge one provides gets embodied in products, one can monitor spillover by taking apart one's competitors' products to see whether it shows up there (Lamming 1993). That would show that in breach of agreement one's partner had allowed spillover to take place. A second major problem is that the balance of interests, to prevent one-sided dependence, is difficult to ensure and maintain. It is sensitive to shifts in competence and external conditions. It is particularly vulnerable to the emergence on the scene of a more attractive partner for one of the players, who will then be tempted to defect and leave others with a gap in performance and worthless specific assets.

Trust, in the narrow sense of expectation that partners will not intentionally create damage even if they have the opportunity and the interest to do so, has several advantages. In contrast with contracting it is cheap, flexible, and self-policing, i.e. requires limited monitoring, since it is driven by internalized motivation. In contrast with governance by mutual self-interest it is less sensitive to contingencies, and requires less monitoring. In comparison with contracting it has the additional advantages of being cheap and flexible. Trust may be already in place when a relation starts, on the basis of kinship, experience in previous contacts, reputation, shared values, and norms of decent conduct. If not, then it will have to be developed in the unfolding of the relation. That indicates a limitation: if not already present, it cannot be effected instantaneously. The main problem concerning trust is: How far can it go? It should not be blind: most people will break trust when the temptation is strong enough. Friendship and kinship can cause such blindness. Perhaps trust can be conceptualized in terms of thresholds: people will not be opportunistic until temptation exceeds a certain threshold of resistance to temptation, and this threshold depends on values and norms, experience, character, kinship, and friendship. Even so, trust matters. It has its advantages within these tolerance levels.

Network structure and one's position in it represent both a contingency and a set of instruments for governance. If network participants one is linked with have links with one's (potential) competitors, there is a hazard of spillover, unless spillover constitutes no threat because of tacitness, speed of change, or idiosyncratic language. To guard against the risk, if it exists, one may limit information transfer, or attempt to control spillover by contracting, monitoring, hostage taking, or reputation. Conversely, one may need to be careful in establishing links with competitors of partners one already has strong links with. That might cause those partners to restrict information exchange. One can encourage openness by concessions of exclusiveness, but that reduces the variety of sources of learning. Next to spillover, contacts have implications for bargaining position. To have multiple partners in any given type of activity makes one less dependent on any of them. However, for this very reason it may yield a threat that they will hold back from committing themselves to specific investments in a durable relation, which restricts the capital that can be derived from it. Also, it multiplies the costs of set-up and monitoring.

Intermediaries can perform useful services here. In other words, here one designs structure in order to assist governance. One stream of literature on networks suggests that players who span 'structural holes' can gain advantage (Burt 1992). If A and B are potential rivals and are connected only by C, then C can threaten to pass sensitive information that he has from A to B and vice versa, and can thereby extract advantage from both. This is one situation of third-party advantage (*tertius gaudens*). The concept suggests that the third party extorts the parties he connects, by exploiting opportunities for spillover or bargaining. However, as argued in Chapter 5, a third party can also play a beneficial role as a go-between (Nooteboom 1999*b*). He can facilitate communication, reducing the need for specific investments in understanding, reduce risks of spillover, by controlling information flows, offer 'trilateral governance' in lieu of elaborate contracts, build trust, and implement reputation mechanisms. One condition for this is that the third party is allowed to occupy an intermediary position only if breach of confidence would destroy his reputation as an intermediary, and this would be costly for him.

One will seldom employ only one of the forms of governance reviewed above. The challenge is to craft the best mix for the circumstances. That mix has to fit strategies, institutional conditions, and network structure, in so far as these cannot be changed. The mix has to be consistent: a contractual approach may be difficult to reconcile with a trust-based approach. What is a feasible and effective mix depends, in particular, on which forms of governance are enabled, supported, or constrained by the institutional environment and other contingencies. These contingencies are summarized in the next section.

8.3.5 Contingencies

Contingencies cropped up at several points in the analysis. There is no single best way to manage knowledge exchange. Here, contingencies are not understood as given (exogenous) and fixed. They can to a greater or lesser extent be affected or even created. The relevant contingencies can be categorized in several ways. There are those that affect the net rewards of knowledge exchange, and those that affect the efficacy of instruments for governance. Contingencies can be attributed to the institutional environment and to technological conditions. Earlier, it was shown that network structure and position also constitute contingencies (as well as instruments for governance).

Under conditions of complexity and rapid change of technology and markets, there is greater need for knowledge exchange. Liability of spillover may be limited because of rapid change: by the time sensitive information reaches a competitor and he is able to effectively use it to compete, it has changed. In Chapter 9 it will be argued that, especially in early stages of fundamental innovation, knowledge is largely tacit and for that reason less susceptible to spillover (Nooteboom 1998). These conditions militate against the instruments of integration and contracting, and favour the instruments of mutual advantage and trust. However, the volatility may be so large that trust has no time to build up if it is not already in place.

When the market requires standardized products, technology is stable, economy of scale and pressure on costs are high, integration and arm's-length, *ad hoc* contracting, i.e. the absence of interfirm networks, may be the best solution, and trust may matter little.

Further conditions of technology are the following. Tighter co-ordination is needed to the extent that technology is systemic. Teece (1986) and Chesbrough and Teece (1996) argued that then integration is needed even in case of innovation, because then innovation in different parts of the system must innovate in tune. Nooteboom (1999g) countered that, while this is true under incremental innovation, under radical innovation, with creative destruction and novel combinations, systemic coherence is a liability, not a virtue.

Institutional conditions affect the viability and form of networks and the choice of instruments in many ways. A lack of an appropriate legal system and reliable enforcement, as in Russia, for example, reduces opportunities for contracting. Lack of trust may reduce the acceptance of dependence and thereby discourages specific investments, or enforces more legal contracting, raising transaction costs, or may stimulate more integration in large firms. Within the firm, a greater volatility of work, because of short-term labour contracts, individual rewards rather than rewards for teamwork or rewards on the basis of seniority, and resulting high turnover of labour, may frustrate the team work and continuity needed for producing, combining, and applying tacit knowledge. Volatility of firm ownership, because of absence of protection against mergers and acquisition, and short-term profit orientation, imposed perhaps by capital markets, may hinder the development of durable relations within and between firms. This may be bad for incremental innovation. On the other hand, when networks are too durable they may yield obstacles for the novel combinations of radical innovation.

This brings us back to a crucial possible liability of networks: tight and durable networking between firms may block radical innovation. A more volatile market system of independent firms that engage in spot contracting with a variety of players may be better. However, it is not certain that this is the case. Absence of networking between firms will entail either limited specific investments, which may reduce added value, or more integration in large firms to limit the problems of dependence that specific investments entail. Such integration within a firm will limit the flexibility needed for novel combinations even more than networks between firms would do, unless firms can easily be broken up. But such volatility of break-up may limit networks inside organizations, which limits the perspective for joint use and production of tacit knowledge, which may inhibit radical innovation. However, this problem will not arise if absorptive, communicative capacities are so large that specific investments are not needed even where cognitive distance is large and knowledge is tacit.

> The celebrated case of 'Silicon Valley' may serve as an example. The argument might run as follows: the players are highly educated and experienced in bridging cognitive distance, and therefore do not need to make high specific investments in knowledge exchange. Therefore, they do not need durable relations, and therefore they can combine a high rate of innovation with volatile network structure. One alternative explanation would be that the players are cognitively close to each other, so that investment in understanding one partner yields understanding of others. Another alternative explanation would be that knowledge is highly documented rather than tacit. I expect that the first explanation is the best. This is susceptible to empirical testing. Concerning risk of spillover, knowledge is probably highly tacit, but there is threat of spillover through staff being poached. However, because knowledge is tacit, it will take some time for it to yield fruit in the new firm, and more so to the extent that it needs to be embedded and shared in teams and communities of practice. By that time knowledge at the source may have shifted, to render the

spillover innocuous. If for these reasons the threat of spillover is limited, there is no constraint on openness or on the number of partners that one's partners can have. This further enhances the variety of knowledge sources that are being connected in flexible ways. If this account of Silicon Valley is correct, it shows why, and in what respects precisely, it cannot be applied as a universal model of all 'industrial districts'. It can be successfully imitated only under the conditions indicated in the analysis.

Since institutions vary between countries, and different institutions yield different opportunities and forms for generating social capital and controlling social liability, convergence of economic systems under globalization is doubtful. A further step in the analysis would be to trace the effects of institutions more systematically and in more detail. How do national or local institutions affect problems of hold-up and spillover and the efficacy of forms of governance to deal with them, and thereby affect innovative performance in national innovation systems. That will be picked up in Chapter 12.

8.4   CONCLUSION

Learning by interaction entails transaction costs of communication and understanding. The need for relation-specific investments in communication and understanding depends on cognitive distance and communicative ability. The latter is subject to cumulative returns to experience. Dependence as a result of specific investments in communication and understanding yields a risk of hold-up. There may be risks of spillover, as a function of cognitive proximity and the degree to which knowledge is documented. Together, these risks entail problems of governance. Instruments for such governance can be derived from a generalized theory of transactions, which embraces elements from transaction-cost economics and elements from social-exchange theory. This adds trust as an element of governance. Concerning the need for governance and the efficacy of instruments there are many contingencies. There is no single, universal best form of governance. Governance requires a tailor-made mix of instruments, taking into account institutional conditions, technology, aims and characteristics of the collaborators, and the development of the relation.

9

A Heuristic of Discovery

This Chapter presents the central thesis of the book: a general 'logic' or heuristic of discovery. It is proposed to apply at all levels: of people, organizations, and innovation systems. It is intended to explain the difference and the relation between radical and incremental innovation; between exploration and exploitation; between second-order (or double-loop or architectural) learning and first-order (or single-loop or parametric) learning. I am tempted to speak of a general 'logic' of discovery, because we are dealing with general principles of 'abduction' (see Chapter 1). However, the term 'logic' might suggest that the principles are necessary, in the sense that they must and always will be followed, and that is not the intention. It is better to speak of a 'heuristic': a feasible, effective, and generally efficient procedure for conducting exploitation in a way that also yields a basis for exploration. However, while the process on average will yield the best results, it is not necessary: there are alternative routes to successful innovation, such as random trial and error, but they will fail more often, and will generally be less effective and efficient. Perhaps the heuristic also represents general principles of self-organization. The general principles are later embodied in causal systems that are specific for the level of innovation systems (Chapter 12) and organizations (Chapter 13).

9.1 PRINCIPLES

This first paragraph indicates the basic principles of the procedure, derived from preceding Chapters. Inspired by the notion of the hermeneutic circle, as a model of meaning change, and Piaget's stages of cognitive development, I propose that the core principle is that structures develop (exploration) from application (exploitation) in a variety of contexts. Ideas, institutions, organizational routines, 'social technology', first settle down to into some 'best practice' or 'dominant design'. This serves as a prototype for applications and variations in different contexts. That shows up the limits of validity as well as indications for novel combinations, which break down existing structures. This leads to a next round of convergence to a dominant design. In other words, there is an alternation of variety of content and variety of context.

9.1.1 Selection and Learning

In Chapter 1 it was noted that the paradox of exploitation and exploration cannot be solved on the basis of rational choice among alternative options, because of (radical) uncertainty: we are dealing with a problem of abduction. We need to find out what the options are. How can we act on the basis of available knowledge and other competencies (exploitation) in a way that yields insights into how to acquire new knowledge and competencies (exploration)? How can we gather elements and directions for Schumpeterian novel combinations?

Chapter 4 discussed evolutionary economics, as an attempt to explain innovation in terms of entrepreneurial ventures selected by markets and other institutions. But, as discussed in Chapter 3, while entrepreneurial ventures are subject to much failure, they are not blind and random. Also, the selection environment is not only a natural environment, but is also to a large extent socially constructed. As discussed in Chapter 4, through learning from experience one may be able to evade elimination by the selection process, and through innovation, political action, and rhetoric one may change the selection environment to one's advantage. It is part of entrepreneurship to transform institutions. The same issue was encountered in a different form in Chapter 3, in the difference between the 'positioning' view of firm strategy, derived from the work of Michael Porter, and the perspective of 'strategic intent' derived from the work of Prahalad. Entrepreneurs do not merely take the market as a given environment in which they seek a niche, but seek to create markets.

In the discussion of the literature on management and organization, in Chapter 2, and in Chapter 4 attempts were shown to explain organizational development in terms of 'punctuated equilibrium', but it remained unclear how punctuation comes about. There have also been attempts to explain organizational development by evolutionary selection of ideas generated more or less at random in the organization.

Chapter 6 gave a discussion of selection at the level of individual cognition, in 'neural selectionism'. This indicates how in partial overlap, selection, and modification of neuronal groups, by modulation of synaptic connections, mental categories may develop in interaction with the physical and social environment.

Darwinian evolution is one way to solve the paradox of exploitation and exploration: ways of exploitation proliferate at random, and the ones that fit best are selected out. The selection of novelty (exploration) is a phenomenon at the population level. There is no prior design to anticipate change in the environment. Perhaps we can usefully look at organizations in this way: create a redundancy of routines and pick out the one that turns out to perform best. This will be further explored in Chapter 13.

However, such blind, random generation of novelty involves much duplication and failure, and is quite inefficient. Goal achievement is pure luck. While this seems adequate for the development of categories as a basis for reflective thought, in neural selection, once we have achieved that we can transcend the blind process of random trial, error, and reinforcement. We have intellect, language, and communication. While rationality is certainly bounded it is not absent. While there is radical uncertainty, we can make reasonable inferences from experience about what might be a good thing to try, and then learn from its failure, in a process of abduction. We can search, and on the basis of experience, intellect, and debate we can hypothesize, argue, and make inferences, in virtual 'internalized' action and speech rather than actual action and speech. Thus, inference, argument, and debate can replace actual by virtual selection, at least to some extent. We can base our decisions on the analysis of scenarios, and the investigation of the robustness of strategies, as Shell Oil Company learned to do. Only when uncertainty is so radical as to preclude such inference and informed speculation, random generation of variations and selection and reinforcement according to success is the only option left. And even then we can devise a heuristic of exploration which yields a solution to the problem of abduction. That is what this Chapter seeks to do.

Furthermore, as analysed in Chapter 8, learning is leveraged by interaction with others, whereby we exploit complementary cognitive competence (absorptive capacity), based on differences of experience in different markets or technologies.

The approach taken here is inspired by the general principles or 'functional invariants', discussed in Chapter 6, which Piaget identified in his theory of the cognitive development of children. Novel mental competencies are developed ('accommodation') in the process of trying to fit experience into existing competencies ('assimilation'). The process of assimilation has stages of 'generalization, differentiation, reciprocation'. This process of assimilation that yields accommodation may provide a model for a more general process of exploitation that yields exploration. Piaget himself claimed a wider validity for his principles, beyond the cognitive development of children, as a general 'logic' of the development of knowledge, called 'genetic epistemology'. However, while taking my inspiration from Piaget, I do not agree with all his views on cognitive development, as indicated in Chapter 6, and I give my own interpretation, development, and application of these notions.

9.1.2   Consolidation

Chapters 1 and 2 discussed the notions of 'technological paradigms' (Dosi 1984, Dosi *et al.* 1988), and 'industry recipes' (Spender 1989) in industries, 'dominant designs' (Abernathy & Utterback 1978) and 'technological regimes' (Teece 1988) in technologies, and 'dominant logics' (Bettis & Prahalad 1995) in organizations. They are partly embodied in rule-based procedures, such as 'performance programs, routines, or scripts'. In Chapter 6, in cognitive science, we encountered 'paradigms' (in the sense of exemplars to be emulated), 'mental models' (Johnson-Laird 1983), 'scripts' (Abelson 1976, Shank & Abelson 1977). In Chapter 7 we encountered 'prototypes' (Rosch 1977) and 'stereotypes' (Putnam 1957). These all indicate that across all these fields of technology, organization, knowledge, and language novelty becomes consolidated in a standard practice, which provides the basis for efficient exploitation.

However, novelty does not spring forward ready-made and out of the blue. This happens only in the ancient Greek myth of the goddess of war and wile Pallas Athene springing fully armed from the brow of Zeus, the chief of the gods. Novelty (novel concepts, practices, products, technologies) at the outset tends to be incompletely determinate. It emerges as a groping around with improvisations that need to crystallize and achieve consolidation in best practice, on the basis of experience with success and failure.[1]

Schumpeter recognized this in his distinction between invention and its realization in a viable practice. It is only after consolidation that geniuses can be distinguished from fools. When a person acquires a new practice, this tends to be ill-defined and messy, with encumbrances from previous practice, and lapses back into more familiar practice. This is most pronounced in the case of learning from practice: a novel way of doing things seems to suggest itself, but it is not clear how or why precisely it should work. It happens even in areas that appear to be quite determinate and purely deductive, such as mathematics. The mathematician Gauss once exclaimed: 'I have got my result; but I do not know yet how to get it' (Popper 1973: 16). This move to consolidation reflects a passage from tinkering to understanding, from intuition to knowledge, from tacit to codified knowledge, from technology to science. But in formal learning too, based on codified knowledge, the phenomenon of initial lack of clarity, confusion, and stumbling arises, and practice is needed for the novel activity to be mastered smoothly. Examples were given in Chapter 1. A further example is the following:

> When building construction shifted from wood to iron and later steel, in the nineteenth century, this was first attempted as a mere functional substitution of a new material in the script of wood construction. But 'chunks' of technological practice remained the same. For example, heating and cooling as a method to harden wood seems similar to heating and cooling to harden iron. But, unlike wood, metal can be welded. At first, wedge-shaped connections required for wood construction were retained, while for metal they do not make functional sense, so that this 'chunk' in the practice of construction was later dropped (Mokyr 1990). In Chapter 1, this phenomenon of lingering elements from old technologies was called 'hysteresis'.[2]

Repeated trials and applications, supported by ancillary innovations in tools, methods, and materials, are required to find out what properly belongs to the novel practice and what not. This yields increasing efficiency from a process of narrowing down, in a reduction of variety; by elimination of what step by step is found out to be redundant, inefficient, or counter-productive. This is associated with the concept of 'first-order', or 'single-loop' learning, discussed in Chapters 1 and 2: learning to conduct an existing practice more efficiently.

Note that the outcome need not be optimal and need not be unique. Several candidates may compete for dominance, or on the basis of ongoing improvements an old practice may compete, and alternatives may coexist for a long time.

---

[1] Because of this, Kuhn (1970) criticized the Lakatosian view that existing theories should not be surrendered until a viable alternative has been developed. To demand this is like inviting someone to box with his hands tied behind his back, or like a grown-up man boxing with an infant. No alternative emerges in well-developed, determinate form, and to demand that is to block its emergence.

[2] Piaget called it '*decalage*'.

A well-known example of an old technology keeping up for a long time with a novel one is the prolonged existence of sailing ships next to steamships (Rosenberg 1972).[3]

The speed of the process depends on the need for standardization. In the case of network externalities, for example, that pressure is great. The famous example, discussed in Chapter 1, is the race towards the technical standard for video recorders. The emergence of one outcome among possible alternatives is influenced by current institutions and flukes of chance and coincidence: what happens to be around in the form of adequate materials, skills, instruments, organization, infrastructure, attitudes, habits of thought, and other institutions. In other words, it needs to be embedded in existing institutional arrangements (see Chapter 5). That is why a given technology may yield different practices in different countries or even in different organizations within an industry. Barley (1986) gives an example of how the use of electronic scanning devices is organized differently, with different results, in different hospitals. The outcome often is not predictable and may not be intended. Development may be locked into a path that later turns out to be suboptimal or even counter-productive (Arthur 1989, David 1985).

Methods of making iron and steel have developed and improved over the centuries. The technology required the development of bellows to achieve sufficient heat. The bellows could be driven by alternative sources of power (water, steam). Crucial for making steel was the proper mix of iron and carbon. For a considerable period of time the English Bessemer practice competed with the German open-hearth process. In the long run the latter prevailed because it allowed for the use of scrap iron and low-grade fuels. A complication that was resolved only after a long time was that the phosphorus in most iron ore contaminated the steel, so that ore with high phosphorus content could not be used (Mokyr 1990). Countries with easy access to ore with low phosphorus content had an advantage.

In the history of technology science has often followed from the 'tinkering' or trial and error of technology, and the externalization of tacit knowledge, rather than leading technology. Mokyr (1990: 170) claimed that up to 150 years ago the majority of inventions have been used before people understood why they worked. This occurred in agricultural technology, mechanical machinery, metallurgy, the textile industry, and shipping. Increasingly, from the second half of the nineteenth century, scientific understanding came to feed technological development. An example is the invention of telegraphy, which required the theoretical notion of electromagnetic waves invented by Maxwell in 1865 (Mokyr 1990: 144). Chemistry was also to a large extent guided by science. Nevertheless, the reverse order of practical tinkering preceding understanding still occurs, as has been exhibited in the information-technology revolution (Dosi 1984).

Why does consolidation take place? It results from a drive towards efficiency and standardization of operation, application, and production. At first, the drive is toward feasibility, in the form a working model. But the innovation also has to be fitted into

[3] This is illustrated in Turner's paintings of steamships next to sailing ships.

systems of use, production, and distribution, and when appropriate systems are not in place, they need to be developed. Alternatively, an inferior innovation with better fit in existing systems may win.

> A nice illustration is the development of radar, prior to and during the Second World War (Checkland & Howell 1998, van der Voort 1999). The underlying invention, much earlier, was due to Maxwell, who proposed the principle of electromagnetism on the basis of mathematical analysis, in 1864. Hertz's empirical proof and the construction of the first oscillator-transmitter followed in 1886. In 1901 Marconi established wireless communication, and predicted the use of short wavelengths for radio detection of objects. The Germans were the first to build an effective detection device, in the thirties. However, in contrast with the Germans, the British incorporated radar technology into an elaborate and sophisticated information system of radar and visual detection points. This served to identify incoming aircraft, establish their position, altitude, and direction, and to connect this with a system of sending out and guiding its own aircraft to intercept the enemy. Distinction between friend and foe was established by a procedure whereby a friendly plane upon receipt of a radio beam returned a much more powerful pulse, to show up as a stronger blip on the radar screen. It was that effective system of use rather than the basic innovation that made the British win the Battle of Britain. During this development, British radar technology remained inferior to that of the Germans in terms of accuracy and range.

The occurrence and speed of efficiency and standardization depend on competitive pressure. As novelty becomes diffused, and patents wear out and the competencies involved become less tacit and more imitable, competition increases and exerts pressure to produce more efficiently, by utilizing economies of scale and scope. Economy of scale demands expansion. It typically entails division of labour, with specialization of labour across different linkages in a chain of production and distribution. This requires systematization and standardization, which entails that tacit knowledge be externalized into documented knowledge (Nonaka & Takeuchi 1995), so that it can be efficiently incorporated in standard operating procedures and specifications of systemic linkages.

> An example, given in Chapter 1, is the British invention, in the seventeenth century, of detailed technical drawings and written specifications for the construction of ships. This allowed the transformation from tacit knowledge of building ships, in procedural memory, to codified knowledge, in declarative memory. This in turn allowed for clearer contracting with shipyards, considerably reducing transaction costs, and classroom instruction of designers and builders.

The outcome of consolidation serves as a platform for expansion and new applications. It provides the paradigm to be followed along a technical trajectory. Next to the achievement of efficiency in exploitation, this is the second rationale for consolidation. It will be argued that this expansion, called generalization, provides the basis for exploration, for accumulating experience as input for the next novelty. The transformation of tacit to codified, documented knowledge, in consolidation, is part of this. Such codification serves to abstract know-how from the specific context in which it has developed. This is needed for the transfer of knowledge for efficient exploitation in new contexts. In consolidation tacit knowledge is partly transformed to codified knowledge and partly lost. In application in novel contexts new tacit knowledge is added again.

9.1.3   Tenacity

While consolidation is needed for efficient exploitation and for generalization, it can develop into lock-in or inertia.

> The US car industry settled down into an industry recipe of 'Fordist production': large volumes of standard products with price-oriented, 'arm's-length' supplier relations. This proved vulnerable to competition from a different, Japanese, industry recipe of quality production with intensive co-operation with suppliers.

Why this inertia? Why stick to established practice in the face of failures? Clearly, inertia can be disastrous. But directly after a novelty has settled down, and 'come into its own', one could not possibly step straight on to the next novelty. Such a leap is difficult to imagine. Entrepreneurship may consist of radical jumps into the dark, with a large risk of failure and a small chance of successful radical innovation. At the aggregate level of the economy such jumps are beneficial when the weight of incidental success exceeds the weight of frequent failure. But at the level of the firm they are generally ill-advised. It is counter-productive to drop and replace practices too soon, before one knows their limits and possibilities for replacement. That would lead to random drift rather than improvement (Lounamaa & March 1987).

Kuhn (1970) not only noted, descriptively, that scientists tend to stick to the 'puzzle solving' of 'normal science', but also indicated, normatively, that a certain amount of theoretical tenacity is rational. First, there is a principle of economy: we do not and should not surrender theory at the first occurrence of a falsifier indicating that our theory is not perfect. It is rational to wait until the cumulative weight of anomalies becomes excessive in some sense. But there is more: It is only by ongoing tests of theory that we find where its real strengths and weaknesses lie. Even Popper (1970: 55) recognized this, in spite of his drive to keep science open to criticism:

I have always stressed the need for some dogmatism: the dogmatic scientist has an important role to play. If we give in to criticism too easily, we shall never find out where the real power of our theories lies.

But, in the spirit of his critical rationalism, Popper elsewhere says (1970: 52): 'in my view the "normal" scientist, as Kuhn describes him, is a person one ought to feel sorry for'.

We need to exhaust our theories to a sufficient extent, before we give them up, not only to recoup our investment in them, so to speak, but also to develop the motivation for a novel alternative, through an accumulation of anomalies. This has been recognized also in the literature on organizational learning. There is a trade-off between the need to adapt and the costs involved in terms of uncertainty as to whether novelty will be successful, and uncertainty about the organizational repercussions (March 1991). To make the step to novel practice one must be prepared to 'unlearn' (Hedberg 1981), in the sense of no longer taking established procedures for granted. Thus, a condition for innovation generally is that there is perceived need, mostly from external pressure, a threat to continued existence, or a shortfall of performance below aspiration levels, as has been the dominant view in the literature on organizational learning (see the survey by Cohen & Sproull 1996).

However, this is not a necessary condition: one may stumble, so to speak, on novelty without seeking it to repair bad performance. Nor is it a sufficient condition. While necessity may be the mother of invention, that may also need a father. Above all, we need to accumulate experience to find out what elements are eligible for preservation in the exploration of novel combinations, and what other elements, and from where, to combine them with. This point does not yet seem to have been appreciated in the literatures on innovation and organizational learning. Thus, a certain amount of conservatism is rational, but of course it can easily become excessive and block innovation.

The basic idea deriving from this is that before we can replace any practice, of theory, technology, or organization, we first need to pursue its potential, in a range of applications in a variety of contexts. We need to do this in order to build up the motive for change, to discover limits of validity, and to gather indications as to how to change it and what elements to preserve from it, and how, in a novel practice. We do not know beforehand which elements are robust under changing contexts, and hence worth preserving, before we have tried it. This is how we might conduct abduction and reconcile exploitation and exploration: while employing the practice we are at the same time exploring its limits and opportunities for its change and replacement. Or, to put it more succinctly: as in crime, the transgression of existing principles requires motive, opportunity, and means. Before the need for replacement of an existing practice arises such a move would be wasteful, and before opportunity and means arise it would be impossible.

This puts the notion of 'inertia' of organizations into a new perspective. Inertia is not only needed for co-ordination and control, for the sake of efficiency in exploitation. It also represents the principle of tenacity: the need to preserve existing principles in order to find out where and why they fail and how they might be replaced, as a contribution to exploration.

Lakatos (1970) proposed that since we replace a theory only in the light of an alternative we should consider not isolated theories but a sequence of them in a 'scientific research programme'. That is characterized by a 'hard core' of explanatory principles, surrounded by a 'protective belt' of subsidiary assumptions. The latter vary from one theory to the next, within the programme, in contrast with the core, which is maintained tenaciously. The process of theory development is governed by a 'negative and positive heuristic': rules about what to do and what not to do. The negative heuristic indicates that the core should not be subjected to criticism. The positive heuristic indicates that changes in the protective belt, in the generation of novel theories, should not be '*ad hoc*' and should be 'progressive'. This means that novel theory should increase empirical content, by adding 'novel facts' predicted by the theory, and that additions or modifications in the protective belt should be coherent with the core principles. However, this maintenance of the hard core and the negative heuristic is conservative, and can cause excessive inertia.[4]

Nevertheless, Lakatos's account may contribute to our understanding of a process of exploitation that contributes to exploration. Protection of the hard core accompanied by additions and modifications in the protective belt may help in the process of finding out where the real strengths and limitations lie, as we move from one application and extension or modification to another. However, we are not only looking for exploitation of existing principles but also for a procedure in which incremental steps lead up to a radical shift. The negative heuristic seems to foreclose that. Note that the principle of tenacity is conservative only in a limited sense: it seeks a basis for change by seeking applications in novel contexts that may generate insights into the need, opportunity, and means for radical change. This is the principle of generalization. It is this combination of tenacity and generalization that reconciles exploitation and exploration, as will be shown.

9.1.4 Generalization

Let us see how exploration is likely to proceed, if because of competitive pressures it needs to proceed effectively and efficiently. The most straightforward way to explore the limits of effectiveness or validity of an existing practice, and at the same time survive through ongoing exploitation of available resources, is to generalize application of the practice to novel contexts. This is what we see in individual development as well as development of firms and markets: attempts are made to carry a successful practice into neighbouring areas of application. This second stage I call the stage of 'generalization'.

Consolidation provides the basis for generalization: for carrying the practice to novel contexts. This enables us to profit from the variety of context. This can only be done if sufficient flexibility for adaptation is allowed there. For this, dominant designs may operate as prototypes, in the sense discussed in Chapter 7. Deviations are allowed in details, while sufficient similarity to the prototype is maintained to preserve the identity of the dominant design. This can yield a variety of manifestations that in principle may have no feature in common, while each preserves sufficient resemblance to the prototype, in chains of family resemblance (Wittgenstein). Language shows how this can work, as analysed in Chapter 7.

If the objective is to conduct exploitation in such a way that it contributes to exploration, we should seek to do it in a way that optimizes both profit from exploitation and

---

[4] Weintraub (1988) reconstructed 'neo-Walrasian' economics as a Lakatosian research programme, and claimed that it is progressive. Nooteboom (1993*b*) opposed this view, arguing that the Lakatosian framework is used to mask or legitimize excessive conservatism in economics.

the gathering of the elements of discovery: motive, opportunity, and means. More specifically, these elements of discovery are the following. First, insight into limitations of current practice. Second, identification of elements of current practice that can be preserved in novel combinations because they do not form the cause of such limitations and are persistently effective. Third, elements from other, neighbouring practices with which they can be combined with a reasonable prospect of useful and workable novelty. Fourth, insight into architectural principles by which these elements can be combined with a reasonable chance of success in utilizing their potential. For all this we need variety of context. We need the movement from one context of application to another in such a way that the next novel context is sufficiently close to afford viable exploitation and sufficiently different to yield novelty of tests and novelty of insight where limitations and opportunities for improvement lie. This is related to the notion of cognitive distance discussed in Chapters 3 and 8. We need sufficient distance to yield novelty, but distance should not be so large as to preclude comprehension. Note that generalization is not automatic. It may be blocked by exit or entry barriers, which deprive progress of its source of variety.

In evolutionary theories a variety of ecological niches perform selection on a variety of life forms (phenotypes) generated by sets of genes. Here, in contrast, we see a life form adapting its cognitive and organizational structure and behaviour as it moves across a variety of contexts, and passes the results of such learning on to others.

I propose that this 'logic' bears a resemblance to the hermeneutic circle of the application and change of meaning in the use of language, as discussed in Chapter 7. This should not come as a surprise. As suggested in Chapter 4, rather than seeing the process of cognitive change as a process of Darwinian evolution, in a biological metaphor, it is more fitting to compare it with change of meaning in language, in a linguistic metaphor. After all, it is by communicative interaction with others that we learn, and change of knowledge is thereby associated with change of meaning. Thus, it is not unreasonable, in fact quite straightforward, to compare exploitation and exploration in business systems with the way word meanings shift (exploration) as they are used (exploitation) in different sentences, in the context of different discourses. This metaphor will be explored more systematically in a later Section.

In a business setting, the contexts across which a practice is generalized may be new markets for existing products; for example, new segments in domestic markets, foreign markets, new technological conditions of production (labour, materials, components, machinery, tools), or new conditions of markets (use, competition) and distribution systems. New contexts may also entail new applications of existing technology, or of forms of organization or governance, in new products or new organizations. In all cases one will encounter differences of context that may necessitate or may suggest modifications, which lead to differentiation. In the case of firms, 'neighbouring practices' from which one may derive inspiration for change may be competing products, alternative technologies with similar uses, alternative distribution systems, new practices, or needs of customers.

An example of generalization is the use of mills for a variety of purposes: grinding (grains, seeds), pumping, sawing, and spinning. Another is the use of steam engines for moving mills, trains, ships, and cars (Mokyr 1990, de Vries & van der Woude 1995). Radar was applied not only for the detection of enemy aircraft, but also for range finding for artillery on battleships, and for the detection of submarines. It was improved for use also in aeroplanes, for detecting ground targets, and for ground control of landing. After the war, applications proliferated to relay stations for telephone and television, control of home appliances, data handling.

I propose that there is an underlying, pervasive 'imperialistic' drive to utilize resources in novel contexts, in all living systems.[5] This drive may be innate in people because of its evolutionary advantage in providing the basis for learning that I claim here. Such imperialism also has an economic rationale. Extension of an existing practice to wider fields of application carries the potential reward of economy of scale and scope.

Exploration of novel applications across contexts can to a greater or lesser extent be done virtually rather than actually, by thought experiments, scenarios, simulation of prototypes, and inspection or 'reverse engineering' of practices or products used elsewhere. As discussed in Chapter 8, there is great leverage in communication with others, at an appropriate cognitive distance, fitting to one's communicative ability. But as in all speculation it will at some point need to be put to the test of reality. That is where the surprises occur from which we can learn.

9.1.5   *Differentiation*

It is to be expected that as one moves through a variety of novel contexts, the practice needs to be differentiated to fit to them, or novel opportunities for improvement may present themselves. This is the next stage, of 'differentiation'. One may need to adjust to a different availability of material inputs and tools, competencies of people, acceptance of products produced. Note that this adaptation is not guaranteed. In a seller's market without much competitive pressure the incentive to adapt and improve may not be sufficient.

When steam engines were transferred from their application in pumping, manufacturing, and trains to propelling ships, a problem was that the residues from boiling sea water clogged up the engine, until the water that was turned into steam was separated from the water used for cooling (Mokyr 1990). Later applications of radar required the shift to shorter micro-wavelengths, which sharpened the abilities of radar and allowed for a smaller device, to be built into a wider range of apparatus (van der Voort 1999).

Here, the process of narrowing by eliminating redundancies, and the reduction of variety of practice, in the first stage of consolidation, is reversed into a process of

---

[5] This can perhaps be associated with Schopenhauer's 'will to live', as a tendency to assert oneself as widely as possible, and Nietzsche's 'will to power', i.e. the will to master, on which the will to knowledge is based.

widening into different versions and extensions of the novelty, with increasing variety. This third stage I call the stage of 'differentiation'.

> It does not seem a coincidence that the geographical discoveries in the fifteenth to the seventeenth centuries preceded the surge of scientific and technological discoveries in Europe. Perhaps they reflect the challenges and opportunities of generalization that I propose here as crucial for innovation. Conversely, part of the explanation as to why the tremendous early technical progress in China came to stagnate after 1400 may lie in the halting of geographical exploration, because of a decision by the imperial court in 1430 (Mokyr 1990: 231).

A proximate form of differentiation is to rearrange elements of an existing practice into novel versions for novel contexts. For this, one may tap into memory of previous applications or experience with trials at the stage of consolidation. This is a process of problem solving, defined as seeking recourse to known ways of doing things (Holland *et al.* 1989: 11). The potential and the success of this depend on what is available from previous experience in (organizational and personal) memory, on the inventiveness in problem solving of the people involved, and on communication and co-operation between them.

> As reported in Chapter 1, an example of innovation by means of a fall-back to previous experience is the case of aspirin (acetyl salicic acid). After it was first discovered it was replaced by a substitute (sodium salicyc acid), which became the dominant product until a Bayer chemist fell back on the old alternative when a patient suffered from the side effects of the dominant product (Mokyr 1990: 122). An example of differentiation after the main principles had been established is the differentiation of ship design by the Dutch, in the sixteenth century, into thirty-nine different designs for different purposes (de Vries and van der Woude 1995).

9.1.6 Reciprocation

A wider, more 'distant' form of adaptation is to adopt elements from foreign practices encountered in the novel context. Their success and similarity indicate that they may be potential sources for this. Similarity entails having elements in common (inputs, outputs, ways of doing things), serving similar markets. Failures of the existing practice are compared with successes of the practices with which it has come into contact, which yields insight into patterns of failure and potential alternatives. Speculations and experiments arise concerning promising adoption of elements from such neighbouring practices. Transfer can also go the other way: elements from existing practice are transferred to a foreign practice encountered in the new context. This transfer is called 'reciprocation' (to adopt that term from Piaget).

> An example given in Chapter 1 was the combination by the Portuguese of the triangular lateen sails of the Arabs with the square sails of northern European ships, to make for the best combination of manoeuvrability and speed. The windmill is a reciprocation between the watermill, which yielded the technology of horizontal shaft, transmission, and gears, and the sail as an instrument for using wind power (Mokyr 1990: 45).

Going back to my linguistic metaphor, reciprocation is akin to metaphor in language: transferring an element from one concept to another; seeing something in the light of something else.

> An example given in Chapter 1 was how Henry Ford adopted the idea for an assembly line from the filling of boxes according to order slips at a mail-order firm. Nonaka and Takeuchi (1995) tell the story of how a beer can served as a metaphor in the design of a copying machine.

Differentiation and perhaps also reciprocation can be seen as 'incremental' innovations: variations upon a theme. But they may lead to more radically novel combinations. People can conduct reciprocation by themselves, but it is tremendously enhanced in social interaction and communication, along the lines discussed in Chapter 8.

9.1.7   Radical Innovation

Recombination of elements from different practices can lead to 'accommodation' in the form of novel combinations (Schumpeter), yielding 'radical' or 'large' or 'macro' innovations, which produce 'saltation' or 'punctuation'. For Schumpeter such innovations were exogenous and random. The great challenge is to specify a process by which they arise. But for this we need the further development of conceptual tools. I propose that it is the structural difference, or 'distance', or previous unrelatedness of elements in the novel combination, rather than economic consequences, that characterizes radical or macro inventions. Small incremental or 'micro' inventions, which might be called 'improvements' because they are more proximate, can have larger economic consequences than radical ones. Generally, more radical, distant novel combinations encounter greater problems in turning ideas into realities, because they are more likely to require instrumental technologies that are not available, or changes in the system of use, production, or distribution in which they are embedded.

> This is what Mokyr (1990) called the 'Leonardo effect', discussed in Chapter 1. Leonardo da Vinci conceived many ideas (such as a flying man) that could not be realized for lack of means to realize or even test them. Other impracticable radical ideas in history were those of the submarine and the internal-combustion engine (both in the seventeenth century). Emmanuelle Conesa (2000) discusses the case of the development of an SSTD: a supersonic, single-stage, transatmospheric craft. It is a cross between a rocket and an aeroplane: a vehicle that takes off and lands as a plane, but which, like a rocket, goes beyond Mach 8 in speed and flies beyond the atmosphere, but in a single stage, without the waste of jettisoning rocket segments. Development requires a radical shift in infrastructural technologies of measurement and experimentation and scientific knowledge to support it. Beyond Mach 8 there are no installations capable of reproducing the combination of speed, pressures, and temperatures that would obtain. The way out might be computer simulation, but the scientific knowledge of the relevant formulae is insufficient. The required infrastructural knowledge and technology need to be shared across many different locations and activities, and thus require standardization.

Innovation does not necessarily have to follow problem solving, and may precede it, or may even precede generalization. But it is usually inspired by a change of context (generalization), in an accumulation of perceived failure and hints for improvement through comparison with and transfer from other practices.

Reciprocation between distant practices requires a leap of imagination. The role of chance increases: we are in the field of serendipity, but it is the serendipity of the prepared mind. The role of the principle of imperialism appears again: in exploring new directions one may hit upon opportunities for transfer that one was not looking for.

> This is the 'King Saul effect' (Mokyr 1990: 286), discussed in Chapter 1. Looking for a better dynamo for bicycle lights, Philips Company hit upon the development of an electric shaver. Petrol at first was a useless by-product in the derivation of lubricants from crude oil, before it was developed into a fuel for the internal-combustion engine. Bessemer invented his steel-making process while trying to solve problems with a spinning cannon shell (Mokyr 1990: 116).

A radically novel combination is not easy to identify as an opportunity, since it literally does not make sense; it cannot be interpreted in terms of existing practices, and therefore extends beyond established meanings and corresponding categories. That is why it is often a lonely, personal affair: it is difficult to make sense of the hunch even to oneself, let alone others. A handful of people stumbled upon X-rays, but only Madame Curie saw what it might mean, and what its implications and uses might be.

How, then, do novel combinations arise? As the area of application of an existing practice is expanded, problems accumulate in the ongoing process of differentiation and reciprocation. *Ad hoc* additions and modifications mess up the clarity and efficiency of the practice, and increase complexity, resulting in loss of efficiency and diminishing returns: it becomes increasingly difficult to make further additions or modifications while maintaining coherence. Duplication arises, with opportunities for economy of scale foregone. Unsolved failures to perform are accumulated. This provides an incentive to consider a clean-up through dropping rather than through only rearranging elements, in novel structures, in Schumpeterian creative destruction. Above all, existing architecture of the practice imposes limits on the novel elements brought in. It is needed to preserve systemic coherence, but it prevents realization of the true potential of new elements. Thus, pressures build up to break down the architecture to realize the potential of novelty. Experience has accumulated as to which novel combinations of elements, gathered in reciprocation from a variety of old practices, might be successfully combined, and by which architectural principles. There is a basis for reasonable hunches. Such, I propose, is the process of abduction.

Next, when success in novel architectures emerges we are back at the beginning: the need for consolidation. But this also is not guaranteed: no new practicable synthesis may arise, and development may end in chaos.

9.2   A CYCLE OF DISCOVERY

The different stages together make up a cycle of discovery. I propose it as a general process of which the hermeneutic circle and Piaget's stages of development are special cases.

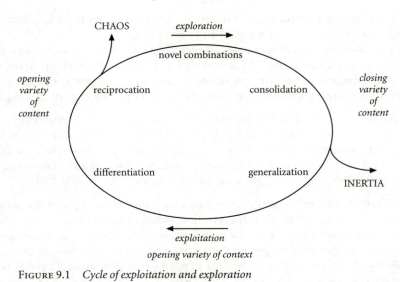

FIGURE 9.1   *Cycle of exploitation and exploration*

9.2.1   The Cycle

The different stages make up a cycle of discovery, as illustrated in Figure 9.1.

The process can be characterized succinctly as an alternation of variety of content and variety of context. In consolidation variety of content is closed down to enable efficient production and a clear paradigm as a platform for generalization. This opens up variety of context, which yields insight into misfits, and into needs and opportunities for adaptation. Note that after consolidation development may end in inertia, because of lack of incentives or opportunities for generalization or differentiation. At the stage of novel combinations, in novel architectures, these may not settle down, and may get stuck in an unresolved chaos of trials, errors, and ongoing misfits that may lead to the development petering out or being dropped.

The cycle of discovery was built up on the basis of a logic of its own. But its similarity was noted to the hermeneutic circle discussed in Chapter 7 (Figures 7.2 and 7.3). This consisted of the old idea that sentence meaning is built up from word meaning (and the meaning of discourse is built up from sentence meanings), but added to that the idea that application of words in different sentences, or different discourses, yields shifts of word meaning. In Chapter 7 this was developed further on the basis of Roman Jacobson's theory of poetics, modified on the basis of Ricoeur's work. Selections from conceptual ('paradigmatic') repertoires are made and combined in the linear ('syntagmatic') order of sentences and discourse, but the new combinations of words in sentences (and sentences in discourse), in different contexts of action, can trigger metaphoric additions or shifts in paradigmatic repertoires. The similarity with the cycle in Figure 9.1 is no coincidence. I propose that both the cycle in Figure 9.1 and the hermeneutic circle are manifestations of the same, generalized process by which application of concepts in different contexts yields the motivation and the material and hints for novel concepts, in an alternation between variety of content and variety of context.

9.2.2 Centre and Periphery

The cycle also appears to be related to an important theme in studies of cultural change: the reversal between centre and periphery in the renewal of culture (Lotman 1990). In Figure 9.1 consolidation constitutes the centre, and generalization takes us to the periphery, to meet challenges of differentiation and to utilize opportunities for exchange leading to novel combinations. If there is no internal generation of variety as a source of innovation it can only come from outside, and enter at the periphery.

> I return to the case of the stagnation of science and technology in China in the fifteenth century, after a period in which it produced many innovations far ahead of Western civilization. Chinese trade had reached as far as southern Africa. The explanation is that variety from the periphery was blocked out by the emperor's ban on foreign trade. Rigid internal bureaucracy and control blocked internal variety, and robbed of both sources of variety innovation stopped. Lotman (1990: 145) reconstructs the renaissance in Italy in these terms: 'Italy as a crossroads was saturated by foreign influences in the fifth century: Germans, Huns, Goths, Ostrogoths, Byzantines, Longobards, Franks, Arabs, Normans, Magyars . . . [Italy] absorbed this flood . . . [these influences] formed themselves into a whole. The result was . . . a burst of cultural activity unheard of in the history of civilization: the Renaissance'.

Lotman (1990: 146) identifies the following stages in the assimilation of the foreign coming in from the periphery:

1. Imported texts 'keep their strangeness . . . [are] limited to an élite, and [are] idealized by it'.
2. 'Links are restored with the past . . . the new is interpreted as an organic continuation of the old'.
3. The claim arises that at home the foreign really comes into its own; achieves its true meaning and potential. Compare this with the proposition above that present practice has to be broken down and rebuilt to let the new achieve its true potential.
4. The new has been entirely dissolved, and becomes the new centre (in what we might call the dominant logic).

Lotman also suggests the link to the hermeneutic circle, indicated above (Lotman 1990: 162):

the central sphere of culture is constructed on the basis of an integrated structural whole, like a sentence, whereas the peripheral sphere is organized like a cumulative chain organized by the simple joining of structurally independent units . . . the first to be a structural model of the world and the second to be a special archive of anomalies

9.2.3   Optimality?

In a procedural sense the proposed 'logic' or heuristic of discovery is optimal: it provides exploration while maintaining exploitation; it minimizes destruction in the process of creation. It is not optimal in the substantive sense of resulting from the equation of marginal cost and revenue. That could not be, because neither would be known. However, being optimal in some looser, procedural, sense, it need not yield a unique or optimal outcome. It allows for path dependence and suboptimal outcomes, and the path taken depends on context and coincidence. Different firms can develop different structures even in the same industry. As indicated before, 'logic' is put between quotation marks, because it is a heuristic rather than a logic in the sense of indicating a sequence of stages that is logically or epistemologically inexorable. It is a heuristic in the sense that it is generally the best answer to the problem of abduction, the best way of exploring while maintaining exploitation.

However, stages may overlap: there is generalization during consolidation, differentiation during generalization, exploration of novel combinations during reciprocation. Stages may even be skipped or reversed. The argument only indicates that then progress, in the form of successful renewal, is more risky. That is the issue of abduction. But it is certainly conceivable that one might hit upon successful novelty more directly, without one or more of the intervening stages. Innovation can occur less systematically, more randomly and spontaneously (Cook & Yanow 1996), when an obvious opportunity presents itself without much exploration. But as a general rule one needs to accumulate failures to build up the need for change, as well as hints in what directions to look: indications as to what changes could be made with some chance of success, and how. More random jumps would have the advantage of reaching the market faster, if they succeeded, and, to the extent that competition takes the form of races to the market, greater risks might be taken in more drastic leaps. Indeed especially small firms do exhibit such reckless behaviour, and thereby they do contribute to the dynamic of economies. But in the case of pure trial and error the risk of failure would be very high. Also, note that technological opportunities may affect the order and length of stages. For example, as indicated before, by simulating the performance of devices on computers rather than actually building prototypes and testing them, one may engage in virtual rather than actual generalization and differentiation, and in that sense skip those stages in the process of searching for viable novel combinations.

The process is not automatic: outside contingencies as well as organizational structure or culture, or lack of talent in people or teams, may block transition to a next stage. Consolidation may be limited because of alternatives persisting side by side. Generalization may be blocked because of a monopoly maintaining an exclusive hold, or because of lack of access to novel contexts (recall the case of the stagnation of the Chinese empire). Differentiation and reciprocation may be blocked because there is insufficient motivation or capability to modify an existing practice. One may get stuck in inertia. There must be a basic interest in solving problems and making things work. While need is not a sufficient condition, it is often necessary. This corresponds with

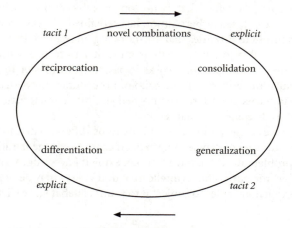

FIGURE 9.2   *Cycle of knowledge*

the notion in the literature on organizational learning that failures are needed to force a willingness to relax existing practice and explore variations or alternatives. In this way, as Schumpeter argued, crises help creative destruction. This brings in one of the contingencies: in markets with little competitive challenge the process may halt because of insufficient pressure.

The process of learning or discovery may not even be intended. Note that the process of exploration is triggered by the will to expand success, rather than the will to learn. But the experience accumulated in expansion in fact yields a basis for learning.

9.2.4   A Cycle of Knowledge

I indicated that in the stage of radical innovation through novel combinations the tinkering of technology often precedes scientific understanding, and knowledge at that stage is typically tacit. Something new is found to work, but one does not know why, or even how, so that one does not know its proper conditions, usage, and potential. It is part of the process of consolidation that this becomes clear, and knowledge becomes explicit. That provides the basis for more systematic application, division of labour, economy of scale, instruction by specification of standard operating procedures, and the specification of contracts that provide the basis for generalization in novel contexts, at a distance. This is illustrated in Figure 9.2.

Note that Figure 9.2 specifies two kinds of tacit knowledge: tacit 1 and tacit 2. The first obtains in architectural restructuring and is the more fundamental: knowledge cannot be made explicit because it is incomplete or non-existent. Later, during generalization, knowledge becomes tacit 2 as a result of routinization: the knowledge is absorbed into practice to become self-evident and is no longer subject to conscious reflection until emergencies trigger attention to it. It may become routine to such an extent that it becomes a reflex that is no longer subject to conscious reflection. Routinization is efficient, as Herbert Simon has explained: it frees up scarce capacity for conscious attention to novelties that are more urgent than routine activities.

Note that it is possible to pass directly from tacit 1 to tacit 2, without the route through explicitness: a practice that works is passed from master to apprentice by example and emulation, entirely in the realm of procedural knowledge, without formal instruction in terms of declarative knowledge. This characteristically obtains in small craft firms, as discussed in Chapter 3.

When emergencies arise, and practice needs to be differentiated to fit novel contexts, then tacit 2 knowledge can become explicit again to engage in rational problem solving. This is problematic if the stage through explicit knowledge was never passed. Then considerable 'maieutic' effort (intellectual midwifery) may be required to make the knowledge explicit, in order to subject it to rational debate (see Chapter 3).

9.3   CONCLUSION

I propose a heuristic cycle of discovery, which shows a way of resolving the paradox of exploitation and exploration. It is based on an alternation of variety of content and variety of context. It is also accompanied by an alternation of tacit and codified knowledge. The cycle is proposed as an alternative to traditional search models as well as evolutionary models of learning. Rather than a biological metaphor of evolution it employs a situated-action theory of cognition and learning, discussed in Chapter 6, and the notion of the hermeneutic circle, discussed in Chapter 7. The basic idea is that new meanings, ideas, and competencies are generated from practice across a variety of contexts. In order to explore novelty one must exhaust present practice: accumulate incentives for as well as directions of change, experimenting with minor change to build up to major change. The context offers scaffolding (Chapter 6), by yielding directions for change and indicating elements for novel combinations, from parallel practices encountered in novel contexts, in a metaphoric process. Radically novel combinations at first are indeterminate, and need to settle down into dominant designs before they can provide a platform for a further round of generalization, differentiation, and reciprocation, to lead up to a next round of novel combinations.[6]

---

[6] Compare this with the description of novelty by Hegel (quoted by Kauffman 1966*a*: 20): 'This indeterminate apprehension of something unknown' and 'This gradual crumbling which did not alter the physiognomy of the whole is suddenly interrupted by the break of day that . . . all at once reveals the edifice of a new world. Yet what is new here does not yet have perfect actuality [translation of "*Wirklichkeit*"]'. To reach a fuller understanding and substantiation of the new insight entails 'an immensely tangled path and an equally immense amount of exertion and toil'. In other words, one may have a general grasp of a concept when it is first proposed as an abstraction, but it becomes 'actual' (in German, 'wirklich') and one understands it in a more real sense only when it has been fully developed in all its implications, ramifications, manifestations, and anomalies *vis-à-vis* other concepts. Certain basic principles (categories) cannot be simply discarded or knocked over by incidental anomalies, but must be adopted, lived through, and out-

A crucial point here is that exploitation and exploration are complements rather than substitutes: one can continue exploitation in a way that contributes to exploration, at least up to the point that a breakdown of architecture occurs to form novel combinations.

grown. Kauffman (1966*a*: 21) argued that this yields the correct interpretation of Hegel's identification of the 'actual' ('*wirklich*', which also means 'operational') with the rational, and that it should not be interpreted as a defence of the status quo, as Popper, for example, did. The cycle of discovery reminds us of Hegel's notion of science as a circle 'that returns into itself, that presupposes its beginning and reaches it only in the end' (Kauffman 1966*b*: 237).

10
An Elaboration with Scripts

This Chapter attempts to increase precision and analytical grip, to prepare for applications of the heuristic cycle of discovery to organizations and innovation systems. The step of radical innovation, or 'saltation', or 'punctuation', may still seem to be something of a mystery. Also, we need to make the heuristic more determinate, to hook it causally on to what actually happens in organizations and markets. I use the notion of scripts for this elaboration, at the different levels of people, organizations, and industries, technological systems, or innovation systems. However, it is important to note that the theory is not 'about scripts'. It is about the heuristic of learning as set out in the previous Chapter, but scripts are used as a preliminary and probably highly imperfect construct to elaborate the workings of the heuristic.

10.1 INTRODUCTION

First comes a summary of the use of scripts in earlier chapters. I reconsider their application at the level of individual cognition. Next, I consider alternative ways of conceptualizing processes in organizations and industries, and conclude that scripts may provide the best model yet.

10.1.1 *Summary of Scripts*

As discussed in Chapter 6, a script consists of sequences of nodes that represent component activities that generally can be performed in different ways, represented by a range of possible 'substitutions' into a node. A script can have alternative branches for different contexts. The notion is derived from cognitive science, where it has been used as a model of cognitive structure for rule-based behaviour. I indicated that I would use it as a model of practices at different levels, of individuals, teams and divisions within firms, firms, industry supply chains, and national innovation systems. The links between levels arise as follows: lower-level scripts substitute their activities into nodes of higher-level 'superscripts'; substitutions into a node of a script in turn have the form of scripts. One reason for this choice of modelling was to solve the multilevel problem identified in Chapter 1. I use this hierarchical structure of scripts, superscripts, and subscripts to model a range of institutional environments, or selection environments. For a given set of practices, represented as a script, its institutional environment is represented by the superscripts in which it is embedded. The script model was mentioned in the discussion of a theory of interactive learning in Chapter 8. Absorptive capacity was modelled as the range of phenomena that can be fitted into cognitive scripts. In Chapter 3 it was announced that scripts would be used to model competencies of firms, and in Chapter 5 it was announced that they would be used to model multilevel institutions.

10.1.2   Generalization of Scripts

In Chapter 9 the process of exploitation and exploration was compared to the hermeneutic circle: the process of letting words shift in meaning as we use them in varying sentences, in various discourses. Can this analogy be used for further elaboration?

At the level of individual learning, the heuristic of discovery can be interpreted in terms of the selectionist neural framework discussed in Chapter 6 (on the basis of the work of Edelman). There, categorization, memory, and meaning are seen as rooted in patterns of activation between units (neurons). The different stages of the cycle of discovery, of consolidation, generalization, differentiation, reciprocation, and accommodation can be interpreted as follows. Consolidation can be seen as the settling down of neural connections into a stable neural net. Generalization can be seen as the activation of the pattern in novel contexts. Differentiation can be seen as the generation of a variety of patterns because of small shifts in the strengths of connections between neurons. Reciprocation can be seen as cross-connections between different nets, where connections within the net are extended to outside units. Here, reciprocation is connected with the psychological notion of association. As discussed in Chapter 8, it is tremendously leveraged in communication between people. Radical novel combination can be seen as the reconstitution of connections across a new collection of units from previously unconnected nets. At the level of concept formation, perhaps this neural process can be seen as underlying the generation of a variety of competing, alternative variations of a script, and recombinations of nodes from different scripts.

In linguistic terms the syntagmatic axis can perhaps be seen as the axis of a script, and syntagmatic slots into which selections from paradigmatic repertoires are projected or substituted can perhaps be seen as the nodes in the script.

At the level of organizations the process can perhaps be extended to the formation and use of scripts that represent organizational processes or competencies. When we move to organizations and markets or innovation systems, we need some conceptualization of organizational process and market process to hook the heuristic of discovery on to. Could some generalization of the notion of a script be used for this? That would be a very attractive move, because the same notion would then apply to the different levels of aggregation: people, firms, and innovation systems, and this would help to realize our ambition for a multilevel theory. But before we start applying the script notion to organizations, let us consider alternatives.

10.1.3 Organizational Grammars?

For processes in organizations, March and Simon (1958) employed the notion of 'performance programs', and Cyert and March (1963), Levitt and March (1988), and Nelson and Winter (1982) used the notion of 'routines'. As March and Simon (1958: 142) themselves indicated, the term 'program' suggests too much rigidity and lack of adaptiveness. Pentland and Reuter (1994: 484) noted that the term 'routine' may suggest too much 'automatism' and 'mindlessness', but nevertheless they stuck to the term. Gioia and Poole (1984) and Barley (1986) applied the notion of scripts in organization studies. The nodes here replace the looser term 'chunks' employed by Weick and Roberts (1993). The term 'chunking' is familiar in artificial intelligence.

More recently, Pentland and Reuter (1994) and Pentland (1995) applied the concept of 'grammar' to elucidate organizational routines. I agree with Pentland and Reuter (1994) that we need a conceptualization that offers the following features:

1. It represents a collective capacity to perform recognizable sequential patterns of action.
2. It allows for a variety of sequences that can nevertheless be seen as functionally similar.
3. It is made up of building-blocks of actions (chunks, nodes) which allow for different, alternative ways of performing the action, constrained by the context.
4. While it imposes restrictions and directions on actions, the sequence of actions is not automatic or mindless, but constitutes 'effortful accomplishment'.

To satisfy these conditions, Pentland and Reuter (1994) and Pentland (1995) preferred the grammar metaphor to the script model. A grammar prescribes how noun phrases and verb phrases are properly ordered, and how words for substitution into phrases are to be selected from a lexicon. The noun and verb phrases serve for chunking, as the nodes do in a script. Pentland and Reuter (1995: 543) proposed that '[generative] grammars form a complete superset of scripts: there is no script that cannot also be expressed by a grammar'.

I propose that it is the other way around: the concept of a grammar is much richer, and thereby more restrictive, than the notion of a script. A script is no more than a sequence of nodes that represent chunks of activity. This can encompass a grammar: a syntagmatic axis into which items are substituted from a lexicon, according to rules of syntax. Pentland and Reuter's formulation of generative grammars in terms of verb and noun phrases into which words are substituted from a lexicon carries most of the problems of the representational–computational view in cognitive science that was criticized in Chapter 6. The suggestion that ranges of meanings for words are fixed (not open-ended), completely specifiable, and independent of the context and the sentence into which they are substituted is not tenable. Their approach ignores the hermeneutic circle; the fact that meanings are open-ended and subject to development in ranging across contexts.

Furthermore, in addition to the requirements specified by Pentland and Reuter, from the perspective of learning the conceptualization of organizational process should also:

5. allow for levels of more and less fundamental change: 'lower-level' innovation of components versus 'higher-level' innovations of the structure that contains the components;
6. permit the notion of parallel structures that can exchange components, in reciprocation;
7. show how novel structures can arise as novel combinations of components from different previous structures;
8. allow for a multilevel theory: for connecting learning at the individual, organizational, and industrial levels;
9. represent causal sequences, in means–end relationships.

These properties are offered by scripts, as will be discussed in more detail later, and not by grammars. The grammar metaphor imposes undesirable restrictions, as follows: Its restrictions with respect to the sequencing of nodes are too rigid and independent of context. Innovation often entails reversals of order, to suit the demands, opportunities, and restrictions of a specific context, which in grammar would not be permitted (you do not adapt grammar to the subject of speech).

> For example, in a service-restaurant script (Shank & Abelson 1977) people select their food after they are seated and they pay after eating, but in the innovation of a self-service restaurant selection and paying precede seating. While at first such a reversal of order would seem peculiar, it does not seem to be as strictly forbidden as a reversal of verb and noun phrases would be in grammar.

The second objection is that we should allow for probabilistic rather than deterministic structures: alternative orderings may be permitted with different probabilities of selection and combination. A grammar does not seem to permit that. A third objection is that the notion of basic 'atoms' or 'primitives', taken from the lexicon, does not apply in the present context. In organizational practices there are more levels of nesting activities within activities, beyond a lexicon of primitives. Every activity can be broken down further into constituent activities, all the way down into the neurophysiological functioning of brains.

10.1.4   *Organizational Scripts*

I will proceed with scripts as representations of organizational processes and competencies, because they seem to offer a minimal and most general model. This will be done in a way that provides a basis for a multilevel theory of people, firms, and industries or innovation systems.

At the organizational level, the script yields a further specification, a minimal extension, of the notion of an organizational routine (Cyert & March 1963, Nelson & Winter 1982) or social technology (Nelson & Sampat 2000). It gives a representation of the use of technologies and other resources, embodied in assets and used by people, as substitutions into a node, embedded in an organizational structure of co-ordination (the script).

The notion of a script serves well to further clarify the notion of competence as the efficient use of resources, as discussed in Chapter 3. Here, the script represents competence and substitutions into the nodes of the script represent resources. This implements the idea that the use of technology requires an organizational competence, and that technological competencies are embedded in organizations. The script represents how competence in general and knowledge in particular are socially constructed and embedded. The script notion is also consistent with Stinchcombe's (1990) reconstruction of a skill as a set of options for action plus principles to choose from them. Here 'skill' is close to 'competence', as it should be. The range of a node represents the options for action, and the script represents the principles for action.

Scripts help to elaborate the analogy between the cycle of discovery and the hermeneutic circle. As suggested above, scripts can represent linguistic structures in the sense that the axis of a script represents the syntagmatic axis, and activities substituted into the nodes of a script represent selections from paradigmatic repertoires in language. The similarity between meaning shift and discovery is that they can both be triggered by unusual, 'impertinent' combinations, or 'collisions', of items selected from paradigmatic repertoires, in a specific context. This is related to reciprocation.

One objection to scripts, raised in Chapter 6, is that scripts are too rigid if we interpret them as completely determined and as single. To meet this objection, three important provisos are made. First, I allow for a repertoire of scripts, in the same way that we allow for a repertoire of meanings for a word, which vary and from which different forms may be selected according to the context. A prototype, stereotype, or paradigmatic exemplar, in the sense discussed in Chapter 6, which guides selection across contexts, may represent this repertoire. Thus, there are different levels of repertoire: repertoires of substitutions for each node of a script, and a repertoire of structures for the script. Any node has a repertoire of possible substitutions, called its extension or range. Some substitutions may be the standard or prototype, but alternatives are allowed by family resemblance. The prototype is a default, applying only for as long as it serves its purpose as a standard. When misfits accumulate across contexts, it may be replaced. In a restaurant script cash is being replaced by credit cards, and chip cards (electronic purses) offer yet another alternative, which has not yet been widely accepted. The range is constrained by the context and by the competencies of the people who contribute actions to the node.

Second, the script need not consist of only one linear stretch, but may be composed of several branches for different conditions, and these may even connect back into the trunk, thus incorporating non-linearities. In other words, the script is generalized into a stochastic network of nodes representing activities.

Third, allowance is made for different 'strengths' of connections between nodes, by analogy to different strengths of synaptic connections in neural nets. These represent different probabilities of activation, depending on the contingencies of context. In other words, I understand scripts in a way that is consistent with the notions of connectionism, parallelism, and selection discussed in Chapter 6. Branches with weakened connections that are 'selected out' need not disappear, but may be recalled for activation when conditions require. In procedural memory this remains subconscious, in declarative memory the dominant script is conscious. As a result, the constellation of nodes, including strengths of connections, depends on experience, and thus varies between people to the extent that they have different experiences. On the other hand, to the extent that people share experience and a social, institutional context of sense making, as in an organization, the scripts they hold will overlap. It was noted in Chapters 2 and 3 that perhaps the most basic function of a firm is to act as a focusing device. Here, that is rendered as a set of organizational scripts that ensure coherence between individual activities and the scripts underlying them. Nevertheless, personal scripts also extend into personal lives and conditions. When people are called upon to act they will do so on the basis of the script that they select from their repertoires, according to their interpretation of the exigencies of the context, and this is always idiosyncratic to some extent.

At the organizational level a script is a framework for connected actions: a connected sequence of activities into which people substitute activities according to their organizational roles, which are in turn structured as scripts. Thus, there are scripts at multiple levels, with subscripts and superscripts. In other words, scripts become recursive: they are nested. There are scripts beyond the boundaries of organizations, and at higher levels. Scripts may extend across firm boundaries, where firms become intertwined in forms of organization 'between market and hierarchy'. They also include 'idea-innovation chains' between research institutes and firms, and between training institutes and firms. There are scripts for supply chains of firms supplying goods and services to each other, and distribution channels to customers. Here, nodes represent entry points where firms substitute their goods or services. Scripts at the level of industries represent common understandings of how connections are and should be, in shared industry recipes (Spender 1989). There are different levels of script within an organization, corresponding to divisions, subsidiaries, departments, teams, or communities of practice (Brown & Duguid 1996). There are different functional scripts within organizations, corresponding to different functions of production, administration, marketing, and finance. We have organizational scripts that express the co-ordination of activities between people or between departments or teams in the organization, scripts according to which people substitute their actions into organizational or team scripts, scripts for chunks of such activities, all the way down to mental scripts.

Scripts may be supported by documents that specify the standard script or prototype, but this generally functions as a default. When conditions invalidate it, it may be replaced or adapted. This is not guaranteed, however; there may be inertia. Scripts may also be tacit, which increases their inertia.

For example, in the payment node of a restaurant script any form of payment in turn requires the activation of a subsidiary practice, such as signing a cheque. At some point we arrive at processes of activating and controlling muscles, in which deliberate choice no longer appears.

10.1.5   Co-ordination

I distinguish three kinds of co-ordination: technical (alignment of standards), cognitive (crossing cognitive distance), and motivational (governance, alignment of purpose, and motivation).

At the level of the organization the probability of selecting a specific variant or branch of a script depends on the repertoires of scripts that the individuals hold, and cues from the context. These cues from context yield scaffolding, as discussed in Chapter 6. They include discussion with team members (or customers, or suppliers) gestures, hints, demonstrations, and meaningful looks. When organizational scripts are codified they are analogous to declarative memory in people. When such explicit documentation is lacking, it is analogous to procedural memory in people.

In organizational scripts, ranges of activities that are allowed as substitutions into a node are constrained by input and output constraints on the node: what one has to deal with as input coming in from a preceding node and requirements on output going into a following node. The allowed range for substitution is part of a person's organizational role.

At the connections between nodes not only technical issues of co-ordination occur, but also cognitive issues of learning by interaction and associated issues of governance. These were discussed in Chapter 8. Issues of learning by interaction entail problems of cognitive distance and communication. Issues of governance refer to the question of how people can be motivated to take each other's and the organization's interests to heart. These issues arise in connections of nodes within as well as between organizations. However, within organizations cognitive distance is shorter, and continuity of relations tends to be greater than between organizations, and this facilitates understanding and joint purpose. This is connected with my thesis of the 'firm as a focusing device'.

To the extent that the constraints are loose, the activity is relatively 'stand-alone'. To the extent that they are tight, activities are systemic. In a 'systemic innovation' (Teece 1988), an innovative substitution into one node would make the operation of other nodes infeasible. To be allowed as a substitute, adaptations would also need to be made in other nodes. Note that this can refer to producer scripts (production-systemic) or user scripts (product-systemic). An example of a systemic product is telecommunication, where a (sufficiently large) firm can offer a system of different components of hard- and software. One can, in principle, have stand-alone technologies producing systemic products and vice versa.

Constraints on nodes may be idiosyncratic or standardized. In the context of transaction-cost economics, we can render the notion of 'dedicated assets' as the tailoring of some asset to fit a substitution into a node of a transaction partner's script, in order to satisfy restrictions that are specific to the firm in question. The notion of assets that are complementary between two scripts is rendered as assets that yield substitutions into nodes in both scripts; economy of scope is rendered as different scripts having shared nodes or substitutions. If constraints on nodes are standardized they require less dedicated investments. Standardization requires codification and documentation. To the extent that scripts are tacit, co-ordination requires close interaction. It is easier to extend scripts across boundaries of firms when constraints are standardized and documented. Within the constraints of a node, the range of substitutions may be prescribed or left to the professional discretion of the worker. However, it is important to note that because of the nestedness of scripts, at some level prescription must stop and performance must be left to the discretion of the worker. Thus, the operation of organizational scripts indeed requires 'effortful accomplishment', and is not routine in the sense of being automatic or mindless (Pentland & Reuter 1994).

10.1.6 Organizational Cognition

As suggested in Chapter 8, a script can also be interpreted as constituting 'absorptive capacity' (Cohen & Levinthal 1990): activities that can be assimilated by substitution into the script. For people this means: what fits the individual's categories of thought. For organizations it means: what fits in organizational practices.

The notion of a script offers a precise idea of what organizational cognition may be, beyond individual cognition. Organizational cognition is embodied in organizational scripts, while individual cognition is substituted into nodes. The script specifies how an organization has competence in the form of established practices, with people contributing actions to chunks of organizational practice (Weick & Roberts 1993). Individual know-how operates at this lower level of aggregation. Individual knowledge is operative only in the context of the constellation of other people in the organization. Organizational knowledge is constituted from the cognition of people in their contributions to nodes, the restrictions on those contributions, the architecture of the nodes in an organizational script, and the knowledge about those scripts. These are documented to a greater or lesser extent in organization charts, blueprints, standard operating procedures, job descriptions, and the like. This yields organizational know-how. This cognitive identity of the firm is closely associated with the culture of a firm (Cook & Yanow 1996). People within the organization dispose of bits of information about this, and hold multifarious supplementary knowledge, but no one knows everything. Organizational culture in Schein's (1985) sense of a deep structure of basic categories of perception, interpretation, and evaluation helps to provide the basis for co-ordination. These categories yield common understanding and thereby reduce the number of things that have to be discussed and regulated for the sake of technical, cognitive, and motivational co-ordination. More precisely, the basic, shared categories that constitute the 'focus' of the firm guide basic principles of script architecture, the collection of nodes, and restrictions on nodes.

Emphatically, this does not entail that a person's personal knowledge is exhausted by what he contributes to a node of an organizational script, according to the role assigned to him. According to the principle of recursiveness, what a person contributes derives from the scripts that constitute his categorical apparatus, which also include his cognition 'qua persona' (Ring & van de Ven 1994). This yields spillovers from personal experience into his organizational role, and this constitutes a source of both error and innovation. This is my rendering of the notion of 'fluctuations' (Gleick 1987; Nonaka & Takeuchi 1995) as a source of both error and innovation. The scope for this depends on how strictly the individual's organizational role is specified and monitored, which is less to the extent that his role demands autonomy, for example as a 'knowledge worker'.

At all levels, situations may arise for which nothing like a script is available, as discussed in Chapter 6: not all activity is so rule-based as to be captured in scripts. That is what brought Shank and Abelson to their analysis of 'storytelling' to complement the notion of scripts. Moreover, as discussed in Chapter 6, even that is not enough: there are also mental representations of spatial images and musical themes that seem to be neither like scripts nor like stories. In addition, where scripts did rule, they may break down. This is how I understand the final stage in the heuristic of discovery: the stage of radical innovation. At that stage script processing has to be replaced by storytelling. The cycle of discovery entails a cycle of the building and breakdown of scripts.

10.2   INNOVATION

The notion of scripts can also be used to clarify notions of innovations, with levels, degrees, and types of innovation.

10.2.1   *Levels and Degrees of Innovation*

Scripts constitute institutions, in the sense, discussed in Chapter 5, that they are part of a selection environment. They select the lower-level activities substituted into them. If activities do not fit the conditions for substitution, they are rejected. But, as discussed in Chapter 5, such selection restrictions can be broken by innovation that transforms the script.

The notion of a hierarchy of scripts allows for innovation at different levels: those of individual, organizational, and industrial scripts. This corresponds with different levels of institutions: at the level of categories of thought, at the level of organizational procedures, at the level of industrial structure, and even higher levels of legal and other societal frameworks.

The script concept also allows for different degrees of innovation (at any level):

1. Changes in the repertoires of substitution into one or more nodes, which might be called 'parametric' change (Langlois & Robertson 1995).

2. Changes in the architecture of the script, which might be called 'architectural change' (Henderson & Clark 1990). One kind of architectural change is less radical: a change in the configuration of existing nodes: a reordering. An example was the change from a service to a self-service restaurant.
3. Radical architectural change consisting of novel architectures of nodes from different scripts. This appears to come close to Schumpeterian novel combinations, which entail creative destruction in terms of the dismantling of existing scripts.

This formulation may suggest that a radical architectural innovation preserves the existing ranges of substitution into the nodes that are reconfigured. This is not intended. As will be argued in more detail later, reconfiguration of nodes will in general entail a redistribution of substitutions over nodes.

As indicated in Chapter 7, the script notion can also be used to reconstruct the notion of metaphor. A metaphor provides a link between two previously unconnected fields of meaning (Miall 1982, Neisser 1987). Metaphor can be interpreted as substitution across scripts: a term that is normally substituted in a node in a 'base' script, in literal reference, is substituted into a different 'target' script. It is relevant to establish this connection, because it entails that the principle of reciprocation has the same logical form as metaphor. In other words, something very much like metaphor is one of the principles of abduction. This confirms the idea, in the existing literature, that metaphor is an instrument of learning and innovation (e.g. Nonaka & Takeuchi 1995).

Radical architectural innovation, as defined above, may yield a good definition of the notion of 'radical innovation' that plays such a big role in the innovation literature. That is a matter of choice of terminology. The alternative would be to characterize the radicality of innovation according to the level at which the change takes place, such as the level of an industry or even a constellation of industries. Different degrees of innovation can arise at all the different levels of people, organizations, and industries or innovation systems. Note that an innovation that is radical in the first sense, at the level of a firm, for example, may constitute only a minor innovation at a higher level; a mere novel substitution into a node in a higher-level industry script—and vice versa.

> Consider the case, discussed in Chapter 1, of the transformation of tacit knowledge in shipbuilding, in the seventeenth century, into the use of technical drawings of ship design. At the level of ship design it may be seen as a mere 'externalization', as defined by Nonaka and Takeuchi (1995), i.e. a codification of tacit practice. At the level of the industry it caused a radical transformation of industry scripts by reducing transaction costs and by allowing instruction to be brought from the shipyard into a classroom. The designer of a ship no longer needed to participate in the supervision at the yard, because the design could be contracted out to a builder according to precise specifications that formed the basis of a contract. At the level of the industry it was a radical innovation, which contributed to the competitive advantage of the British over the Dutch.

I propose the following choice of terminology. An architectural innovation will be indicated as a radical degree of innovation, and a high level of innovation will be indicated as an innovation with a wide 'scope'. The analysis provides a more precise specification of what in the innovation literature has been called the distinction between innovations 'new for the firm, new for the industry or new for the world'. It also clarifies how 'mere adoption' of something that is widely diffused in an industry may at the firm level require a major architectural innovation in organizational scripts to absorb it.

10.2.2   *Types of Innovation*

We can distinguish producer and consumer scripts. Among other things, a consumer script expresses the fact that some product has value to a user only to the extent that it fits into the user's scripts. That represents part of the product's selection environment.

> An illustration of an elaborate user script is the information system in which the British embedded radar technology. Different radar stations were coupled with each other and with visual detection points to yield input into a system of interpretation and screening, in order to identify aircraft, distinguish between friend and foe, establish height, position, direction, and speed, and to guide aircraft to interception.

Another part of the selection environment is the industry (supply-chain) script into which the product also has to fit, such as supply channels, distribution channels, and procedures for installation, maintenance, and repair. Acceptance of a new product is risky to the extent that it entails an architectural change in consumer or supply-chain scripts. A product is a configuration of 'affordances', i.e. properties that it offers to afford the performance of user scripts. This may entail substitution into a node of a user script, such as a material input, or an instrument. But it can also constitute a node for the user to substitute actions into, such as a machine that he needs to operate. Thus, we might see a car as an input into a consumer script for travelling (with different forms for holiday and work), but we might also see the car as imposing a driving script on the consumer.

A physical product is the output of a process of physical transformation. We can distinguish between a process innovation, which entails a change of producer script, and a product innovation, which entails a change of consumer script. A service product, however, is itself a production script, with customers contributing actions to some of the nodes, in what is often called the 'front-office' part of the producer script. Radical innovation of a physical product can be defined as one that can no longer be fitted to a user script, and requires the user to adopt or develop a novel script. A product innovation may be incremental in the sense that it constitutes a novel substitution into one or more nodes. But a radical service innovation entails a radical change in a producer script to accommodate different activities of the consumer (or industrial customer). Here, the consumer may be the innovator, rather than the producer, if he is allowed to play that role.

What complicates matters further is that many products have aspects of both goods and services, as the car example showed. Even for goods the consumer may be involved in the production process, such as the specification of the configuration of the product that he wants. One of the important implications of information and communication technology is that it allows for such moves. Conversely, it allows services to become more like goods. It used to be customary to characterize services as things that cannot be produced on stock, and that require a coincidence in time and place of production and consumption: the customer is present when the doctor examines or operates on him. Now, increasingly, a customer may access some services at his discretion of time and place, through remote access to a database (e.g. the Internet) or an expert system, which embodies the diagnostic and consulting skills of a specialist, to the extent that the latter's tacit, procedural knowledge can be codified.

10.3   THE HEURISTIC OF DISCOVERY

The heuristic of discovery, developed in Chapter 9, can now be further specified in terms of scripts, to show in more detail how the principles of discovery work.

10.3.1   *The Heuristic Embodied*

The problem of abduction now is: How can a script function as a selection environment, in the form of an organizational practice within the firm, or in the form of a techno-economic paradigm in an industry, and yet be transformed as the script functions? In terms of scripts the heuristic of discovery can now be specified as follows:

Consolidation. Old scripts have been broken up, and in that sense competencies have been destroyed. There is no longer a dominant design that operates as a selection environment, or as a paradigmatic exemplar (or prototype) to guide adaptations across contexts. A novel, emerging script is indeterminate in the sense that the identification and sequencing of nodes (architecture), and effective substitutions into them are unstable: best practice is not yet clear. The novel script is messed up with mismatches between elements combined from earlier scripts, in attempts at novel combinations. Nodes or substitutions are included that do not fit well, or nodes are put in an inappropriate order. But there is no existing norm or model to identify this, and increase in effectiveness or efficiency is a matter of learning by experimenting. As experimentation proceeds, more insight is gained from repeated trials in the context in which the script was first conceived and found to be successful to some extent. By experimentation, the best selection and sequencing of nodes are established, and this yields a dominant design. Efficiency increases through the elimination of redundant nodes and inappropriate substitutions, and a narrowing down to optimal and parsimonious procedures. This proceeds along 'experience curves' (Yelle 1979). This is my rendering of the notion of 'first-order' (or 'single-loop') learning. Once such a dominant design has been established, it functions as the new selection environment for lower-level activities.

Generalization. Next, the script is applied in novel contexts. In economic contexts this entails that a technology is applied in new areas, or products are exported to new markets, or production is relocated. Further streamlining of the dominant design occurs, and on the basis of expanded demand economies of scale are reaped, and specialization occurs: the breaking up of nodes into specialized pieces. Generalization is driven by a possibly instinctive imperialistic drive in life forms to extend their territories; to expand areas of application, to apply ideas to new fields. In economic contexts there is also pressure from competition: as novelty wears out and diffuses, initial partial monopolies erode, competition by new entry increases, and a pressure arises to reduce costs by economy of scale and scope. Demand increases, as consumers become aware of, familiar with, and confident about new products. This produces market opportunities to achieve economy of scale. The resulting fall in price further stimulates demand. The dominant design provides a prototype upon which variations can be made, depending on the context.

Differentiation. As the script is applied in novel contexts, differentiation occurs to adapt to those differences. Subsidiary forms, left over from the period of experimentation prior to consolidation, may be revived. The most proximate form of differentiation, preserving architecture, is parametric change through different substitutions into nodes in different contexts; for example, to adjust for differences in capabilities or desires of customers, capabilities of labour, sources of energy, available materials, technology of maintenance and support, technical standards, etc., in different countries. This will typically develop into a branching of a general script into different branches for different contexts. Together, the stages of generalization and differentiation can be seen as incremental innovation, which is cumulative: building upon past performance.

Reciprocation. As anomalies and misfits accumulate, the limits of the script's potential become visible, and observations accumulate which indicate that elements (nodes) from other practices (scripts), performing similar functions, appear to perform better. They are seen to eliminate shortcomings or offer opportunities for satisfying different demands. This leads to the borrowing of novel substitutions from those nodes, and next the adoption of entire nodes, in metaphorical transfer.

Novel combinations. As differentiation and reciprocation proceed, scripts become messy, inefficient, and inconsistent. Novel substitutions or nodes put strain on the script's architecture: they do not fit in the existing ordering of nodes and associated conditions imposed on inputs into and outputs from nodes. Above all, novel substitutions are not utilized to their full potential, because of constraints imposed by existing architecture. To allow for their full utilization, constraints have to be modified, but this has implications for the substitutions allowed in other nodes. This yields a proliferation of alternative branches for different contexts. As a result, the same nodes appear at different locations in the architecture, different nodes have overlapping substitutions, opportunities for utilizing economy of scale are missed, and there is an accumulation of anomalies. As a result of increasing structural complexity there are

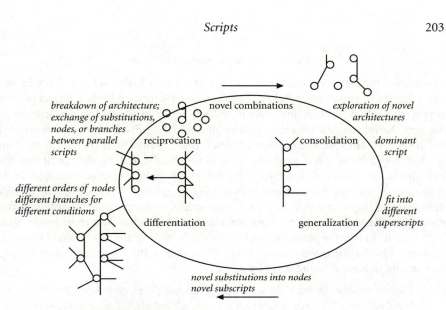

breakdown of architecture;
exchange of substitutions,
nodes, or branches
between parallel
scripts

novel combinations

exploration of novel
architectures

reciprocation

consolidation

dominant
script

different orders of nodes
different branches for
different conditions

differentiation

generalization

fit into
different
superscripts

novel substitutions into nodes
novel subscripts

FIGURE 10.1   *Cycle of script formation*

diminishing returns in further importation of novelty. All this yields pressures for a more fundamental redesign. Changes reverberate through the architecture, in several iterations, leading up to a novel architecture. Substitutions are reassembled into new nodes, and nodes are reconfigured into new architectures. Here, we are back at the initial stage of consolidation. At the beginning of this stage knowledge is largely tacit. During consolidation a novel technological regime develops (dominant design), with documented knowledge and standardized procedures (Boisot 1995).

> One example is the innovation of self-service in retailing (Nooteboom 1984). In service, customers are stationary, waiting at a counter, while the staff scuttle about to collect the orders. In self-service this is switched: customers walk along the aisles to select the goods and the staff are stationary at a checkout. Advantages are the following: Time spent by customers is substituted for time spent by staff. One can have a larger shop surface with more goods (in the case of service this would be prohibited by the need for staff to run up and down over-long distances). Shelves can be stocked at times of low custom, thus improving the utilization of both labour and space. Walking through the shop, customers may receive an impulse to buy more than they would have without inspecting the shelves. Inspecting the goods on the shelves is more enjoyable for the customer than waiting at the counter. An enabling condition was that customers became sufficiently familiar with the goods so that they no longer needed advice from attendants.

The elaboration of the cycle of discovery in terms of script formation is illustrated in Figure 10.1.

10.3.2   *Industries, Firms, and Users*

Processes at the firm level and the industry level are linked. The industry level, i.e. the constellation of competitors, users, suppliers, distributors, and other, lateral players supplying enabling constraints, constitutes part of the institutional environment of the firm. Novel substitutions into nodes of industrial scripts, by firms offering novel products, typically (but not necessarily) result from architectural changes at the firm level, although these will in general not yet have consolidated. To the extent that the industrial script cannot accept the novel substitution without changes elsewhere in its structure, the innovation has trouble in gaining acceptance. Thus, there may be lack of fit with existing user scripts or distribution scripts, or competitors may block entry. As a result, the early use of an innovation may not occur where it is most productive, but where its fit into the prevailing architecture is feasible with a minimum of systemic changes. This explains why innovations often realize their potential only in due course, and in areas distant from first usage.

> Consider the development of the semiconductor industry (Teece 1988, Stoelhorst 1997), mentioned in Chapter 1. It started with the transistor as a substitute for the vacuum tube—in the script model: a novel substitution into the node of amplification, in scripts representing the architecture of a radio. But its potential went further: its greater reliability, greater speed, lower power use and lower heat dissipation opened up opportunities for much more complex electrical systems. But the manual soldering of the connections between the discrete components formed a bottleneck: it was expensive and generated too many errors. Ultimately, the answer was to make a range of components (resistors and capacitors next to amplifiers) in the same silicon technology, and integrate them in an overall system including connections between them. This constituted a major architectural change.

I noted that scripts could also be used to represent the competence of consumers, or of users more generally. Some products can be seen as requiring fit in user scripts, while others can be seen as requiring consumers to fit their competencies into a node of a script imposed by the product. The heuristic of discovery also applies to user scripts. In the case of a novel use, users have to settle on their dominant pattern of use, in a process of consolidation. As products are applied in novel ways user competence will be differentiated. Users may reciprocate their competence when making comparisons with the practices of other users, or comparing the use of one product with that of another. This may engender new user practices, or desires for new practices. In this way the heuristic of discovery can also be used to model preference formation. That also is seen as essentially a social process: it is typically by comparison with use processes of relevant other users that preferences are formed, through a process of reciprocation. Burt (1987) found that in the diffusion of innovations, imitation or 'contagion' does not just arise from contagion by contact, as is assumed in most models of diffusion. Imitation depends on who is already using the innovation. In particular, it depends on whether he is 'structurally equivalent', i.e. on whether he occupies a similar position in social networks. Only then is he likely to serve as a role model. Here, structural equivalence can perhaps be associated with similar or shared 'superscripts' into which user scripts are embedded.

10.3.3 Self-organization

In Chapter 4 it was suggested, and this suggestion was repeated in Chapter 9, that for the issue of exploitation and exploration the perspective of self-organization may be more fitting than the perspective of evolution.[1] The notion of self-organization emerges from the literature on complex adaptive systems. For a recent survey, see Khalil and Boulding (1996). Perhaps the heuristic of discovery set out in Chapter 9 and elaborated in this Chapter can be seen as constituting general principles of self-organization.

Khalil (1998: 11–18) defined 'natural order' as an order for which there is no agent who stands outside it to manipulate the order. This is what Dupuy (1998) called an 'autonomous system'. Khalil distinguished two kinds. One kind is 'systems' that have mere 'structure', i.e. a set of elements and relations between them which can entail order in the form of deterministic chaos, irreversible thermodynamics, non-linear dynamics, etc. Here, elements interact chaotically or 'stochastically', but without any organizing purpose, and as a result the system is not adaptive. Another kind of natural order is 'complexes' that have 'organization', which entails a unifying set of goals shared by the members of the set that allows for 'organic' interaction and adaptation. The difference between market and organization according to Khalil is that markets entail stochastic interaction on the basis of separate, individual self-interest, while organization entails 'organic' interaction on the basis of common goals.

Compare this with my characterization of an organization as a 'focusing device', as discussed in Chapter 3. However, there the 'focus' relates not only to common purpose but also to joint perception and understanding, in a reduction of cognitive distance. As I do in this book (Chapter 5), Khalil adopts notions from Aristotelian causality, and characterizes organization as including final causes (the joint purpose). But the question of course is: How does the organic interaction in an organization work? How does it deal with the problem of exploitation and exploration? Khalil does not answer that question.

A basic intuition in complexity theory is that adaptive or self-organizing systems have a hierarchy, or different levels. Dupuy (1998: 71) proposed that the appropriate method to study social systems is neither 'top-down', with a subordination of elements and their relations to the totality, nor 'bottom-up', with a deduction of the properties of the totality from those of fully specified elements. 'The whole and its parts are mutually determined, and this co-determination explains the complexity of living things'.

Compare this with my proposal of rejecting both methodological individualism and methodological collectivism, in favour of 'methodological interactionism'. The

---

[1] However, perhaps evolution itself can be seen as a process of self-organization.

notion of a script offers a model of a 'whole' (the script) that incorporates 'parts' in the form of nodes. The nesting of scripts offers a hierarchy of different levels. My proposal of a cycle of discovery entails a circular causality between the whole and the parts. The stage of consolidation yields a new whole (script), in the form of a competence that guides efficient use of resources (substitutions into nodes) and provides a basis for generalization. This is how the 'whole' regulates the 'parts'. However, as applications spread across novel contexts, differentiation and reciprocation occur, which put the whole under increasing pressure, until it breaks down and novel 'wholes' (architectures of scripts) are formed, with novel combinations of parts from previous wholes (nodes from different scripts). This is how the 'parts' determine the 'whole'.

Dupuy (1998: 73) proposed that 'the most fundamental concept in the theory of autonomous systems is the emergence of behavior proper to the system (*eigenbehaviors*)'. This is also known as 'systemic effects'. Dupuy assigns this to an 'endogenous fixed point', which is as much an effect as a cause in the system. The identity of the whole is not transcendent but emergent from itself. In crowds, it is 'produced by the crowd although the crowd believes itself to have been produced by it'. It may be connected with the *leader*. Love of the leader spreads by contagion, which creates his leadership (Dupuy 1998: 74). Leadership is not built on any intrinsic features of the leader, but is a systemic effect. I add that this makes it understandable how a leader can function without any apparent capabilities (as in the case of royalty). His capability as an 'endogenous fixed point' is produced for him by the crowd, but for the leader to function this cannot be recognized, and so the myth is created that his leadership is invested in him from some external fixed point. This could be God in the case of royalty and shareholders in the case of a firm. While the fixed point is in fact endogenous and emergent, it is masked as external and transcendent.

Compare this, again, with my notion of the firm as a focusing device. Here, it is not necessarily only the leader who constitutes the endogenous fixed point. It may also reside in organizational culture, in the form of symbols, myths, heroes, and rituals. The shared categories (of perception, interpretation, and evaluation) that form the focus of the firm constitute 'endogenous fixed points', which emerge in the organization itself. They are emergent, systemic effects. As noted by Dupuy (1998: 78), this was recognized by Hayek, who 'echoes Durkheim's claim that the categories of human thought are irreducible to individual experience and cannot be recapitulated by any form of consciousness'. This perspective further underpins the notion of 'methodological interactionism' proposed in this book.

Zeleny (1998: 125) proposed that social systems:

are networks characterized by inner co-ordination of individual action achieved through communication among temporary agents. The key words are co-ordination, communication, and limited individual life span. Co-ordinated behaviour includes both co-operation and competition.

This echoes Khalil's idea that complex systems entail organization in the form of shared purpose. Zeleny (1998: 135) defined social organization as:

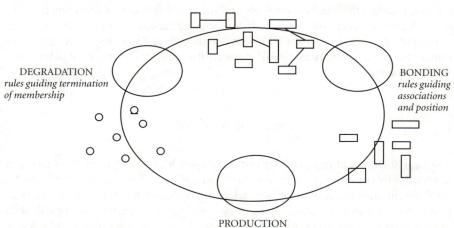

FIGURE 10.2 *Zeleny's circular causation*
Source: Zeleny (1998: 136).

a network of interactions, reactions, and processes involving, at least: production (the rules and regulations guiding the entry of new living components), bonding or linkage (the rules of guiding associations, functions, and positions of individuals during their tenure within the organization), degradation or disintegration (the rules and processes associated with the termination of membership).

This is illustrated in Figure 10.2.

Compare all this with my proposal of a heuristic of discovery, and compare Figure 10.2 with the representation of my cycle of discovery in Figure 10.1. I have modelled co-ordination in terms of scripts, with the nodes as the temporary elements. At the level of organizational scripts, the nodes entail actions by people. As explained before, the individuality of the people involved, whose organizational activities entail scripts that overlap with their scripts 'qua persona' (Ring & van de Ven 1994), is crucial. It is a source of both error and innovation.

So, if my theory of discovery fits into concepts and theories of complexity and self-organization, what does it add? I propose that, as already indicated, it adds the insight as to how circular causality between whole and parts might work, in an alternation of variety of content and variety of context, which goes together with an alternation of top-down and bottom-up causality. On the basis of trial and error, variety of content narrows down to a dominant design, which acts as a prototype for proliferation across different contexts (top-down). This yields new variety of content through the shedding of old parts and the adoption of new ones, leading on to a breakdown of the whole (bottom-up), and a reconfiguration of a novel set of parts into a tentative new whole that again needs to consolidate. I show how this process can combine exploitation and exploration: they provide the basis for each other. I move beyond a general concept of self-organization that applies across natural and social systems, by founding the process in human characteristics of knowledge, language, and communication, discussed in Chapters 6 and 7. In Chapter 8 I elaborated the role and workings of communication, in the crossing and reduction of cognitive distance, and the issues of governance that it involves.

10.4   CONCLUSION

The heuristic cycle of discovery set out in Chapter 9 can be elaborated in terms of scripts. For this purpose the script notion was modified to allow for different branches for different conditions, probabilistic selection, openness to change, and variety of interpretation and application. A recursive nesting of scripts was proposed, with industrial scripts, organizational scripts, scripts for teams or communities of practice, scripts for people contributing their actions or ideas, going down into neural structures in the brain. This provides the basis for a multilevel theory of people, organizations, and industries or innovation systems. It also enables a distinction between different degrees of innovation: parametric innovation through novel substitutions into nodes, novel ordering of existing nodes, radical innovation through novel assemblies of nodes from different scripts. It also enables a distinction between consumer and producer scripts, as a basis for discussing different kinds of goods and services according to their relation to such scripts. The script notion can be used for a coherent, systematic, multilevel elaboration of the notions of institutions, selection environments, organizational processes, competencies, and skills.

Perhaps the heuristic of discovery can be seen as constituting general principles of self-organization.

11

Integration and Disintegration

In industries the cycle of discovery is associated with a cycle of organizational integration and disintegration. However, (dis)integration also depends on a host of other factors, related to the institutional environment. In this Chapter, those are specified and it is shown how they connect with the cycle of discovery.

11.1   A CYCLE OF (DIS)INTEGRATION

Some stages in the cycle of learning and development require integration of activities, with strong ties, and others require disintegration, with loose ties among a variety of autonomous units. The connection between the cycle of discovery and the cycle of integration and disintegration depends on a number of conditions concerning market, technology, and institutions.

11.1.1   *Discovery, Integration, and Disintegration*

Radical innovation, with novel combinations, entails a redefinition and a reconfiguration of nodes into novel scripts, and hence requires a break-up of existing scripts (creative destruction). This entails organizational disintegration. That may in turn entail the break-up of a firm, or decentralization into highly autonomous units. The connection between change and disintegration is in line with a long-standing tradition in the management and organization literature. It has been said long ago that stable, predictable environments require a 'mechanistic', bureaucratic structure, while volatile, unpredictable environments require a looser, organic structure (Burns & Stalker 1961, Emery & Trist 1965, Thompson 1967). More recently, Stinchcombe (1990) proposed that variety of information sources requires organizational disintegration.

In the present discussion, 'integrated structure' is synonymous with 'mechanistic' and 'bureaucratic' structure, and 'disintegrated' structure is synonymous with 'organic' structure. This could cause misunderstanding. R. M. Kanter (1983) used the term 'integration' to refer to conceptual integration of what was previously separated; the crossing of boundaries; the break-up of existing, rigidly 'compartmentalized', structures. Here, by contrast, the term 'integration' is used to refer to organizational integration: co-ordination and the limitation of autonomy. For integration in the sense used by Kanter I use the Schumpeterian term 'novel combinations'.

Note that, as discussed before, I evade talk only of small versus large firms, because one can have connected firms in industrial districts and disconnected units within 'virtual firms'. It is the degree of integration of activities that counts, in different forms of organization between market and hierarchy. In Chapter 5 (Figure 5.1) a distinction was used between integration of property in the sense of claims to residual profit, and integration of residual decision rights. The most extreme form of organizational disintegration is autonomous units, under separate ownership, which engage in pure, arm's-length market transactions. Separately owned units can become more or less integrated, in the sense of losing autonomy of decision making and freedom of choice, by more or less constraining governance of interfirm relations. This can entail more or less long-term, more or less detailed contracts; mutual dependence through dedicated investments or exchange of hostages, or other switching costs; routinization; building of trust. Next, units can become integrated under unified ownership, within a single firm. Within the firm, units can be more or less integrated in terms of centralization and hierarchical control. This depends on the tightness, rigidity, and type of co-ordination. These more detailed aspects of (dis)integration go beyond the scope of this book (for an exposition, see Nooteboom 1999g).

In terms of scripts, the size of an organization is determined by the throughput of scripts (scale), the number of nodes, and the extent to which nodes of scripts lie within the boundaries of the firm. The strength and tightness of linkages between the nodes determine the degree of integration. Economy of scale occurs when cost of node capacity increases less than proportionately with throughput. Economy of scope depends on the extent to which different practices have shared substitutions (overlapping extensions of nodes) or shared nodes. Economies of integration depend on the extent that outputs from one practice serve as inputs for another and carry transaction costs.

There still is a significant difference between large and small firms, but it concerns not so much technical efficiency as governance and management of meaning. As indicated in transaction-cost economics, hierarchy yields opportunities to claim information for monitoring and possibilities for conflict resolution which exceed those among independent firms. As proposed in Chapter 3, the core function of a firm is to act as a focusing device and to provide shared meanings; to align perceptions, interpretations, and evaluations in order to achieve a common goal. However, both governance and common perception and understanding can also be achieved to a varying extent in various forms of organization between market and hierarchy.

The proposition now is that in industries the cycle of discovery is associated with a cycle of organizational integration and disintegration, as illustrated in Figure 11.1.

Broadly speaking, the generation of novelty, at the stages of reciprocation and architectural innovation (novel combinations), requires more or less disintegrated structures, in highly decentralized firms, with a high degree of autonomy, or industrial districts of independent firms. Consolidation and generalization require more or less integrated structures, within firms or in tightly connected networks of firms. Differentiation requires an intermediate mode, with loosely co-ordinated networks or large

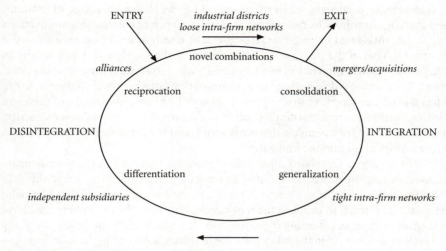

FIGURE 11.1   *Cycle of integration and disintegration*

firms with relatively independent subsidiaries. However, this is a broad generalization that is subject to many technological, organizational, and institutional contingencies.

11.1.2   Contingencies

Let us consider radical, architectural innovations (novel combinations). The need for disintegration depends on whether the innovation is competence-enhancing or competence-destroying (Abernathy & Clark 1985).

> In their study of technological discontinuities in passenger-airline transport (1924–80), Portland cement (1872–1980), and minicomputers (1956–80), Tushman and Anderson (1986) identified a series of six competence-enhancing and two competence-destroying discontinuities. As one would expect, the latter are more favourable to new entrants and the former to incumbent firms. Only two competence-destroying discontinuities were found. One was the switch to the process of burning powdered coal as fuel in cement (1896), which made the existing know-how for wood-fired kilns obsolete. The other was the use of integrated circuits in minicomputers (1965), which rendered the assembly of transistor-based computers obsolete. They both occurred relatively early in the development of the industries. The switch to semiconductor memory in 1971 was competence-destroying for memory manufacturers, but not for the computer manufacturers who used it. The two competence-destroying discontinuities were largely pioneered by new firms, while the six competence-enhancing discontinuities were almost exclusively introduced by established industry members (p. 455). As predicted, the ratio of entries to exits declined after competence-enhancing discontinuities. Contrary to prediction, entry-to-exit ratios were higher before than after competence-destroying discontinuities (p. 457).

Competence-destroying innovations are said to be to the advantage of entrants, and thereby contribute to disintegration, while competence-enhancing innovations perpetuate integrated incumbents. However, the question is: Whose competence is destroyed? That of the producer, the consumer, or the supply chain as a whole? In Chapter 10, radical innovation was identified with architectural innovation: a novel script. Thus, at the industrial level radical innovation entails a novel consumer script, a novel producer script, a novel supply-chain script, or any combination of these. An innovation that destroys consumer competence, i.e. requires a novel consumer script, has a large risk of failure, unless this novel script, and the consumer's introduction to it, are incorporated into the innovation.

The implications for relative advantage of an entrant versus an incumbent firm are no longer straightforward. If the innovation entails a novel producer script, this is to the advantage of an entrant, unless of course the innovator was an incumbent who transformed himself to produce the innovation. However, the incumbent may have gained advantages in collecting the experience that yields novel combinations, along the cycle of discovery. On the other hand, he may have got stuck in the inertia of consolidation and generalization, and then the entrant is at an advantage. Destruction of consumer competence or supply-chain competence may be to the disadvantage of an incumbent, because he has vested interests in the old structure. However, precisely for that reason the incumbent may be in a better position to tailor the new institutions to a form of innovation that suits his purpose. Recall the discussion, in Chapter 4, of the fact that the selection of innovations is to a greater or lesser extent socially constructed. Incumbents may be at an advantage here.

Taking into account the role of distance discussed in previous Chapters, we find that novel combinations are promoted by a constellation of separate, relatively small, weakly connected, spatially proximate units in complementary activities ('industrial districts' or autonomous units in large firms). In such constellations, a number of requirements are satisfied. Sufficient cognitive proximity is needed to be able to understand each other, and trust is needed to do without complex, detailed, costly, constraining contracts, and to contain risks of spillover. These requirements are satisfied on the basis of shared norms and values of conduct, the bonding of family, clan, or friendship, an efficient reputation mechanism, the 'shadow of the future' from expected dealings with each other in the future, or shared routines. Sufficient cognitive distance to offer each other novel insights is achieved through variety in activity and experience. There is sufficient spatial proximity to allow for frequent and varied contacts, and for intensive interaction in partial joint production, needed for the transfer of tacit, procedural knowledge, which is characteristic of the early stages of innovation. Here, competition is not on price but on novelty.

Opportunity for disintegrated structures is also related to the absence of disadvantages that they have in other stages of development. Small, independent units are not so good at orchestrating many parts of a system to innovate in tune (Teece 1986, 1988, Chesbrough & Teece 1996), but, since we are dealing here with radical innovations, in 'novel combinations', which break up existing systems, that yields no obstacle. Tacit, procedural knowledge has the disadvantage of lacking the basis for formalized procedures with documented communication that is needed for large-scale production, with specialization in different departments. But at the early stage of innovation both the opportunity and the need for large scale are absent. There is no opportunity because the market is still small. There is no need because as a result of initial monopoly, pressure from competition on costs is weak.

Large, integrated firms can survive or indeed create the discontinuities of novel combinations by means of decentralization of highly autonomous divisions or even individual 'intrapreneurs', with sufficiently weak ties. But there are limits to the variety that can be created and sustained in a large firm. How can one foresee the kinds of variety that might become relevant? In the extreme case, to create that variety the large firm would have to engage in practically everything, allowing for any combinations, and what then remains of the notion of an organizational script? It would become a script with no limitations to nodes and their substitutions, no architecture, and one could no longer speak of a firm. It seems necessary to also maintain a readiness to mop up successful small innovators, in order to tap into a variety of independent firms that would be hard to reproduce within the firm. Moreover, to benefit from their advantages of integration large firms must also maintain a capability for systemic alignment, with strong ties, in the later stages of consolidation and in the stage of generalization. In this way it is conceivable that a large firm combines the best of two worlds. While it is not easy to perform this balancing act (Nooteboom 1989), it is conceivable, and indeed appears to be achieved by firms such as the 3M company and INTEL. However, an illustration of how difficult this is is given by the recent federalization of IBM, which was instituted to compete with more flexible, specialized, and independent firms. This subject of ways to combine exploitation and exploration within a firm will be taken up in Chapter 13.

At the stage of consolidation, with the search for a dominant design, it is important that there is flexibility to try out various combinations and forms, and that misfits are efficiently weeded out. Here also lies the strength of the variety and autonomy of small, independent units. We run into a second restriction in the mimicry of industrial districts by large firms. The efficiency in the elimination of failures, in *ex post* selection, becomes doubtful because of the possibility of propping them up with cross-subsidization from successful products in a portfolio.[1] Depending on the selection environment of markets and institutions such practices are not necessarily weeded out.

> Examples of small firms running ahead in commercialization are: semiconductors and computer-aided design (Rothwell & Zegveld 1985), microcomputers (Langlois & Robertson 1995), self-service retailing (Nooteboom 1984).

On the other hand, at the stage of generalization, after consolidation, integrated structures are better at large-volume production and distribution of novel products in

---

[1] In that sense they are not efficient from a societal perspective, but that of course still leaves the possibility for their existence.

wider world markets. A dominant design has emerged. Tacit, procedural knowledge has been developed into declarative, documented knowledge, which allows for transfer across larger distances. At the same time, increase of scale is feasible with the growth of demand, and is necessary to reduce costs as a result of increasing competition, as patents wear out and imitation increases. Competition has shifted from novelty to price. This favours larger production units, integrated distribution channels, spreading of risks, access to finance, and the umbrella of a brand name, on the basis of penetration into extended markets. This in turn favours a larger, more international, and more integrated firm, with tight control of interfaces between nodes in scripts. Integrated structures are better at the development of coherent systems of connecting technologies, distribution systems, industry structures, supporting infrastructure, and technical and commercial standards, yielding the configuration of a novel techno-economic paradigm.

Next, as generalization turns into differentiation and reciprocation, comparative advantage shifts again to a greater variety of scripts, in more autonomous divisions, subsidiaries, or independent firms, to give room for the generation of variety by reciprocation, in preparation for the next round of more fundamental innovation. Differentiation of products and processes also contributes to an escape from pure price competition between identical products that developed from generalization. Small firms, or independent units within large firms, are better at product differentiation in niche markets, where they do not run into disadvantages of small-scale production and can benefit from flexibility and proximity to customers.

11.1.3   Internationalization

The product-cycle theory of Vernon (1966) suggests that when multinational companies (MNCs) invest in other countries, this is based on standardized technology, organization, and management, so that in the host countries we should find no R & D or design, and only simple, standardized production with cheap labour. This is contradicted by recent research. Not only production but design and development also are transferred to host countries, and subsidiaries of MNCs demand, and are given, considerable room for local differentiation of product, production, and distribution (Bartlett & Goshal 1989, Storper 1997, Glimstedt 1999). MNCs are said to 'tap into' local complementary competencies (Bartlett & Goshal 1989, Glimstedt 1999). The MNC 'appears to use its tentacles to acquire from each country its excellence in research rather than to decentralize its brain' (Archibugi & Michie 1997: 189, quoted in Glimstedt 1999: 10). Rather than cloning their products and processes the MNCs specialize by location (Storper 1997). Conceivably, the latitude for foreign subsidiaries to adapt products and technologies is not given by design but results from sheer inability of headquarters to co-ordinate across a multitude of countries.[2] However, empirical research into patent data confirms that increasingly firms conduct R & D

---

[2] Personal communication from Richard Whitley.

abroad, to adjust and develop their products and technologies abroad, tapping into local competencies and resources (Cantwell and Piscitello 1999*a*/*b*).

The cycle of discovery and (dis)integration would explain such phenomena. Like the old industrial life-cycle theory of innovation to which it is related, the product-cycle theory of internationalization neglects the importance for discovery, and ongoing innovation, of exploration by differentiation and reciprocation. If MNCs are to survive through combining exploration with exploitation they must allow for decentralization and differentiation. As explained in the theory of knowledge, expounded in previous Chapters, they must employ external economy of cognitive scope and indeed 'tap into' complementary competence, including cognitive competence, in the host country.

As explained in the new internationalization literature, this has implications for national policy. One should try to employ incoming foreign direct investment (FDI) from advanced foreign companies as an occasion for contributing one's local resources and competencies to serve the functions of differentiation and reciprocation, and thereby benefit from complementarity between the foreign and the domestic (Glimstedt 1999). This suggests that rather than convergence of economic systems across the globe, specialized local conditions, including institutions, may provide a basis for competitive advantage of nations.

11.1.4   *Timing and Emphasis*

The speed at which pressures for integration and disintegration arise, along the cycle of innovation, depends on the duration of the cycle, and the extent of integration depends on the need and the type of standardization.

At the level of idea formation by individuals the cycle can be quite fast: it can turn around in an hour or a day. Product cycles vary enormously. In financial services and some fashion goods the cycle can be a year; in cars, computers, and machine tools two to four years; in major construction projects five to seven years; in pharmaceuticals and telecommunications infrastructure ten to fifteen years (Quinn 1992). The key question is not just how long the cycle is, but whether there is a mismatch between the cycle for the product and the cycle for production. Generally, production systems have long cycles if they are embodied in large sunk investments in the form of dedicated hardware (such as factories). They have short cycles when they entail craft production with tools that can easily be replaced or professional work on the basis of knowledge or skill that can easily be updated.

If the cycle of the production system is long, because of a large, fixed, sunk cost in durable hardware, and the product cycle is short, there is a problem. This problem can be solved at least to some extent if novel products can be made by novel assemblies of components, according to an enduring technology of assembly, or if the production system has the flexibility to adapt product forms in small batches because it is programmable.

Organizational change requires restructuring of organizational scripts, involving a redistribution of people across tasks or a reconstitution of tasks, goals, motives, perspectives, shared meanings. In industrial districts it requires entry and exit of firms and the building of new network relations. Such developments tend to take a long time, especially if they require a change of the 'deep structure' of organizational culture, such as basic categories of perception, interpretation, and evaluation (Schein 1985). Restructuring of systems of production, supply, and distribution also takes a long time. Increasingly, the problem of inertia lies in organizational culture and distribution systems rather than production technology.

> According to the study of technological discontinuities in the cement industry by Tushman and Anderson (1986) it took twenty-three years to move from the Rotary kiln to the Edison long kiln (1896–1909) and sixty years to move to the Dundee kiln with process control. In the airline industry it took twenty-two years to move from the generation of the Boeing 247, Douglas DC2, and DC3 (with the DC3 as the dominant design, in 1937) to the era of the jet aircraft, with the Boeing 707 (1959). Next, it took ten years to establish the wide-body jets, with the Boeing 747 (1969). In the minicomputer industry it took only two years to move from transistors to integrated circuits (in 1964), and seven years to move to semiconductor memories. The speed of movement to integrated circuits derived from the strong pressure to eliminate the constraints that limited the realization of the potential of semiconductors imposed by the assembly of different components of different materials, as discussed elsewhere.

The duration and prominence of different stages within the cycle can also vary considerably. This depends, for example, on the intensity of competition and its pressure for change. It also depends on how important product differentiation and economy of scale are, and of what type economy of scale is. Product differentiation depends on the type of product and customer. In fashions in prosperous countries product differentiation is essential. Engineering economy of scale is crucial in process industries. Economy of scale in the use of information technology has declined enormously with the advent of microcomputers and user-friendly software. In some markets there is enormous economy of scale in marketing: in brand name, advertising, and distribution.

When product differentiation is crucial, economy of scale is limited or absent, and no major discontinuities in production technology occur, industrial districts can last for long periods of time. This is to be expected in fashion goods, where automation is difficult in some of the activities involved, such as cutting and assembling clothes, which yields a limit to economy of scale, while product differentiation and speedy response are crucial. On the other hand, when economy of scale is crucial and the product is hardly differentiable, large, tightly integrated companies can persist for a long time.

> Illustrations of the longevity of industrial districts are found in abundance in Italy (Malerba 1993): in fashion, shoes, and furniture. These satisfy the conditions: great importance of differentiation, low production economies of scale. As indicated by Malerba, a problem may be that information technology may to some extent be competence-destroying, in that for effective use it cannot be simply attached to existing production but requires its redesign. It may require a change of production scripts. Another consideration is that, as indicated above, there can be large effects of

scale in marketing: distribution channels and brand name. The prediction would be that in fashion-oriented industrial districts there is, or will be, a tendency for the emergence of central, and perhaps dominant, parties that provide this marketing. This is confirmed by the case of Benetton. Here, the economies of scale in marketing and brand name are combined with economy of scale in the provision of the ICT network which co-ordinates flexible, differentiated production with speedy and efficient response to shifts in fashion.

An illustration of the longevity of large, tightly integrated firms is the oil industry. This satisfies the conditions of large economy of scale, in the exploration and production of crude oil, the refining and distribution of oil, and the spread of political risk in having access to crude oil at diverse locations, while the product is hardly differentiable. The prediction is that those firms will be in trouble when product differentiation does appear, as is happening in the chemical industry. Combination of oil with chemicals made sense from the perspective that the feedstock for most chemicals is a derivative from oil (naphta), as long as bulk products that fitted the large-scale-process mode of production dominated the market. But the rationale is disappearing in the short term because of the emergence of low-volume, high-added-value chemical specialities and 'designer chemicals', which require a shift from undifferentiated bulk production far from the market to close market interaction for low-volume specialized products. In fact, there have been intensive debates in Shell Oil Company on whether the organization should effect a turnaround in this direction. It seems that the resistance to this has prevailed, probably rightly so: the transformation would be too big.[3] The expectation now is that Shell will hive off its chemicals division. In the longer term, however, threats emerge also for oil: solar energy, which entails an entirely different production technology and distribution structure; hydrogen fuel, which does not fit the installed base for distribution of oil.

Some markets have a dual structure: a large segment for standardized products and small, niche markets for specialized, differentiated products. Examples are clothing and shoes. For the first segment one would expect more integrated and for the latter more disintegrated structures. And this is indeed what is found.

11.1.5 Collapsing the Cycle?

Do we really need standardization, with the resulting need for integration? Perhaps we can interpret the revolution in the organization of firms that is currently taking place as the disappearance of standards and integration. Then the cycle of innovation would collapse. Can we do without standardization and enduring organizational structure? Can exploration be instant and continuous? Can we do without integration, and retain ongoing disintegration? Bennis (1969) already predicted the death of bureaucracy, because all environments become turbulent, permitting only organic, disintegrated structures (quoted in Buchanan & Boddy 1992: 35).

---

[3] Personal communication from Ernst Homburg, who is conducting a study of the development of the chemical industry.

From the analysis it follows that this is conceivable when efficient production (exploitation) does not require standardization, scaling up, and division of labour, and when the product requires ongoing customization from the very beginning. This is approximated most closely in craft production and professional services, such as consultancy. But even there the paradox of exploitation and reciprocation appears, though in a more limited fashion.

> Take, for example, the consultancy firm Arthur Andersen, which is often proposed as a paradigm example of a flexible firm. Its consultants are highly autonomous, employing their individual knowledge, skill, and creativity to provide custom-made advice. But, even there, attempts are made to safeguard professional standards and quality. For example, this is needed to ensure consistent quality across different locations of a multinational customer. Moreover, measures must be taken so that different consultants make use of each other's experience in order not to reinvent the wheel all the time. Scale is exploited by requiring consultants to contribute their experience to a common pool, and to work together. This requires incentive systems for consultants to volunteer their experience to the common pool. That requires that they be judged and promoted at least in part on the basis of such contributions, weighted by their usefulness, measured by the extent that colleagues make successful use of them. The common pool requires a certain minimal amount of standardization of concepts and procedures in a thesaurus. The question would still be to what extent such fixity of meanings and categories hampers exploration. It would require special measures to allow and prepare for shifts of meaning, which requires a certain amount of standardization of definitions and procedures.

Another way to escape the cycle is not to engage in production at all, but to act as an orchestrator of the productive activities of others. ICT increasingly yields the opportunities for this.

> Quinn (1992) gives the example of a company in custom-made ASICS (Application Specific Integrated Circuits). They interface with clients directly by means of ICT, to determine functional specifications. They then employ their own specialized software to convert this into photo masks, which are sent by ICT to a company in Japan for etching; next, to a company in Korea for dicing and mounting; next, to Malaysia for assembly, from where the chip is flown directly to the customer. A similar example in sports shoes is Nike. Another example is Benetton: it also performs the task of orchestration, by means of ICT, of a decentralized network of individual producers and retailers.

Rather than refuting the cycle of innovation, these examples show how the orchestrator conducts exploration by flexibly exploiting the productive competencies of different companies, in shifting configurations, and thereby tries to escape the need and the dangers of inertia. The risk of inertia as a result of standardized, more or less fixed systems for efficient production is hived off to other players. But, even here, the focal, orchestrating firm must be careful to both maintain and develop its core competence of orchestration.

When standards are not embodied in hardware that represents a large sunk cost (such as cables and switches in telecommunication systems), but in software (as in communication by radio), and it is possible at low cost to translate between different standards by slotting in translation software, then there would seem to be no need for any dominant design. Competing, differentiated standards may remain differentiated from the start, in ongoing differentiation and reciprocation.[4] However, that would imply that the competing standards would not be appropriable, and how then do firms obtain the reward for their investment and risk taking? This conundrum is in fact with us: some firms freely distribute their system via the Internet. One explanation is that in doing so they quickly obtain a large user base, which gives them detailed information on usage and preferences, down to individual users, which provides a basis for further added-value services geared to individual preferences. It is, so to speak, not the technical system but the customer base that becomes the core competence.

> An example is the famous case of American Hospital Supplies (AHS). They started with dedicated hardware in the form of terminals that captured customers. New intermediaries who provided an interface for linkage with other suppliers broke this captivity. But AHS had meanwhile added services, partly based on their accumulated knowledge of client wishes and procedures, and thereby created ongoing customer captivity.

Does this invalidate the cycle of innovation? Perhaps it does. But the logic underlying the cycle still helps to analyse the conditions for such instant exploration.

11.2   FURTHER DETERMINANTS

It is important to note that the stage in the cycle of innovation yields only one determinant of (dis)integration, and there are many other qualifying or modulating conditions. It has already been mentioned that the speed of the cycle and the salience of its stages can vary between industries, as a function of economy of scale and differentiability of products. But there is more. First, there are institutional effects. Second, there are effects following from transaction costs, or, more generally, problems of co-ordination. These problems can be solved in several ways, and these alternatives have implications for organizational integration or disintegration.

11.2.1   *Institutional Effects*

The theme of organizational (dis)integration of economic activities goes back to Adam Smith and Marshall. The latter included the role of location and distance, in agglomeration effects, in his notion of industrial districts. Here, I collect more recent insights into the causes of and reasons for (dis)integration. At this point, recall again

---

[4] This insight emerged in a discussion at the Netherlands Institute for Advanced Studies (NIAS) with Henrik Glimstedt.

TABLE 11.1   *Conditions of (dis)integration*

Aristotelian cause	Interpretation	Aspects
final	incentives	dependent on firm size or profitability, short- or long-term results, status, reputation effects, etc.
efficient	labour	flexibility of hiring/firing, duration of employment, education/training
material	material inputs	need for backward integration, as a function of obstacles to access to inputs
formal	knowledge, technology	scale and scope, bridging institutions, tacitness, level of abstraction, speed of change, systemic or stand-alone, flexibility, modularity, availability of standards
conditional	time and space	transaction costs as a function of physical and communication infrastructure
	chains	supply-chain structure
	regulation	contract and property law, appropriability, anti-trust law, etc.
	categorical	ethics and habits of collaboration or domination, 'exit' or 'voice', trust or mistrust, consensualism vs. individualism

that, as indicated in Chapter 5 (Figure 5.1), forms of integration can be ordered along two dimensions: integration of financial ownership (claims to residual profit) and integration of decision rights (claims to residual decisions). Note that there are degrees of integration along both dimensions, between market and hierarchy. One can have more or less integrated relations in terms of duration, exclusiveness, and number of activities involved.

For the causes/reasons of (dis)integration I employ a taxonomy of causes, inspired by Aristotle, which is close to the taxonomy of institutions developed in Chapter 5. There, I proposed that institutions provide enabling conditions, i.e. they affect the causality of action, for which I employed the multiple causality of Aristotle. Here, I analyse the effects of institutions on organizational (dis)integration (see Table 11.1).

All these factors have to be taken into account in applying the cycle of discovery and its implications for (dis)integration in different industries, countries, or innovation systems. I will discuss them in the order presented in the table.

If incentives are based on firm size, one will be more motivated to integrate than when they are based on innovation and quality in collaboration with outside partners. If they are short-term, one will be more oriented to *ad hoc*, flexible, price-oriented, arm's-length interfirm relationships. If they are long-term, one will be more oriented either to long-term, intensive relations, with mutual investment in competencies, or to the build-up of firm-specific competencies.

When hiring and firing of labour is flexible and not tied to long-term employment, one will be more inclined to hire labour rather than preserve flexibility by sourcing from outside firms. This is an advantage especially in the stage of break-up of architectures (scripts). On the other hand, workers will be more willing to engage in firm-specific learning and team formation, and to transfer their knowledge to colleagues, when their job is more assured. This is an advantage in consolidation, generalization, and differentiation. These points confirm the cycle of (dis)integration indicated in Figure 11.1.

When inputs (materials, components, machines, and instruments) are not available in sufficient quality, or are supplied only by a monopolist upon whom one threatens to become dependent, one will tend to make rather than buy them. The first situation (lack of supply) is likely to occur in the early stages of development, so this contributes to the tendency towards integration in the trajectory from innovation to consolidation. The second situation is likely to occur when the upstream industry is in the stage of consolidation and generalization, with concentration and increase of scale.

Concerning knowledge and technology, the incentive to integrate clearly depends on economies of scale or scope. This arises particularly in consolidation and generalization. However, scope effects may yield a reason for integration at the stage of differentiation, contrary to the prediction in Figure 11.1. The reason would be that joint production of differentiated products would yield efficiency advantages of scope.

Bridging institutions serve to facilitate transfer, exchange, or joint production of knowledge. An example is the Fraunhofer Institute in Germany.

The question whether the technology is systemic or stand-alone is relevant as follows: When innovation is incremental, i.e. preserves architecture (of a script, for example), and the technology is systemic, in the sense that there are strict conditions on the inputs and outputs of nodes, and these are not standardized, then the different parts of the architecture must innovate in step, to preserve their systemic coherence, and this tends to require more integration (Teece 1988, Langlois & Robertson 1995).

Frankel (quoted in Teece 1988: 270) argued that the lack of vertical integration in Britain, as compared with the US, in iron and steel in the second half of the nineteenth century and in the textile industry in the first half of the twentieth century explains the lag of Britain behind the US. This is in line with the present analysis.

On the other hand, when the innovation is radical, in the stage of architectural break-up, this condition drops out, and architectural coherence becomes a liability. This is in fact the reason for expecting a more disintegrated structure in that stage of innovation, as illustrated in Figure 11.1.

Separability of technology is related to the issue of systemic versus stand-alone technology, but is not only technical: To what extent can a needed part of some organization be pried loose from the rest to form an element of a new configuration? The reasons for inseparability can be technical, but can also be related to organizational issues of decision and ownership rights. When this is not possible, it can obviously form an obstacle for disintegration, but also for integration: when one wants to integrate by taking over some part of an existing organization but it cannot be pried loose (Nooteboom 1999*a*).

Poor infrastructure of transportation and communication provides a disincentive for sourcing from far away, because of the risks of delay in delivery, and would thus contribute to integration. This is particularly important when just-in-time supply is crucial, as is the case where there are many differentiated product forms, for which the cost of buffer stocks would be prohibitive.

The most deeply rooted elements of the institutional environment are the categorical conditional causes: categories of perception, understanding, and evaluation; language, ethics, and habits concerning co-operation, domination, loyalty, the good life, status, prestige. Some of these are related to motivation and incentives (final cause) concerning management, employment, collaboration, and rivalry.

> Walker (1993) characterizes the development of the British innovation system along the following lines: After Britain blazed the trail of the industrial revolution it entered a persistent, long-term decline of its manufacturing and production of technology, compared to other countries. It shifted from machinery and cars to food-related processing and especially service sectors: retailing, finance, property. This was connected with the importance of London as a financial centre. But Walker suggests that it was also related to the perception of manufacturing as yielding low job status compared to trade and finance. Also, similarly to the US, there is an orientation towards short-term profit. This is related to the importance of stock markets as a source of finance (in contrast with the importance of banks in Japan and Germany), and a corresponding liberal regime of financial markets, with easy trading in assets and mergers and acquisitions. This yields pressure towards short-term profits, and this can more easily be reconciled with trade and services than with manufacturing. This is a clear case of how basic notions of achievement and prestige connect with motives and goals, which form an important determinant of economic structure.

11.2.2   Co-ordination

The issue of (dis)integration is closely related to problems of co-ordination, as discussed in Chapters 5 and 8. Here, I briefly review the main points. There are problems of co-ordination in a technical sense, of how to align competencies, and problems relating to agency, i.e. intentions and motivation. Here, I focus on intentions rather than competencies.

As discussed in Chapter 8, differentiated products yield a higher profit margin than standardized products. However, differentiated products tend to require differentiated investments, specific to the product. This entails specific investments and the resulting problems of dependence and hold-up, unless technology is flexible. Earlier, in Chapter 3, I gave the reasons why firms need outside sources of cognition, to compensate for the cognitive myopia caused by co-ordination and cognitive focusing within the firm. For this they need to bridge cognitive distance, to achieve sufficient mutual understanding between disparate sources of knowledge. In Chapter 8 it was shown that this entails investments that are 'specific' to the relation, in the sense discussed in transaction-cost economics. A certain durability of the relation is required to set up and recoup the investment. Dependence as a result of specific investments yields the risk of hold-up. Another problem of co-ordination is spillover: the unintended flow of information and knowledge to competitors. Of course collaboration always involves a flow of knowledge, but the question is what the net benefit of loss and gain of knowledge will be. One will want to constrain flows of knowledge that jeopardize competitive advantage and are not needed for the gain of knowledge. When the problem of spillover arises, it entails problems of agency. To what extent are network members motivated not to steal competitive advantage from their partners and to guard against spillover to the partner's competitors. Information and knowledge can play the role of hostages. Yielding sensitive knowledge whose appropriability one wishes to retain makes one dependent on the ability and effort of the partner to maintain confidentiality. It yields the recipient power: he may threaten to divulge it to your competitors.

Chapter 8 offered a toolbox of forms of governance: evasion, integration, contracting, mutual self-interest, trust, and network structure. The degree to which integration will be used as a solution depends on the extent of the problem and on the viability of alternative instruments for governance. That depends, especially, on the institutional environment. This will be further explored in the chapter on innovation systems (Chapter 12).

11.3   THE COMPUTER INDUSTRY

Many conditions have been indicated that affect organizational (dis)integration, and it would be useful to show how all this works out in specific industries. For an illustration I review the electronics and computer industries.

11.3.1   Description

I employ the account given by Malerba, Nelson, Orsenigo, & Winter (1998). I use only their account of (dis)integration phenomena, not their theory. They reject the transaction-cost perspective in favour of the older 'quite different perspective' of the 'growth of the market', in terms of economies of scale and learning from specialization. But this is a false choice: the two perspectives can very well be combined, as I attempted to show earlier, in Chapters 5 and 8. The issue of integration and disintegration is clearly essential in studies of innovation systems, and while transaction costs are not the whole story, or even the most important part of the story, concerning the question of whether to integrate activities in a firm or distribute them in a network, they still are relevant. Furthermore, as I also indicated, if we see innovation systems as systems that produce innovation and learning from interaction between organizations, we cannot leave out the perspective of the co-ordination and governance of interorganizational relations. This is illustrated by the fact that accounts of national innovation systems repeatedly refer to the importance of co-ordination in the production and diffusion of innovations. For example, Walker (1993) identifies weakness in capabilities of co-ordination as a major problem in the British innovation system.

In accordance with theoretical expectations, the computer industry began with small firms, who purchased the early components in the open market (1950–8). With the advent of transistors in 1962 (Tushman & Anderson 1986: 454), some computer producers integrated into components, but this did not really get under way until the emergence of integrated circuits soon after (1964). At that point all producers wholly or partly integrated into integrated circuits (Malerba *et al.* 1998: 4). Malerba *et al.* give three reasons. First, integrated circuits 'embedded system elements and thus required close co-ordination of both components and systems'. Second, semiconductors were 'strategic' and were kept in house for fear of spillover. Third, there were fears of shortages of various key semiconductor components.

11.3.2 *Analysis*

The reasons given by Malerba *et al.* would also appear in my analysis: the arguments of consolidation, systemic integration, and scale; the spillover argument and the argument of access to inputs, as discussed above (see Table 11.1). However, I would add some qualifications and some new points. I noted before, on the basis of the work of Stoelhorst (1997), that the step towards integrated circuits, in contrast with semiconductors, constituted a radical, in the sense of an architectural, innovation. The transistor could be seen as a novel substitution into an established script, while the integrated circuit constituted a new script. This was forced by the fact that without that step, with semiconductor technology applied only to one component, that technology could not realize its full potential. Thus, it was not until integrated circuits that one could speak of a radical innovation, with its subsequent need for consolidation in a dominant design and a drive for efficient, large-scale production. Next to the sheer shortage of supply of quality components, there is also a transaction-cost interpretation of integration: the components at that time were specific; the technology had not yet settled down in standardized specifications, and hence supply entailed specific investments. Given the impossibility of concluding reliable contracts, and given the bent towards either legal governance or direct control in US and UK systems of innovation, this also may have led to the choice of integration. The argument for integration to control spillover would, according to our analysis, be valid only if the knowledge involved were reasonably explicit and documented (which is plausible: blueprints of designs), and speed of change were not so great as to eliminate the threat of spillover (which I don't know).

Next, according to Malerba *et al.*, 'with the full development of the semiconductor industry, and the introduction of microprocessors, very large integrated circuits, and RAM and ROM memory devices, disintegration took place' (p. 4). The reasons Malerba *et al.* give for this are that:

because the new demand for semiconductors coming from personal computer producers had grown rapidly; in response, a variety of highly advanced components were introduced by several merchant microelectronics firms. A key firm—INTEL—emerged as the industry leader for microprocessors, thus determining the de facto standard in the semiconductor industry to which computer producers, out of necessity, complied

Again, I would augment rather than contest this. First of all, after consolidation one would expect standards to appear, which lessen the problem of specific investments, which facilitates outsourcing. In subsequent generalization one would expect further opportunities for economy of scale for specialized producers. When next the product (integrated circuits) differentiates, as indicated, use of a single main supplier (INTEL) would make sense to achieve scale in combination with differentiation, if there is also large economy of scope, which militates against separate specialized producers of differentiated products. This I don't know. Also, one would expect users to militate against such monopolization. Did INTEL succeed in achieving this position because of strong economy of scope or unique competencies of technology and speed? I can make a prediction: with such integration at the stage of differentiation and subsequent reciprocation I would expect a slowdown in the development of further radical innovation unless novel entrants appear or INTEL achieves a high degree of disintegration.

> Burgelman (1996) and Stoelhorst (1997) recount how INTEL moved into RISC while corporate strategy was not to do it, on the ground that it would cannibalize existing products. This could happen because 'the product champion disguised the product as a co-processor rather than a stand-alone one . . . By the time management caught on, he had lined up a (non conflicting) customer base' (Burgelman 1996: 416). RISC had been invented at IBM, but had lain dormant. What usually happens in cases like this is that the internal entrepreneur cannot have his way and leaves to start up for himself. In this case there was enough allowance for deviation and redundancy for the innovator to stay.

Tushman and Anderson (1986) proposed that semiconductors were competence-destroying for incumbent firms assembling older components. Thus, the emergence of semiconductor memories was competence-destroying for the makers of them. But semiconductors and integrated circuits were not competence-destroying for computer assemblers who were not integrated into the old technology of components.

Malerba *et al.* also consider integration of computer makers into software. The explanation they give here is that at first IBM could achieve market power by bundling them, but this was broken down by anti-trust authorities. Without contesting that, I would, here also, add a consideration of governance. Similar reasons for integration may at first have applied: paucity of competent and sufficient suppliers, and dedicated investments for dedicated software. As standards developed, there was a better basis, also for IBM, to outsource the software.

Perhaps the most important conclusion from this case study is that, given the complexity of causation, for a proper analysis we need more detailed information. Complicated as the analysis may already be, there are further details to be taken into account, but they go beyond the scope of this book (see Nooteboom 1999*g*).

11.4   CONCLUSION

Associated with the cycle of innovation there is a cycle of organizational integration and disintegration. Stages of consolidation and generalization generally go together with more integration, while differentiation, reciprocation, and novel combinations generally go together with more disintegrated structures.

It has been recognized that (dis)integration of organization depends on much more than just the stage of the cycle and the type of competencies destroyed. It depends on characteristics of technology, such as flexibility, whether it is systemic or stand-alone, the extent to which knowledge is tacit (even after consolidation in a dominant design), speed of change. It depends on a variety of elements in the institutional environment. Both those elements and characteristics of technology are relevant for governance: instruments chosen to control hold-up and spillover risks, depending on institutions that affect transaction costs, such as legal instruments, basis for trust, technology available for monitoring, and attitudes towards collaboration and rivalry ('exit' and 'voice').

I conclude that some factors may run counter to the predictions of the relation between stages of innovation and organizational integration given in Figure 11.1. First, in confirmation rather than contradiction of the cycle, movement along the cycle may stall for several reasons. Scale effects combined with non-differentiable products may cause a stop at large, tightly integrated companies, as in the oil industry. Strong needs for differentiation combined with low effect of scale and lack of radical, competence-destroying process innovations may allow disintegrated structures such as industrial districts to live on.

Other factors appear to move in contradiction with the cycle. Scope effects can induce integration at the stage of differentiation. The issue of (dis)integration will then be settled by other conditions: degree to which technology is systemic, governance conditions. Problems of inseparability can form an obstacle for both disintegration and integration.

Other factors, however, confirm the predictions: flexibility/training of labour, access to inputs, economy of scale, tacitness of knowledge, speed of knowledge change, need for external economy of cognitive scope, protection against spillover, degree to which technology is systemic. Remaining factors mostly neither contradict nor support the predictions, but are complementary to them: incentives, bridging institutions, flexibility of technology, infrastructure, (part of) regulation, categories.

TABLE 11.2   *Determinants of (dis)integration*

	Disintegration	Integration
stage in the cycle, with conditions:	novel combinations competition on novelty → low need for scale tacit knowledge high speed of change → low need for spillover control labour flexibility cognitive scope	consolidation/generalization competition on price → high need for scale explicit knowledge low speed of change → high need for spillover control training systemic technology
unless:	prevented by inseparability	prevented by inseparability
stage in the cycle with conditions:	differentiation/reciprocation little scope stand-alone standards easy governance	differentiation/reciprocation high scope systemic few standards strained governance
governance:	collaboration, consensus, voice trust long-term perspective	rivalry, individualism, exit mistrust short-term perspective

They have effects on transaction costs, and hence on governance, and hence on costs and opportunities of disintegration.

The results indicate that there is a systemic coherence between the determinants of (dis)integration. They are summarized in Table 11.2.

In fact, the intricacies of systems of governance and innovation are even greater than already indicated. For the study of specific industries and firms a more advanced, detailed, in-depth analysis is needed to take complications into account. The next Chapter will analyse the effects of institutions on innovative performance.

Part III

APPLICATION

12

Innovation Systems[1]

For an analysis of innovation systems, this chapter applies the results from previous Chapters. From Chapter 8 it adopts the analysis of learning by interaction and associated forms of co-ordination. The basic idea here is that innovation arises from interaction between firms. From Chapter 9 it adopts the cycle of discovery, and the elaboration in terms of scripts from Chapter 10. This extends existing life-cycle theories of innovation. From Chapter 11 it adopts the corresponding cycle of integration and disintegration. An attempt is made to identify 'generic types' of innovation system. Two types are identified that reflect differences between 'Anglo-Saxon' and other systems, in Japan and continental Europe, with the possible alternative of a 'third way'.

12.1 DEFINITION AND FOCUS

This paragraph gives a characterization of innovation systems and indicates the focus of this Chapter.

12.1.1 *Institutions and Innovation*

The literature on business systems studies the effects of different institutional frameworks on the structure of economic organization (Whitley 1999). The literature on innovation systems studies the effects of institutions and organization on innovation. (For a review of national innovation systems see Nelson (1993).) Innovation systems are systems of organizations and institutions that produce, select, and diffuse innovations. The literature supplies many examples of institutional effects on innovation and the diffusion of innovations.

> Chapter 5 gave an example, in the Netherlands, of the effect of regulations for the establishment of enterprises on Schumpeterian novel combinations. Here, institutions take the form of entry barriers in existing industries and limitations to the setting up of novel industries across existing industry boundaries.
>
> There is a suggestion that US institutions in the form of financial markets and markets for corporate control provide incentives for short-term profits that may jeopardize R & D aimed at longer-term innovation (Mowery & Rosenberg 1993).

[1] I thank Richard Nelson, Richard Whitley, and Rogers Hollingsworth for their comments on an earlier version of this Chapter. Of course, the usual disclaimer applies.

A well-known feature of the 'Japanese system' is the system of 'life-time employment', although this is not as strict as often suggested, and is expected to erode (Odagiri & Goto 1993). Odagiri and Goto note how the Japanese management system also includes a high degree of interaction between R & D and production, which may be eroded as a result of a shift to foreign production. The Japanese financial system, with limited influence of shareholders and with intertwined interests and governance of firms and banks, has allowed for a more long-term orientation, but this also is expected to be eroded as a result of globalization of financial markets.

In the analysis of business systems or innovation systems organizations are seen as institutional arrangements in a wider institutional environment. The latter is more or less durable and culturally and socially embedded, and yields varieties of capitalism (Hollingsworth & Boyer 1997, Whitley 1999). According to an emerging view in the literature, innovations arise in particular from interactions between firms and other organizations (Lundvall 1985, 1988, 1993). This connects with the literature on 'corporate social capital' (for a survey, see Leenders and Gabbay 1999). Networks, within and between firms, generate social capital, defined as follows (Leenders & Gabbay 1999: 3): 'The set of resources, tangible or virtual, that accrue to an organization through social structure, facilitating the attainment of goals'.

Increasingly, there is recognition that networks not only create positive outcomes (social capital) but also negative ones (social liability) (Brass & Labianca 1999, Gargiulo & Benassi 1999). Linkages between firms can enhance both the diffusion and the generation of innovations. But a possible liability is that networks can become so tight, exclusionary, and durable that they create inertia.

This Chapter adds to the literatures on business systems and innovation systems by analysing by what mechanisms different institutions have effects on innovation. Too often, in both literatures, effects of institutions on economic outcomes are postulated without giving insight into the underlying mechanisms, down to the behaviour of firms. For example, Walker (1993) claimed that in the UK there is too little diffusion of innovations, because of a lack of interfirm networks. Why is this? What institutions cause such a liability, and by what mechanism? It is proposed here that forms of co-ordination between firms form a crucial part of that mechanism. The central proposition is that innovation outcomes, at the level of firms, are to a large extent determined by the forms of co-ordination used for interfirm relations, and that these forms of co-ordination are conditioned by institutions that vary between countries. This Chapter also contributes to the literature on corporate social capital by analysing how social capital can be managed, and how this depends on the institutional environment.

12.1.2   National systems?

The customary term is 'national innovation systems'. There are arguments in favour and arguments against that (Nelson & Rosenberg 1993). A powerful argument against it is that increasingly technologies and markets cross national boundaries, and this argument is more powerful the smaller and more internationally oriented the country is. For the Netherlands, for example, it would be ludicrous to consider that country in isolation. On the other hand, a greater or lesser part of the institutional environment is country-bound, since it derives from national cultural histories, and entails more or less path dependence, as has been argued in the 'varieties of capitalism' literature (Hollingsworth & Boyer 1997, Whitley 1998).[2]

Chapter 5 proposed categories of perception, understanding, and evaluation, embedded in language, as the 'deep structure' of institutions, and differences in that will not disappear easily. Between countries, complex and shifting patterns of partial convergence and partial divergence are to be expected. Convergence will be greatest where the product or technology in question is least embedded in fundamental categories of perception, understanding, and evaluation. In Chapter 6 reference was made to the work of Lakoff and Johnson (1980, 1999), who claim that for abstract categories, such as the good, the true, and the beautiful, etc. we employ metaphors based on primary, physical categories such as movement, location, grasp and touch, volume, mass, up or down, in or out, containers, etc. In other words, cognition is rooted in bodily experience (Lakoff & Johnson 1999). Since we have a shared evolution in a shared physical environment, with limited variations in climate, food, etc., our primary, physical categories are likely to be shared to a large extent. Higher-level cognitive and cultural categories vary to a greater extent because they are derived, secondary, and based more on discourse than on objective nature. They are more likely to vary across cultures. Thus, material goods and technology are likely to be perceived and to develop more similarly across cultures than norms and values.

An illustration given in Chapter 5 was the Dutch consensus-based 'polder model', which has yielded social agreement on policies of wage restraint. Currently this is under pressure from a much faster increase of managers' income, from higher salaries and share options, than workers' income. The argument in defence of it is globalization: elsewhere managerial salaries are higher and Dutch salaries cannot be out of step too much, for fear of a drain of managerial talent. But it threatens to break up consensus on wage restraint, with the unions planning to increase their claims now that management has fallen out of step.

An example of convergence which retains some difference is the following: In a recent study in the automobile industry in the US and Japan, de Jong, Nooteboom, Vossen, Helper, and Sako (1999) found a striking similarity between Japan and the US in the variables that characterize those relations, and in the causal relations between them. The study was based on a large data set on buyer–supplier relations, collected by Susan Helper and Mari Sako. The evidence clearly indicates that in the US buyer–supplier relations have turned around from short-term, arm's-length relations, with an emphasis on price, to more durable, co-operative relations, focused on joint production of added value on the basis of complementary competencies. There were only

---

[2] From an evolutionary perspective, national institutions can perhaps be seen as species that have developed along different evolutionary branches, and this provides large obstacles for jumping to a different branch. In other words, there is likely to be path dependence in the evolution of institutions.

minor differences left, but on closer inspection they may be significant. One difference was that the average level of transaction-specific investments by suppliers was lower in Japan than in the US. This runs counter to the standard story that in Japan buyer–supplier relations have more depth and are more dedicated. The second difference was that the effect of the attractiveness of the buyer on the level of those investments by the supplier was less in Japan than in the US. The third difference was that the effect of 'future perspectives', based mostly on the level of commitment of the buyer to the supplier, was higher in Japan. These differences can be explained as follows. The expected effect of buyer value on specific investments follows from the opportunity for the best suppliers to choose the most attractive buyers, and engage in more specific investments for them, leaving the less attractive buyers to the less attractive suppliers. The latter have less incentive to tie themselves down with specific investments, needing to maintain an opportunity to switch to a more attractive buyer later. If in Japan suppliers are more captive, inside vertical business systems (*keiretsu*), with less scope for choice of customers across the boundaries of such systems, we would expect the effect of buyer value to be less. There is less incentive for suppliers to compete for the most attractive buyers by engaging in more specific investments, so that the average level of specific investments is lower. With a limited choice of buyers, suppliers can only be enticed to engage in specific investments by being offered better conditions in terms of a durable relation, guaranteed by high commitment. Thus, specific investments depend only on the expected duration of the relation, i.e. future prospects fed by buyer commitment. Summing up: Japanese relations are more durable, with more commitment, which does by itself contribute to higher levels of dedicated investments, but because of lack of competition this does not yield a net effect of higher levels of dedicated investments.

The remaining difference between the US and Japan may be important. Relations need to be long enough to recoup specific investments and to build up co-operation; to achieve mutual understanding, trust, and joint development. But relations may also be too long, causing undue rigidity and lack of the variety that is needed for innovation (Nooteboom 1998). Thus, the development in the US may have captured the advantages of co-operative relations while maintaining more choice, flexibility, and variety of relations, which we would expect to favour innovation.

In this Chapter the focus is on the effects that the institutional environment has on innovative performance through the modes of co-ordination that it enables and supports. In other words, modes of co-ordination are taken as an intermediate variable between institutional environment and innovative performance. An important issue of co-ordination is whether innovative activities take place within organizations or between them, in what type of interfirm linkage, with what mode of governance. The design and governance of interfirm relations is a large subject, which is treated more extensively elsewhere (Nooteboom 1999a). Here, use is made of the results from that research, with a focus on patterns of organizational integration and disintegration in relation to innovation.

An example of the effect of institutions on organizational integration or disintegration in the history of the US system of innovation is the effect of anti-trust regulation (Mowery and Rosenberg 1993). At first it was lax, which stimulated large firms to grow and innovate by taking over innovative small firms. When anti-trust policy shifted to restrict this, there was more growth of small, entrepreneurial firms. The entry of such firms was further enabled by a liberal regime of property-rights protection, which allowed small firms to enter market niches, an active venture-capital market, and military-procurement policies that were open to small firms. A weakness in the US, identified by Mowery and Rosenberg, is lack of diffusion of innovations, particularly in robotics and computer-integrated manufacturing. Mowery and Rosenberg detect changes in the US system: a lesser importance of military procurement and a more liberal anti-trust policy since the Reagan administration, which may shift the emphasis back away from small entrants towards larger firms. This is expected to be enhanced by a policy aimed at more appropriability of innovations, which yields fewer entry opportunities and may exacerbate the lack of diffusion. They also detect a tendency to learn from Japanese buyer–supplier relations, in a shift from arm's-length, short-term contracting aimed at lowest price towards more durable relations aimed at the utilization of complementary competencies for the sake of efficiency and quality (cf. Nooteboom 1999a/d 1998).

12.2   CYCLES

The basic proposition is that the cycle of discovery, developed in Chapter 9, plays an important role in innovation systems. This paragraph summarizes the earlier 'life-cycle theory' of industrial dynamics, and shows what the cycle of discovery has to add.

12.2.1   *Life Cycles and Punctuated Equilibria*

As indicated in previous Chapters, a familiar theory in the literature on innovation systems is the theory of life cycles. Interpreted broadly, this includes the concepts of dominant designs (Abernathy 1978, Abernathy & Utterback 1978), technological trajectories and regimes (Nelson & Winter 1977), technological guideposts (Sahal 1981), and technological paradigms (Dosi 1982), which have already been discussed in earlier Chapters. Similar ideas were offered by Freeman, Clark, and Soete (1982) and Davis, Hills, and Laforge (1985). As in general, in industrial dynamics and evolutionary economics there have been few successful attempts to explain the origins of novelty. The Schumpeterian term 'novel combinations' merely labels our ignorance. It has not been explained by what path such combinations come about. Attention has concentrated on how exogenously created variety provides the basis for population dynamics in processes of selection.

The general idea of earlier life-cycle theory is that in the initial, turbulent stage disintegrated structures of independent units of activity prevail, trying out different forms and variations of a novel technology or product, which are then selected out to converge to the dominant design. As discussed before, competition then leads to a shift to process innovations to increase efficiency. The pressure towards a dominant design also depends on the extent to which the technology entails network externalities or complementary technologies or systems that are specific to the technology.

As indicated before, a distinction has been made between competence enhancing and competence destroying innovations (Abernathy & Clark 1985). Tushman and Romanelli (1985) and Romanelli and Tushman (1994) analyse such technological discontinuities in terms of punctuated equilibria. However, while this theory suggests an explanation of how the discontinuities come about, such an explanation is not forthcoming; they are simply assumed to arise somehow, and remain as exogenous as they did in earlier theory. Thus, Gersick (1991: 19) stated:

The definitive assertion in this paradigm [i.e. punctuated equilibria] is that systems do not shift from one kind of game to another through incremental steps: such transformations occur through wholesale upheaval. The discussions [in previous sections of the article] should help to explain why incremental changes in a system's parts would not alter the whole. As long as the deep structure is intact, it generates a strong inertia, first to prevent the system from generating alternatives outside its own boundaries, then to pull any deviations that do occur back into line. According to this logic, the deep structure must first be dismantled, leaving the system temporarily disorganized, in order for any fundamental changes to be accomplished. Next, a subset of the system's old pieces, along with some new pieces, can be put back together into a new configuration, which operates according to a new set of rules

This is unsatisfactory, for several reasons. First, we should get our sources right. According to Gould and Eldredge, the originators of the theory of punctuated equilibrium, punctuation is not to be confused with saltationism: the idea that change arises from some discontinuous transformation (Eldredge & Gould 1972, Gould 1989). It arises from 'allopatric speciation': small populations, isolated at the periphery or outside their parents' habitat, develop into a new species. There is no discontinuity in this; just a development that is abrupt only on a geological timescale.

Second, if apparent discontinuities occur this does not eliminate the need to explain where they come from. The crucial question is when and how the 'deep structure' breaks down, and, above all, how one finds out what 'subset of old pieces', and what 'new pieces' one should 'put back together', and according to what 'new configuration'.

As discussed in Chapter 9, for discontinuities we require motive, opportunity, and means. In socio-economic evolution, the issue of *motive* has been recognized in the literature, typically with reference to the ideas of Thomas Kuhn, discussed before (March 1991, Hedberg 1981, Cohen & Sproull 1996, Gersick 1991, Tushman & Romanelli 1985). One needs to encounter a crisis of misfits before one is willing to surrender the investment of past practice. In the literature *opportunity* has received less attention. It arises from new varieties of demand and other conditions (institutions, access to markets) offered in novel contexts. *Means* arise from the new varieties of resources (knowledge, experience, inputs of labour, capital, materials, and components), which yield elements for novel combinations and indications for their architecture. The most developed ideas that I could find for the causes of innovation did not go very far. Consider the following quote from Gersick (1991: 29), which refers to Kuhn (1970), Gould (1989) and Prigogine and Stengers (1984). It sums up what still needs to be explained.

The new direction does not emerge all at once; instead, a catalytic change opens the door to it. Kuhn described critical insights that sometimes show the way to novel paths of investigation, leading to new paradigms. Gould described initial mutations that thrust a group of organisms into a new mode of life, thereby subjecting them to novel selective pressures, which then work toward full emergence of the new species' [and] systems' particular histories matter, because histories determine the unique array of information and conditions from which system members can select their new direction—the jumping-off place for the transition

I propose that the cycle of discovery set out in Chapter 9 explains how this might work.

12.2.2 The Cycle of Innovation

The cycle of discovery proposed in Chapter 9 can be seen as an extension of the life-cycle theory of industrial dynamics, indicated above. The old 'cycle' is not really a cycle: it moves from novel combinations to dominant designs and then stalls at the mystery of the next innovation. It cannot explain the fact that dominant designs precede innovations as much as they follow them. I propose that after consolidation in a dominant design the cycle continues. Consolidation (the establishment of a dominant design and efficient production) provides a platform for applications in novel contexts (generalization). This opens up variety of context. In new contexts, the need and opportunity are encountered to adapt the system to local conditions (differentiation). Parallel practices are found that in some respects perform better, and here one finds the means for change: indications of which parts to drop and which new parts to incorporate (reciprocation), and indications as to what new configurations might work. The cycle of discovery constitutes a process of abduction: motives, elements, and directions are gathered for a novel system that has some chance of yielding improvement. When applied to innovation and diffusion, the cycle of discovery (see Figure 9.1) is as illustrated in Figure 12.1.

In Chapter 10 the cycle was elaborated in terms of scripts. Architectural change was defined as change of script structure, and parametric change as change of substitutions into nodes of scripts. The architecture of scripts may be compared with the 'deep structure' that Gersick proposed. It is through novel substitutions into the nodes of an existing architecture, and through altering the order of nodes for different conditions, and through incorporating elements from parallel scripts, that exploration takes place while exploitation proceeds. Admittedly, discontinuity still obtains at the point when architecture breaks down, and configurations of novel scripts are tried. However, reasons and causes of such discontinuity as well as ways to cross the gap have been indicated. Increasing complexity of *ad hoc* add-ons yields a spaghetti structure which is difficult to co-ordinate and causes diminishing returns of further add-ons. Duplications of nodes at different points of the architecture entail that economies of scale are foregone. Most important of all, constraints imposed by the existing structure prevent novel activities from utilizing their full potential. This experience, built up in the process, gives hints in what directions to seek a novel configuration: take the most

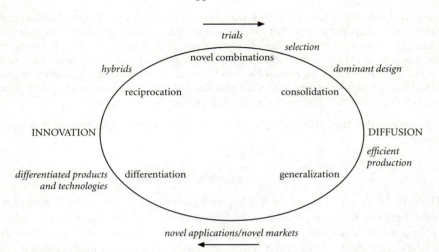

FIGURE 12.1   *Cycle of innovation and diffusion*

promising novel component activities, try to design a structure around them that allows maximal utilization of potential, while pooling similar activities to improve co-ordination and enable economy of scale. Success is not guaranteed, but the process of redesign is not blind or random.

As discussed in Chapter 9, the cycle of discovery purports to represent a fundamental heuristic of discovery that applies at all levels: individual cognition, organizational learning, and innovation. In this Chapter the focus is on the latter: transformation in an industry. This refers to the development of a product, process, technology, or combination of these, new to the industry. There may be wider technological complexes that in their turn go through the cycle. In terms of scripts that would be rendered as follows: Cycles for subscripts yield novelty fed into the nodes of a superscript, which contributes to the cycle of that. In other words, architectural innovation at the subscript level yields differentiation on the level of the superscript.

> For example, in the computer industry there were cycles of development leading from vacuum tubes to transistors to integrated circuits to microprocessors (Stoelhorst 1997, Malerba *et al.* 1998, Tushman & Anderson 1986). These represented elements (nodes, subscripts) of computers (superscripts) that developed from mainframe computers to minicomputers to personal computers.

In this way learning and innovation at different levels can be conceived of as a nesting of cycles. Discovery by people in organizations contributes to organizational cycles, which contribute to industrial cycles. At any level, the cycle is contingent upon its institutional environment. Within the firm movement along the cycle depends on the institutional arrangements of the firm: organizational structure, process, and culture yield forms of co-ordination (with a certain tightness, type, and scope) that determine the conditions for exploitation and exploration in the firm. They determine the extent to which a firm is flexible or inert—is able to achieve the stages of consolidation, differentiation, reciprocation, and novel combinations in novel architectures. That is the subject of Chapter 13. The performance of firms and the appropriateness of their forms of co-ordination, in different stages of the cycle, depend on the institutional environment, including conditions such as competitive pressure. At the level of an industry, movement along the cycle depends on how institutions enable or inhibit the stages of the cycle. That is the subject of the present Chapter. As stated, the emphasis lies on how institutions enable or constrain modes of co-ordination within and between firms.

In Chapter 11 it was proposed that associated with the cycle of discovery there is a cycle of organizational integration and disintegration (Figure 11.1). Here, we see a connection with the literature on industrial districts or networks: for novel combinations, relatively disintegrated structures are at an advantage. However, this does not necessarily entail networks of different firms. It may entail 'virtual organizations' of loosely coupled, highly autonomous entities. Figure 11.1 hides a complex set of factors that affect the timing and degree of integration and disintegration. These were discussed in Chapter 11 (see Table 11.2). Predictions concerning (dis)integration, indicated in Figure 11.1, should take into account contingencies which vary between industries and countries.

12.3 INSTITUTIONS AND INNOVATION SYSTEMS[3]

This paragraph proceeds with an analysis of how the institutional environment affects innovative performance, with modes of co-ordination and organization as an intervening variable. First, it considers the effects of institutions on problems and instruments of co-ordination. Next, it proceeds to set up two 'generic types' of innovation system, in terms of the way in which they deal with issues of co-ordination within and between firms, and it explores the merits and feasibility of an alternative 'third way'.

12.3.1 Institutional Effects

In the context of this book, in the discussion of co-ordination the focus is on learning and innovation: on the utilization of complementary sources of knowledge and the joint production of new knowledge. A central feature in this is the management of cognitive distance. This has implications for where one should locate the boundary of the firm, how to co-ordinate activities within the firm, and how to co-ordinate across boundaries of the firm. One cannot effectively deal with co-ordination in terms of two

---

[3] Parts of this Chapter appeared in 1999 in an article in *Research Policy*, with the title 'Innovation and Inter-firm Linkages: New Implications for Policy'.

separate issues of intra- and interfirm co-ordination, as if the boundary of the firm is given and fixed. Issues of co-ordination and the boundary of the firm constitute one integrated issue. As conditions change, both modes of co-ordination and the boundary of the firm are subject to shift.

As discussed in Chapters 5 and 8, and summarized in Chapter 11, co-ordination needs to take into account risks of hold-up and spillover. The forms of governance considered in Chapter 8 were: evasion of risk, organizational integration, contracting, mutual self-interest, trust, and network structure. There is no space here to give a complete inventory of all the effects that institutions may have. The discussion is limited to a number of salient effects. The goal is to give sufficient examples to support my claim that to a large extent the effect of institutions on innovative performance operates through forms of co-ordination. First, I review some effects of institutions on problems of governance, and then their effects on forms of governance.

Educational systems and the infrastructure of information and communication condition *spillover*, by determining the degree to which knowledge can be codified and by determining opportunities for communication. Professional organizations affect professional allegiance, which also affects spillover between professionals from different firms. Centrally negotiated agreements on vocational training, made compulsory for an entire industry, can discourage free riding in vocational training and the poaching of staff.

Inclinations towards *opportunism*, legal *contracting*, *self-interest*, loyalty, and *trust* are affected by categories of perception, understanding, and evaluation that form the deep structure of institutions. This includes inclinations towards autonomy or community, individualism or collectivism, consensus or authority. It includes attitudes of exit (i.e. to exit from a relation, fire people, or sell firms when expectations are not met) versus voice (i.e. to signal discontent and try to redress its causes (Hirschman 1970)).

> Voice plays an important role in Japan, but also in the Netherlands. There, decision making involves a lengthy process of consensus making, and for this reason the Dutch have been called the 'Japanese of Europe'. This constitutes both social capital and liability. On the negative side it slows down decision making; on the positive side it engenders wide support of decisions once they are taken. Currently it is viewed positively as the 'polder model', yielding a consensus to scale down social security and increase flexibility of labour. In the past it was seen negatively as a 'Dutch disease' of stickiness and slow adaptation, and will no doubt be seen in this way again when the negative effect prevails.

Forms of co-ordination also are conditioned, i.e. enabled and constrained, by institutions. An indicative (non-exhaustive) summary is given below.

Evasion of dependence may be forced by institutional conditions: if there are no viable forms of co-ordination for reducing risks of dependence. This would obtain when there is no adequate legal basis (for ownership, contract, liability, association), no trust, radical uncertainty of conditions, no sense of community and solidarity, no kinship.

Co-ordination by *integration* depends on legal forms of ownership, and on opportunities to buy and sell firms or parts of them. These are conditioned by the system of corporate control. These include: constraints on takeovers, conditions for their finance, the structure and demands of capital markets (concentration of share ownership, short- or long-term profit orientation), structure, tasks and roles of directorates, and incentives for managers. Do directorates only represent shareholder interest or also the interests of other stakeholders? Do they have a supervisory or an advisory role (Nooteboom 1999e)? Integration is also conditioned by the role and strength of labour unions, constraints on hiring and firing people, and whether labour conditions are established by firm or by industry.

Co-ordination by legal *contracting* is conditioned by the availability of appropriate laws (of ownership, contract, liability), the reliability of their enforcement (independence of the judiciary, efficiency of the police, absence of corruption), price and quality of lawyers. It is also conditioned by opportunities for efficient search, for preparing contracts, monitoring compliance, and covering risks of default. This includes credit ratings, notaries, information and communication infrastructure, systems of insurance, the patent system.

Co-ordination by mutual *self-interest* is also conditioned by opportunities for monitoring, by constraints on collaboration (from government competition policy), the efficiency of reputation mechanisms, constraints on hostage taking (share ownership is a form of hostage taking, and in some countries there are constraints, e.g. on share ownership by banks). It also depends on the structure and roles of unions, and trade, industry, and professional organizations.

Co-ordination by commitment and *trust* is conditioned by relations of friendship, kinship or clans, norms and values of decent behaviour, orientation to voice rather than exit, lack of mobility, etc.

Co-ordination by *network structure* (exclusiveness of relations, go-betweens) is conditioned by the presence and orientation of industrial, trade, or professional organizations, the role of banks and other commercial intermediaries, the rigours of competition policy.

While technology should probably not be counted as an institution, it creates a number of important contingencies. Technology conditions the degree to which knowledge is tacit, the communicability of knowledge, and the speed of knowledge change, and thereby affects conditions of spillover. It also affects opportunities for monitoring and hence contracting. Markets determine opportunities from demand and pressures from competition for product differentiation, and technology determines how flexibly this can be performed. The two together determine the need for specific investments, which in turn determines problems of hold-up. The degree to which technology is systemic determines the need for technical co-ordination. These effects of industry and technology can confound effects of institutional systems. It may be that effects of interindustry differences (for given institutions) exceed those between institutional systems (for a given industry).

12.3.2   Innovative Performance

For the implications for innovative performance, one should take into account the different types, levels, and degrees of innovation, as discussed in Chapter 10:

- *Types*: product, process; technological, commercial, organizational, institutional innovation
- *Levels*: within a team, in the firm, at the level of an industry or an entire economic system
- *Degrees*: incremental/radical, parametric/architectural

For the present purpose we only need a characterization of incremental as opposed to radical innovation. As proposed in Chapter 10, I consider an innovation radical when it is architectural (Henderson & Clark 1990), when it entails a reconfiguration of scripts, with nodes from previously separate scripts (Schumpeterian 'novel combinations'). An innovation is incremental when it is parametric, i.e. preserves architecture and represents a novel substitution into existing nodes of a script. An incremental product innovation entails a novel feature of an existing product or a novel way of performing part of a user activity; for example, adding books to the product assortment of a supermarket. A radical product innovation entails a novel user practice; for example, the shift from service to self-service retailing. An incremental process innovation entails the use of a new material or component, or labour from a new source, in an existing production process. A radical process innovation entails a different organization of production; for example, the shift to assembly-line production; the introduction of robots to replace manual production. A radical industrial innovation entails the redesign of chains of production, supply, and distribution; for example, the merging of banking and insurance.

It seems fairly obvious that interfirm networks enhance the diffusion of innovations, as well as incremental innovation, and the arguments will not be set out here. However, one might expect that tight, durable network relations between firms limit the flexibility of configurations of activity, needed for the Schumpeterian 'novel combinations' of radical, architectural innovation, whereas more volatile systems of autonomous firms yield better opportunities for new configurations.

Networks are found in Japan and certain European countries such as Germany (Gelauff & den Broeder 1996), supported by institutions that favour durable relations, based on voice. A more volatile system of autonomous firms, based on exit, is found, for example, in the US. The expected difference regarding the performance in radical innovation is consistent with the prevailing view that the US are more entrepreneurial in the Schumpeterian sense. According to the argument, this would be a result of the lack of tight and durable interfirm networks, easy entry for newcomers, and easy break-up of large firms.

But what about the specific investments needed for differentiated, high-value products? In a system with only *ad hoc*, short-term interfirm relations there would be no opportunity to recoup the investment. By the logic of the analysis previously set out, this would either lead to lack of such investments or integration in large firms to safeguard the investment. The former would yield lack of high-value-added products. The latter would yield even greater lack of flexibility in the configuration of activities than in the case of interfirm networks, unless firms are easily broken up and sold. The US system satisfies that requirement. But if firms are easily broken up, this tends to go together with flexible labour, with easy hiring and firing. Both aspects of volatile business systems reduce the prospect of durable jobs. These obstruct team building and investment in firm-specific human resources, which might jeopardize the development, sharing, and joint production of tacit knowledge that may be needed especially for radical innovation. Along this line of argument the superiority in radical innovation of volatile, exit-oriented systems of innovation is not as evident as it seemed at first sight. In view of the importance of this issue, I will elaborate on it, in a comparison between the US and Germany.

12.3.3   Innovation Systems

We can now reconstruct innovation systems by piecing together consistent configurations of institutions, the forms of co-ordination that they allow for, and the implications for innovative performance, and see to what extent these configurations fit empirical, observed systems. Clearly, this is in principle quite complex. The good thing about that is that it may accommodate the rich variety of systems that we in fact observe. Complexity is reduced by the fact that there is considerable systemic coherence between institutions themselves and in configurations of compatible forms of co-ordination. A predilection for consensus decision making is difficult to reconcile with authoritarianism, élitism, or an orientation to exit rather than voice. A tendency towards highly detailed and strict legal governance of relations is difficult to reconcile with an orientation towards trust, and it is difficult to reconcile with the unpredictability of contingencies involved in innovation.

By way of illustration a comparison is given between the US and Germany. There are three reasons for this choice. First, I can build on earlier work on this comparison (Gelauff and den Broeder 1996). Second, this choice allows me to utilize a comparative study by Steve Casper of the US and German biotechnology industries. Third, the differences between these two systems seem to be so clear and salient that one is tempted to see them as prototypes or generic systems. The UK system has important similarities to the US system. The Japanese and some European systems have important similarities to the German system. One has to beware of myths here, and further empirical research is desirable to check whether propositions concerning institutions, forms of co-ordination, and innovative performance are empirically correct, and how these vary between industries.

The lore is that US institutions are oriented towards autonomous agents, *ad hoc* contracting, exit, entailing easy buy and sell, hiring and firing, entry and exit, limited trust, and an inclination towards legal contracting. If this is true, then, according to the logic of the analysis, the US system would be prone to co-ordination based on a mix of the following forms: evasion of specific investments, integration into larger firms, legal contracting, non-exclusive and short-term interfirm relations. The composition of the mix would depend on the industry. Focus of buyers in their relations with suppliers would tend to be on low cost, achieved by bargaining under the threat of alternative partners, which requires abstention from switching costs due to specific investments. Whatever risks of opportunism are left are covered by legal contracting.

The expected performance of this system can be characterized as follows: low production costs due to competitive bidding for standard components and products, high transaction costs due to low trust and extensive legal contracting. Absence of specific investments leads to absence of switching costs, which enables exit, with intensive price competition, but also leads to low quality in the sense of undifferentiated, standard products, to the extent that technology is inflexible. Detailed contingent contracts are less feasible in turbulent environments of radical innovation, and if feasible would yield a straightjacket that frustrates the open-endedness required for collaboration in innovation. Low trust not only increases transaction costs, but also inhibits the information exchange required for such collaboration (out of fear of spillover). This limits collaboration to partners within the own firm, which yields the need to integrate contributing activities in the firm. But this reduces cognitive distance and thereby the variety and flexibility of sources of complementary competence and cognition. However, easy break-up of firms maintains flexibility of novel combinations, but the uncertainty and short-term orientation of intra-firm networks inhibits teamwork and the joint development and sharing of tacit knowledge. Performance is consequently strong in standardized products (limited specific investments) and product differentiation tends to occur in industries with flexible technology. The system is strong in: efficient, low-cost, large-scale production, high volatility of entrepreneurship, and creative destruction. It has limited strength in: the diffusion of innovation, high-added-value, differentiated products under inflexible technology, and innovations entailing much tacit knowledge that requires durable relations within and between firms. When the complementary knowledge from different sources needed for the novel combinations of radical innovation is explicit and therefore easily portable, then the US-type system can yield the basis for radical innovation through novel combinations.[4] If, on the other hand, complementary knowledge is tacit and embedded in people, teams, organizational structure, or culture, it can be acquired only through close and durable relations, with specific investments in mutual understanding and close co-operation.

Some of these predictions are consistent with the diagnosis of the US system offered by Mowery and Rosenberg (1993): too little diffusion and adoption of technology, at least in certain industries. However, under some conditions short-term orientation

---

[4] I owe this insight to a discussion with George Gelauff of the Dutch Central Planning Bureau.

and high volatility of entry, exit, and labour turnover need not form an obstacle, as is illustrated in the example of Silicon Valley, discussed in Chapter 8. Players may be highly experienced in crossing cognitive distance, and therefore not need to make high specific investments in knowledge exchange, and therefore do not need durable relations, and therefore can combine a high rate of innovation with volatile network structure. Concerning risk of spillover, while knowledge is probably highly tacit, there is threat of spillover through staff being poached. However, because knowledge is tacit, it will take some time for it to yield fruit in the new firm, and more so to the extent that it needs to be embedded and shared in teams and 'communities of practice'. By that time knowledge at the source may have shifted, to render the spillover innocuous.

Consistent with its institutions, oriented towards voice, durable relations, close ties, employee involvement in decision making, relations between unions, employer associations, and educational systems, Germany, by contrast, employs the following forms of co-ordination. Specific investments, more or less tight, exclusive and durable network relations, within and between firms and other organizations, co-ordinating intermediaries, and a mix of legal contracting, mutual interest, commitment, and trust, with the composition depending on the industry. This yields strength in high-value-added production, high quality, differentiated products, diffusion, incremental innovation, and radical innovation that requires the production, use, and exchange of tacit knowledge. Now, knowledge tends to be more tacit in the early stages of the cycle of discovery, so that the German-type system may have an advantage in that stage, i.e. at the early stages of the emergence of radical innovation. Exclusiveness, or small numbers of relations per activity, has its function in reducing set-up costs of relations, reducing risks of hold-up because of specific investments. It thereby encourages such investments, and limits risks of spillover. Note, moreover, that there is more variety as a source of innovation in linkages between firms than in linkages within firms. But this variety may also be limited because of the exclusiveness of relations, which limits new entry into the network, and variety within the network may erode (and cognitive distance may become too small) when the linkages last too long.

It was noted that when technology is flexible there is less need for specific investments in order to achieve differentiated products, and then, *ceteris paribus*, the US-type system has an advantage. This is important, because information and communication technology has the effect of enabling flexible production, of both services and goods; in particular, flexible manufacturing systems, including computer-aided design and computer simulation for virtual instead of physical testing of prototypes. This yields the prediction that the US-type system will be superior when this condition applies, as is likely in an increasing number of industries.

Note that in both systems there are both large firms and industrial-district-type forms of organization. However, compared to Germany, in the US large firms are more easily broken up and labour turnover is higher, and interfirm relations in industrial-district-type arrangements are less durable, more volatile, in exit-oriented relations (as in Silicon Valley).

The differences between the two systems are summarized in Table 12.1.

Application

TABLE 12.1   *The US and German systems*

	US: contractual, multiple	Germany: relational, exclusive
characteristic	formal, extensive contracts multiple, short relations	limited, implicit contracts lasting, more exclusive relations
mode of conduct	'exit'	'voice'
culture/institutions	individualistic, large firms, legalistic	groups, networks of firms, group ethic
mediating variables		
specific investments	low	high
switching costs	low	high
value of the partner	low	high
room for opportunism	low	high
inclination to opportunism	high	low
performance outcomes		
production costs	low	higher
transaction costs	higher	lower
product differentiation	low	high
incremental innovation	low	high
creative destruction	high	low?

Source: Nooteboom (1999*d*).

Summing up: The US system has the advantage when even in early stages complementary knowledge is explicit and documented, production technology is flexible, and required durability of employment, firm-specificity of knowledge, and the need for building durable teamwork are low. The German system has the advantage to the extent that the reverse applies: production technology is inflexible, and knowledge is more difficult to codify, and is more firm- or relation-specific, so that durability of relations between and within firms is needed.

A striking confirmation of some of these expectations is given by Casper's (1999) comparative study of the biotechnology industry in Germany and the US. In that industry there is a dual structure. On the one hand, there are volatile organizational structures in biotechnology, which produce novel designs of products and processes. On the other hand, there is the more stable structure of the pharmaceutical industry, which carries such novel products through procedures of testing and regulatory approval and into efficient production, marketing, and distribution. One would predict that the US system is better at the first type of activity, because it requires more volatility. This is what Casper finds. One would also predict that when as a result of tacitness of knowledge more intimate, durable relations of corporate governance are required the German system has the advantage. This is precisely what Casper also finds. The type of biotechnology that has recently developed in Germany has that characteristic.

12.3.4   A Third Way?

There is a policy implication for continental European countries, particularly for the Netherlands, which seems to be at the forefront in following Anglo-American systems of financial and corporate control, under the rallying cry of 'shareholder value'. Before we gravitate further towards the Anglo-American system we should be aware that we cannot adopt one part of the system (e.g. shareholder value in corporate governance) without the other (easy break-up of firms and short-term labour relations).

Policy measures against interfirm linkages may well result in further concentration and conglomeration, and from the perspective of both static and dynamic efficiency that may be worse than networks. This connects with an ongoing debate on the benefits of mergers and acquisitions. The weight of criticism of mergers and acquisitions increases when the resulting integrated firms cannot easily be broken up. We should be aware that the easy break-up of firms needed for radical innovation in the US system may have detrimental effects on the commitment of labour to firm-specific training and teamwork which may also be needed for radical innovation, as discussed above.

A central policy question is whether there is a viable intermediate system between the US and German systems (a 'third way'), that has the advantages of both without the disadvantages. This third way would adopt from the relational German-type system its in-depth co-operation, with specific investments, differentiated products, and intensive exchange of knowledge. However, it would combine this with the greater flexibility and multiplicity of relations from the US-type system. In short, whereas the US system was characterized by 'contractual and multiple' forms of co-ordination, and the German system by 'relational and exclusive' forms, the third way would be characterized by 'relational and multiple' forms. This is summarized in Table 12.2.

How can such a system work; what are the institutional and technological prerequisites? It was noted before that the problem of spillover disappears in a world of radical speed of change in complex technologies and markets (Nooteboom 1998). Then, there is no longer any limit to the number of partners in co-operation. That offers more *possibilities* for multiple relations. And in such a world there is also a greater *need* of multiple, non-exclusive relations: competition more and more becomes a race to the market with new products. To have any chance of winning the race one must limit oneself to core competencies, which implies co-operation with others. In that situation one needs more variety of sources for co-operation, rather than a few exclusive ones.

How is that goal realized? Multiplicity of relations entails multiplication of set-up costs of relations and of the costs of specific investments. The first problem may be mitigated by declining costs of contact between firms, as a result of the further development of information and communication technology. That may be expected to further decrease the costs of setting up and entertaining a network linkage. The second problem lessens if flexible technology also is a salient part of the new world, because, as discussed, products can then be differentiated without specific assets.

TABLE 12.2   *A third way*

	relational, multiple
characteristic	limited, implicit, contracts; open, multiple relations
mode of conduct	'voice'
culture/institutions	networks, group ethic, use of 'go-betweens'
intervening variables	
specific investments	high
switching costs	middle
value of the partner	high
room for opportunism	high
inclination to opportunism	low
performance outcomes	
production costs	low
transaction costs	low
product differentiation	high
incremental innovation	high
creative destruction	high

Source: Nooteboom (1999*d*).

Suppose, however, that technology is not that flexible. In principle, in view of specific investments a relation need not last longer than needed to recoup those investments. As the theory of repeated games tells us, a danger may arise when one establishes beforehand when a relation is to be ended. It is precisely in the uncertainty about the end, and the possibility of an ongoing relation, that it may be in one's self-interest to refrain from opportunism. Yet these two principles can be reconciled. One can make firm agreements for a duration that does not exceed the time needed to recoup the investment, and yet keep the option open for renewed continuation if the relation fits the new conditions and yields attractive prospects. That gives more flexibility than now, in the German-type system, for the reconfiguration of relations when the gales of creative destruction gather. This is indicated in Table 12.2 by taking switching costs as of 'middle' height.

Clearly, there must be a fit between the 'third way' and existing institutions. If trust is not already in place, on the basis of well-developed and shared norms of conduct, as part of the institutional environment, and has to be built up in each relation, then the time needed to do that, and to recoup the specific investment that it constitutes, can pose a problem. The minimal duration of a relation then is determined by the longest of the following two: the time needed to recoup specific investments and the time needed to build trust and recoup the investment that it represents. If the latter is decisive, then a possible solution is that the source of trust is not sought within a given

relation, but in a larger group of potential partners that can enter upon varying relations among each other. And that, it seems, is exactly the function of the Japanese enterprise groups (*keiretsu*). Clearly, the institutional environment must be there to enable
such systems. The advantage of such groups is that on the one hand there are trust
and durable relations within the group, and on the other hand competition between
the groups is maintained. This by itself does not imply that the Japanese system is
ideal. The possibly excessive duration of relations and the relative exclusiveness of,
especially, vertical buyer–supplier relations yield an obstacle to innovation, since they
curtail the variety of contacts that is a source of innovation (Nooteboom 1998).

Along these lines, policy should seek to establish a reconciliation between co-
operation (durable linkages) and competition in the sense of multiplicity of relations,
a greater ease of entry and exit in networks. For this, relations should be sufficiently
durable but no more than needed to recover the specific investments needed for high
quality of products and collaboration in innovation. The use of third parties as 'go-
betweens', to mediate between would-be partners as an 'engine of voice', might be an
important part of the system. The question is who would perform such roles, and how
that would be enabled by the institutional environment.

Clearly, there are more questions concerning the institutionalization needed to
support a 'third way'. There is no space to pose and answer all those questions here.
That would constitute a subject for further study.

12.3.5   Country Specialization

While the third way might be optimal, it may not be necessary, and it is not likely
to be feasible for all industries in all countries. It depends on the type of industry, the
stage of its development, and the institutional environment. For a given country it
might be approached in some industries but not in others. The analysis, together with
other considerations, such as geographical location, may provide a basis for explaining industry specialization across countries. In view of differences in institutions,
enabling different forms of co-ordination, and the fact that different industries tend
to require different forms of co-ordination, it is not self-evident that all countries
should aim at the same 'most profitable' or 'most promising' emerging industries.
One should choose industries in which one has comparative institutional advantage.
This should be taken into account next to traditional elements of comparative advantage, such as availability and price-of-production factors.

As noted in Chapter 11, rather than convergence of economic systems across the
globe, specialized local conditions, including institutions, may provide a basis for
competitive advantage of nations. However, in the process of utilizing the opportunities of complementary competencies between foreign and domestic firms institutions
are likely to develop in directions that are hard to predict and may or may not yield
greater or lesser convergence. Institutions are subject not so much to design as to a
process of change that may also satisfy our cycle of discovery. Through reciprocation
between incoming and domestic institutions novel combinations may arise. This need

not yield an equilibrium of institutional convergence any more than innovation in general yields an equilibrium.

Another way to look at country specialization is to look at 'stage specialization': specialization in terms of the stages of the cycle of discovery, for any given industry. Conditions in one country might be conducive to the volatility required for the stage of radical, architectural innovation, in novel combinations. In another country they may be more conducive to the stages of consolidation and generalization. Other countries might be more expert at differentiation of products across different markets. Rather than trying to be good at all stages in all industries, one might establish linkages with other countries with complementary institutional competencies at different stages.

For an illustration, let us reconsider Casper's (1999) comparative study of the biotechnology industry in Germany and the US. In some branches of the industry the knowledge required for innovation is more documented and the building of durable linkages in teams within firms and durable relations between firms may be less important. In other branches, where knowledge is more tacit, and there is a greater need for specific investments, with greater drawbacks of detailed legal governance, durable networks between firms and durable employment relations within firms may be more important. One country might be better equipped, institutionally, for the one and another country for the other. Or one country is better at dealing with the volatility of biotechnology, while another is better at developing efficient systems for the production and distribution of drugs and gaining regulatory approval of new drugs, in the pharmaceutical industry. Rather than trying to be good at all stages in all industries, countries might more profitably seek patterns of complementary institutional advantage between countries. One country might supply novel drug designs, to be carried through regulatory approval and efficient production and distribution in another country.

In fact, it is probably such a strategy that multinational firms are following in their internationalization policies. Moving through cycles of discovery, they seek to shift their activities to where conditions are most conducive to the stage in hand. Governments should determine at what stages in what industries their institutional advantages lie, and construct policies accordingly. From that perspective they might determine where weaknesses lie, and where changes at the surface level of institutions needed to reduce them are feasible and fitting in the deep structure of institutions. One might then attract foreign firms that fit in such a strategy, either because they fit or because they can help to achieve desirable shifts in institutional surface structure.

12.4   CONCLUSION

The cycle of discovery developed in Chapter 9 has been applied to modify and extend the life-cycle theory of innovation and industrial dynamics. With that theory it shares the notion that radical novelty arises in a state of flux and confusion, which needs some time to settle down in a dominant design. I add that this is accompanied by the transformation of tacit, procedural into explicit, declarative knowledge (see Figure 9.2). The dominant design and declarative knowledge allow for the co-ordination needed for division of labour to attain economy of scale. It provides the basis for the specification of standard operating procedures, contracts and co-ordination at distance, allowing for generalization to novel contexts. To the life-cycle theory I add the subsequent stages of building up experience in a variety of new contexts, to gather the experience needed for abduction towards the next novelty. Thus, the circle is closed, to show not only how novelty gets settled and diffused, but also how it arises.

As in the punctuated-equilibrium view I recognize discontinuities, but try to eliminate the mystery of the origin of punctuation by showing how experience can build up to it along the cycle of discovery. I also recognize that innovative discontinuities yield creative destruction of competencies. When they destroy competencies or resources of production or organization in existing firms, this yields an advantage to new entrants. But when they destroy user or supply-chain competencies or resources, large incumbent firms may be at an advantage.

In spite of the complexity of institutional and other effects, an attempt was made to sketch generic systems of governance in the context of innovation. There has been an emphasis on co-ordination between firms because that is required if we see innovations systems as systems of interaction between organizations, and this aspect is not well developed in the literature. The suggestion was introduced that in government policy one might look at country specialization not just in terms of industry specialization but also in terms of stage specialization, i.e. specialization in the stages in the cycle of discovery.

In Chapter 13 I proceed to a closer analysis of what goes on within and between organizations, and the implications for the management of firms.

13

Organizational Learning

The results from previous Chapters are now applied to an analysis of organizational learning, i.e. the generation, transformation, and transfer of knowledge and ideas in and between organizations. First, a comparison is made between the cycle and earlier treatments of similar issues in the literature. The issue of organizational learning is linked with the notion of entrepreneurship. It is argued that different notions of entrepreneurship connect with different stages in the cycle of discovery. Next, the structure and process of organization are analysed from the perspective of learning, and the implications are considered for the development of organizations and the management of learning.

13.1   COMPARISONS

First, the cycle of learning and discovery, called 'the cycle' from now on, is compared with other discussions of knowledge processes found in the literature, as discussed in Chapter 2: Nonaka and Takeuchi (1995), Choo (1998), and Volberda (1998). Attempts are made to fit their views into the cycle. This serves to test the value of the cycle as an integrative framework.

13.1.1   *Knowledge Conversion*

As discussed in Chapter 2, Nonaka and Takeuchi (1995) offered a view on how novelty emerges from different stages in the conversion and combination of knowledge. Part of their story can be fitted into the present cycle, as follows: They proposed that explicit knowledge is combined with explicit knowledge (*combination*) for efficient and systematic utilization. In the present cycle of discovery this occurs at the stages of consolidation and generalization, as discussed in previous Chapters. Next, as a practice spreads, in generalization, it is *internalized* into tacit, routinized practice. New tacit knowledge accrues, in *socialization*, in the new contexts encountered in the processes of differentiation and reciprocation. One of the examples Nonaka and Takeuchi presented was a cook's skill in kneading dough, to infer the proper design of a bread-baking machine. According to Nonaka and Takeuchi such combinations of tacit knowledge are next *externalized* to yield explicit, codified designs for approval by top management. My story differs here: I unpack the process of making novel combinations. But then, as the trial and error of novel combinations converges on a dominant

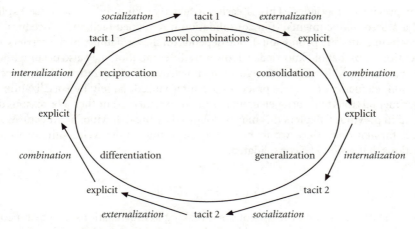

FIGURE 13.1   *Cycles of knowledge conversion*

design, in consolidation, tacit knowledge is indeed externalized, with some loss in abstraction, into codified knowledge.

Figure 13.1 illustrates how the conversions of knowledge proposed by Nonaka and Takeuchi can be built into the cycle of discovery. What this adds to their analysis is the explanation of the rationale of the cycle. It explains how the conversions of knowledge relate to stages in a discovery process, why they occur in the order indicated, how this combines exploitation and exploration, how each stage enables the next, and why and how transitions between the stages take place.

As noted before, in Chapter 9, the cycle implies that there are two kinds of tacit knowledge. First, in the emergence of novelty knowledge is tacit because there is lack of understanding of how and why precisely new things work. It is only through further experimentation and trial and error in application that such understanding emerges and knowledge gets codified. This is needed to abstract from the specific context of discovery, as a basis for generalization to novel contexts. Later, codified and documented knowledge often becomes routinized, subsiding into tacit knowledge in the sense of subsidiary awareness (Polanyi 1962), at the stage of generalization. In contrast with the first type of tacit knowledge, this second type often was once codified and documented, prior to routinization, and may be reconstructed as such, if the routine has not subsided too much into 'second nature'. However, in consolidation knowledge may never get codified, and may be transferred as tacit knowledge. In other words, tacit knowledge may be internalized as such and then develop into a routine. It may remain in procedural memory, without ever entering declarative memory. As discussed in Chapter 3, this is what typically happens in crafts or professions, where the master transfers tacit knowledge to the apprentice.

When the need for differentiation is encountered in novel contexts, knowledge may be externalized again to design adaptations through novel combinations of knowledge from previous experience. This is easiest when that knowledge was once explicit and is stored in documents. If in consolidation it remained tacit and procedural (as happens in crafts and professions), one depends on the availability of the carriers and practitioners of that old knowledge. However, differentiation may also occur without externalization, with combinations of tacit knowledge, in socialization. Next, in reciprocation, elements of outside practices are internalized, largely by socialization, in experimental trials to transfer elements from one practice to another. For reasons discussed in previous Chapters this may be followed by breakdown of architectures and search for new ones. Here, we are back at the beginning of the cycle, with novel combinations that need to be consolidated.

13.1.2   *Sense Making*

Choo (1998) focuses on processes of sense making in organizations, in which people construct knowledge and generate ideas: 'the organization provides a physical, social and cultural context so that the experience and growth of this knowledge takes on meaning and purpose' (p. 105). Here, the paradox of exploitation and exploration appears as a paradox of limiting and maintaining ambiguity. The basic scheme that Choo proposes for understanding organizations and managing information is a 'knowing cycle' of sense making, decision making, and knowledge creating. Sense making and decision making are connected by 'premise control'. The relation between sense making and knowledge creation is described in a way that provides a link with the work of Nonaka and Takeuchi.

Sense making must tap into the mental models and experiences of individual members of the organization. The resultant shared interpretation provides a framework for joint organizational action. This view shows how the personal, tacit knowledge of individuals may be unlocked and converted into explicit knowledge that moves organizational innovation. It helps to get away from the old top-down view of planning that 'management knows' and can tell people what to do. It recognizes that it is often the people working at the interfaces with technology, customers, competitors, suppliers, and other outside partners who know what the options are for elements to be brought together in new organizational action. In terms of the cycle from Chapter 6, they are channels of reciprocation.

Choo identifies a 'success trap', which is close to the notion of 'inertia', and a 'failure cycle' (see the quotations in Chapter 2). This is close to what in this book, and elsewhere, is called the 'chaos' of unending attempts at novel combinations (see Figure 9.1).

Further elements from Choo's analysis, relevant to the present discussion, are the following:

1. the distinction between cognitive 'elements' (preferred types of information and data) and 'operators' (methods by which information is ordered and arranged to make sense) (p. 90). This may be similar to the notion of nodes in a script, discussed in Chapter 10;

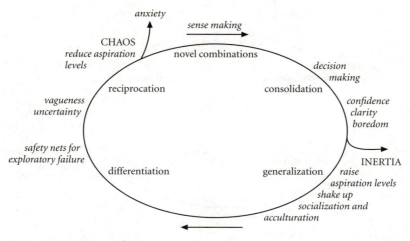

FIGURE 13.2   *Sense making*

2. the reference to Hayek's notion that we should let the context carry some of the representational and computational load (p. 116) and the reference to Vygotsky's 'activity theory' as an underlying theory of knowledge and language (p. 224). This entails the idea that activity systems are mediated (in language, technology, collaboration) in particular contexts, and are provisional (forever subject to development), pragmatic (purposive and object oriented), and contested. This point is close to the approach taken in this book, in the situated-action theory discussed extensively in Chapter 6, with the notion of scaffolding provided by the context of action.

Some elements from the work of Choo can be incorporated into the cycle of discovery, presented in Chapter 9, as illustrated in Figure 13.2. Note that the 'reduction' or 'slowdown' of socialization and acculturation, as a shake-up to break away from inertia (see the quotation from Choo in Chapter 2), connects with the need for organizational disintegration, as a condition for exploration, discussed in Chapter 11.

Not everything from Choo's analysis can be incorporated in the cycle, and the cycle goes beyond his analysis. In particular, Choo's cycle of information search for the solution of a problem, in terms of initiation, selection, exploration, formulation, collection, presentation, leading up to resolution of the problem (see Chapter 2), applies only when a clearly defined problem arises. It frequently does, but that does not apply to discovery. Choo does not seem to recognize what in earlier Chapters was called the problem of abduction. The availability of a clear problem that merits search for information, and criteria for relevant information, cannot be taken for granted. The main point of the discovery procedure is finding out where problems lie, which deserve priority, what might be promising or viable elements of a solution, where they

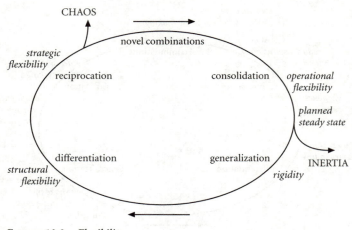

FIGURE 13.3   *Flexibility*

are to be searched for, and what the architecture of a new solution might be. Choo does give a clue here: search is serial rather than parallel, i.e. alternatives in the neighbourhood of the problem symptom are searched for first. The cycle of discovery presented in Chapter 9 is proposed as a theory of how this proceeds: how the motivation, elements, and directions for change are accumulated in applications that branch out from the 'neighbourhood' of existing practice.

13.1.3   Flexibility

Volberda (1998) makes a distinction between different types of flexibility: steady state, operational, structural, and strategic. They are defined by their location in a two-by-two matrix that crosses variety of (managerial) capabilities and the organization's responsiveness to such capabilities. Operational flexibility entails low variety of capabilities and fast response, structural flexibility entails high variety and slow response, and strategic flexibility entails high variety and fast response. Rigidity, which here is called inertia, entails low variety and slow response. Figure 13.3 yields an attempt to integrate this into the cycle of discovery.

While Volberda's typology of flexibility has considerable appeal, I have a problem with the suggestion that capabilities for change are the prerogative of management, as discussed in Chapter 2. Volberda also yields another typology of alternative flexible forms: rigid, planned, flexible, chaotic. Examples of the flexible form are the social network firm and the 'cluster organization', and 'regional cluster organization' (presumably what in the economic literature is called 'industrial districts', going back to the work of Marshall). In the chaotic firm: 'innumerable initiatives are impossible to implement . . . [there is] no distinct technology, stable administrative structure, or basic shared values (so that) the organization is controlled by the environment' (p. 214). I prefer this approach to the previous one. Here, chaos seems to be ascribed not to lack of controllability but to lack of coherence.

According to Volberda the key challenge for management is to establish the right kind of flexibility at the right time, when conditions demand it. Here, I would say that this is to be done according to the demands of the stage of development, as illustrated in Figure 13.3. The crucial question then is how organizations are to achieve this, in organizational structures, processes, and management. In the next paragraph this will be analysed from the perspective of entrepreneurship.

13.2   ENTREPRENEURSHIP

Production of novelty, or exploration, is clearly related to the notion of entrepreneurship. Thus, there must be a relation between entrepreneurship and the cycle of discovery. There is a variety of notions of entrepreneurship and the suggestion sometimes is that one of them must be 'the correct' notion. Here, it will be shown that different types of entrepreneurship may be seen as belonging to different stages in the cycle of discovery.

13.2.1   Variety of Concepts

In Chapter 3 it was noted that different notions of entrepreneurship emphasize different things, in different combinations (cf. Hébert & Link 1982, Chell *et al.* 1991, Thurik 1996, van Praag 1996):

- innovation (Bentham, Thünen, Schumpeter, and perhaps Say)
- creative destruction through novel combinations (Schumpeter)
- the identification and utilization of possibilities for consumption and production (Cantillon, Smith, Menger, Mises, Hayek, Kirzner)
- the configuration and management of production factors for efficient production (Say, Marshall, Mises)
- the provision of capital (Marshall)

According to Schumpeter entrepreneurs form an élite, while according to (other) Austrian theorists (especially von Mises) entrepreneurship is widely dispersed. Some theorists emphasize the acceptance of risks (Cantillon, Say, Knight) and the role of fundamental, unpredictable uncertainty (Cantillon, Knight, Menger). Associated with different roles of entrepreneurs different characteristics, resources, or competencies have been identified: imagination, alertness, perceptiveness, open-mindedness; judgement, sense of realism; risk acceptance, risk reduction; supply of capital or other resources; perseverance, ambition, or need for achievement, independence, charisma, strength of personality; capability of leadership, managerial capability. I propose that rather than any single notion or characteristic of entrepreneurship being universally 'true', regardless of context and conditions, different notions fit different stages in the cycle of discovery.

There are cases of entrepreneurship that are difficult to assign to either the Schumpeterian or the Kirznerian type, because they contain elements of both. Schumpeterian entrepreneurs build on inventions that were already there and in that sense also 'merely' utilize existing potential. Moreover, there are different levels of innovativeness: radical and incremental, innovations of principle and innovations of application, in different fields or contexts. An important type of innovation, between Schumpeterian entrepreneurship and entrepreneurship according to (other) Austrians, is product differentiation. It can be reconstructed as bridging gaps between supply and demand in Lancasterian product-characteristics space (Lancaster 1966), by offering novel combinations of available product characteristics. This is Austrian in that no new characteristic appears, and gaps are bridged in characteristics space by varying intensities of characteristic in the mix. Differentiation becomes more Schumpeterian when it consists of the addition of a new product dimension, shifting the positioning of existing products and preferences (Péli & Nooteboom 1999).

According to the cycle of discovery, without innovations of application (in differentiation, reciprocation) creative destruction (novel combinations) would not take place. Diffusion does not consist in a simple mechanical working out of a single innovation. Generally, new contexts or new applications require adjustment or reinvention. Is this secondary innovation Schumpeterian or Kirznerian? The whole notion of equilibrium, and the distinction between equilibrating (Kirznerian) and disequilibrating (Schumpeterian) entrepreneurship becomes problematic. The point of the cycle is that in the combination of exploitation and exploration, in consolidation, generalization, differentiation, reciprocation, and novel combinations in novel architectures, diffusion lays the basis for the next innovation. What is supposed to be equilibrating is at the same time disequilibrating in the sense that it prepares for the next innovation. As discussed in Chapter 3, entrepreneurship can be seen in both the creation and the realization of potential. The cycle of discovery entails that the realization of potential lays the basis for new creation of potential. Thus, along the cycle we find a combination of the two types, with the emphasis shifting from Schumpeterian to Kirznerian, as pointed out by Cheah and Robertson (1992).

13.2.2   A Cycle of Entrepreneurship

There is not any single 'true' type of entrepreneurship, but a whole range of types, corresponding with the different stages of the discovery process proposed in Chapter 9 (Figure 9.1). Rather than being alternatives between which one must choose, these types are complementary: they build upon each other. In combination with the corresponding cycle of integration and disintegration illustrated in Figure 11.1, this idea reflects the notion of 'dynamic complementarity', first proposed by Rothwell (1985, see also Rothwell 1989). According to this notion, small and large firms have different roles to fulfil in innovation, and are complementary to each other.

The stages of consolidation and generalization, with their shift to more systemic integration, increase of scale, division of labour, and co-ordination would connect with Say's and Marshall's notions of entrepreneurship. In differentiation, practices are further adapted to differences in demand. It entails the realization of existing potential, but also entails learning and conceptual change, leading up to a next innovation, and this is part of Austrian entrepreneurship according to Menger and Hayek. Reciprocation, which has the logical structure of metaphor, is more Schumpeterian in that it explores elements for novel combinations. Schumpeterian entrepreneurship fully comes into its own (but goes beyond Schumpeter) in accommodation towards novel combinations in novel architectures, where existing structures of action (scripts) are broken down and from the debris novel practices are experimentally built up, to survive, die, or be improved in the subsequent stage of consolidation.

But the point of the discussion here is not to fit in existing notions of entrepreneurship without overlap and gaps, and thereby reduce the cycle of discovery to existing notions of entrepreneurship. The point is to provide a new perspective beyond existing notions of entrepreneurship, and to deduce types of entrepreneurship that were not recognized before. The following types of entrepreneurship then emerge:

In differentiation:
• Adaptation of practices to a diversity of demand or available inputs, while maintaining the basic elements and architecture of existing practice. The need and opportunity for this derives from attempts at generalization to novel contexts. This requires some degree of perceptiveness, imagination, and resources, scope for initiative and the courage to use it. It requires a certain amount of decentralization.

In reciprocation:
• Importation of elements from 'adjacent' practices that in novel contexts appear to be better in some respect of product or production, while maintaining the architecture of the practice in hand. The requirements from the previous stage apply to a higher degree: imagination to produce metaphorical ideas for novel combinations. In an existing firm, it requires an organizational structure and culture that allow for that.

In accommodation:
• Recombination of elements from diverse practices in a new architecture. If the origin of ideas lay inside a large, integrated organization, this will often require a spin-off. This stage requires exceptional imagination, heterodoxy, courage, and organizational autonomy.

In consolidation:
• Trials of new combinations. This requires risk acceptance, determination, perseverance, and charisma and leadership to bring other people along, including suppliers of capital.

- Efficient selection of failures. This requires sense of realism, judgement, or an efficient selection environment.
- Adapting existing systems of application to allow the innovation to achieve its fullest potential. It may require standardization, large-scale production, utilization of scope. This requires influence, resources, management, co-ordination.

In generalization:

- Further standardization, increase of scale, internationalization (export, foreign investment). A Chandlerian or Weberian marshalling and rational direction of coherent systems of specialized resources. This requires a variety of resources, including international experience and contacts, ability to co-ordinate.

Let us review how the process works, at the level of an industry. We need to show how firms seeking their own self-interest generate discovery in markets. At the industry level, if at any stage incumbents failed to utilize any opportunity produced by preceding stages, sooner or later some firm would enter from somewhere in the world to do it, if there were no entry barriers to prevent that. Note that when the logic of discovery is applied to the market, it is pervaded by competition. But shifts occur between different types of competition, and competition is seldom perfect. The drive behind competition is that entrepreneurs at all stages try to distinguish themselves from others, and thereby push profits above marginal costs. They do this by the following activities:

- differentiating their products (at the stage of differentiation);
- adding novelties in the form of features from other contexts (in reciprocation);
- coming up with novel combinations (accommodation);
- developing the most efficient form of a novelty (consolidation, substage 1);
- effecting wider systemic changes to utilize the full potential of a novelty (consolidation, substage 2);
- implementing scale, scope, and efficient production;
- carrying the novelty to new contexts through exports and foreign investment (generalization).

Competition does not take the form of everyone doing the same thing and pushing prices to marginal costs, but rather replacing products and practices by ones that are better, being more efficient, or satisfying preferences more closely, or generating novel perspectives for production or consumption.

A firm is not likely to survive and make a profit if it does not contribute to this process. To do so, it will have to offer the type of entrepreneurship which is appropriate to the stage to which it aims to contribute, as deduced above. It is not likely to succeed if it tries to organize large-scale production before knowledge about it has become documented to provide the basis for division and co-ordination of labour. The chance of failure is large in carrying a practice to large-scale and novel markets before it has proved its feasibility and worth. Novel combinations which are a leap in the dark, in random trial, may succeed but are less likely to do so than trials informed by experience. Such experience is derived from the failures of existing practices, insight into opportunities for variations in different contexts, and experiments with novel combinations of elements from practices that have similar elements or architectures.

13.3   ORGANIZING FOR EXPLOITATION AND EXPLORATION

Given the requirements of entrepreneurship, appropriate to the stages of the cycle, how should organizations be structured and how can they adapt their structures, to solve the paradox of exploitation and exploration?

13.3.1   *Exploitation and Exploration*

The core problem of how to combine exploitation and exploration can now be formulated as follows: How can one organize so as to satisfy the different requirements of different stages in the discovery process?

The literature proposes that in the development of new firms there is a process of routinization or bureaucratization, which accords with the notion of consolidation. Volberda (1998: 217–18) formulated it as follows:

[first] . . . flexibility . . . is created from . . . chaotic international expansion activities . . . [later] the flexible organization faces a crisis. It must become more efficient in its operations to extract greater benefit from the changes that it introduced previously, and to exploit its existing knowledge and opportunities

As discussed in Chapters 2 and 11, the business literature also identifies shifts between disintegration and integration. Organizational scholars have indicated that the appropriate form depends on the volatility of conditions. Under volatile conditions of rapidly changing technology and markets the more disintegrated form is best, and under more stable conditions the more integrated, centralized form is often best. Consistent with this, in Chapter 11 a cycle of integration and disintegration was proposed, in connection with the cycle of discovery. Integration is needed for consolidation and generalization, but subsequently different degrees of disintegration are needed for differentiation, reciprocation, and novel combinations. In Chapters 9 and 11 it was concluded that along the cycle exploration can be combined with exploitation, and this contributes to the resolution of a paradox, but for this firms have to deal with the alternation of integration and disintegration. How can this be done?

Nonaka and Takeuchi proposed that management should be conducted 'middle-up-down'. It is a job of middle management to tap tacit, experiential knowledge coming from below, where internalization and socialization take place, and externalize it to generate proposals to be put to management, and to facilitate the combination of different areas of explicit knowledge at lower levels. For exploring innovative, novel combinations, Nonaka and Takeuchi recommend a 'hypertext' organization, by analogy to windows processing on computers. This is somewhat like a flexible form of matrix organization: cross-functional and cross-departmental groups are formed *ad hoc*, according to the opportunity at hand, like opening windows on the computer.

As noted in Chapter 2, Volberda (1998) identifies several ways to solve the paradox of exploitation and exploration. One is separation in place: one part of an organization engages in exploitation, another in exploration. There is horizontal and vertical separation. In horizontal separation one division or department, typically R & D, preferably in collaboration with marketing, engages in exploration, and another, typically production, engages in exploitation. The problem here is of course how to govern the interface. There is the perennial frustration of marketing people that production people are 'not willing' or 'not competent' to deliver what market opportunities call for, and the equally perennial frustration of production people that marketing people are too dense to appreciate what is technically feasible and cost-effective. Vertical separation can go two ways. Management yields scope for exploration to take place 'below', where people interact with the market and with sources of technology, labour, inputs, to utilize the opportunities they meet, and management tries to maintain sufficient coherence to prevent waste through duplication and mismatch. Alternatively, management lays claim to choices of direction and content, and co-ordinates staff in the execution of their vision.

Many organizational scholars have dealt with this theme (e.g. J. D. Thompson 1967). In economics it was discussed by Aoki (1986), who made a distinction between a horizontal and a vertical 'information structure'. In the vertical structure management co-ordinates workshops but is incapable of adequate monitoring of emerging events in markets and technologies. In the horizontal structure production decisions are co-ordinated among semi-autonomous shops, which can better respond on the spot to emerging events. The former is typically American (the 'A firm'), Aoki proposes, and the latter typically Japanese (the 'J firm'). In the A firm there are clear job specifications, and standard operating procedures. Problem solving is relegated to supervisors, repairmen, and engineers. In the J firm, duties are not specified in detail, and workers rotate across jobs so that they become familiar with a wide range of activities, as a basis for horizontal co-ordination. Decentralization is also carried across the boundaries of the firm to suppliers, who are given more scope for initiative. The weak spot of this arrangement is that in spite of rotation the insight needed for effective co-ordination may be too limited. Moreover, suppliers may have divergent strategic orientations that are at odds with the firm's focus on core competencies or activities.

If it is correct that exploitation is associated with relatively integrated structures and exploration with more disintegrated structures, this sheds further light on the tension between exploitation and exploration. The part of the organization that is oriented towards exploitation is oriented towards structure, co-ordination, standards, stability, preservation of boundaries, efficiency. The part that is oriented towards exploration is oriented towards process, autonomy, breaking standards, change, crossing boundaries, novelty. The one sees the other as bureaucratic and non-entrepreneurial, and is itself seen as erratic, wasteful, disorganized, and inefficient.

Another separation between exploitation and exploration proposed by Volberda is separation in time: exploitation occurs at one time, and exploration at another. This yields the 'oscillating' (Burns & Stalker 1961) or 'ambidexterous' (Duncan 1976) or 'two-state' (Shepard 1967) mode, with a to-and-fro from disintegrated, loose, and open to integrated, tight, and homogeneous, and back again. The question is how people can be so flexible as to cope with the implied uncertainty and instability.

A third type of separation is the following: separation according to seniority. One form is that junior staff are trained in exploitation, subject to strict standards of efficient production, and may proceed to more autonomous, varied, exploratory work after they prove their ability and mastery of standard work and accumulate experience as a basis for it. The disadvantage of this is that senior people may have become too committed to or entrenched in past or existing concepts, standards, and procedures. Thus, the reverse approach is also conceivable, where junior people are allowed to generate novelty, on the basis of the freshness of their insights, and the senior people help to implement ideas in efficient production, on the basis of their experience.

> An illustration is a Dutch computing-services firm (Pink Elephant), which started out with the management of computer systems, and later branched out into consultancy. The first activity is geared to efficient, standardized procedures (exploitation), and the second is more geared to innovative, tailor-made solutions, which are more exploratory. Junior staff enter in the first activity and may be promoted to the second.

A fourth type of separation is based on a dual internal labour market. Routinized exploitation is relegated to temporary staff, who are hived off when their skills have become redundant or obsolete, if they are unable to adjust. Exploration is conducted in an ongoing fashion by highly skilled core workers. The danger of this form is that exploration is no longer informed by experience in exploitation. An example is massive back-office clerical work in administration or simple programming, which is typically located in low-wage countries with little job security.

13.3.2 A Selectionist Approach

Chapter 2 discussed Burgelman's (1996) view of the generation and utilization of ideas in a firm as a Darwinian selection process. Could this yield a solution to the paradox of exploitation and exploration? How cognitive selection might work at the level of the person, in neural processes of cognition, is indicated in Chapter 6: the selectionist process in the formation of neural nets that embody cognitive categories, proposed by Edelman (1987, 1992). This is based on a principle of redundancy: for each practice alternative ways of doing things are generated, and those ways are reinforced that turn out to be successful. In other words, each form is oriented towards efficient exploitation, and structural change in exploration is effected at the population level by selecting those that are most apt to the task at hand. But, contrary to the suggestion from the term 'neural Darwinism' employed by Edelman, this selection is not quite

Darwinist. The units selected here are neural networks. They can not only be rein-forced or weakened by strengthening or weakening synaptic connections, but also overlap and in synaptic adaptations can generate novel combinations of parts of net-works. Or at least that is how I understand Edelman's work.

Of course a big difference between neural networks and organizations is that we are not dealing with neurons but with people. And the notion of a 'garbage can' of ran-domly generated ideas seems to deny human capabilities of rational inference. Whilst rationality is no doubt bounded, it is not totally absent. Nevertheless, some degree of randomness and redundancy for *ex post* selection on the basis of proven success may be part of the solution. This is the case especially when uncertainty is so large as to limit rational, systematic exploration.

In Chapter 10 cognitive and organizational networks (and competencies and institutions) were rendered as scripts, with people substituting activities into nodes, according to their skills and their organizational roles. These activities in turn spill over into activities and experiences of those people in other contexts. There is ongo-ing metaphorical transfer from those outside activities into organizational activities, depending on how tightly organizational roles are restricted and monitored. This yields a source of variety, which generates mistakes, accidents, and innovation. In second-order learning, and radical novel combinations, scripts break down; rule-based behaviour turns into less structured storytelling (Shank & Abelson 1995), improvisation, and play. It can turn into chaos. The pooling of nodes from a variety of scripts, accumulated in the process of reciprocation, without a clear architecture, yields redundancy from which trials of novel combinations can arise. Here, in the selection from trials, at the stage of novel combinations and the early stage of con-solidation, the discovery process is at its most Darwinian.

Redundancy, to create a pool of variety for selection, can be created in different ways. One is to duplicate several subsidiaries, divisions, or departments, or jobs and skills. However, such redundancy is inefficient and difficult to manage.

> Burgelman (1996: 415) employed the example of INTEL. At first, the company tried to maintain a disintegrated structure by 'forming relatively small business units and creating a bottom-up strat-egic planning system. However, that became very unwieldy . . . The system is now more top down'.

One way of duplicating skills is to rotate personnel. That has the added advantage of creating connections between different areas of knowledge, as a basis for hori-zontal co-ordination without management intervention, as indicated above in the account given by Aoki (1986).

Redundancy and trials to some extent can be virtual rather than real. People and organizations have memory, and they communicate, so that not every alternative needs to be actually practised and rehearsed in the firm. Alternative modes may be remembered as practices that performed well in the past. In other words, there can be redundancy in the mind of alternative concepts that can be triggered into action when circumstances require it. Or ideas are gleaned from what others do, in other organ-izations, to the extent that this can be understood at a distance. That forms the basis for comparison; for metaphoric transfer. Moreover, while under radical uncertainty one cannot forecast, one can construct scenarios, i.e. plausible possible futures, and explore what actions would work under what conditions, to see what actions are robust under a variety of futures.

> As indicated before, that is what Shell Oil Company developed in the seventies, and what helped it through the oil crises. Note that scenarios have a double function. One is to anticipate the future even if it is radically uncertain. The second is to reduce redundancy and yet maintain a variety of options. This operates through the investigation of the robustness of strategies across scenarios: find out what elements of strategy and corresponding elements of corporate structure appear in best strategies in different scenarios and focus on the building and maintenance of those elements. This helps to determine what actual redundancy should be built in, to select from as conditions require. On the basis of scenario analysis contingency plans were prepared, to be selected for implementation as conditions arose. This was combined with variety, and partial redundancy, of subsidiaries, divisions,and competencies. At the time, when I was involved in this, I could not understand the rationale of what I perceived as enormous waste of duplication. Now I do. I am not sure, however, how much of that redundancy was actually planned and how much arose from the process of different divisions carving out their niches and claiming to be unique while in fact causing considerable duplication. Part of that must have been dysfunctional, but to some extent it may have had the selectionist rationale expounded here.

13.3.3 Punctuated Equilibrium

A variant of evolutionary theory is the theory of punctuated equilibrium, as discussed in Chapter 4. In the context of organization (Tushman & Romanelli 1985, Romanelli & Tushman 1994), it remains unclear what the origin of punctuation is. According to the original theory, in biology, punctuation (which is abrupt only in the perspective of geological time) arises from allopatric speciation, i.e. from a subpopulation that became isolated from its parent population. Could this yield a model to solve the paradox of exploitation and exploration? That would mean that part of the organization is shielded from the rest and allowed to develop on its own in a separate niche. This would be a specific instance of the thesis that disintegration is required for the emergence of radical innovation or transformation ('a new species'). We could see spin-off firms as a population of routines that gets 'isolated from its parent population'. This might be mimicked by a department gaining autonomy within a firm, in so-called 'skunk works'. The separate divisions of the 3M company come to mind. This form brings us back to the principle of separation in place of exploitation and exploration.

Interestingly, the cycle of discovery, discussed in Chapter 9, can be interpreted in terms of allopatric speciation. The stage of generalization yields migration to new niches, in which new species may arise. This requires separation: there must be allowance in the new niche for escape from the selection environment that applies in the parent environment. In organizational terms, this requires decentralization and autonomy; in other words, disintegration.

13.3.4   Scaffolding and Collaboration

Another potential principle, that may be derived from the logics of knowledge and language studied in Chapters 6 and 7, is the principle of scaffolding in the situated-action theory of knowledge and language. Meanings of words are ambiguous and open-ended. They are ambiguous in that there is a range of possible meanings, in a paradigmatic repertoire, and it is the context which disambiguates; which determines which option is the 'correct' or relevant one. They are open in that variation across contexts may yield shifts in the paradigmatic repertoire; in other words, in usage of words meanings may shift.

In Chapter 9 it was noted that in the cycle of discovery the stage of consolidation often entails codification of tacit knowledge. This involves abstraction: a disembedding from context, to allow for transfer to novel contexts, in generalization, in which context-specific tacit knowledge is added again. Abstraction entails ambiguity: a range of possibilities, and which possibility is to be chosen depends on the context. The addition of context-specific knowledge, to enable application and to offer new possibilities, in reciprocation, constitutes scaffolding.

How does this translate to firms? It might help us to understand better what the celebrated roles are of suppliers and customers in the development of products and technology. Chapters 3 and 8 discussed the notion of 'external economy of cognitive scope'. To the extent that the environment (markets, technology, institutions) is complex and volatile, one needs complementary, external intelligence to help identify, understand, and evaluate opportunities and threats. This contributed a cognitive dimension to the reasons and modes of interorganizational relations. The argument was supported by the situated-action theory of knowledge and language set out in Chapter 6. The cognitive argument for interfirm collaboration is now extended with a selection argument and a scaffolding argument. In selection, the population of modes of behaviour from which unpredictable futures may select need not all be maintained (in memory or in reality) in the firm itself but may be spread across different participants in a network. Moreover, the network may be adapted to yield adjustments in such populations, to vary the scope of variety subjected to selection. Scaffolding indicates that one can leave standard operating procedure incompletely specified, to leave it open to choice and variation, in so far as this is consistent with the need for co-ordination, which depends on how systemic the technology is.

Summing up: In extension of earlier arguments, in Chapter 11, or perhaps I should say in a reformulation of them, disintegration of organizations is needed to allow for allopatric speciation, and to allow for scaffolding in novel contexts.

13.3.5   Revitalization By Take-over

There is also the possibility of revitalization and the evasion of inertia through absorption of novel variety by merger or acquisition. Typically, more bureaucratic and often large organizations acquire innovative and often small and young firms. This may also contribute to the solution of a transition problem in the new, entrepreneurial firm. As discussed in earlier Chapters, after innovative success, at the stage of consolidation, the entrepreneur will often need to transform himself from entrepreneur to manager, and to introduce some degree of bureaucracy into his organization. He may not be able to take this hurdle, and takeover by a managerially more competent firm may be a welcome solution. This may revitalize the firm which takes over, but of course its bureaucracy may also stifle the innovativeness of the firm taken over. In any case, in due course cognitive distance will tend to be eliminated, so that a new injection of novelty will be required. I will return to the development of the entrepreneurial young firm in a later section.

13.3.6 Contingencies

Note that the problem of combining integration and disintegration depends on contingencies of industry, technology, and market, as indicted in Chapter 11. In some cases the need for integration and stability is less, and therefore one can more easily maintain exploration. In other cases the need for exploration is less, and one can more easily maintain exploitation.

> Tushman and Romanelli (1985: 195) recount the case of ATT: 'during the period from 1913–1976, ATT either controlled its environment or was shielded from competitive pressures. Under the stable and/or predictable conditions, a myriad of convergent, incremental decisions and actions bolstered ATT's strategic orientation and resulted in an effective and highly inertial organization'.

The problem is greatest when tight and enduring integration has to be combined with frequent and radical disintegration. This is the case when technology enables strong economy of scale, competition compels that it be utilized to mimimize costs, it entails large and highly dedicated, sunk investments that are inflexible, i.e. cannot be employed for different product forms, while products need to be differentiated and changed frequently. It is difficult to manage this, but it is possible.

> Chapter 1 mentioned the example of Ericsson, reported by McKelvey and Texier (2000). Ericsson made radical innovations in mobile telecommunication, surviving the corresponding transformation of products, production, and organization.

At the other extreme, there are limited problems when efficient exploitation does not require large, durable, sunk, inflexible assets. Technology can be adaptable in two ways. First, it is flexible: investments are not dedicated and can be used for a variety of product forms. This can be achieved either on the basis of modularity of parts and flexible assembly, or on the basis of flexibility in the primary process of production. For example, the use of flexible, programmable machinery allows for a variety of products without high costs and delays of switching from one product form to another. The use of computer-aided design and performance simulation of virtual prototypes is much faster and more flexible than manual design, building, and physical testing of

TABLE 13.1   *Industry contingencies*

Industry	Product cycle	Product differentiation	Production cycle	Dedicated assets	Scale/ sunk costs
Artisan/ craftsman	short	high	short	low	low
Fashion goods	short	high	short	low	high
Trades	short	high	medium	medium	medium
Banking/ insurance	medium	medium	medium	medium	high
Professional services	increasing	increasing	long	high	high
Bulk/process manufacturing	long	low	long	high	high
Piece/batch manufacturing	short	high	long	decreased	high

real prototypes. A second basis for adaptability is that investments are not large and costly, or are not sunk, and their replacement does not require much change of skill or organization. Table 13.1 gives a survey of different conditions for different industries.

The Table illustrates the advantage of small, artisanal producers. They have a general set of skills and tools which command a wide scope of tailor-made product forms, so that exploration can more easily be combined with exploitation, and inertia is less likely to be a problem. Of course, a condition is that there is a demand for such speciality products, in spite of their high price, either because there are no competing products on the basis of efficient, large-scale production of commodities, or because there are niche markets where a high relative price for specialities is viable. The decline of many artisanal activities was caused by the emergence of cheaper, bulk commodities. Nevertheless, the principle applies. No doubt the often reported re-emergence of small business is at least in part a result of this principle.

The manufacturing and distribution of fashion goods is also characterized by a short product cycle and high product differentiation. To cope with this assets must be flexible, and increasingly this is achieved by means of information technology, to adapt forms, materials, colours, and distribution quickly to changing tastes. Economy of scale is needed to compete. This combination of the need to compete with low costs with the opportunities offered by ICT has eliminated independent artisans in a number of fashion industries. The prototypical example is Benetton.

At the other extreme we have bulk or process industries (materials, fuels, base chemicals, and foodstuffs), with a long product cycle, dedicated, inflexible production systems, with high economy of scale and high sunk costs. For these reasons firms tend to be inertial, but this does not matter because the product is hardly differentiable and hardly changes. As indicated before, the crucial condition is that product and production cycles are synchronized. This forms at least part of the explanation of the longevity of oil and chemical companies. However, such industries encounter problems if products develop shorter cycles and become more differentiable. In parts of the chemical industry this has happened with the emergence of chemical specialities and 'designer chemicals'. To cope with this ways must be found to make production technology more flexible.

Problems are predicted when product and production cycles are out of sync. Table 13.1 shows two cases. One is the production of unit goods or batches, such as cars and consumer electronics. Differentiation and the speed of change of products have increased enormously, and, to cope with this, survival in these industries required either flexible assembly of modular components or flexible processes of design, testing, and production, both with the help of automation. In this way solutions to the problems appear to have been found. A second case is professional services, such as consultancy. Differentiation and change of the product are increasing, while the production process has typically had a long cycle, and entailed high sunk costs, considerable economy of scale, and highly dedicated investments, since it involved the education and training of specialists. To survive, firms in such industries will need to make expertise more flexible and adaptable, either by modularizing it or by widening the scope of application. Both are happening. Modularization takes place by offering consultants software tools for piecing together their work from standard elements. Scope of application is achieved by pooling consultants' knowledge by means of software tools, whereby they contribute their experience to a common pool in which colleagues can search, and by posting their problems so that colleagues can pitch in. In chapter 11 I gave the example of Arthur Andersen.

13.4   DEVELOPMENT AND LEADERSHIP

This paragraph turns to questions of development and leadership. How do firms develop? In development, how do they cope with the problems of exploitation and exploration; of integration and disintegration? How do they deal with the demands of entrepreneurship?

13.4.1   Development of Firms

New firms typically arise from a successful innovation, arising of its own accord or as a spin-off from another firm or a research institute. Typically, a spin-off arises because the innovation does not fit in the structure, strategy, competencies, or culture of the parent organization. The new, independent firm struggles with making the innovation technically and commercially viable. Thus, organizational development at the start is closely related to the cycle of discovery: the firm tries to survive the stages of innovation and consolidation. The task of the leader is to achieve internal and external credibility, to inspire, and to direct the formation of culture, in the sense of a coherent set of mental categories, as defined by Schein (1985) and summarized in Chapter 2. The personal categories of the leader form the template for culture to develop, to the extent that they are confirmed in success.

Next, existing or adapted categories must serve to support the demands of further development: selecting the most promising novel combination, testing, developing, and marketing it. Next, if success emerges, the innovation must be carried through to consolidation and efficient production, typically with economy of scale based on specialization and division of labour. After consolidation, at the stage of generalization, the emphasis shifts further to exploitation: efficient production, distribution, and internationalization, typically at a rapidly increasing scale, to satisfy demand, to reduce costs, and to fight off new entrants to the market.

A well-known hurdle in the literature on the growth of the firm arises when the innovating entrepreneur has to delegate responsibility, systematize, and formalize the organization after the innovation proves its worth (Nooteboom 1994). Increase of scale entails delegation and division of labour, with appropriate means of measurement and control, and this requires standardization and the transformation of tacit into explicit, documented knowledge. The entrepreneur, in the sense of the risk taker and charismatic leader, often finds it difficult to become a manager and engage in this type of activity. The perseverance and stubbornness that were a virtue in getting the firm on track may form a liability in keeping it on track. As Leonardo da Vinci said, men of genius start great works, and industrious people finish them. In the terms of Witt (1998*b*): the entrepreneur will have to shift from 'cognitive leadership' to 'governance' (and back again, later). Contrary to what Witt claims, cognitive leadership does not always yield better performance than governance. It performs worse in the systematization, rationalization, and increase of scale associated with the stage of generalization.

> An example is the Dutch computer-service company BSO (now called Origin). After its first success, it attempted to expand in a cell-division process, with cells dividing into further autonomous cells as growth occurred, in an attempt to replicate the entrepreneurial form with which the enterprise started. However, the ensuing lack of coherence, costs of duplication, and unutilized opportunities for economy of scale and scope forced the company to change its structure. It required the replacement of the original entrepreneur to make the switch.

Next to efficient production the focus may shift to efficient distribution and the financing of expansion, which has implications for ownership and control. In other words, the Schumpeterian entrepreneur has to become a manager, or hire one. As a leader, what culture should he now try to develop? To what extent can that be achieved on the basis of the culture that has meanwhile emerged? Is he the right one to achieve it? Is he able to see his shortcomings and let someone else do the managing? Is he capable of surrendering that authority?

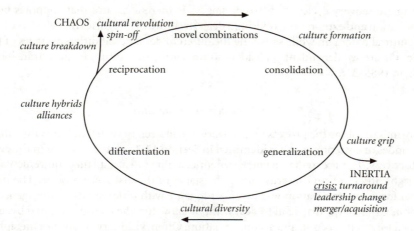

FIGURE 13.4   *Organizational development*

If the leader and the firm succeed in innovation and fail in consolidation or generalization, a new manager has to come in or the firm is taken over by an established firm. As indicated above, that firm may in fact be using this acquisition to revitalize its own culture and pull it out of a state of inertia. Then the problem is how to incorporate such foreign bodies without destroying their novelty and dynamism. Alternatively, the innovative firm, aware of the stumbling block, may choose to hive the innovation off, by selling itself or a licence.

If the firm survives, the culture that has survived all the stages so far is likely to take a strong hold. Successes turn into myths and the leader into a hero. The risk now becomes a risk of inertia. The question is whether incumbent management is able to turn itself and the culture around, and thereby destroy their own myths; to deconstruct their heroism. It would be preferable if it could, because in the stronghold of existing culture an outsider would have a much harder time achieving the turnaround.

> Tushman and Romanelli (1985: 180) tell the story of Singer: 'Singer . . . in its diversification into high technology products and markets has engaged in "recreation". No longer does the company intend to be perceived as a producer of quality sewing machines and furniture. Traditional Singer values and images, as well as products and markets serviced, structure, and control systems, have been fundamentally altered in rapid order'.

Such turnaround consists of loosening dogma; of adapting the product to novel markets and conditions of competition, to allow for differentiation, and next to allow for foreign influence for exploring novel combinations (reciprocation). This is likely to require alliances, and perhaps a merger or acquisition.

The process is illustrated in Figure 13.4.

Again the question arises: How can an organization cope with such transformation? Moreover, when organizations survive into large firms, how can they accommodate multiple discovery cycles in different stages? Is there a culture that supports both exploitation and exploration, offering a deep structure of categories that yield a coherent cultural paradigm while satisfying the different demands at different stages of the cycle? Or are we dependent on leaders to transform the culture in stage transitions (Schein 1985: 326)?

13.4.2   Modes of Leadership

If a firm is to follow the process of discovery, it will need to switch between the different modes of entrepreneurship identified in Section 13.2, related to stages in the cycle of discovery. To the extent that entrepreneurial ability satisfies all the requirements, in the right order, a firm can grow along the stages of the discovery process. The divisional form of organization was invented to cope with differentiation after generalization. Often, large firms fail to deal with, or allow for, the disorder created by, and needed for, reciprocation and accommodation. Often, visionary creators of metaphor lack the daring, charisma, and stamina to carry it into radical new combinations. Radical innovators often do not have the means, stamina, patience, and perseverance to take the venture through consolidation. They often fail to cope with the transition from daring, charismatic, visionary leadership to rational, systemic delegation and co-ordination. Takeovers, alliances, spin-offs, and break-ups of firms help to overcome such problems of transition between the stages of the discovery process.

Alternatively, a firm may survive by continually shifting its portfolio of activities such that it can maintain its entrepreneurial mode, by phasing activities in and out of its portfolio as they enter and leave the stage in which it specializes. This is the notion of 'stage specialization' introduced in Chapter 12. Thus, we can have firms that specialize in generating novel innovations, or in testing them, or in bringing them up to large-scale and systemic, rationalized production and global distribution, or in differentiating them. This may be more important and fundamental than specialization in specific products or markets. As discussed, differentiation and to a greater extent reciprocation, accommodation, and early consolidation require disintegrated structures, and here industrial districts have a comparative advantage over tightly integrated large corporations. Different firms that specialize at different stages can enter a relation of symbiosis.

> An example is the relation between small, diverse, specialized biotechnology firms and large pharmaceutical firms. The first yield the novel combinations and the second yield the lengthy process of regulatory approval of new drugs, the systemic, large-scale production and marketing of novel products, and the spread of risk across a portfolio of products.

The best illustration of symbiosis is of course the industrial district, discussed in Chapters 11 and 12. Here, different firms specialize in different stages of the development cycle, and shift activities between them to move between stages. Some firms specialize in R & D or other forms of experimentation with novel combinations, some specialize in consolidation and production, some in large-scale and distant marketing, distribution, exports, some in incremental improvements and differentiation.

Another approach, proposed in Chapter 11, is to act as an orchestrator: one co-ordinates activities between other firms who offer activities associated with the stages: one activates them or transacts with them only when needed. In industrial districts there is a risk of a central player adopting this role, as Benetton did in the design, production, and distribution of fashion clothing.

Most authors approach the problem as if management knows what should be done, and it is a problem of how to get the organization along. For Nonaka and Takeuchi the organization produces ideas from which management selects. But how does it know what to select, and why? On the basis of what does it select? Volberda focuses on how management engineers the right flexibility of the organization. This can perhaps be seen as lifting the task of management to a higher, 'meta' level: management does not know what the right direction is, but it knows what type of flexibility is needed under what conditions. Choo moves more explicitly towards the question of how management can exert 'premise control' so that the organization will move in the right direction of its own accord. That line is pursued in this Chapter. The question now is how management does that, and how they know what the right premises are.

13.5   MANAGEMENT OF LEARNING

To deal with exploitation and exploration, which options for structure and process can management use? How can it manage the transfer and development of knowledge and competence?

13.5.1   *Knowledge Transfer*

Here, I build on Chapter 10, to analyse processes of knowledge transfer in terms of scripts. Organizational scripts can be codified and documented up to a point by inspection, analysis, and mapping of processes of production, administration, and communication in firms. However, this has its limits, because of lack of knowledge or 'causal ambiguity' (Lippman & Rumelt 1982). In organizations, as in people, scripts may be tacit, not known explicitly to anyone. One may be able to observe what happens, but that does not necessarily imply that one understands what is going on. In organizations, people participate in a node of a script, perhaps without anyone grasping the script as a whole. That is the equivalent of tacit knowledge at the level of the organization: what actually happens could not be codified. As noted before, the distinction between tacit and documented knowledge is closely related to the distinction between 'procedural' and 'declarative' knowledge (Cohen & Bacdayan 1996, Cohen 1991). At the stage of accommodation scripts break up. As discussed in Chapters 6 and 10, rule-based codes break down into storytelling (Shank & Abelson 1995).

Corresponding to the distinction between procedural and declarative knowledge, there are different ways of obtaining (learning) or transferring (teaching) a script. With tacit knowledge one needs to learn procedurally, as an apprentice, by imitating observed behaviour of one or more 'masters', in a community of practice (Brown & Duguid 1996), and trying it out in practice, subject to correction by that community. When knowledge is documented, one can learn declaratively, by studying some codification of the script, in a blueprint, algorithm, formula, or standard operating procedure. A necessary condition for this is that the practice has settled down in a dominant design. However, since, because of the principle of recursiveness, at some level of nesting tacit elements are inevitable, formal training is never completely successful if it is not accompanied by socialization in a community of practice. Here, socialization is not taken in the specific sense employed by Nonaka and Takeuchi (exchange of tacit knowledge), but in the usual sense of people being embedded in social structure and culture. It follows that training always requires some degree of socialization. The distinction between the two types of learning was already recognized by Penrose (1959).

The script model enables us to be more precise about why practices are never completely reducible to documented knowledge. The principle of recursiveness, with substitutions into nodes being themselves subscripts, implies that practices (scripts) have an inevitable tacit component at some level in the nesting of subscripts. Complete, declarative transmission of a practice would yield a regress: one would need to specify all subscripts and superscripts, but in any finite explanation one cannot keep on explaining the terms of the explanation. At some point one must rely on unspecified, local, tacit knowledge embedded in the context. Good practice, with all its inveterately tacit elements, its rich experience with specializations for different contexts, with corresponding 'work-arounds', cannot be completely canonized into written procedures, manuals, or training programmes, without any unspecified residual (Brown & Duguid 1996). It is one of the pitfalls of management to think that it can be. The inadequacy of that view is illustrated when processes break down because people 'work to rule'. It is also illustrated in the insight that for diffusion of knowledge in a firm it may be better to rotate staff than to issue written rules or procedures (Cohen & Bacdayan 1994).

There is a further reason why competence often requires that at least at some level of nesting (sub)practices are tacit. This can be explained by Simon's principle of bounded rationality. Since our capacity for rational evaluation is limited, it is efficient to routinize practices to some extent, by developing them into tacit knowledge and focusing rational evaluation on novel challenges.

Generally, when firms grow large, with the need for and opportunity of delegation and specialization in different activities in different departments, procedural knowledge with its direct, face-to-face visual and oral co-ordination and communication no longer suffices. Ways of doing things must be made explicit and explainable, i.e. must be turned into declarative knowledge, and must be documented to form instructions and standard operating procedures across departments or subsidiaries. In other words, transformation into declarative knowledge and codification are required for diffusion over large distances and many people. But this documentation can only be achieved (and then not fully, as argued before) after a dominant design has emerged at the stage of consolidation. Formalized procedures in large-scale organization and division of labour can work only after consolidation.

While tacit knowledge is productive and in any case inevitable, it can provide an obstacle to learning, as discussed in Chapter 3. It is difficult to criticize and replace an element of practice when it is tacit. There is a paradox involved: when knowledge is tacit, one is not aware that it is a basis for action. It tends to seem self-evident, and to question it would be called 'impractical'. This is the cause of well-known problems in the transfer of novel technology to small firms, where knowledge tends to be more tacit, as discussed in Chapter 3. The small size of the organization allows for it, since control can take place in direct visual and oral contact, which lessens the need for formal, documented standards and procedures. This enables small firms to be flexible and to offer relatively high levels of motivation, which is part of their competitive advantage. However, one problem with tacit knowledge is that one cannot simply argue that novel technology is better. One needs to first make the entrepreneur aware, by externalization, of what he is doing and why, for him to become receptive to an alternative. (See Chapter 3 for further details.)

People may have a stake in maintaining the tacitness of their knowledge, because it enhances their power. Thus, it is understandable, for example, that accountants resisted automation, for its ability to encode their tacit expertise. As a result, when automation pushed through they lost status and salary, and had to move into less codifiable consultancy.

13.5.2 Development of Competence

The functioning of people in nodes of organizational scripts is governed by their ability to react to events. This 'reactivity' (Saraph 1994) is close to the notion of absorptive capacity, discussed in Chapter 8. The difference is that reactivity entails not only ability to make sense, as absorptive capacity does, but also the added ability to translate that into appropriate action. In other words, it is also close to the notion of 'competence' (see Chapter 3). The difference is that reactivity does not entail ability to utilize resources in general, as competence does, but such ability in response to specific phenomena. A well-developed (richly structured) form of reactivity is based on a 'repertoire': activities that may serve as substitutions into nodes, and a choice procedure for selecting among them. This is similar to Stinchcombe's (1990) rendering of skill as a repertoire of routines plus selection principles.

The choice procedure for a repertoire requires cognitive capacities: perception (awareness, sensitivity to stimulus), interpretation (meaning creation, understanding, knowledge), and evaluation (goal congruence). The scope of a repertoire refers to the number of options, which may be narrow or wide. The choice procedure may be flexible, i.e. variable under change of conditions, or strict. To the extent that the complexity of choice is greater one will expect higher levels of professional competence. Implementation requires skill, commitment, and energy. This varies, with varying needs for training and experience. As discussed above, codified, declarative knowledge can be learned more quickly if the necessary absorptive capacity is there, than tacit, procedural knowledge, which requires socialization and the building of interaction and experience. Complexity is greater when the activity is involved in different nodes of a script, and in different scripts within a firm. People are also involved in many scripts outside their role in the firm, 'qua persona' (Ring & van de Ven 1994), and therefore have a range of repertoires. Reciprocation may yield a carry-over of substitutions or nodes between inside and outside scripts, but this is restricted to the extent that choice procedures are restricted in organizational role. Such reciprocation may be a source of both error and innovation. People may be rotated across nodes or scripts.

Efficient performance of a script requires appropriate substitutions, which requires appropriate repertoires. A crucial question for management is this: how to guide the development of repertoires so as to achieve an adequate balance between continuity for the sake of good performance (exploitation), and adaptation of repertoires and the configuration of scripts for the sake of survival under changing conditions (exploration). To affect reactivity of staff one needs reactivity to that reactivity. Reactivity to one's own reactivity constitutes self-awareness (Saraph 1994).

Should management manage the reactivity of workers by specifying their repertoires? Traditional notions of planning are based on that perspective. How does management obtain the appropriate meta-reactivity (reactivity to workers' reactivity)? For that, it should have self-awareness; reactivity to its reactivity to the reactivity of workers. On what learning would that be based? Or should it subject its meta-reactivity to the people's reactivity to that, and then react to that reactivity? In other words, should it govern by feedback to its governance? Or should management rather govern on the basis of the self-awareness of people; on the basis of people's reactivity to their own reactivity, according to their own processes of discovery?

The building of repertoires can proceed in different ways:

Specification. This entails the imposition of coded contents of repertoires that are to be adopted. This clearly requires declarative knowledge of the scripts involved. In innovative activities, after invention and at the beginning of the consolidation stage, this is impossible, because the performance is not yet determinate, and is largely tacit. Next, when it is beyond that stage, some tacit knowledge gets lost in the transcription. The result constitutes a mere datum for the recipient, and his performance depends on his capacity to absorb it and transform it into information, and from there into performance. If, for example, the perception, interpretation, or choice in a prescribed repertoire conflicts with similar procedures in the recipient's existing repertoires, it literally does not make 'sense'. Apart from these complications, prescription may work when the need for continuity is paramount.

Clearly, this mode is the most appropriate when the organization finds itself at the stages of consolidation and generalization. Crucial here are stability and either tight co-ordination or finely tuned teamwork in communities of practice. Here, the danger of inertia is large, because staff must adhere to strict specifications; their scope to adapt is restricted.

Imitation. This entails an exemplar of model performance that is demonstrated for people to imitate. This idea is derived from the analysis of prototypes in language, in Chapter 7. Perhaps this can be accompanied by some documentary support: there may be combinations between this mode of imitation and the previous mode of pre-scription. Imitation can happen at an earlier stage of development than prescription, when knowledge is still procedural rather than declarative, but not too early, because the performance requires a certain amount of stability to be imitated. It entails that the recipient forms his own repertoire through imitation of model performance. Since a given performance can be achieved on the basis of different repertoires, in other words repertoire is underdetermined by its performance (in the same way that theory is underdetermined by its predictions), this may lead to considerable deviations from the model as circumstances change. The recipient may have imported elements from repertoires in other scripts, probably including scripts from his personal experience.

According to the perspective of social constructivism, cognitive categories, which are part of repertoires, develop in interaction with the physical and social environ-ment, according to the stages of development in the cycle of learning. People react to their activities by learning to adapt to novel conditions. Importation from other scripts (reciprocation) provides a source of variety. Management may want to affect this self-reactivity of people, and the question comes up again as to whether this is to be done by specification of a repertoire (for people to adapt their repertoires), or the setting of models for imitation. Management may want somehow to restrict the direc-tion of change, to maintain sufficient continuity, or to guide the change in the direc-tion of certain overarching goals. Full repertoires for affecting the change of reactivity seems unlikely: one would have to be able to predict what cannot be predicted. More likely would be simple institutions to restrict or guide the change. Here, one thinks of the role of culture as an institution: certain models of conduct, embodied in myths, may provide indications for goal selection, and certain rituals may confirm certain practices for adapting repertoires.

This form is most appropriate at the stage of differentiation: the dominant design is not imposed as a rigorous order but as a theme to be varied. A certain amount of com-petition between staff or divisions might be invigorating here.

Management of meetings. Since, according to the theory, cognitive categories develop from interaction with the physical and social environment, one can influence change of repertoires yet more indirectly, by governing the environment in which people develop their categories. A main instrument here is the pattern in which people communicate and meet. This can be achieved literally through official and social meetings, through rotating people across jobs or through changing organizational structure. In this way also one could affect the balance between continuity and change. Since the effects of these instruments are very indirect, they are very difficult to predict.

This form is most appropriate at the stage of reciprocation. Meetings might be guided by indications of what sources of new elements might fruitfully be tried, derived from earlier experience in reciprocation or from indications in the preceding stages of generalization and differentiation. How would management know this?

Indications on whom to bring together with whom might be derived from success in similar but not identical contexts. One might rotate staff, between sales or marketing and R & D and production, for example, so that they could see their activities in another light; or from an exploitation-oriented part to an exploration-oriented part, when stabilization of chaos and consolidation are needed; or vice versa, when there is a need to open up to variety. Meetings might include customers and suppliers with experiences with different products and technologies. Use might be made of tools of information and communication to facilitate such exchange. The problem may be more motivational than technical. To let colleagues profit from valuable experience one requires trust that they will not free ride and advance their careers at one's expense. Incentive mechanisms have to be well aligned with the goal. In Chapter 11 the case of Arthur Andersen was given as an example.

Management of redundancy. When scripts break up, and people revert to story-telling, there are several risks. In incoherent trials one can easily bet on the wrong horse. Trial and error can lapse into chaos. Loss of standards can yield lack of selection. The first can be fought by creating redundancy in parallel trials. The second requires the opposite: a limitation of variety. The third may be fought by bringing in prospective users. Clearly, these demands are paradoxical. Of course they are. This is precisely the reason that my theory (and earlier life-cycle theory) favoured disintegrated structures of industrial districts. Here, the process is at its most Darwinian.

13.5.3   Management of Meaning

The problem of stage transition is evaded when the firm specializes in a specific stage of the cycle. The problem then is to identify novel projects to feed into that stage, and to identify and serve recipients of projects coming out of that stage. Typically, for such a strategy of stage specialization one should be embedded in a network with different partners specializing in different stages, to pass projects along to each other. Another way to avoid the problem is to operate with redundancy, with alternative ways of doing things existing side by side, to let the fittest survive. But that requires ruthless selection, which within an organization can be very difficult. The 'market' tends to be better at this, and again we arrive at disintegration, in the form of industrial districts or other networks. Within firms it might work, if the firm can cope with a variety of views, and disagreement, and people are able to be flexibly reallocated across projects according to their success.

Chapter 1 mentioned the studies by de Woot *et al.* (1978) and Bourgeois (1985), which indicated a negative relationship between top-manager consensus concerning choices and performance, and the studies by Dess (1987) and Hrebiniak and Snow (1982) which found the reverse. In the light of the present analysis this is not surprising: it depends on the stage in the cycle of development. At the stage of consolidation and generalization such consensus is beneficial, but at the stage of exploring novel combinations for radical innovation it is not to be expected nor desirable, until chaos lasts too long and some convergence for consolidation becomes necessary for survival. This is confirmed by the fact that Bourgeois's study referred to firms in volatile environments, where I would indeed expect consensus to have a negative effect on performance.

Fiol (1996) distinguished between the content and the framing of communication. The latter refers to how something is expressed (as examples, she mentions 'breadth', 'rigidity'). In this way 'collective learning can occur in the absence of shared meaning' (p. 177). This calls to mind the distinction, discussed in Chapter 7, between extension (reference, content; what a term refers to; the truth value of a proposition) and intension. Intension or sense refers to the way in which reference is identified. It is related to categorization: how something is recognized as belonging to a class or how the truth of a proposition is determined. In Chapter 7 the view was discussed at length that generally there are no necessary and sufficient conditions for class membership, independent of context, and that shifts in meaning occur as contexts change. There are family resemblances rather than shared, essential characteristics. Categorization is guided by prototypes or paradigms or exemplary cases that operate by default, i.e. are provisional—subject to change as the context requires. This is conveyed by symbols, slogans, myths, or role models.

Chapter 7 discussed the notion of the hermeneutic circle, in which the meaning of a whole depends on the meaning of the parts, but also vice versa: meanings of terms shift in their use in discourse. I connected this with Roman Jacobson's theory of poetics. From existing paradigmatic repertoires we select items to be put together in a syntagmatic structure, and this may modify the paradigmatic repertoires through novel connections, suggested by metonymy or metaphor, or by proximity or juxtaposition in the syntagmatic structure, similarity of sounds, or rhythmic connection. In the present context of management of meaning the hermeneutic circle is not just a metaphor but a model: it may tell us how the management of meaning might take place. The question is how it can be employed as a cycle of meaning in speech communities to effect the development cycle at the level of the organization. For novel ideas and practices in organizations we need the organizational equivalent of poetry.

Combination of exploitation and exploration now becomes an issue of how to allow for shifts in paradigmatic repertoires while maintaining an ability to achieve syntagmatic coherence. In the script approach it was noted that towards the stage of reciprocation, and certainly at the stage of novel combinations, scripts fall apart. To use the terminology of Shank and Abelson (1995): scripts are replaced by storytelling. The question then is how we can stimulate the breakdown of existing scripts and guide the construction of new ones. Is there a way, and a need, to create some coherence in storytelling?

Metaphor plays a central role. In the discussion of the cycle of development it was noted that reciprocation is structurally equivalent to metaphor: the carry-over of an element from one script to another. Here, we concentrate on metaphor in the literal sense: the use of language to shift perceptions, interpretations, and evaluations. While management of meetings provides or withholds opportunity for novel combinations, metaphor acts as a trigger to see something in terms of something else. It highlights some features and hides others (Pondy 1983). An example used by Nonaka and Takeuchi (1995) is the use of a beer can to trigger a new approach to the design of a copying machine. Chapter 1 mentioned Ford's metaphoric transfer of the principle of an assembly line from a mail-order firm to car manufacturing.

At the stage of generalization, after consolidation, metaphor can be used to loosen existing concepts and show that something different is less different than it appears, so that discontinuity is made more understandable and acceptable (cf. Gioia *et al.* 1996). At that stage it can be used to show that more complexity and diversity are required; that the world (the market, the firm) is not as simple as it seems (cf. Boland, Tenkasi, & Te'eni 1996). This may help the escape from inertia. Conversely, in a state of chaos, with ongoing proliferation of novel combinations, metaphor may be helpful to achieve more coherence. There, it may be used to reduce complexity and uncertainty; to simplify and to give a new sense of a shared direction (Pondy 1983). Both may be needed in the communication between management and workers, and may then work in both directions: management shifting the orientation of workers or vice versa. It may be needed within boards of directors, perhaps through the intervention of a consultant.

> Smircich (1983) tells us about an organization where two quite different cultures were combined by merger. The problem of disagreement was so large that an 'ethic of apparent harmony' developed to disarm this disruptive force. But this led to immobility, because problems of disagreement were hidden.

The focus has been on cognitive issues, but related to these there are of course also motivational issues of control: How does one ensure fruitful, constructive collaboration? Previously, the deep structure of organizational culture (in Chapter 2) and of institutions (in Chapter 5) was identified as the basic categories of perception, interpretation, and evaluation. The latter includes normative issues of behaviour. Hence management of meaning also includes issues of motivations and behavioural control. However, that constitutes a voluminous subject that goes beyond the scope of this book.

13.6   CONCLUSION

The art of management will largely consist of finding innovative novel combinations of the structural and processual elements discussed above. They are summarized in Table 13.2. The structural choices are: specialization at some stage of the cycle and symbiosis with other organizations at other stages, maintenance of variety and redundancy by means of external relations, absorption of variety by merger or acquisition, spatial separation of exploitation and exploration, separation in time, internal redundancy. Choices for the development of competence are: through specification, imitation, management of meetings, management of redundancy, management of

TABLE 13.2   *Ways to deal with exploitation and exploration*

Organizational structure

Do not try to combine: select a specialization and let products and technologies move through it, and seek symbiosis with other firms that specialize in other stages of development

Scaffolding and collaboration: maintain openness, ambiguity, external cognitive scope; spread redundancy, scaffolding.

Combine by separation in place, with horizontal or vertical co-ordination

Combine by separation in time: oscillation

Selection: maintain redundancy

Competence building

Specification

Imitation

Management of meetings

Management of meaning

Symbols, slogans, myths

Metaphor

meaning. The latter entails the use of paradigmatic exemplars expressed through symbols, slogans, myths; metaphors to make discontinuity more continuous or vice versa, to share and shift functional perspectives, to inject exploitation into exploration or vice versa.

> An example of an inventive combination is the practice at the 'Central Book House', in the Netherlands. It buys and supplies books for the book trade. It has three core divisions, which need to be tightly integrated:
>
> 1. the assortment of books, which must offer a high degree of differentiation to customers, in terms of composition and size of packages;
> 2. logistics for efficient and fast delivery;
> 3. information technology to enable 2 and to collect and provide strategically vital information as to what books are read by whom where at what price, for 1 and for customers (both publishers and shopkeepers).
>
> Clearly, efficient exploitation is crucial. But so is exploration, to keep up with developments in reading habits, technologies of information processing and dissemination, changes in publishing. Because of the systemic coherence of the three divisions, innovation must occur in step. To achieve this while maintaining efficient exploitation, the following solution was found. The organization

is basically exploitation oriented. But there is a permanent R & D team of eight people, recruited at different moments (two new people every half year) from the three different departments, and moving out after two years, not going back to their own division of origin but on to one of the others. Moving out from exploration, back into exploitation, they carry responsibility for implementing innovations they have helped to develop. One can see the advantages. One is that exploration is based on experience in exploitation, and is conducted with a view to the expected responsibility for implementation to be taken on later. The different divisions each contribute to both exploration and its implementation, to protect systemic coherence. There is turnover in the team to maintain variety and ongoing influx of experience from exploitation. According to our taxonomy in Table 13.2 it is a case of combining exploitation and exploration through spatial separation with both horizontal and vertical co-ordination, in combination with management of meetings. It looks like the hypertext form recommended by Nonaka and Takeuchi, with the important difference that the cross-functional team for exploration is always in place, albeit with a varying composition, and the production departments know in advance when they will lose and gain people.

Are there problems? It seems that the assumption in the system is that the cycle of innovation is two years. If it turns out to be longer a person moving out of the R & D team has nothing new to implement in the division he joins, at least not an innovation to which he contributed. Is this an incentive or a disincentive to see to it that something new comes out within the two years? What if people are valuable but do not want to move out of exploration and back into exploitation, and if their competencies support that preference? What guarantees that one will always find people who have the skills and interest in both exploitation and exploration? What guarantees are there that rivalries between the divisions will not be carried into the development process? Is this prevented by the prospect of having to move into another division after the two years in exploration? Does this form make the organization 'immortal'? Can it survive a shift to electronic publishing and ordering through the Internet?

14
Conclusions and Further Research

This final Chapter reviews to what extent the preceding analysis helps to answer the questions specified in Chapter 1, and to explain the stylized facts supplied in Chapter 1 and elsewhere. For this, it summarizes the research questions and the answers provided in this book. It next discusses priorities for further research. The main such priority is empirical testing of the many propositions set out in previous Chapters. Hypotheses are presented and ways of testing them are indicated.

14.1 ANSWERS

This paragraph considers to what extent the results from past Chapters can answer the research questions and explain the stylized facts.

14.1.1 *Research Questions*

The research questions are repeated below, in Table 14.1. The first is the central question for this book.

14.1.2 *Continuity and Change*

How can the questions concerning continuity and change (Research Questions 1, 2, 4, 7, and 12) be answered and how can the corresponding phenomena be explained? According to the heuristic of learning, expounded in Chapter 9, the fundamental logic of these phenomena is as follows. First, novelty needs to consolidate in dominant designs. This is needed for efficient exploitation and for application in novel contexts. The latter provides insights into where its strengths and limitations lie, which yields the motivation for adaptation and suggests elements for novel combinations and indications for their configuration (Questions 1 and 4).

The process consists of several stages, moving from proximate to more radical change. First, there is incremental change, with adaptations to different contexts made on the basis of past experience (differentiation). Next, elements are adopted from other practices encountered in new contexts (reciprocation). The process satisfies the conditions of ongoing exploitation for survival in the short term while yielding the exploration needed for survival in the longer term. Syncretic accumulation of elements from different practices causes strain on existing architectures of configuration,

Table 14.1 *Overview of research questions*

1. What are the sources and conditions of paradigm switches, punctuations, or radical innovations?
2. How can we identify paradigm switches and punctuations? (Are they the same?). How can we demarcate incremental and radical innovation? How can we operationalize 'discontinuity'?
3. What are the meaning and role of 'paradigms' here?
4. How do novel combinations arise? How are they related to radical innovation and creative destruction?
5. Why does a dominant design arise, and how?
6. How can we explain when and why dominant designs follow or precede innovation, and when and why technology (tinkering) follows or precedes science (understanding)?
7. What is the relation between diffusion and innovation? Is diffusion a mere 'working out' of the innovation, or does it also prepare for the next innovation? Does it tend towards equilibrium or does it prepare for ongoing disequilibrium?
8. Why and how do companies internationalize? Is this purely to diffuse innovations or also to develop them?
9. When and why are small firms (or 'industrial districts') more successful in innovation and learning than large ones (or multinational enterprises), or vice versa? How do small and large firms relate in innovation and diffusion?
10. How do firms develop, and how can they survive? How does this relate to entrepreneurship?
11. How are organizational integration and disintegration related to innovation? How does this connect with the issue of firm size in relation to innovation?
12. How can firms combine first- and second-order learning, or exploitation and exploration?
13. How and why does inertia arise? When is it bad and when not? How is this related to dominant designs?
14. How can inertia be evaded or overcome, to proceed with further innovation or learning?
15. How and when does metaphor work as an instrument of innovation? How does this relate to the notion of innovation by 'novel combinations'?
16. When, and on what, is consensus among top management good for firm performance and when disagreement?
17. What is the role of interfirm interaction in innovation and learning?
18. What are the conditions for learning in collaboration between organizations?
19. How random or systematic is novelty? How does it happen that search yields results in unexpected directions? How prepared does one have to be in order to invent? How does this preparation take place?
20. How can we explain fits and misfits of novelty? What are the conditions for survival?
21. How can we explain hysteresis: old technologies staying on as parts of new technologies?
22. How are all these phenomena of innovation and learning connected between the levels of people, organizations, and innovation systems?

and yields pressure (motive) and indications (means) for more radical, architectural change, in novel combinations. This shows the continuity in the process of change (Question 2), and indicates that the notion of equilibrium does not make sense (Question 7). In the process of diffusion there is change, and experience is built up for the next innovation. In other words, in the process that is supposed to yield equilibration the seeds are sown for disequilibrium. The processes of differentiation and reciprocation show how novel combinations (Question 4) constitute radical innovation.

> An example discussed in Chapter 1 is the succession of naval technical trajectories in the fifteenth to eighteenth centuries. The adoption by the Portuguese of the Arab lateen sail for the sake of greater manoeuvrability, in combination with the existing use of square sails for the sake of speed, is an example of reciprocation yielding an architectural innovation or novel combination. It arose from travel (generalization) which brought the Portuguese into contact with Arab heritage in shipbuilding. Another example is the combination of principles of construction from dike building with those of shipbuilding, in the Netherlands. In combination with external pressures this yielded the new design of the 'flute' ship. That also arose from the demands of novel contexts; in this case the need to open up trade in the Baltic and circumvent the trade cartel of the Hanseatic League, and the ensuing need to sail around Jutland. That form of ship was next differentiated into many different ship designs for different purposes. It is not clear whether and how this in turn led to a new architectural innovation. However, it is clear that the Dutch decline was exacerbated by their lagging behind the English in the adoption of teak wood and the use of drawings and corresponding specifications in shipbuilding.

The notion of scripts was introduced in the theory of knowledge discussed in Chapter 6, and was used in Chapter 10 to elaborate the heuristic of discovery. Differentiation is specified more precisely as novel substitutions into nodes of a script, or different branches of scripts for different contexts. Reciprocation is specified more precisely as the transfer of some substitution from a node of one script to another script, or the transfer of a whole node from one script to another. Radical change is specified as change of script configuration, with a redistribution of substitutions across nodes.

14.1.3   Science, Technology, and Dominant Designs

Why and how do dominant designs arise (Question 5)? Does science precede technology or vice versa (Question 6)? Do dominant designs follow or precede innovation? Cases for both are found in history. The cycle of discovery can explain this.

Novelty often first arises through tinkering, with a great deal of trial and error, at the stage of novel combinations in new architectures. It is not yet understood why or even precisely how novelty works. Knowledge is largely tacit and procedural rather than explicit and declarative. It is only as selection proceeds that novelty 'comes into its own': becomes better understood and systematic, and integrated with other understanding, in the process of consolidation. This is often where technology develops into science, and dominant designs follow innovation. But next, science and dominant designs provide the basis for more widespread and systematic application. They serve to abstract novelty from the specific context in which it arose, so that it may be generalized to new contexts. That, I proposed, provides the basis for new technology to develop. Thus, science and technology follow each other and provide the basis for each other.

It is in the process of consolidation that the evolutionary theory of innovation is at its best: the selection environment of markets and institutions selects out from alternative trials of a novel practice those forms that fit best in existing systems (scripts) of production, distribution, and use. However, there is an incentive to change the selection environment, i.e. to change the superscripts and scripts of usage so that they may assimilate the innovation. Thus, innovation in production and products tends to go together with organizational and wider institutional innovation, and attempts to come out on top in the new 'negotiated order'.

> Examples indicated in Chapter 1 were the emergence of the VHS standard in videos, Ford's assembly-line production, the DC3 in aeroplanes, the IBM 370 in computers, and the Fordson tractor. A more extended illustration of the process of the negotiated order, given in Chapter 4, was the battle between alternative designs of a hearing aid (single- and multiple-channel cochlear implants). This was used as an illustration of how the selection environment, if one wants to employ that term from evolutionary theory, is endogenous: subject to influence by innovation, political action, and rhetoric.

14.1.4   *Internationalization*

The theory also yields a perspective on internationalization strategies of multinational corporations (Question 8). While firms expand internationally primarily to leverage investments and success in technology, products, brand names, distribution, customer base, organization, in fact this process may contribute to learning and innovation, by generating the process of generalization to novel contexts. There is evidence that multinational companies are now consciously using internationalization as an innovation strategy by tapping into competencies in host countries. A condition for this is that the firms allow for decentralization and autonomy ('disintegration'), to enable adaptation to local conditions, in differentiation and reciprocation, and allow novelty to develop even if it threatens to cannibalize existing activities.

These conditions are more likely to be satisfied when the firm employs local partners, in joint ventures or non-equity alliances, than when it engages in green-field investments or takeovers. Often, one sees that such alliances ultimately result in the local partner taking over the activity, when it no longer needs the input of know-how or other resources from the foreign partner, while it is in a better position and more motivated to exploit the success of the locally emerging novelty. This may be beneficial if it is the only way to force expansion of the novelty, in spite of its cannibalization of products in the home market of the foreign partner.

> An illustration is the Japanese joint venture between Xerox and Fuji (Lorange & Roos 1992). It was intended by Xerox as a sales channel for its existing photocopying machines, but in time

technology spilled over to Fuji, which enabled it to develop its own type of copier, tailored to local demand. Xerox initially saw this as a threat in the form of a new competitor that might jeopardize its own sales and development in the home country. However, this was amply compensated for by additional sales, since the new copier was positioned at the low end of the market and was complementary rather than substitutive to Xerox's range, and it effectively prevented Xerox's competitor IBM from entering the Japanese market. Would Xerox have blocked this development if it had wholly owned the venture? Would it have tried to block development if the local product had been in more direct competition with its own products?

14.1.5 Paradigms and Inertia

What is a paradigm, and how does it work (Questions 2 and 3)? The term is often used to denote a dominant design or, as I would say, a script or superscript which provides the selection environment for practice, if one wants to use that term from evolutionary theory. Such a paradigm provides inertia. What is the role of inertia (Question 13)? While an excess of inertia is bad, since it blocks exploration, some inertia is needed, not only to achieve efficient exploitation, but also to provide a platform for generalization and thereby open up the process of exploration. This was called the principle of tenacity.

The original meaning of 'paradigm', however, is that of an exemplar: a canonic example to be followed or emulated. Often, application and further development of novelty (generalization) proceeds on the basis of a paradigm in that sense. That arises in the form of a dominant design from the stage of consolidation. This is effective because it yields the basis for generalization by association rather than programming. This is related to the function of prototypes in language, as discussed in Chapter 7. By setting an example to be emulated, with possible variations, rather than giving precise and rigid specifications of action, it provides the basis for exploitation while allowing for the variety required for exploration (generalization, differentiation, reciprocation). In other words, in this sense of the term, a paradigm helps not only to provide a basis for exploitation but also to do so in a way that allows for exploration and thereby overcomes inertia (Question 14).

> The case discussed in Chapter 1 was Adam Smith's pin factory in economic theory, as an exemplar of economy of scale by specialization. However, when interpreted too literally or strictly the example can become too constraining. To take the example of the pin factory: there are other types of economy of scale than those associated with division of labour; for example, engineering economy of scale related to the size of a container in process or transport industries (with the resulting rule that a doubling of size yields a 20 per cent reduction of unit costs).

As discussed in Chapter 13, firm culture includes role models, such as the founder of the firm or other 'heroes' from the firm's past, or tall stories of mythical success. These can be interpreted as exemplars in the management of exploitation and exploration, as part of premise control, to guide innovative behaviour, to allow for change while giving it some direction.

14.1.6   Consensus

When is top-management consensus good and when bad for firm performance (Question 16)? The evidence, summarized in Chapter 1, was mixed: sometimes consensus was good and sometimes not. The theory in this book suggests that in the stages leading up to radical innovation diversity is good for the production of innovations, while towards and after consolidation and during generalization consensus is good. Note that innovation does not necessarily lead to good financial or growth performance. Both dissent and consensus are good, but at different stages, and their proper succession and alternation in time are good for financial and growth performance. But one can have fairly good financial and growth performance without in-house innovation, by adopting outside innovation.

The outcome also depends on what the consensus or dissent is about. The most relevant issues in my theory, where consensus matters in relation to the stage in the cycle of discovery, are: products to be developed, production method/technology to be used, organizational structure, and style or culture to be chosen. In consolidation there should be reasonable consensus on product, with dissent on production and organization. In generalization there should be reasonable consensus on product, production, and organization. In differentiation there should be allowance for dissent on product, and perhaps organization, which widens to issues of technology and intensifies in stages of reciprocation and novel combinations.

14.1.7   Firm Size and (Dis)integration

There is mixed evidence concerning the relation between firm size and innovation (Question 9). As indicated in Chapter 1, the evidence shows that while small firms participate less in R & D than large firms do, when they participate they do so more intensively. There is also evidence, though more limited, that they do so more efficiently. In the adoption of externally produced innovations (diffusion) small firms tend to lag behind. I argued that it is more useful to conduct the analysis in terms of organizational (dis)integration than of firm size, because increasingly the structure and boundaries of firms are becoming fuzzy. An approach in terms of degrees of (dis)integration allows for decentralized or even virtual large firms and more or less integrated structures of small firms (industrial districts or networks). This leads to the question concerning the development and survival of small firms (Question 10) and the relation between innovation and organizational (dis)integration (Question 11).

> An illustration given in Chapter 1 was that while in some areas micro-electronics was developed by small firms (Silicon Valley), in other areas (Boston) it was developed by large firms. Large firms have survived radical innovations in pharmaceuticals, in mobile telecommunication (Ericsson), and in household machinery (Singer) (Question 14). On the other hand, there are many examples of the inertia of large firms, which caused them to fall behind in innovation (Question 13). One was the case of the Ford automobile company that lagged behind in the move towards product differentiation. Other examples were ATT and the Dutch Philips Company.

Most of the evidence seems to indicate that in novel combinations of technologies disintegrated structures are more favourable and in subsequent efficient and large-scale utilization and diffusion integrated structures are more efficient. That was already explained by the life-cycle theory of innovation, but in this book the explanation is carried further on the basis of the heuristic of learning, in Chapter 11. Disintegrated structures are better in offering the variety needed to generate unusual and unexpected novel combinations, and yield efficient selection of superior outcomes and the death of inferior ones, without the protection of cross-subsidization from established successful products or processes. The extended cycle of innovation in this book suggests that after consolidation and generalization disintegrated structures again have the advantage in the incremental innovation and exploration of product differentiation and reciprocation.

> Most of the evidence appears to confirm the expectations. Where large firms survived or created radical innovation, this was often achieved through disintegration (Question 14): by setting innovation apart in separate development teams or divisions (3M Company), or co-ordination of highly independent units of design, production, and distribution (Benetton). IBM is an example of a company that needed to disintegrate in order to survive the radical innovation of personal computers. In Chapter 1 a meta-analysis by Damanpour (1991) was mentioned of twenty-three survey studies of the correlations of the adoption and implementation of a variety of internally and externally generated innovations with a range of organizational variables. The main outcome was that centralization had an almost universal negative effect, and formalization mostly had a negative effect, with some exceptions for service innovations and innovations in not-for-profit organizations. This is explained by the considerations given above.
>
> An example of a company which needed to integrate in order to survive after an initial period of innovation is BSO, a Dutch company in the field of provision of IT services. It was first structured as a set of independent 'cells', which were split up in independent new cells when they became too big. At the time the company boasted that it did not need co-ordination, marketing, and the development and efficient use of resources. But it ran into problems this way, and had to be taken over and restructured to achieve some co-ordination in order to survive.

There were, however, remaining empirical anomalies. An anomaly that appears to contradict the need to disintegrate is the long-term survival of fairly tightly integrated oil companies. An anomaly that appears to contradict the need to integrate after innovation is the prolonged existence of many loosely structured industrial districts (e.g. in fashions and furniture, in Italy for example). These anomalies can be explained by a more extended analysis, given in Chapter 11, which takes into account a number of contingencies that modulate the relation between (dis)integration and stage in the innovation cycle.

If economy of scale is large, and the product is not susceptible to differentiation (it is and remains an essentially homogeneous good), and no radical innovations appear that challenge existing firm and industry structure (scripts), then tightly integrated structures may survive.

This may explain the case of the oil industry. However, there may be other causes contributing to the survival of a company like Shell Oil Company; in particular, its use of scenario planning to anticipate possible futures. The explanation I gave entails the prediction that if a radical innovation were to occur that upset production or distribution scripts, or if opportunities and needs for product differentiation were to arise, the oil companies would disintegrate or die. The prediction is that this will happen, unless they are powerful enough to block entry of the novelties involved. The first will occur when novel sources of energy or novel feedstocks for chemicals arise and prevail which require different production and distribution structures (such as agricultural feedstocks for degradable plastics, and hydrogen or solar energy to replace oil). The latter is already arising in the chemical industry, with the emergence of a demand for and technology of designer chemicals and other chemical specialities. As it happens, concomitant problems are indeed emerging for the chemical divisions of oil companies.

If, in contrast, economy of scale is and remains small, and there is a demand and technical opportunity for ongoing differentiation, then industrial districts may persist for long periods of time. This is expected to be the case for fashion industries, where differentiation is needed to maintain distinction in fashion, to the extent that there are also obstacles to mechanization and automation as a basis for economy of scale in differentiated production. This is partly the case in clothing and leather because of the properties of the materials involved. This explains the longevity of industrial districts in fashion industries. However, there is an important qualification: effects of scale in brand name, advertising, distribution, and exports may yield the ascendance, and ultimate dominance of a member of the network or district which focuses on these functions.

This also yields a prediction. In internationalizing (or globalizing) fashion markets industrial districts will come to be dominated by marketing and distribution firms. Actually, this prediction is already confirmed by the Benetton case for fashion clothing and by IKEA for furniture.

14.1.8   Learning by Interaction

Increased outsourcing of activities by firms is explained by the need to focus on core competencies and to maintain flexibility. The analysis, in Chapter 3, adds the consideration of learning, on the basis of the principle of external economy of cognitive scope. This follows from the interactionist, constructivist, situated-action theory of learning: firms need outside, complementary sources of cognition to the extent that the environment is complex and changing (Question 17). The theory also specifies conditions for such learning by interaction (Question 18).

Learning by interaction requires on the one hand sufficient cognitive distance to yield novelty, and on the other hand sufficient proximity to enable understanding.

These results together explain the stylized fact, noted in Chapter 1, that especially in high-tech industries firms 'move to the middle' of intensive, durable (but not too durable) alliances with outside partners. This keeps the middle between both ends of the spectrum of organization: the integration of mergers and acquisitions ('hierarchy') and the disintegration of *ad hoc*, arm's-length transactions ('market').

Cognitive distance depends on absorptive capacity. This is typically limited in the traditional small firm, in contrast with the small firm that arises as a start-up, or spin-off, from a large firm by highly educated and experienced, entrepreneurial specialists. This explains the empirical finding that the former type of firm associates little with centres of formal learning and research, such as universities and research institutes. Absorptive capacity can be increased by cumulative experience and R & D. Thus, in order to profit from cognitively distant sources one may need to conduct the appropriate R & D needed to understand and evaluate such sources.

This explains the phenomenon, also reported in Chapter 1, that outside collaboration for learning need not imply that internal R & D decreases: it may be needed to maintain understanding of cognitively distant sources. Thus, focus on core competencies need not mean surrender of a wide range of R & D to maintain absorptive capacity. The core competence refers primarily to organizational competence to target, produce, and market products. Issues concerning cognitive distance and absorptive capacity were analysed in more detail in Chapter 8.

14.1.9 Indeterminacy

While each stage in the cycle of discovery provides the basis for the next one, and the sequence of stages provides the basis for exploration during exploitation, they are neither necessary nor sufficient for innovation, as discussed in Chapter 9. They are not necessary: novelty can also arise in a more Darwinian fashion through selection of random, uninformed trials, in blind trial and error. However, in that way there is much waste of foregone opportunities for exploitation and gambles of novelty that are not informed by experience and insight. The stages are also not sufficient: one stage does not necessarily produce the next one. That depends on external pressures and internal capabilities. Especially in the absence of competitive pressure, and with lack of opportunities to explore new contexts, people, firms, industries, and countries may rigidly stick to existing concepts and procedures (inertia).

> One illustration of this is the stagnation of technical development in China when the country was closed off from trade in the fourteenth century. People, firms, and industries may be unable to change in spite of pressures and opportunities, and then are not likely to survive. There are many examples of the death of firms and the decline of nations that were unable to adapt. One is the Dutch East India Company, with its decline in the eighteenth century. It was unable to adapt to the changed conditions, due in particular to the emergence of English competition. An opportunity for averting decline by a merger between the Dutch and English East India companies was not realized.

When generalization does occur and leads to differentiation and reciprocation, this does not necessarily lead to novel architectures, especially when there is no pressure to do so, when novel architectures are not needed for streamlining, efficiency, or full utilization of the potential of novelty.

> Perhaps an example is the innovation of self-service retailing, which started and consolidated in the general food trade and expanded to other trades, then cafés, restaurants, and hotels. It picked up new elements on the way, but the basic logic of it does not seem to have changed. It could be adapted to novel contexts, and adopt new elements in doing so, without losing much of its efficiency or limiting the utilization of potential. However, perhaps trading on the Internet, which is likely to transform the structure of trade, can be seen as a novel combination of self-service and communication technology that will yield novel architectures to fully utilize new potential and realize efficiencies.

These indeterminacies are related to the erratic nature of innovation: the phenomena of initial limitation of potential, innovative failure, and hysteresis (Questions 19, 20, 21). Those phenomena are also related to the period of consolidation, with the convergence to a dominant design (Question 5).

The process of change can have the appearance of long stability with intermittent radical change ('punctuated equilibria') along the following lines: In a given context adaptations that entail a break with established regimes, in the form of sub- and super-scripts, are not viable. Adaptation in a novel context, with fewer constraints imposed by the dominant designs resulting from previous innovations, is needed to give novel combinations a chance to emerge, develop, and prove themselves. This seems very similar to the process of allopatric speciation that Gould and Eldredge proposed as the process underlying punctuated equilibrium in biology. Particularly in social structures, deviants are not tolerated, and need to migrate to a secluded niche in order to develop. This preserves local equilibrium for the sake of exploitation, and it explains why innovation often achieves its first success in other areas than those where it later achieves its full potential. After the potential of novelty has been proved, and the limitations on the realization of its potential imposed by incumbent wider structures (superscripts) become manifest, it becomes understandable how punctuation, i.e. a relatively fast and apparently sudden process of breakdown and structural adjustment, can occur in the wider context, outside the context in which the novelty emerged.

14.1.10   Hysteresis, Metaphor, Serendipity, and King Saul

Often, in innovation there is a burden of inappropriate leftovers from previous practice, which was termed 'hysteresis' (Question 21). The examples discussed in Chapter 1 were the inappropriate use of joints in iron construction according to principles left over from the technology of wood construction, and the construction of direction indicators on cars that mimic hand waving. This is explained here in terms of innovations embedded in existing scripts of production or usage that have not yet been fully adapted to completely utilize the potential of the innovation.

The importance of metaphor (Question 15) has repeatedly been noted as part of the processes of learning and innovation. Here, it is associated with reciprocation:

indications for novelty are generated by substitutions of elements from one practice into another. When successful, this causes the second process to be seen in the light of the first (and perhaps vice versa), which shifts meaning and understanding and orients search in a new direction.

> One case discussed in Chapter 1 was Henry Ford's inspiration for the use of an assembly line to make cars, which he derived by analogy to the process at a mail-order firm. Another example is the origin of windmills as a reciprocation between sailing ships and watermills. Both required a radical, architectural change of structure to be utilized.

Novel combinations result from opportunities suggested in the meeting of parallel practices or events in novel contexts (Question 4), but this suggestion through metaphoric transfer will not occur to everyone. It may occur by chance, but even then only to a mind that is prepared; that has the absorptive capacity for it. This is called serendipity.

The King Saul effect entails that search in one field often ends up in innovations elsewhere (Question 19). This is also explained by the process of discovery: when shifting the application of some technology from the field of its first success to novel fields of application one may run into opportunities for novel combinations, in the process of differentiation and reciprocation, in areas outside the focus of attention. Above, reciprocation was seen as yielding a novel element that shifts an existing practice. But it can go the other way: elements from an existing practice are introduced into another and cause transformation there.

> The case of serendipity discussed in Chapter 1 was the discovery of X-rays by Marie Curie. The cases of the King Saul effect discussed in Chapter 1 were Philips's shaver, which resulted from an attempt to develop a new dynamo for bicycle lights, and the Bessemer steel process, which resulted from work on cannon shells.

Apart from the logical equivalence between metaphor and reciprocation, metaphor is part of the management of exploitation and exploration, as discussed in Chapter 13. It offers management another means of premise control: of shifting perceptions or orientations of staff without specifying precisely what they should do or how, and thereby leaving room for exploration while accelerating it, or slowing it down, or changing its direction.

14.1.11   Leonardo and Other Failures

Innovative ideas are viable only to the extent that they fit into existing boundary conditions, such as technologies of production and usage (Question 20). This was unpacked by means of the concept of scripts, in Chapter 10. Organizational scripts (of production, administration, etc.) can work only when the subscripts for activities substituted into them are in place, and output of the scripts fits in superscripts of supply chains and use by customers. As a result, ideas that are viable in principle achieve realization only when input and output conditions are satisfied. Some innovative ideas are impossible to realize under any conditions, because of fundamental constraints in laws of mechanics, for example.

> Cases discussed in Chapter 1 were seventeenth-century ideas of submarines and internal-combustion engines. These reflect the Leonardo effect: the basic ideas were sound, but the needed auxiliary or enabling technologies were lacking. Leonardo's conception of a flying man in the form of a man as a bird, waving wings, does not seem workable under any earthly technology, because of the mechanical constraints imposed by the structure of the human body in relation to gravity. It seems that if gravity were less it might be feasible. Thus, we might be made to fly like birds on the moon, with its lighter gravity. For flight on earth we had to devise the non-human body of an aeroplane. That took centuries to develop.

Another reason for failure is that, while feasible in principle, technically and systemically, i.e. assimilable in systems of use, production, and usage, innovations fail because alternatives, even though they are technically inferior, fit better into existing systems. These are therefore introduced sooner and subsequently block entry to the superior innovation as a result of path dependency and lock-in in systems of production and use. One contributing cause of this may be network externalities.

> Cases discussed in Chapter 1 were the Video 2000 system of Philips, and oil-based internal combustion engines. Technically the Philips system was superior, but the VHS system set the standard by capturing the market more quickly, through the distribution of prerecorded tapes and tapes with play times that fitted demand. At the beginning, hydrogen and electric cars were in principle just as viable as oil-fuelled ones, but the latter were first, and created lock-in through technologies and systems of production and distribution.

Closely related to the Leonardo effect is the phenomenon, indicated above, that initially new products or technologies cannot realize their full potential; not because they are insufficiently developed in themselves, but because they do yet not fit well into industrial superscripts or user scripts. Realization of their full potential requires change of those scripts. This is an important contributing factor to architectural change at the higher level of superscripts, if the full potential of the novelty under consideration is sufficiently attractive.

> The case discussed in Chapter 1 was that of integrated circuits: they were necessary for semiconductor technology to achieve its full potential.

14.1.12   The Multilevel Issue

The notion of scripts, used in Chapter 10 to elaborate the heuristic of discovery, with its different levels of organizational scripts, subscripts for actions of people, and superscripts of supply chains, helped to develop a multilevel theory of learning and innovation (Question 22). The cycle of discovery applies at all levels, but with widely different cycle times, with faster turnaround at lower levels: people go through learning cycles more quickly than organizations, and they go through cycles more quickly than industries. At any stage of the cycle at one level there are multiple iterations of the cycle at the lower level.

14.2   EMPIRICAL TESTING

While the foregoing analysis was anchored in stylized facts, as indicated in the previous paragraph, this is not the same as systematic, pointed empirical testing. Such testing is a priority for further research. This paragraph specifies testable hypotheses derived from the analysis and also specifies how they can be tested.

14.2.1   Stages of Innovation

The central challenge is to test the central thesis of the cycle of innovation and learning:

> H1: Innovation follows the stages of novel combinations, consolidation (dominant design), generalization, differentiation, and reciprocation.

Ideally, a test would trace the emergence and development of innovations and learning to see whether they follow the sequence of these stages, whether each stage emerges from the one that precedes it in the theory, and whether processes that follow the sequence are more successful than processes that don't. One question then is how to identify those stages. In innovation studies, differentiation could perhaps be identified in terms of the variety of product dimensions and variety of markets, if it concerns a product, or variety of applications, if it concerns a technology. Reciprocation could perhaps be identified in terms of flows in input–output tables, licensing or cross-licensing, R & D co-operation, exchange of staff, and alliances or joint projects. However, one should ensure that this indeed refers to combining technologies, not just extending the mix of products in a portfolio. Architectural innovation, in novel combinations, could be identified in terms of new patents, new product announcements, share of sales in new products, and new firm entry. Consolidation could be identified in terms of firm exits, market concentration, increase of scale, decrease of profit margins. Generalization could be identified as number of markets or applications, sales volume, exports and other forms of internationalization.

In organizational learning, differentiation could be identified in terms of variety of products, markets, product divisions or subsidiaries, and R & D sites. Reciprocation could be identified in terms of acquisition or sale of licences, cross-functional, cross-regional, or cross-divisional teams or communication, or number and types of linkages with outside partners such as customers and suppliers (various forms of alliance). Architectural innovation might be identified in terms of R & D expenditure, patents, new-product announcements, percentage of sales in new products, new market entry, and new divisions or teams. Consolidation might be identified in terms of divestments of products and assets, takeovers of competitors, increase of scale, division of labour, and increase of efficiency. Generalization might be identified as increase of sales, market share, exports, foreign direct investment, takeovers, joint ventures, or non-equity alliances in other markets or technologies.

Empirical tests could also focus on patterns of variety (difference between units), volatility (change of units), and averages (across units) predicted by the theory. In novel combinations: relatively high volatility and variety in number of firms, firm size, profits, sales, share prices, products, patents, technologies, together with low average firm size, low sales volumes, high average costs, net entry of firms, large perceived market, and technological uncertainty. In consolidation: a reduction of variety and volatility, in all these respects, higher average firm size, sales, share prices, lower average costs and profit margins, together with net exit of firms, a shift from product to process innovations and investments, and lower perceived market and technological uncertainty. In generalization: an increase in variety, volatility, and average level of market and sales expansion and profits, with increased market uncertainty. In differentiation: increased variety and volatility in investments, products, and product prices, shift to product innovations, dispersion of R & D, higher local shares of production, labour, distribution, profits. In reciprocation: a continuation of that trend, plus increased variety of costs, technological uncertainty, a shift from takeovers to joint ventures and alliances, in production, distribution and R & D, more local divestments, increased cross-licensing.

In the absence of the opportunity to traverse the full cycle, for lack of data, one could study pairwise relations between stages: Does reciprocation usually precede radical innovation, is it preceded by differentiation, is that preceded by generalization, and is that preceded by consolidation?

A final caveat is that one should take into account the unit of analysis and aggregation effects. The unit of analysis may be an innovation, a technology, or a (division of a) firm. If a technology or a firm contains several different components in different stages of development, the aggregate is likely to confound expectations and results. Then disaggregation is needed to a level where there is homogeneity in stages of development.

14.2.2   Cycle of (Dis)integration

As discussed in the previous Section there is already much evidence that supports the thesis of (dis)integration in relation to stages of innovation. Disintegration can entail industrial-district-type networks of small firms or highly autonomous divisions or subsidiaries of large firms. The hypothesis is that at the stage of novel combinations there will be relative disintegration, in consolidation and generalization more integrated structures, and in differentiation more disintegration, which intensifies with reciprocation and the next round of novel combinations. Disintegration will generally follow the stages of more internal autonomy of divisions, divestment, break-up of joint ventures, looser alliances, and industrial districts. However, concerning the extent and speed of disintegration various contingencies have to be taken into account. For example, the extent and type of economies of scale and scope, speed of product—compared with product cycles, extent of sunk costs, opportunity and need for product differentiation, etc., as discussed in Chapter 11. For example, expanding the discussion on the subject in the previous Section:

H2.1: Large firms can survive or produce radical innovation only by adopting a disintegrated firm structure.

H2.2: Large firms can survive over a long time without disintegration if there has been no radical (competence-destroying) innovation, there is no opportunity for product differentiation, and there are sizeable economies of scale.

H2.3: Industrial districts can survive for a long period of time if product differentiation is of great and ongoing importance, and there are limited economies of scale.

H2.4: Industrial districts of fashion goods that are subject to internationalization will yield integration, in the form of dominance of a large participant who is expert in marketing, distribution, and export.

14.2.3 Overview

The different hypotheses concerning stages of innovation and integration are brought together in an overview in Table 14.2.

TABLE 14.2 *Overview of hypotheses*

	Consolidation	Generalization	Differentiation	Reciprocation	Novel combinations
Population variables					
Concentration	Increasing	High	Decreasing	Decreasing	Low
Product variety	Decreasing	Low	Increasing	Increasing	High
Process variety	Decreasing	Low	Low	Increasing	High
Scale	Increasing	High	Stable or decreasing	Decreasing	Low
Profit variety	Decreasing	Low	Increasing	Increasing	High
Innovation characteristics					
Product	Incremental	Little	Incremental	Incremental	Radical
Process	Radical	Incremental	Incremental	Incremental	Radical
Organization	Radical	Incremental	Incremental	Incremental	Radical
Organization characteristics					
Hierarchical levels	Increasing	Increasing	High	Decreasing	Low
Complexity	Decreasing	Low	Increasing	Increasing	High
Centralization	Increasing	Decreasing	Low	Low	Low
Formalization	Increasing	High	Decreasing	Decreasing	Low

Complexity refers to variety of disciplines, departments, subsidiaries, types of expertise, levels of training.

The notion of hierarchical levels is related to the notion of 'structural differenti-ation' employed by Dewar and Hage (1978), but that includes, next to hierarchical levels, the number of departments, job titles, etc. Here, the latter are not included, and are rather seen as part of 'complexity'. The concept of complexity here entails only *variety* of departments, disciplines, skills, levels of training and education, and not also average *levels* of training and education, as the notion does in the work of Dewar and Hage. While there is a clear expectation that variety decreases in consolidation and then increases with differentiation, reciprocation, and novel combinations, it is not clear what to expect concerning the level of expertise and training. These can be both high and low at the stage of consolidation. On the one hand routinization of work can lower levels of production skill, but on the other hand division of labour can increase levels of specialization and administrative skills. Dewar and Hage found that addition of new activities went together with greater complexity. That accords with my expecta-tion: such addition is associated with reciprocation and novel combinations. In their study of the effects of complexity, centralization, and formalization, among other things, on the adoption of new programmes and services in sixteen social-welfare organizations, Hage and Aiken (1967) found that complexity, decentralization, non-formality, and participation in agency-wide decision making all had a positive effect, as I would expect.

14.2.4   Industry Effects

It was recognized in several places that the speed of progress along the cycle of discov-ery, the weight of different stages in the process, the relative importance of exploita-tion and exploration, and the problem of inertia depend on contingencies related to industries, technologies, and markets. Especially important is the cycle of product change in relation to the cycle of change in production. If products are highly differ-entiable and need to change fast, because of changes in needs or fashion, but the neces-sary change in the technology or organization of production is slow, the problem of inertia is most serious, particularly if there are large economies of scale and invest-ments in production are fixed and sunk. The contingencies were summarized in Chapter 13, Table 13.1. They can be subjected to empirical tests, and they need to be taken into account to control for industry effects in empirical studies of innovation, learning, and organization proposed in other sections of this paragraph.

14.2.5   Sources of Innovative Success

At the firm level one could further test the following hypotheses:

> H3.1: Innovative output is generated by internal and/or external sources of variety.

> H3.2: Innovative input and output, in combination with organizational integ-ration and co-ordination, generate commercial success.

Innovative output could be measured in the usual ways (with all the problems attached to them): patents, citations, number of new products/processes, share in sales of new products. Internal sources of variety might be measured by variety of: competencies, in terms of kinds and levels of training; R & D, in terms of variety of fields in which patents were filed; organization, in terms of number and autonomy of divisions or departments. The number and types of vertical and horizontal alliance (including equity and non-equity joint ventures) might measure external sources of variety.

According to the theory innovative success does not necessarily entail commercial success. We would seek to explain such success, measured by total-factor productivity, profits, and sales growth, as the *combination* (interaction) of internal innovative output or external innovative input with organizational integration and co-ordination. Internal innovative output would be as defined above. External innovative input would be measured as acquired licences, external R & D, mergers, and acquisitions. To test the hypothesis of the need of integration for success against the alternative of innovation without integration, we could employ the following basic mode specification:

$$S = a.Io + b.Io.IC + c.Ii.IC$$

where S is commercial success, Io is internal innovative output, IC is degree of integration and co-ordination, Ii is external innovative input.

The test might be conducted within a single industry, for which we should then take an industry where economy of scale is important. Alternatively, we could conduct the test across industries, with proper control of industry effects; for example, with economy of scale modulating the effect of integration/co-ordination, intensity of competition (entry barriers) modulating the effect of innovation.

14.2.6 *Organizational Forms for Exploitation and Exploration*

One could test propositions concerning ways in which firms can combine exploitation and exploration:

> H4: Firms that are successful in combining exploitation and exploration do so on the basis of one of the forms discussed in Chapter 13, or combinations of them. These involve, among others, spatial separation of exploitation and exploration, separation in time, Nonaka and Takeuchi's hypertext organization, Ciborra's platform organization, orchestration of other firms.

Success in combining exploitation and exploration could be measured by survival across periods of radical innovation as well as consolidation. This study would have a useful exploratory dimension in finding out what creative combinations have been found, beyond known forms. See, for example, the case of the 'Central Book House' discussed in Chapter 13.

14.2.7   *Management of Change and Change of Management*

We could test the following hypotheses:

H5.1: In radical innovation there is a positive association between success and either diversity of opinion among management and diversity of competence and experience of staff, and freedom for diversity of initiatives and teams, or change of management to escape from inertia.

H5.2: In stages of consolidation and generalization there is a positive association between success and either unity of opinion, co-ordination, and strict procedures, or change of management to escape from chaos.

One could also test the use of metaphor in different stages and transitions between stages:

H6.1: Use of metaphor by staff, within the firm and between firms, is largest (pervasive, persistent) at the stage of reciprocation.

H6.2: Use of metaphor by management is largest in successful consolidation (escape from chaos, see Figure 9.1 in Chapter 9) and in successful transition from generalization to differentiation (to escape from inertia). In the first case metaphor is used to increase coherence and in the latter to loosen established ideas and to encourage thinking in new directions.

14.2.8   *Management Consensus*

The theory also yields the following hypotheses:

H7.1: Diversity of views, both between management and staff and between managers among themselves, on products to be produced and technologies to be used is beneficial at the stages of reciprocation and novel combinations, in the sense of generating good innovative performance.

H7.2: Consensus of views, both between management and staff and among managers themselves, on products to be produced, with dissent on technology and organization of production, is beneficial at the stage of consolidation, in the sense of achieving high market share and efficient production.

H7.3: Consensus on product, technology, and organizational structure and style/culture to be used is beneficial at the stage of generalization, in the sense of generating good financial and growth performance.

In cases where firms from different industries are combined, there should be control of industry variables such as economy of scale and intensity of competition.

14.2.9   *Cognitive Distance*

The hypotheses of cognitive distance are as follows:

H8.1: Cognitive distance has an inverted U-shaped effect on effectiveness of learning by interaction (this reflects the notion of an optimal cognitive distance, see Chapter 3, Figure 3.1).

H8.2: Increasing absorptive capacity, which increases optimal cognitive distance, can increase comprehensibility.

I focus on testing the hypothesis at the level of the firm. For effectiveness of learning we might take the usual measures of innovative output, indicated before, and total-factor productivity. For the measurement of cognitive distance between firms, we might employ one of the methods developed in the literature on knowledge spillovers (Jaffe 1986, Los 2000). There, to measure spillovers, R & D expenditures in class (industry or firm) 'j' are weighted by the relevance of that R & D for class 'i', in terms of the proximity of knowledge. A proxy used for the measurement of this proximity is the relevant input–output coefficient, on the assumption that R & D is directed most at resources which entail the greatest share of total costs, which ignores product innovation, or the assumption that R & D expenditure will be directed most at technologies that are close, with 'closeness' being interpreted as 'having similar input structures'. Another measure is the extent to which patents cite each other. A further class of more elaborate measures is: Euclidean distances, correlation coefficients or cosines between pairs of vectors representing inputs (Los 2000), shares of patent classes in total patents in the firm or industry, or locations in a multidimensional space spanned by dimensions of product-field classifications of R & D expenditures. In the case of individuals, a much more elaborate method would be to extract 'mental maps' and devise distance measures for them. For ease of inspection a multidimensional space of vectors representing relative positions may be projected into a two-dimensional mapping of mutual distance by means of 'multi-dimensional scaling' (Los 2000).

Allowance was made for investment in absorptive capacity, yielding an upward shift of the curve for understanding. If the knowledge involved is primarily tacit and procedural, absorptive capacity depends on cumulative direct interaction. If knowledge is primarily explicit and declarative it may depend on cumulative R & D. One could test the effect of investment in absorptive capacity as follows: Suppose that the curves for novelty and understanding as functions of cognitive distance are as follows:

$$N = a.d, U = b - c.d$$

where N is novelty, d is cognitive distance, U is understanding.

The effect of R & D or cumulative interaction on understanding may reside in parameter b or c or both.

Then for effectiveness (E), as product of novelty and understanding, we have:

$$E = N.U = a.b.d. - a.c.d^2$$

One could test the effect of both cognitive distance and investment in understanding (I) by using explanatory variables I.d and I.d^2 and testing their interaction effects. This may indicate whether there is an effect at all, and whether it resides in b, or c, or both.

If it is in b, then the effect of I.d should be significant. If it is in c, then the effect of $I.d^2$ should be significant. Investment in understanding might be measured as R & D, or an appropriate part of R & D, or, preferably, cumulative R & D, or cumulative interaction, depending on whether the knowledge involved is more explicit or tacit.

14.2.10 *Firm Size, Tacit Knowledge, and Patenting*

According to part of the theory, smaller firms have more tacit knowledge and lower absorption capacity (provided they are of the traditional type, not spin-offs from large firms or set-ups by highly trained people). There is little need to test the implication that small firms generally deal with partners at small cognitive distance: that has been amply shown in the literature. But there are interesting implications for patenting.

According to the general view in the literature, small firms patent more than large ones because they do not have the alternative means for appropriation that large firms have. That may be so. But, on the other hand, if knowledge in small firms is more tacit, as proposed here, then this provides some protection against spillover. According to the cycle of discovery, knowledge is also more tacit in the early stages of radical innovation, and thus the stage in the cycle should be included in patent research. Note that the relation between tacitness and firm size now has at least two dimensions. First, according to the arguments from scale in transaction costs, in small firms co-ordination can take place by direct supervision, so that there is no need to codify and document knowledge for co-ordination across more specialized functionaries and larger distances. Second, according to the cycle of innovation there is correlation between firm size and stage of innovation: at the stage of radical innovation knowledge is more tacit and firms tend to be smaller. Furthermore, according to the theory of effects of scale in transaction costs small firms have relatively higher set-up costs of patenting. If patenting entails a fixed set-up cost this will yield a relatively high cost per unit of sales for a small firm with a small volume of sales associated with the patent. This effect would be less after the first time a patent had been filed. Also, the threat of litigation in case of patent infringement is less credible from small firms.

This yields the following hypotheses:

> H9.1: Small firms tend to patent less than large firms do, but once they have patented their propensity to patent will increase.

> H9.2: All firms tend to patent less prior to consolidation, at the stages of radical innovation and experimentation (reciprocation), and more during consolidation and generalization.

15

Summary

15.1   PURPOSE AND SCOPE

The purpose, scope, and methodology of the book are set out in Chapter 1. Twenty-two research questions are specified. The central issue concerns the relation between stability and change; between exploitation and exploration; between learning to do existing things better and learning to do new things. Exploitation is needed to survive in the short term, by efficient production. Exploration is needed to survive in the long term, through innovation and adaptation. How can they be combined?

An important line running through the book is a social constructivist, interactionist view of learning and innovation. Knowledge, in the wide sense of perception, interpretation, and evaluation, depends on categories (or mental maps, or schemas) that have been developed in interaction with the social and physical world. In fact, the book aims to replace both the methodological individualism of economics and the methodological collectivism of (some) sociology with methodological interactionism. For this purpose a synthesis is sought between economics, sociology, and cognitive science.

In the area of learning and innovation we are confronted with a proliferation of partly overlapping concepts and bits of theory, whose coherence and consistency are not clear. How can we deal with this? My answer is: by delving more deeply for more fundamental principles that will unify phenomena across different fields. Such principles are sought in part I, in the literature on management and organization (Chapter 2), economics (Chapter 3), evolutionary theory (Chapter 4), institutional economics (Chapter 5), theory of knowledge (Chapter 6), and language (Chapter 7). The results are used in part II to develop a theory of learning by interaction (Chapter 8), a heuristic cycle of discovery (Chapter 9), with an elaboration in terms of scripts (Chapter 10), and a cycle of organizational integration and disintegration related to the cycle of discovery (Chapter 11). These show how exploitation and exploration can be combined; how they complement each other. The principles of discovery also constitute principles of self-organization. These results are applied in part III, for an analysis of innovation systems (Chapter 12) and organizational learning (Chapter 13). The final Chapter (14) reviews the answers to the research questions specified in Chapter 1 and specifies hypotheses for further, more empirical, research.

15.2   LEARNING AND INNOVATION

In economics, there has been an enormous recent growth of literature on bounded rationality, asymmetric information, incomplete contracts, and knowledge. However, as discussed in Chapter 3, this has not dealt with learning in any important sense. It is mostly learning in the limited sense of increase of productive efficiency (experience) or the acquisition of knowledge by transfer (spillover) of information. The implicit theory of knowledge is not acceptable. To achieve knowledge, information must be assimilated in a cognitive framework that is able to absorb it. This notion of absorptive capacity has been adopted in modern economics, but the implications of the underlying notion of knowledge are not yet fully developed there.

In contrast with the field of economics, in the field of management and organization a large literature on learning has developed that is consonant with the social constructivist, interactionist theory of knowledge indicated above. Part of this is reviewed in Chapter 2. The literature has recognized the need for exploration alongside exploitation. Exploration goes beyond rational choice from a known set of alternatives, and thus entails radical uncertainty. That is why economics was ill-equipped to deal with it. It entails that, rather than knowledge of alternatives preceding action, action reveals alternatives. The central problem is a problem of abduction: How does one proceed into the unknown in a way that has some chance of yielding the discovery of viable options? And how does one survive in the process? How can one explore while maintaining exploitation; how can one exploit in a way that contributes to exploration? How can one create with a minimum of destruction?

If knowledge indeed depends on categories (or mental maps, or schemas) that have been developed in interaction with the social and physical world, then different people and groups, in different environments, develop different meanings, views, and understandings of the world to the extent that they have not interacted. This has important implications for the purpose and working of the firm and of interfirm relations. Firms exist not only, and not primarily, to limit transaction costs, but to act as a focusing device: to align perceptions, interpretations, and evaluations (and hence motivation) in order to achieve a common goal. This focus yields myopia and requires complementary cognition in outside sources. Thus, interorganizational relations are needed not only for reasons of static efficiency or flexibility, but also for deeper reasons of learning. This is more pronounced to the extent that technology and markets are complex and variable. However, interfirm relations then entail cognitive distance that may obstruct understanding. This distance should be large enough to yield novelty of cognition but small enough to enable comprehension. Comprehension can be improved with improved absorptive capacity. This explains the fact that one needs research not only to develop technology oneself but also to comprehend and evaluate outside partners.

The notions of 'absorptive capacity' and 'cognitive distance' are further analysed in Chapter 8, in an attempt at the development of a theory or a logic of learning by

interaction, in terms of cognitive and communicative mappings. Chapter 8 also analyses the implications for the governance of interfirm relations. It attempts to connect
the fields of interorganizational learning and governance.

15.3 EVOLUTION AND INSTITUTIONS

Evolutionary theory is reviewed in Chapter 4. This perspective has its uses in economics and organization. The variant of evolutionary theory called 'punctuated equilibrium' is interesting for its explanation of prolonged periods of stasis punctuated
with sudden change, since that is also what we often observe in technology and in
industry structure. Evolutionary theory may be applied to markets, in the selection of
firms or parts of firms, and it may be applied to the selection of ideas and proposals
within the firm. The evolutionary perspective has the merit of demonstrating the
crucial importance of diversity at the level of the firm to explain structural change at
the population level of industries, and diversity of views within the firm to explain
innovation at the level of the firm. Above all, in the context of the present book, it
shows how novelty can emerge from the functioning of existing forms of life, without
prior design and choice, by means of selection from a redundant set of forms. This
may provide a basis for a solution of the paradox of exploitation and exploration. But
this is not the only solution.

Evolutionary theory also entails many problems. There are pitfalls in its application
even in biology. Thirteen points are collected in which socio-economic evolution is
different from biological evolution. The most important problems, in the context of
this book, are the following: Evolutionary theory has no explanation to offer of processes of adaptation and learning by firms and people. It focuses on population-level
change as a result of selection among firms that tend to be looked on as inert. It
neglects the sources of novelty and focuses on selection. That is particularly serious
if learning and adaptation of life forms, in ontogenetic as opposed to phylogenetic
development, are themselves immersed in, entwined with, the selection process. And
that is what I propose: exploration takes place in the process of exploitation. The selection environment is endogenous. From misfits in the selection process we can learn,
and either adapt our capabilities to the selection environment or change the environment by innovation, political action, or negotiation. Either way, we may escape selection. The notion of 'co-evolution' has been proposed for this, but it does not seem
adequate.

In economics and organization the selection environment consists of institutions.
These are analysed in Chapter 5. I adopt the sociologist's view that institutions not
only regulate but also constitute behaviour, offering directions and enabling conditions. Thus, institutions not only select but also support and enable behaviour, in ways
that are very unlike biological evolution. Rather than trying to make an inventory of
institutions, I look at institutionalization as an activity. Social entities are institutions

to the extent that they enable/constrain action. In other words, institutions affect the causality of action. This is elaborated on a basis of a multi-causal theory of action derived from Aristotle. Institutions are themselves institutionalized to a greater or lesser extent, i.e. enabled/constrained by institutions at other levels. This allows for a hierarchy of different levels of institutions. Organizations are themselves institutions in the sense that they enable/constrain action within them, but are themselves institutionalized by their institutional environment.

The economic selection environment includes laws, regulations, customs, as well as language and basic categories of perception, understanding, and morality. Institutionalized conditions include markets (of products, finance, labour, and other inputs), infrastructure, knowledge, and technology, and associated incentives, constraints, and enabling conditions. Thus defined, the selection environment is to a large extent subject to change by innovation and political action. Innovation shifts technology and market conditions, and political action shifts laws and rules. Parts of the selection environment are socially constructed and form a negotiated order. A prime example is the criteria by which novel technology is judged and selected by regulatory agencies and markets. They have a common cognitive basis with the technology that is to be selected, and are subject to rhetoric and negotiation.

Different levels of institutions are proposed, with a deep structure of basic categories of perception, interpretation (understanding), and evaluation (value judgements), which produce a surface structure of rules that enable and constrain behaviour. The deep structure is not easily changed, and yields enduring institutional differences between countries. The surface structure is more amenable to a certain amount of convergence, but subject to the constraints from the deep structure, which will tend to prevent complete identity of institutions even at the surface level.

Chapter 5 also discusses different brands of institutional economics. It criticizes transaction-cost economics from the perspective of learning and innovation. However, it preserves important notions from that theory, such as notions and instruments for the governance of interfirm relations. It summarizes an attempt at a wider theory of interfirm relations which combines elements from transaction-cost economics with a perspective of social exchange and a perspective of learning by interaction. It focuses on the dynamics of innovation and learning and includes trust next to opportunism.

15.4   SITUATED ACTION

The theory of knowledge and language employed in this book is elaborated in Chapters 6 and 7. Constructivist, interactionist theory is underpinned by the non-mainstream, 'situated-action' theory of knowledge and language, in contrast with the 'computational–representational' view. It does not deny mental representations in any form, but stresses the mutual interaction between mental structure and context-specific behaviour. This further contributes to the development of 'methodological interactionism' to replace both the economist's methodological individualism and the sociologist's methodological collectivism.

In the situated-action perspective, knowledge is seen as the internalization of action in physical and social contexts. In ontogenetic development children learn to distinguish objects, and attach significance to them with help from the mother. This leads to pointing, which leads to reference and speech, which leads to internal speech (Vygotsky), which accompanies internalized, virtual action, which develops thinking. Self-awareness has a basis in bodily functions and develops from imagined reactions of others to the self.

Categorization and meaning cannot be captured in universal, context-independent, necessary and sufficient conditions. They are open-ended: categorization is subject to family resemblance and is guided by prototypes, or stereotypes that serve as defaults, subject to revision as experience accrues in novel contexts. Context provides a scaffold for understanding in several ways. It helps to disambiguate meanings in ways that would not be possible in lexical restrictions specified apart from context. It also contributes to the change of meaning and understanding. The mother scaffolds the development of categories in the child, and hopefully teachers do the same for their pupils. This underpins our notion of institutions as enabling constraints.

Recent theory of neural selectionism is found to offer a view of how the properties of meaning indicated above might be embedded in neural structures and processes (Edelman). It may also yield a possible model for solving the paradox of exploitation and exploration by means of redundancy plus selection. Exploitation generates a variety of parallel, alternative practices, which may both adapt and be selected according to their adequacy in possibly changing contexts and thereby allow for exploration without interrupting exploitation.

15.5   HERMENEUTIC CIRCLE

Chapter 7 discusses the hermeneutic circle (Gadamer, Jacobson, and Ricoeur): the meaning of a whole depends on the meaning of the parts, and vice versa. Thus, sentence (or discourse) meaning depends on word (or sentence) meaning, and word (or sentence) meaning shifts across sentences (discourses). This has been further elaborated as the selection from paradigmatic repertoires for combination in linear, syntagmatic structures, where new meanings of elements can arise as a result of contiguity in the sentence. This operates through metaphor. The cycle of discovery, developed in Chapter 9, and the hermeneutic circle have in common the idea that change of understanding and practice arises from an alternation of variety of meaning and variety of context. Novel contexts (sentences, discourses, action contexts) yield unorthodox 'collisions' between disparate elements, which cause elements to be seen in a new light and may yield a redistribution of sense across concepts, in new categories and ontologies. In this way the intersubjective order of language (Saussure's *langue*) is disturbed by context-specific, idiosyncratic usage (*parole*).

15.6   A HEURISTIC OF DISCOVERY

Chapter 9 is the central chapter of the book. It develops a heuristic of discovery, or second-order learning, or exploration, along the following lines. First, any novelty of concept, practice, or technology when it arises is incompletely determinate. It was discovered partly by chance, coincidence, and trial and error, and partly by design and inference based on previous experience, as a novel combination of elements from a diversity of past practices. It is ill understood why it works or even how precisely it works best, because it cannot at first be fitted into existing meanings, categories, and understanding of causality. In other words, at that stage knowledge is largely tacit. Some time is required for consolidation; for developing best practice, and preferably also understanding of why it works. This is typically accompanied by externalization or codification of tacit knowledge. This yields a system of practice. It is difficult to imagine how one can jump directly to the next novelty without exploring its limits of validity and collecting indications as to what elements from what existing practices should be combined in what way. Of course, blind, random combinations would be a way to proceed, but success would be swamped by failure. That may be the way it works in biological evolution, but in cognitive and socio-economic evolution we have the benefit of being able to learn from imagination, inference, and experience. But that does require the accumulation of experience on which to base imagination and inference. Also, in order to survive, in jobs and markets, we must maintain our functioning (exploitation) as we engage in exploration, and we need to build the motivation to change on the basis of an accumulation of failure. We need this for our own readiness to engage in the stress and uncertainty of conceptual change, and we need it in firms to build acceptance of change by workers and owners.

Consolidation provides a platform for generalization of the practice to novel contexts, since we have then found its best practice, which makes it worth while to generalize, and one hopes that we understand why it works, so that we can efficiently transfer it to others. In other words, in consolidation tacit knowledge has a chance of becoming explicit. Generalization opens the new practice up to a variety of contexts, where it is likely to meet new insight into limitations and inspiration for improvement from parallel practices in the novel context. This results in differentiations of the practice, and reciprocation with parallel practices, in the form of exchange of elements.

As adaptations to varying contexts accumulate, in increasingly syncretic structures, complexity increases, which complicates and slows down the grasp and co-ordination of the whole. Diminishing returns arise in further additions to the structure. Duplication of elements in different places in the structure yields opportunity costs in economy of scale foregone. The old structure imposes constraints, to preserve the functioning of old parts, which thwarts the full utilization of the potential of novel elements. All this yields pressure on present systemic coherence for a more radical, architectural change, with fewer elements and more clarity of structure, with more economy of scale as a result of concentration of similar activities and fewer obstacles to realizing the potential of novelty. Indications as to what elements to combine by what architectural principles are given, to a greater or lesser extent, from preceding experience with differentiation and reciprocation. Now we arrive at the beginning of the cycle, with a novel combination searching for consolidation.

This process seems homomorphic to the hermeneutic circle in language. Here, as there, novelty arises from a variety of selection from paradigmatic repertoires, in different configurations in different contexts of action, which yields unanticipated juxtapositions of elements, which may yield shifts of meanings, i.e. a reconstitution of paradigmatic repertoires. There also appears to be a connection with Margaret Archer's cycle of 'morphogenesis': structure conditions/enables action, which under sufficient openness to transfer from or towards outside contexts may yield a transformation of structure.

The heuristic satisfies the condition of maintaining exploitation in a process of exploration. However, this procedure is not necessary for the generation of novelty, nor is its success guaranteed. Novelty may be achieved in random novel combinations that are not based on experience in selection. And transition between stages in the cycle may stall. There may be insufficient incentive to differentiate, because of either lack of external pressure (competition) or lack of opportunity (demand). Internal systemic coherence and closure to the outside may yield insufficient incentives or opportunities or allowance for the differentiation and experimentation needed for innovation. Novelty may keep cycling in a prolonged chaos of rival forms, with a long delay before consolidation is achieved through selection among alternatives. Convergence is not logically necessary.

In Chapter 10 the cycle is further elaborated in terms of scripts: network structures (architecture) of nodes representing component activities. The network represents structure and the nodes represent insertion points of agency. We recognize producer scripts and consumer scripts. We propose a nested structure of scripts, with component activities also satisfying (sub)scripts, and organizational scripts substituting activities in industrial (super)scripts. Here, organizations are corporate actors, substituting their actions in higher-level structures, such as industry supply chains. Differentiation is reconstructed as novel substitutions into nodes of an existing script in novel contexts, initiated by idiosyncratic action; reciprocation is reconstructed as importation of substitutions into nodes, or whole nodes, from parallel practices encountered in the context. Novel combinations, in radical, 'architectural' innovation are reconstructed as a restructuring of scripts from elements and architectural principles derived from a diversity of scripts encountered in experience. This process operates at all levels, but with different cycle times. At the personal level it constitutes the generation of novel concepts, at the organizational level the transformation of organizational structure and processes, at the industrial level the generation of novel industries, and at the (supra)national level the generation of novel socio-economic paradigms. Higher-level scripts constrain and enable lower-level scripts. They will often resist pressures from below for their architectural change. That is why often novelty first arises in niches where opportunity, inspiration, and lack of constraint permit its emergence, until it generates results that force architectural change more widely to permit full realization of potential. This constitutes the conditions for punctuated equilibrium by means of the equivalent of allopatric speciation suggested by Gould.

15.7 A CYCLE OF (DIS)INTEGRATION

Chapter 11 proposes a cycle of organizational integration and disintegration associated with the cycle of discovery in innovation systems, and explores further factors affecting degrees and forms of (dis)integration. This includes issues of governance, which are developed in the context of a generalized theory of transaction relations, discussed in Chapter 5.

Disintegrated structures tend to be favoured in the stages leading up to novel combinations and the selection process leading to consolidation. This is because of the need for a variety of elements for novel combinations, the need to develop outside the regimentation of established systems, and the need for efficient selecting out of misfits. Integrated structures are favoured later, in the generalization that follows consolidation. This is because increased demand yields the opportunity and increased competition yields the need for an increase of efficiency through increase of scale, and the need for an administrative basis for setting up and co-ordinating expansion for generalization.

The speed of the cycle and the salience and duration of stages are contingent upon factors that vary between industries and technologies. If there is no effect of scale, disintegrated structures may subsist without replacement by integrated structures, especially if there is an ongoing opportunity and need for product differentiation. On the other hand, if economies of scale are large and the threat of new competition is low because of entry barriers, and there is little opportunity for product differentiation, integrated organizations may subsist without being replaced by or breaking up into disintegrated organizational structures. The degree of (dis)integration further depends on institutions, such as habits and attitudes regarding work, rivalry, collaboration, individualism or consensus, and other more or less institutionalized conditions, related to incentive structures, markets for products and inputs, type of knowledge and technology (such as degree of tacitness, systemic coherence, modularity). However, most of these reinforce rather than weaken the relation between (dis)integration and the innovation cycle.

15.8 INNOVATION SYSTEMS

In Chapter 12 the analysis of institutions and governance from Chapter 5, the analysis of learning by interaction from Chapter 8, the heuristic of discovery from Chapters 9 and 10, and the cycle of (dis)integration from Chapter 11 are applied to the theory of innovation. It yields a cycle of innovation that extends the existing 'life-cycle' theory of innovation and industrial transformation.

The approach taken builds on the view that innovation arises in particular in inter-action between firms. That entails that forms of co-ordination between firms matter for innovative performance. Therefore, an important part of the effects of institutions on innovative performance is bound up with their effects on problems of governance and with the enabling conditions and constraints that they offer for forms of co-ordination. Preceding Chapters yield the basis for an analysis of these effects. This leads to a comparison between different categorical systems of innovation, which reproduce perceived differences between, for example, the German and the US (and UK) systems of innovation. One is based more on collaboration in networks, in durable relations based on voice, which yields fast diffusion of technologies, incre-mental innovation, and quality production. The other is based more on rivalry, short-term, arm's-length contracting, and exit, which yields more efficient production of standardized products and may yield more radical innovation, but on the condition of easy break-up of firms and interfirm relations. The analysis also provides the basis for exploration of a third way, which might have the advantages of both, without the disadvantages.

15.9 MANAGEMENT OF LEARNING

In Chapter 13 the theories of learning and language from Chapters 6 and 7, the heur-istic of discovery from Chapters 9 and 10, the cycle of integration and disintegration from Chapter 11, and the cycle of innovation from Chapter 12 are applied to the learning organization: its design and management. Here, we return to the crucial issue of how to combine exploitation and exploration. Several options for structural design are discussed. One is separation in place between exploitation and exploration: they are simultaneously conducted at different places in the organization. The separa-tion may be vertical, with management doing the exploration and the 'workers' the exploitation, or the reverse. It may also be horizontal, with, typically, an R & D depart-ment doing the exploration, perhaps together with marketing, and production doing the exploitation. Note, however, that there are conditions, to the extent that the motiva-tion, experience, and material for exploration arise from exploitation, as we proposed in our heuristic of discovery. Furthermore, one needs to see to it that the results of exploration have some chance of feasible implementation in exploitation and that people in exploitation are sufficiently motivated and able to perform such imple-mentation. How does one deal with these issues of transfer? One may solve this by means of a permanent development team, with a rotation of staff recruited from opera-tional departments, who after a while return to (other) operational departments to take responsibility for exploitation. This is especially attractive if the systemic coher-ence of the different operational departments is high, so that close co-ordination in the implementation of exploration is required.

Another solution is to specialize at a particular stage of the cycle, and shift technologies or products into and out of the organization when they enter and leave that stage. Then one would have one permanent structure that is either integrated or disintegrated. This is in fact one of the central features that make industrial districts work, and allow them to persist across different stages of ongoing cycles.

Yet another approach is separation in time: a fluctuating organization that integrates and disintegrates as required. This may suggest that exploitation can be stopped to conduct exploration, which goes against our proposition that exploration arises in the process of an exploitation, which is subject to fragmentation and experimentation at the stages of differentiation and reciprocation. Thus, we should envisage a process in which a fixed group of people shifts its mode of work along these lines, with more loosening of ideas and practices in some stages, followed by more co-ordination and focus in other stages. Alternately loosening and strengthening connections between people may do this. That would require people to switch their orientations, routines, and habits. Particularly for knowledge workers, such as scientists or consultants, it may also take the form of integration and disintegration in the mind-sets of people in a fixed organizational structure, where they alternately concentrate on the convergence of efficient production and the divergence of exploration. The problems are compounded when an organization is involved in different activities (products, technologies) at different stages of development.

Another option is redundancy, combined with selection. Here, the firm becomes like a population of practices, in the sense of evolutionary theory. There is ongoing, constantly renewed proliferation of diversity, in parallel practices that are selected out for exploitation as the technological and market conditions require. The problem with this is that it can entail much waste of resources in more or less random varieties of practice. However, variety and selection may be partly virtual rather than actual, in the form of conceptual prototypes that are pre-tested artificially, in scenario analysis and computer simulation. Analysis of components or competencies that are robust under a variety of possible futures can reduce the scope of actual redundancy, to make it feasible without too much waste of resources.

Concerning the management of competencies one has several options. One can specify the content of competence (prescribe its scripts), or set conditions which it must satisfy to cohere in the system (organizational scripts), give examples or role models to be emulated, or manage meetings through which people adapt to each other (which includes rotation of people across jobs).

Whichever structure of organization and mode of competence creation one chooses, appropriate management of meanings, employing metaphor, metonymy, symbols, slogans, and myths, must support this. Metaphor can serve to make exploration acceptable, by showing how novelty connects with existing practice, or on the contrary trigger coherence by showing similarities.

Bibliography

ABELSON, R. P. (1976). 'Script Processing in Attitude Formation and Decision Making', in J. S. Carroll and J. W. Payne (eds.), *Cognition and Social Behavior* (Hillsdale, NJ: Erlbaum), 33–45.

ABERNATHY, W. J. (1978). *The Productivity Dilemma: Roadblock to Innovation in the Automobile Industry* (Baltimore: Johns Hopkins University Press).

—— and J. M. UTTERBACK (1978). 'Patterns of Industrial Innovation', *Technology Review*, 81: 41–7.

—— and K. B. CLARK (1985). 'Innovation: Mapping the Winds of Creative Destruction', *Research Policy*, 14: 3–22.

ACS, Z. and D. AUDRETSCH (1990). *Innovation and Small Firms* (Cambridge, MA: MIT Press).

—— and D. AUDRETSCH (1991). 'R & D, Firm Size and Innovative Activity', in Z. Acs and D. Audretsch (eds.), *Innovation and Technological Change* (Ann Arbor: University of Michigan Press).

ACZEL, P. (1990). 'Replacement Systems and the Axiomatization of Situation Theory', in R. Cooper, K. Mukai, and J. Perry (eds.), *Situation Theory and its Applications* (Stanford, CA: Stanford University Press), 1–31.

ALCHIAN, A. (1950). 'Uncertainty, Evolution and Economic Theory', *The Journal of Political Economy*, 43/1: 211–21.

AMIN, A. (1989). 'Flexible Specialisation and Small Firms in Italy: Myths and Realities', *Antipode* 21: 13–34.

ANDERSEN, E. S. (1992). 'The Difficult Jump From Walrasian to Schumpeterian Analysis or Characterising Schumpeter's Analysis: Dynamics, Development or Economic Evolution?', unpublished paper for the International Joseph A. Schumpeter Society Conference, Kyoto, August.

AOKI, M. (1986). 'Horizontal vs. Vertical Information Structure of the Firm', *American Economic Review*, 76/5: 971–83.

ARCHER, M. S. (1995). *Realist Social Theory: The Morphogenetic Approach* (Cambridge: Cambridge University Press).

ARCHIBUGI, D. and J. MICHIE (1997). 'Globalization of Technology: Towards a New Taxonomy', in D. Archibugi and J. Michie (eds.), *Technology, Globalization and Economic Performance* (Cambridge: Cambridge University Press).

ARGYRIS, C. and D. SCHÖN (1978). *Organizational Learning* (Reading, MA: Addison–Wesley).

ARTHUR, B. (1989). 'Competing Technologies, Increasing Returns, and Lock-in by Historical Events', *Economic Journal*, 99: 116–31.

AYER, S. (1965). *The Vakyapadiya of Bhartrhari, with the Vrtti* (Deacon College, Poona).

BAKER, W. E. and D. OBSTFELD (1999). 'Social Capital by Design: Structures, Strategies, and Institutional Context', in R. Th. A. J. Leenders and S. M. Gabbay, *Corporate Social Capital and Liability* (Dordrecht: Kluwer), 88–105.

BALDWIN, L. and J. T. SCOTT. (1987). *Market Structure and Technological Change* (Chur: Harwood).

BARLEY, S. R. (1986). 'Technology as an Occasion for Structuring: Evidence from Observation of CT Scanners and the Social Order of Radiology Departments', *Administrative Science Quarterly*, March, 78–108.

BARTLETT, C. A. and S. GOSHAL (1989). *Managing Across Borders—Transnational Solutions* (Boston, MA: Harvard Business School Press).

BAUMEISTER, R. F. and L. S. NEWMAN (1995). 'The Theory of Stories, the Primacy of Roles and the Polarizing Effects of Interpretative Motives: Some Propositions about Narratives', in R. S. Wyer jun. (ed.), *Advances in Social Cognition* (Hillsdale, NJ: Erlbaum), 97–105.

BENNIS, W. G. (1969). *Organizational Development: Its Nature, Origins and Prospects* (Reading, MA: Addison–Wesley).

BERGER, P. and T. LUCKMANN (1967). *The Social Construction of Reality* (New York: Doubleday).

BETTIS, R. A. and C. K. PRAHALAD. (1995). 'The Dominant Logic: Retrospective and Extension', *Strategic Management Journal*, 16/1: 5–14.

BIJKER, W. E., T. P. HUGHES, and T. J. PINCH (1987). *The Social Construction of Technological Systems* (Cambridge, MA: MIT Press).

BLAIR, J. M. (1972). *Economic Concentration* (New York: Harcourt, Brace, Jovanovitch).

BLEEKE, J. and D. ERNST (1991). 'The Way to Win in Cross-border Alliances', *Harvard Business Review*, November/December, 127–35.

BODEN, M. A. (1979). *Piaget* (Fontana).

BOISOT, M. (1995). *Information Space: A Framework for Learning in Organizations, Institutions and Culture* (London: Routledge).

BOLAND, R. J., R. V. TENKASI, and D. TE'ENI (1996). 'Designing Information Technology to Support Distributed Cognition', in J. R. Meindl, C. Stubbart, and J. F. Porac (eds.), *Cognition Within and Between Organisations* (London: Sage), 245–282; first published in 1994 in *Organization Science*, 5/3.

BOURGEOIS, J. (1980). 'Performance and Consensus', *Strategic Management Journal*, 1: 227–48.

—— (1985). 'Strategic Goals, Perceived Uncertainty and Economic Performance in Volatile Environments', *Academy of Management Journal*, 28: 548–73.

BRASS, D. J. and G. LABIANCA (1999). 'Social Capital, Social Liabilities, and Social Resources Management', in R. Th. A. J. Leenders and S. M. Gabbay, *Corporate Social Capital and Liability*, (Dordrecht: Kluwer), 323–40.

BRESSON, C. DE. (1987). 'The Evolutionary Paradigm and the Economics of Technological Change', *Journal of Economic Isssues*, 21: 751–61.

BROUWER, E. (1997). 'Determinants of Innovation: The Message from Alternative Indicators', (University of Amsterdam doctoral dissertation).

BROWN, J. S. and P. DUGUID (1996). 'Organizational Learning and Communities of Practice', in M. D. Cohen and L. S. Sproull (eds.), *Organizational Learning* (London: Sage), 58–82; first published in 1991 in *Organization Science*, 2/1.

BRUNER, J. S. (1979). *On Knowing: Essays for the Left Hand* (Cambridge, MA: The Belknap Press; first published in 1962.

BUCHANAN, D. and D. BODDY (1992). *The Expertise of the Change Agent* (New York: Prentice-Hall).

BURGELMAN, R. A. (1996). 'Intraorganizational Ecology of Strategy Making and Organizational Adaptation', in J. R. Meindl, C. Stubbart, and J. F. Porac (eds.), *Cognition Within and Between Organisations* (London: Sage), 405–38; first published in 1991 in *Organization Science*, 2/3.

BURNS, T. and G. M. STALKER (1961). *The Management of Innovation* (London: Tavistock).

BURT, R. (1982). *Toward a Structural Theory of Action* (New York: Academic Press).

—— (1987). 'Social Contagion and Innovation: Cohesion Versus Structural Equivalence', *American Journal of Sociology*, 92: 1297–1335.

—— (1992). *Structural Holes: The Social Structure of Competition* (Cambridge, MA: Harvard University Press).

CALDWELL, B. J. and S. BOEHM (1992). *Austrian Economics: Tensions and New Directions* (Deventer: Kluwer).

CANTWELL, J. A. and L. PISCITELLO (1999*a*). 'The Emergence of Corporate International Networks for the Accumulation of Dispersed Technological Capabilities', *Management International Review*, special issue, 1: 123–47.

—— (1999*b*). 'Spatial Distribution and Agglomerative Tendencies of MNCs' Technological Activities in Europe: A Comparison Between Foreign-Owned and Indigenous Firms', unpublished paper for the Conference of the European Association for Evolutionary Political Economy, Prague, November.

CASPER, S. (1999). 'High Technology Governance and Institutional Adaptiveness: Do Technology Policies Usefully Promote Commercial Innovation Within the German Biotechnology Industry?', unpublished paper for the Seminar on Institutions and Innovation, Netherlands Institute for Advanced Studies in the Humanities and Social Sciences (NIAS), 15 June.

CASSON, M. (1998). 'An Entrepreneurial Theory of the Firm', unpublished paper for the DRUID conference, Bornholm, 9–11 June.

CHEAH, P. L. and P. L. ROBERTSON (1992). 'The Entrepreneurial process and innovation in the product life cycle', unpublished paper for the International Joseph A. Schumpeter Society Conference, Kyoto, August.

CHECKLAND, P. and S. HOWELL (1998). *Information, Systems and Information Systems* (New York: Wiley).

CHELL, E., J. HAWORTH, and S. BREARLEY (1991). *The Entrepreneurial Personality* (London: Routledge).

CHESBROUGH, H. W. and D. J. TEECE (1996). 'When is Virtual Virtuous? Organizing for Innovation', *Harvard Business Review*, Jan.–Feb., 65–73.

CHOI, C. J. and S. LEE (1997). 'A Knowledge Based view of Cooperative Arrangements', in P. Beamish and P. Killing (eds.) *Cooperative Strategies: European Perspectives* (Jossey, MA: Bass).

CHOO, C. W. (1998). *The Knowing Organization* (Oxford: Oxford University Press).

CIBORRA, C. U. (1996). 'The Platform Organization: Recombining Strategies, Structures and Surprises', *Organization Science*, 7/2: 103–18.

—— (1991). 'Individual Learning and Organizational Routine', *Organization Science*, 2/1, reprinted in M. D. Cohen and L. S. Sproull (eds.) (1996). *Organizational Learning* (London: Sage), 188–229.

—— and P. BACDAYAN (1996). 'Organizational Routines are Stored as Procedural Memory', in M. D. Cohen & L. S. Sproull (eds.) (1996). *Organizational Learning* (London: Sage) 403–30; first published in 1994 in *Organization Science*, 5/4.

—— and D. A. LEVINTHAL (1990). 'Absorptive Capacity: A New Perspective on Learning and Innovation', *Administrative Science Quarterly*, 35: 128–52.

COHEN, M. D. and L. S. SPROULL (eds.) (1996). *Organizational Learning* (London: Sage).

COLOMBO, M. and P. GARRONE (1996). 'Technological Cooperative Agreements and Firm's R & D Intensity: A Note on Causality Relations', *Research Policy*, 25/6: 923–32.

CONESA, E. (2000). 'Organizational Dynamics and the Evolutionary Dilemma between Diversity and Standardization in Mission-oriented Research Programmes: An Illustration', in P. P. Saviotti and B. Nooteboom (eds.), *Technology and Knowledge: From the Firm to Innovation Systems* (Aldershot, Edward Elgar).

Cook, S. D. D. and D. Yanow (1996). 'Culture and Organizational Learning', in M. D. Cohen and L. S. Sproull (eds.) (1996). *Organizational Learning* (London, Sage), 430–5; first published in 1993 in *Journal of Management Enquiry*, 2/4.

Copleston, F. (1962). *A History of Philosophy*, I: 1 (New York: Doubleday).

Cyert, R. M. and J. G. March (1963). *A Behavioral Theory of the Firm* (Englewood Cliffs, NJ: Prentice-Hall).

Damanpour, F. (1991). 'Organizational Innovation: A Meta-analysis of Effects of Determinants and Moderators', *Academy of Management Journal*, 34/3: 555–90.

Damasio, A. R. (1995). *Descartes' Error: Emotion, Reason and the Human Brain* (London: Picador).

Dasgupta, P. and J. Stiglitz (1980). 'Uncertainty, Industrial Structure and the Speed of R & D', *Bell Journal of Economics*, 90/1: 1–28.

—— (1981). 'Entry, Innovation, Exit', *European Economic Review*, 15: 137–58.

David, P. A. (1985). 'Clio and the Economics of QWERTY', *American Economic Review*, 75: 332–7.

Davis, C. D., G. E. Hills, and W. Laforge (1985). 'The Marketing/Small Enterprise Paradox: A Research Agenda', *International Small Business Journal*, 3/3: 31–42.

Dellarosa, D. (1988). 'The Psychological Appeal of Connectionism', *Behavioral and Brain Sciences*, 11/1: 28–9.

Dess, G. (1987). 'Consensus on Strategy Formulation and Organizational Performance: Competitors in a Fragmented Industry', *Strategic Management Journal*, 8: 259–78.

Dewar, R. and J. Hage (1978). 'Size, Technological Complexity and Structural Differentiation: Towards a Theoretical Synthesis', *Administrative Science Quarterly*, 23; reprinted in J. Hage (ed.) (1998) *Organisational Innovation* (Aldershot: Ashgate), 293–312.

Dijk, B. van, and A. R. Thurik (1998). 'Entrepreneurship: visies en benaderingen', in D. P. Sherjon and A. R. Thurik, *Handbook ondernemens en adviseurs in het MKB* (Deventer: Kluwer).

Dosi, G. (1982). 'Technological Paradigms and Technological Trajectories: A Suggested Interpretation of the Determinants and Directions of Technical Change', *Research Policy*, 11.

—— (1984). *Technical Change and Industrial Transformation* (London: Macmillan).

——, C. Freeman, R. Nelson, G. Silverberg, and L. Soete (1988). *Technical Change and Economic Theory* (London: Pinter).

Duncan, R. B. (1976). 'The Ambidextrous Organization: Designing Dual Structures for Innovation', in R. H. Kilmann, L. R. Pondy, and D. P. Slevin (eds.), *The Management of Organization Design* (NY: North-Holland), 167–88.

Dupuy, J-P. (1998). 'The Autonomy of Social Reality: On the Contribution of Systems Theory to the Theory of Society', in L. Khalil and K. E. Boulding, *Evolution, Order and Complexity* (London: Routledge), 61–88.

Eaton, B. C. and R. G. Lipsey (1989). 'Product Differentiation', in R. Schmalensee and R. D. Willig (eds.), *The Handbook of Industrial Organization* (Amsterdam: North-Holland), 723–70.

Edelman, G. M. (1987). *Neural Darwinism: The Theory of Neuronal Group Selection* (New York: Basic Books).

—— (1992). *Bright Air, Brilliant Fire: On the Matter of Mind* (London: Penguin).

Eijck, J. van, and H. Kamp (1997). 'Representing Discourse in Context', in J. van Benthem and A. ter Meulen, *Handbook of Logic and Language* (Amsterdam: Elsevier), 179–237.

ELDREDGE, N. and S. J. GOULD (1972). 'Punctuated Equilibria: An Alternative to Phyletic Gradualism', in T. J. M. Schopf (ed.), *Models in Paleobiology* (San Franciso: Freeman, Cooper, & Co.), 82–115.

EMERY, F. E. and E. L. TRIST (1965). 'Causal Texture of Organizational Environments', *Human Relations*, February, 21–32.

FIOL, C. M. (1996). 'Consensus, Diversity and Learning in Organizations', in J. R. Meindl, C. Stubbart, and J. F. Porac (eds.), *Cognition Within and Between Organisations* (London: Sage), 173–206; first published in 1994 in *Organization Science*, 5/3.

—— and M. A. LYLES (1985). 'Organizational Learning', *Academy of Management Review*, 10/4: 803–13.

FLAVELL, J. H. (1967). *The Developmental Psychology of Jean Piaget* (Princeton, NJ: Van Nostrand).

FODOR, J. A. (1975). *The Language of Thought* (New York: Thomas Y. Crowell).

FOSS, N. J. (1994). *The Austrian School and Modern Economics* (Copenhagen: Handelshojskolen Forlag).

—— (1996). 'The Emerging Competence Perspective', in N. J. Foss and C. Knudsen (eds.) (1996). *Towards a Competence Theory of the Firm* (London: Routledge), 1–12.

—— (1998). 'Firms, Coordination and Knowledge: Some Austrian Insights', unpublished paper for the Workshop 'Recent Developments in Austrian Economics', Max-Planck Institut zur Erforschung von Wirtschaftssystemen, Jena, 7–8 August.

—— and C. KNUDSEN (eds.) (1996). *Towards a Competence Theory of the Firm* (London: Routledge).

FOSTER, J. (1997). 'The Analytical Foundations of Evolutionary Economics: From Biological Analogy to Economic Self-organization', *Structural Change and Economic Dynamics*, 8: 427–51.

—— (1998). *Competitive Selection, Self-organisation and Joseph A. Schumpeter*, unpublished paper for the International Joseph A. Schumpeter Society Conference, Vienna, 13–16 June.

FREEMAN, C. J. (1979). 'The Determinants of Innovation', *Futures*, 11: 206–15.

—— CLARK, J. and L. SOETE (1982). *Unemployment and Technical Innovation* (London, Frances Pinter).

—— and C. PEREZ (1989). 'Structural Crises of Adjustment, Business Cycles and Investment Behaviour', in G. Dosi (ed.), *Technical Change and Economic Theory* (London: Pinter).

FREGE, G. (1892). 'On Sense and Reference' (in German), *Zeitschrift für Philosophie und philosophische Kritik*, 100: 25–50.

FRIEDMAN, M. (1970). 'The Methodology of Positive Economics', in *Essays on Positive Economics* (Chicago: Chicago University Press), 1–43; first published in 1953.

GADAMER, H. G. (1977). *Philosophical Hermeneutics*, ed. David E. Linge (Berkeley: University of California Press).

GARDNER, H. (1983). *Frames of Mind: The Theory of Multiple Intelligences* (New York: Basic Books).

GARGIULO, M. and M. BENASSI (1999). 'The Dark Side of Social Capital', in R. Th. A. J. Leenders and S. M. Gabbay, *Corporate Social Capital and Liability* (Dordrecht: Kluwer), 298–322.

GARUD, R. and M. A. RAPPA (1996). A Socio-cognitive Model of Technology Evolution: The Case of Cochlear Implants', in J. R. Meindl, C. Stubbart, and J. F. Porac (eds.) *Cognition Within and Between Organisations* (London: Sage), 441–74; first published in 1994 in *Organization Science*, 5/3.

GEACH, P. and M. BLACK (1977). *Philosophical Writings of Gottlob Frege* (Oxford: Blackwell).

GELAUFF, G. M. M. and C. DEN BROEDER (1996). 'Governance of Stakeholder Relationships: The German and Dutch Experience', Research Memorandum 127, Central Planning Bureau, The Hague.

GERSICK, C. J. G. (1991). 'Revolutionary Change Theories: A Multilevel Exploration of the Punctuated Equilibrium Paradigm', *Academy of Management Journal*, 16/1: 10–36.

GIOIA, D. A. and P. P. POOLE (1984). 'Scripts in Organizational Behaviour', *Academy of Management Review*, 9/3: 449–59.

——, J. B. THOMAS, S. M. CLARK, and K. CHITTIPEDDI (1996). 'Symbolism and Strategic Change in Academia', in J. R. Meindl, C. Stubbart, and J. F. Porac (eds.), *Cognition Within and Between Organisations* (London: Sage), 207–44, first published in 1994 in *Organization Science*, 5/3.

GLEICK, J. (1987). Chaos: Making a New Science (London: Penguin).

GLIMSTEDT, H. (1999). 'Constructing the Global, Reconstructing the Local: Reflexive Actors and Economic Action in the Internationalized Context', unpublished paper.

GOULD, S. J. (1989). 'Punctuated Equilibrium in Fact and Theory', *Journal of Social Biological Structure*, 12: 117–36.

GRANDORI, A. (1997). 'An Organizational Assessment of Interfirm Coordination Modes', *Organization Studies*, 18/6: 897–925.

GRANOVETTER, M. (1982). 'The Strength of Weak Ties', in P. Marsden and N. Lin, *Social Structure and Network Analysis* (Beverly Hills, CA: Sage), 105–30.

GRANSTRAND, O., P. PATEL, and K. PAVITT (1997). 'Multi-technology Corporations: Why They Have Distributed Rather than Distinctive Core Competencies', *California Management Review*, 39/4: 8–25.

GRINYER, P. and D. NORBURN (1977–8). 'Planning for Existing Markets: An Empirical Study', *International Studies in Management and Organization*, 7: 99–122.

HABERMAS, J. (1982). *Theorie des kommunikativen Handelns*, (Theory of Communicative Action), pts. 1/2 (Frankfurt: Suhrkamp).

—— (1984). *Vorstudien und Ergänzungen zur Theorie des kommunikativen Handelns*, (Preliminary Studies and Elaborations to the Theory of Communicative Action; Frankfurt: Suhrkamp).

HAGE, J. (ed.) (1998). *Organizational Innovation* (Aldershot: Ashgate).

—— and M. AIKEN (1967). 'Program Change and Organizational Properties: A Comparative Analysis', *American Journal of Sociology*, 72: 503–19.

HAGEDOORN, J. and J. SCHAKENRAAD (1994). 'The Effect of Strategic Technology Alliances on Company Performance, *Strategic Management Journal*, 15: 291–309.

HAMLYN, D. W. (1978). *Experience and the Growth of Understanding* (London: Routledge).

HANNAN, M. T. and J. FREEMAN (1977). 'The Population Ecology of Organizations', *American Journal of Sociology*, 88: 929–64.

—— and J. FREEMAN (1984). 'Structural Inertia and Organizational Change', *American Sociological Review*, 49: 149–64.

HART, O. (1990). 'Is Bounded Rationality an Important Element of a Theory of Institutions?', *Journal of Institutional and Theoretical Economics*, 146: 696–702.

—— (1995). *Firms, Contracts and Financial Structure* (Oxford: Clarendon Press).

HAYEK, F. VON (1976). *Law, Legislation and Liberty: The Mirage of Social Justice* (Chicago: University of Chicago Press).

HÉBERT, R. M. and A. N. LINK (1982). *The Entrepreneur* (New York: Praeger).

HEDBERG, B. L. T. (1981). 'How Organizations Learn and Unlearn', in P. C. Nystrom and W. H. Starbuck (eds.), *Handbook of Organizational Design* (New York: Oxford University Press), i. 3–27.

——, P. C. NYSTROM, and W. H. STARBUCK (1976). 'Camping on Seesaws: Prescriptions for a Self-designing organization', *Administrative Science Quarterly*, 21: 41–65.

HELPER, S. (1990). 'Comparative Supplier Relations in the US and Japanese Auto Industries: An Exit/Voice Approach', *Business and Economic History*, 19: 1–10.

—— (1991). 'Strategy and Irreversibility in Supplier Relations: The Case of the U.S. Automobile Industry', *Business History Review*, 65: 781–824.

HENDERSON, R. M. and K. B. CLARK (1990). 'Architectural Innovation: The Reconstruction of Existing Product Technologies and the Failure of Established Firms', *Administrative Science Quarterly*, 35: 9–30.

HENDRIKS-JANSEN, H. (1996). *Catching Ourselves in the Act: Situated Activity, Interactive Emergence, Evolution and Human Thought* (Cambridge, MA: MIT Press).

HENNART, J. (1988). 'A Transaction Costs Theory of Equity Joint Ventures', *Strategic Management Journal*, 9: 361–74.

HILL, C. W. C. (1990). 'Cooperation, Opportunism, and the Invisible Hand: Implications for Transaction Cost Theory', *Academy of Management Review*, 15/3: 500–13.

HIPPEL, E. VON (1988). *The Sources of Invention* (Oxford: Oxford University Press).

HIRSCHMAN, A. O. (1970). *Exit, Voice and Loyalty: Responses to Decline in Firms, Organisations and States* (Cambridge, MA: Harvard University Press).

HODGSON, G. M. (1993). *Economics and Evolution: Bringing Life Back to Economics* (Cambridge: Polity Press).

—— (1998). *The Political Economy of Utopia: Why the Learning Economy is Not the End of History* (London: Routledge).

HOFSTEDE, G. (1980). 'Motivation, Leadership and Organization: Do American Theories Apply Abroad?', *Organization Dynamics*, summer, 42–63.

HOLLAND, J. H. (1975). *'Adaptation in Natural and Artificial Systems'* (Ann Arbor: University of Michigan Press).

——, K. J. HOLYOAK, R. E. NISBETT, and P. R. THAGARD (1989). *Induction: Processes of Inference, Learning and Discovery* (Cambridge, MA: MIT Press).

HOLLINGSWORTH, R. and R. BOYER (eds.) (1997). *Contemporary Capitalism: The Embeddedness of Institutions* (Cambridge: Cambridge University Press).

HREBINIAK, L. and C. SNOW (1982). 'Top Management Agreement and Organizational Performance', *Human Relations*, 35: 1139–58.

IJIRI, Y. and H. A. SIMON (1977). *Skew Distributions and the Sizes of Business Firms* (Amsterdam: North-Holland).

JACOBSON, R. (1987). *Language in Literature*, ed. K. Pomorska and S. Rudy (Cambridge, MA: Harvard University Press).

JAFFE, A. F. (1986). 'Technological Opportunity and Spillovers of R & D: Evidence from Firms' Patents, Profits and Market Value', *American Economic Review*, 76: 984–1001.

JAKOBSON, (1987). *Language in Literature*, ed. Krystyana Pomorska and Stephen Rudy (Cambridge, MA: Harvard University Press).

JANSSEN, Th. M. V. (1997). 'Compositionality', in J. van Benthem and A. ter Meulen (eds.), *Handbook of Logic and Language* (Amsterdam: Elsevier), 417–73.

JEWKES, J., D. SAWYERS, and R. STILLERMAN (1958). *The Sources of Invention* (London: Macmillan).

JOHNSON-LAIRD, P. N. (1983). *Mental Models* (Cambridge: Cambridge University Press).

DE JONG, G., B. NOOTEBOOM, R. W. VOSSEN, S. HELPER, and M. SAKO (1999). 'How Long-term Supply Relations Work', unpublished paper.

JORNA, R. (1990). *Knowledge Representations and Symbols in the Mind* (Tübingen: Stauffenburg Verlag).

KAMIEN, M. I. and N. L. SCHWARZ (1982). *Market Structure and Innovation* (Cambridge: Cambridge University Press).

KANTER, E. M. (1983). *The Change Masters: Corporate Entrepreneurs at Work* (London: Allen & Unwin).

KAUFFMAN, W. (1966a). *Hegel: Texts and Commentary* (New York: Anchor (Doubleday)).

—— (1966b). *Hegel: A Reinterpretation* (New York: Anchor (Doubleday)).

KHALIL, L. (1998). 'Social Theory and Naturalism: An Introduction', in L. Khalil and K. E. Boulding, *Evolution, Order and Complexity* (London: Routledge), 1–39.

—— and K. E. BOULDING (1998). *Evolution, Order and Complexity* (London: Routledge).

KIRZNER, I. M. (1973). *Competition and Entrepreneurship* (Chicago: University of Chicago Press).

—— (1985). *Discovery and the Capitalist Process* (Chicago: University of Chicago Press).

KLEIN WOOLTHUIS, R. (1997). 'Entrepreneurial Activity Through Inter-organisational Relationships', unpublished paper RENT X, Research in Entrepreneurship and Small Business, Faculty of Technology and Management, University of Twente, Brussels, 20–30 November.

—— (1999). 'Sleeping with the Enemy: Trust, Dependence and Contract in Interorganisational Relationships', (University of Twente, Enschede, the Netherlands, doctoral dissertation).

KLEINKNECHT, A. and J. O. N. REIJNEN (1992). 'Why Do Firms Cooperate on R & D?', *Research Policy*, 21: 1–13.

KNIGHT, F. (1921). *Risk, Uncertainty and Profit* (Boston: Houghton Mifflin).

KOGUT, B. (1988). 'A Study of the Life Cycle of Joint Ventures', in Contractor and Lorange (eds.), *Cooperative Strategies in International Business* (Lexington, MA: Lexington Books), 169–93.

KOHNSTAMM, R. (1998). a column (in Dutch) in NRC/Handelsblad.

KOOPMANS, T. C. (1957). *Three Essays on the State of Economic Science* (New York: McGraw Hill).

KUHN, T. S. (1970). *The Structure of Scientific Revolutions*, 2nd edn. (Chicago: University of Chicago Press).

LAAT, P. B. DE (1999). 'Dangerons Liaisons: Sharing Knowledge within R & D Alliances', in A. Grandori (ed.), *Interfirm Networks: Organization and Industrial Competitiveness* (London: Routledge), 208–36.

LACHMANN, L. (1978). 'An Austrian Stocktaking: Unsettled Questions and Tentative Answers', in L. Spadaro (ed.), *New Directions in Austrian Economics* (Kansas City: Sheed, Andrews & McMeel), 1–18.

LAKATOS, I. (1970). Falsification and the Methodology of Scientific Research Programmes, in I. Lakatos and A. Musgrave (eds.), *Criticism and the Growth of Knowledge* (Cambridge: Cambridge University Press).

—— (1978). *The Methodology of Scientific Research Programmes: Philosophical Papers Volumes 1 and 2*, ed. J. Worrall and G. Curry (Cambridge: Cambridge University Press).

LAKOFF, G. and M. JOHNSON (1980). *Metaphors We Live by* (Chicago: University of Chicago Press).

—— (1999). *Philosophy in the Flesh* (New York: Basic Books).

LAMMING, R. (1993). *Beyond Partnership* (New York: Prentice-Hall).

LANCASTER, K. (1966). 'A New Approach to Consumer Theory', *Journal of Political Economy*, 74: 132–57.

LANGLOIS, R. N. (1998). 'Personal Capitalism as Charismatic Authority: The Organizational Economics of a Weberian Concept', *Industrial and Corporate Change*, 7/1: 195–214.

—— and P. L. ROBERTSON (1995). *Firms, Markets and Economic Change* (London: Routledge).

LATOUR, B. (1987). *Science in Action* (Cambridge, MA: Harvard University Press).

—— and S. WOOLGAR (1979). *Laboratory Life* (Beverly Hills, CA: Sage).

LATSIS, S. J. (ed.) (1980). *Method and Appraisal in Economics* (Cambridge: Cambridge University Press).

LAWRENCE, P. & J. LORSCH (1967). *Organization and Environment* (Boston, MA: Harvard Business School).

LEE, T. and L. L. WILDE (1980). 'Market Structure and Innovation: A Reformulation', *Quarterly Journal of Economics*, 94: 429–36.

LEENDERS, R. Th. A. J. and S. M. GABBAY (1999). *Corporate Social Capital and Liability* (Dordrecht: Kluwer).

LEVINTHAL, D. A. (1996). 'Organizational Adaptation and Environmental Selection', in M. D. Cohen and L. S. Sproull (eds.) (1996). *Organizational Learning* (London: Sage), 195–202; first published in 1991 in *Organization Science*, 2/1.

LEVITT, B. and J. G. MARCH (1988). 'Organizational Learning', in W. R. Scott (ed.): *Annual Review of Sociology* (Palo Alto, CA: Annual Reviews).

LEWONTIN, R. (1983). 'The Organism as the Subject and Object of Evolution', *Scientia*, 118: 63–82.

LINSKY, L. (1971). *Reference and Modality* (Oxford: Oxford University Press).

LIPPMAN, S. and R. P. RUMELT (1982). 'Uncertain Imitability: An Analysis of Interfirm Differences in Efficiency Under Competition', *Bell Journal of Economics*, 13: 418–38.

LORANGE, P. and J. Roos (1992). *Strategic Alliances* (Oxford: Blackwell).

Los, B. (2000). 'The Empirical Performance of a New Interindustry Technology Spillover Measure', in P. P. Saviotti and B. Nooteboom (eds.): *Technology and Knowledge: From the Firm to Innovation Systems* (Aldershot: Edward Elgar).

LOTMAN, Y. M. (1990). *Universe of the Mind: A Semiotic Theory of Culture* (London: I. B. Tauris).

LOUNAMAA, P. H. and J. G. MARCH (1987). 'Adaptive Coordination of a Learning Team', *Management Science*, 33: 107–23.

LOURY, G. C. (1979). 'Market Structure and Innovation', *Quarterly Journal of Economics*, 93: 395–410.

LUHMANN, N. (1988). 'Familiarity, Confidence, Trust', in D. Gambetta (ed.), *Trust Making and Breaking of Cooperative Relations* (Oxford, Blackwell), 94–108.

LUNDVALL, B. A. (1985). *Product Innovation and User–Producer Interaction* (Aalborg: Aalborg University Press).

—— (1988). 'Innovation as an Interactive Process—From User–Producer Interaction to National Systems of Innovation, in G. Dosi, C. Freeman, C. Nelson, R. Silverberg, and L. Soete (eds.), *Technology and Economic Theory* (London: Pinter).

—— (1993). 'User–Producer Relationships, National Systems of Innovation and Internationalization', in D. Foray and C. Freeman (eds.), *Technology and the Wealth of Nations* (London: Pinter).

McCLELLAND, J. L., D. E. RUMELHART, and G. E. HINTON (1987). 'The Appeal of Parallel Distributed Processing', in D. E. Rumelhart, J. L. McClelland, and the PDP Research Group,

Parallel Distributed Processing: Explorations in the Microstructure of Cognition, Volume 1: Foundations (Cambridge, MA: MIT Press), 3–44.

MCKELVEY, M. (1996a). *Evolutionary Innovations: The Business of Biotechnology* (Oxford: Oxford University Press).

—— (1996b). 'Technological Discontinuities in Genetic Engineering in Pharmaceuticals? Firm Jumps and Lock-in in Systems of Innovation', *Technology Analysis and Strategic Management*, 8/2: 107–16.

—— and F. TEXIER (2000). 'Surviving Technological Discontinuities Through Evolutionary Systems of Innovation: Ericsson and Mobile Telecommunication', in P. P. Saviotti and B. Nooteboom (eds.), *Technology and Knowledge: From the Firm to Innovation Systems* (Aldershot: Edward Elgar).

MAHAJAN, V. and Y. WIND (1986). *Innovation Diffusion Models of New Product Acceptance* (Cambridge, MA: Ballinger).

MALERBA, F. (1992). 'Learning by Firms and Incremental Technical Change', *The Economic Journal*, 102: 845–59.

—— (1993). 'The National System of Innovation: Italy', in R. R. Nelson (ed.), *National Innovation Systems* (Oxford: Oxford University Press), 230–60.

—— and L. ORSENIGO (1995). 'Schumpeterian Patterns of Innovation', *Cambridge Journal of Economics*, 19: 47–65.

—— and L. ORSENIGO (1996). 'The Dynamics and Evolution of Industries', *Industrial and Corporate Change*, 5: 51–88.

——, R. R. NELSON, L. ORSENIGO, and S. WINTER (1998). 'Vertical Integration and Specialisation in the Evolution of the Computer Industry: Towards a "History friendly" Model', unpublished paper for the International Joseph A. Schumpeter Conference, Vienna, 13–16 June.

MALMBERG, A. and P. MASKELL (1996). 'Proximity, Institutions and Learning: Towards an Explanation of Regional Specialization and Industry Agglomeration', unpublished paper for the EMOT Workshop, Durham, NC, 28–9 June.

MANSFIELD, E. (1969). *Industrial Research and Technological Innovation* (London: Longmans, Green, & Co.).

MARCH, J. (1991). 'Exploration and Exploitation in Organizational Learning', *Organization Science*, 2/1.

—— and H. A. SIMON (1958). *Organizations* (New York: Wiley).

MASTERMAN, M. (1970). 'The Nature of a Paradigm', in I. Lakatos and A. Musgrave, *Criticism and the Growth of Knowledge* (Cambridge: Cambridge University Press), 59–89.

MEAD, G. H. (1934). *Mind, Self and Society: From the Standpoint of a Social Behaviorist* (Chicago: Chicago University Press).

—— (1982). *The Individual and the Social Self*, unpublished work of G. H. Mead, ed. D. L. Miller (Chicago: University of Chicago Press).

MEINDL, J. R., C. STUBBART, and J. F. PORAC (eds.) (1996). *Cognition Within and Between Organisations* (London: Sage).

MERLEAU–PONTY, M. (1964). *Le Visible et l'invisible* (Paris: Gallimard).

METCALFE, J. S. (1998). *Evolutionary Economics and Creative Destruction* (London: Routledge).

MIALL, D. S. (ed.) (1982). *Metaphor: Problems and Perspectives* (Brighton: Harvester).

MILGROM, P. and J. ROBERTS (1992). *Economics, Organization and Management* (Englewood Cliffs, NJ: Prentice-Hall).

MINSKY, M. (1975). A Framework for Representing Knowledge, in P. H. Winston (ed.), *The Psychology of Computer Vision* (NY: McGraw-Hill).

MINTZBERG, H. (1983). *Structure in Fives: Designing Effective Organizations* (Englewood Cliffs, NJ: Prentice-Hall).

MOKYR, J. (1990). *The Lever of Riches: Technological Creativity and Economic Progress* (Oxford: Oxford University Press).

MOWERY, D. C. and R. N. ROSENBERG (1993). 'The US National System of Innovation', in R. R. Nelson (ed.) (1993), *National Innovation Systems* (Oxford: Oxford University Press), 29–75.

NEISSER, U. (ed.) (1987). *Concepts and Conceptual Development* (Cambridge: Cambridge University Press).

NELSON, R. R. (ed.) (1993). *National Innovation Systems: A Comparative Analysis* (New York: Oxford University Press).

—— and S. WINTER (1977). 'In Search of Useful Theory of Innovation', *Research Policy*, 6: 36–76.

—— and S. WINTER (1982). *An Evolutionary Theory of Economic Change* (Cambridge: Cambridge University Press).

—— and N. ROSENBERG (1993). 'Technical Innovation and National Systems', in R. R. Nelson (ed.), *National Innovation Systems* (Oxford: Oxford University Press), 1–26.

—— and B. N. SAMPAT (2000). 'Making Sense of Institutions as a Factor Shaping Economic Performance', *Journal of Economic Behavior and Organization* (forthcoming).

NEWELL, A. and H. A. SIMON (1972). *Human Problem Solving* (Englewood Cliffs, NJ: Prentice-Hall).

NONAKA, I. (1995). 'The Knowledge Creating Company', *Harvard Business Review*, November–December, 96–104.

—— and H. TAKEUCHI (1995). *The Knowledge Creating Company* (Oxford: Oxford University Press).

NOOTEBOOM, B. (1982). 'A New Theory of Retailing Costs', *European Economic Review*, 17: 162–86.

—— (1984). 'Innovation, Life Cycle and the Share of Independents: Cases from Retailing', *International Small Business Journal*, 3/1: 21–33.

—— (1986). 'Plausibility in Eonomics', *Economics and Philosophy*, 2: 197–224.

—— (1987). 'Threshold Costs in Service Industries', *Service Industries Journal*, 7: 65–76.

—— (1989). 'Paradox, Identity and Change in Management', *Human Systems Management*, 8: 291–300.

—— (1990). 'The Popperian Legacy in Economics: Confusion and Beyond', *De Economist*, 138/3: 256–75.

—— (1991). 'Entry, Spending and Firm Size in a Stochastic Development Race', *Small Business Economics*, 3: 103–20.

—— (1992a). 'Towards a Dynamic Theory of Transactions', *Journal of Evolutionary Economics*, 2: 281–99.

—— (1992b). 'Agent, Context and Innovation: A Saussurian View of Markets', in W. Blaas and J. Foster (eds.), *Mixed Economies in Europe: An Evolutionary Perspective on their Emergence, Transition and Regulation* (Aldershot: Edward Elgar), 33–52.

—— (1993a). 'Firm Size Effects on Transaction Costs', *Small Business Economics*, 5: 283–95.

—— (1993b). 'The Conservatism of Programme Continuity: Criticism of Lakatosian Methodology in Economics', *Methodus*, 5: 31–46.

NOOTEBOOM, B. (1993*c*). 'Transactions and Networks: Do They Connect?', in J. Groenewegen (ed.), *Dynamics of the Firm: Strategies of Pricing and Organisation* (Aldershot: Edward Elgar), 9–26.

—— (1994). 'Innovation and Diffusion in Small Business: Theory and Empirical Evidence', *Small Business Economics*, 6: 327–47.

—— (1996*a*). 'Trust, Opportunism and Governance: A Process and Control Model', *Organization Studies*, 17/6: 985–1010.

—— (1996*b*). 'Towards a Learning Based Model of Transactions', in J. Groenewegen (ed.), *TCE and Beyond* (Deventer: Kluwer), 327–49.

—— (1997). 'Path Dependence of Knowledge: Implications for the Theory of the Firm', in L. Magnusson and J. Ottoson (eds.), *Evolutionary Economics and Path-dependence*, (Cheltenham: Edward Elgar), 57–78.

—— (1998). 'Cost, Quality and Learning Based Governance of Buyer–Supplier Relations', in M. G. Colombo (ed.), *The Changing Boundaries of the Firm* (London: Routledge), 187–208.

—— (1999*a*). *Inter-firm Alliances: Analysis and Design* (London: Routledge).

—— (1999*b*). 'Roles of the Go-between', in S. M. Gabbay and R. Leenders (eds.), *Corporate Social Capital* (Deventer: Kluwer), 341–55.

—— (1999*c*). 'Trust as a Governance Device', in M. C. Casson and A. Godley (eds.), *Cultural Factors in Economic Growth* (Springer).

—— (1999*d*). 'Innovation and Inter-firm Linkages: New Implications for Policy', *Research Policy*, 28: 793–805.

—— (1999*e*). 'Voice and Exit Systems of Corporate Control', *Journal of Economic Issues* 33/4: 45–60.

—— (1999*f*). 'The Dynamic Efficiency of Networks', in A. Grandori (ed.): *Interfirm Networks: Organization and Industrial Competitiveness* (London: Routledge), 91–119.

—— (1999*g*). 'Learning, Innovation and Industrial Organisation', *Cambridge Journal of Economics*, 23: 127–50.

——, J. BERGER, and N. G. NOORDERHAVEN (1997). 'Effects of Trust and Governance on Relational Risk', *Academy of Management Journal*, 40/2: 308–38.

—— and W. CONSTANDSE (1995). 'Het gouden cluster van de Vereningde Oostindische Compagnie' ('The Golden Cluster of the United East India Company'), *Holland Management Review*, 44: 1–5.

—— and R. W. VOSSEN (1995). 'Firm Size and Efficiency in R & D Spending', in A. V. Witteloostuyn (ed.), *Market Evolution: Competition and Cooperation Across Markets and Over Time*, Studies in Industrial Organization, xxix (Deventer: Kluwer), 69–86.

NORTH, D. C. (1990). *Institutions, Institutional Change and Economic Performance* (Cambridge: Cambridge University Press).

—— and R. THOMAS (1973). *The Rise of the New World: A New Economic History* (Cambridge: Cambridge University Press).

ODAGIRI, H. and A. GOTO (1993). 'The Japanese System of Innovation: Past, Present and Future', in R. R. Nelson, *National Innovation Systems* (Oxford: Oxford University Press), 76–114.

OHMAE, K. (1989). 'Global Logic of Strategic Alliances', *Harvard Business Review*, March–April, 143–54.

OSBORN, R. N. and C. C. BAUGHN (1990). 'Forms of Interorganizational Governance for Multinational Alliances, *Academy of Management Journal*, 33/3: 503–19.

OUCHI, W. G. (1980). 'Markets, Bureaucracies, Clans', *Administrative Science Quarterly*, 25: 129–41.

PAGANO, U. (1999). 'Veblen, New Institutionalism and the Diversity of Economic Institutions', unpublished paper for the European Association for Evolutionary Political Economy Conference, November, Prague.

PAVITT, K. (1984). 'Sectoral Patterns of Technical Change: Towards a Taxonomy and a Theory', *Research Policy*, 13: 343–73.

—— (1998). 'Technologies, Products and Organization in the Innovating Firm', *Industrial and Corporate Change*, 7/3: 433–51.

PEIRCE, C. S. (1957). *Essays in the Philosophy of Science* (Indianapolis, IN: Bobbs-Merrill).

PÉLI, G. and B. NOOTEBOOM (1999). 'Market Partitioning and the Geometry of the Resource Space', *American Journal of Sociology*, 104/4: 1132–53.

PENROSE, E. (1959). *The Theory of the Growth of the Firm* (New York: Wiley).

PENTLAND, B. T. (1995). 'Grammatical Models of Organizational Processes', *Organization Science*, 6/5: 541–56.

—— and H. H. REUTER (1994). 'Organizational Routines as Grammars of Action', *Administrative Science Quarterly*, September, 484–510.

PETTIGREW, A. M. (1987). 'Context and Action in the Transformation of the Firm', *Journal of Management Studies*, 24/6: 649–70.

—— (ed.) (1988). *The Management of Strategic Change* (Oxford: Basil Blackwell).

PFEFFER, J. and G. R. SALANCIK (1978). *The External Control of Organizations: A Resource Dependence Perspective* (New York: Harper & Row).

PIAGET, J. (1970). *Psychologie et epistémologie* (Paris: Denoël).

—— (1974). *Introduction à l'épistémologie génétique* (Paris: Presses Universitaires de France).

PIORE, M. and C. SABEL (1983). 'Italian Small Business Development: Lessons for US Industrial Policy', in J. Zysman and L. Tyson (eds.), *American Industry in International Competition: Government Policies and Corporate Strategies* (Ithaca: Cornell University Press).

POLANYI, M. (1962). *Personal knowledge* (London: Routledge).

—— (1966). *The Tacit Dimension* (London: Routledge).

—— (1969). *Knowing and Being* (London: Routledge).

PONDY, L. R. (1983). 'The Role of Metaphors and Myths in Organization and in the Facilitation of Change', in L. R. Pondy, P. J. Frost, G. Morgan, and T. C. Dandridge (eds.), *Organizational Symbolism* (Greenwich, CT: JAI Press), 157–66.

POPPER, K. R. (1973). *The Open Society and its Enemies*, II (London: Routledge & Kegan Paul), first published in 1945.

—— (1970). 'Normal Science and its Dangers', in I. Lakatos and A. Musgrave (eds.), *Criticism and the Growth of Knowledge* (Cambridge: Cambridge University Press), 51–58.

PORTER, M. A. (1980). *Competitive Strategy* (New York: Free Press).

—— (1985). *Competitive Advantage* (New York: Free Press).

—— (1990). *The Competitive Advantage of Nations* (New York: Free Press).

VAN PRAAG, C. M. (1996). *Determinants of Successful Entrepreneurship* Tinbergen Institute Research Series (Amsterdam: Thesis publishers).

PRAHALAD, C. and G. HAMEL (1990). 'The Core Competences of the Corporation', *Harvard Business Review*, May–June, 79–83.

PRIGOGINE, I. and I. STENGERS (1984). *Order Out of Chaos: Man's New Dialogues with Nature* (New York: Bantam).

PUTNAM, H. (1957). *Mind, Language and Reality: Philosophical Papers*, II (Cambridge: Cambridge University Press).

QUINE, W. (1960). *Word and Object* (New York: Wiley).

QUINN, J. B. (1982). *Strategies for Change* (Homewood, Ill.: Irwin).

—— (1992). *Intelligent Enterprise* (New York: The Free Press).

READ, S. J. and L. C. MILLER (1995). 'Stories are Fundamental to Meaning and Memory: For Social Creatures, Could It Be Otherwise?', in R. S. Wyer jun. (ed.), *Advances in Social Cognition* (Hillsdale, NJ: Erlbaum), 139–54.

RICOEUR, P. (1975). *La Metaphore vive* (Paris: Éditions du Seuil).

RING, P. S. and A. VAN DE VEN (1994). 'Developmental Processes of Cooperative Inter-organizational Relationships', *Academy of Management Review*, 19/1: 90–118.

ROCHA, F. (2000). 'Inter-firm Technological Cooperation, Asset Characteristics and R & D Strategy', in P. P. Saviotti and B. Nooteboom (eds.): *Technology and Knowledge: From the Firm to Innovation Systems* (Aldershot: Edward Elgar).

ROMANELLI, E. and M. L. TUSHMAN (1994). 'Organizational Transformation as Punctuated Equilibrium: An Empirical Test', *Academy of Management Journal*, 37/5: 1141–66.

ROSCH, E. (1977). 'Human Categorization', in N. Warren (ed.), *Advances in Cross-cultural Psychology*, I (New York: Academic Press).

—— (1978). 'Principles of Categorization', in E. Rosch and B. B. Lloyd (eds.), *Cognition and Categorization* (Hillsdale, NJ: Erlbaum).

ROSE, S. (1992). *The Making of Memory* (New York: Doubleday).

—— (1997). *Lifelines: Biology, Freedom, Determinism* (London: Penguin).

ROSENBERG, N. (1972). *Technology and American Economic Growth* (White Plains: Sharp Company).

—— (1992). 'Joseph Schumpeter: Radical Economist', unpublished paper for the International Joseph A. Schumpeter Society Conference, Kyoto, August.

ROTHWELL, R. (1985). 'Innovation and the Smaller Firm', First International Technical Innovation and Entrepreneurship Symposium, Utah Innovation Foundation, Salt Lake City, 11–13 September.

—— (1986). 'The Role of Small Firms in Technological Innovation', in J. Curran (ed.), *The Survival of the Small Firm* (Gower).

—— (1989). 'Small Firms, Innovation and Industrial Change', *Small Business Economics* 1: 51–64.

ROTHWELL, R. and W. ZEGVELD (1985). *Innovation and the Small and Medium Sized Firm* (London: Pinter).

RUMELHART, D. E., J. L. MCCLELLAND, and the PDP Research Group (1987). *Parallel Distributed Processing: Explorations in the Microstructure of Cognition, Volume 1: Foundations* (Cambridge, MA: MIT Press).

——, G. E. HINTON, and J. L. MCCLELLAND (1987). 'A General Framework for PDP', in D. E. Rumelhart, J. L. McClelland, and the PDP Research Group, *Parallel Distributed Processing: Explorations in the Microstructure of Cognition, Volume 1: Foundations* (Cambridge, MA: MIT Press), 45–76.

SAHAL, D. (1981). *Patterns of Technological Innovation* (Reading, MA: Addison-Wesley).

SARAPH, A. (1994). 'Toolbox for Tomorrow' (Groningen University, Groningen, the Nether-lands, doctoral dissertation).

SAUSSURE, F. DE (1979). *Cours de linguistigue générale*, lectures given between 1906 and 1911, first published in 1915 (Paris: Payot).

SAVIOTTI, P. P. (1996). *Technological Evolution, Variety and the Economy* (Cheltenham: Edward Elgar).

—— and B. NOOTEBOOM (2000). *Technology and Knowledge: From the Firm to Innovation Systems* (Aldershot: Edward Elgar).

Saxenian, A. (1994). *Regional Advantage: Culture and Competition in Silicon Valley and Route 128* (Cambridge, MA: Harvard University Press).

Schein, E. H. (1985). *Organizational Culture and Leadership* (San Francisco: Jossey–Bass).

Schelling, T. (1963). *The Strategy of Conflict* (Oxford: Oxford University Press).

Scherer, F. M. (1980). *Industrial Market Structure and Economic Performance* (Chicago: Rand McNally).

Schumpeter, J. A. (1909). *Theorie der wirtschaftlichen Entwicklung* (Leipzig: Duncker & Humblot).

—— (1939). *Business Cycles: A Theoretical, Historical and Statistical Analysis of the Capitalist Process* (New York and London: McGraw Hill).

—— (1943). *Capitalism, Socialism and Democracy* (London: Unwin).

Scott, L. M. (1995). 'Representation and Narrative', in R. S. Wyer jun. (ed.), *Advances in Social Cognition* (Hillsdale, NJ: Erlbaum), 165–76.

Shank, R. (1980). 'Language and Memory', *Cognitive Science*, 4: 243–84.

—— and R. Abelson (1977). *Scripts, Plans, Goals and Understanding* (Hillsdale, NJ: Lawrence Erlbaum).

—— and R. Abelson (1995). 'Knowledge and Meaning: The Real Story', in R. S. Wyer jun. (ed.), *Advances in Social Cognition* (Hillsdale, NJ: Erlbaum), 5–81.

Shanon, B. (1993). *The Representational and the Presentational* (New York: Harvester (Wheatsheaf)).

—— (1988). 'Semantic Representation of Meaning: A Critique', *Psychological Bulletin*, 104/1: 70–83.

—— (1990). What Is Context?, *Journal for the Theory of Social Behaviour*, 20/2: 157–66.

Shepard, H. A. (1967). 'Innovation-resisting and Innovation-producing Organizations, *Journal of Business*, 40/4: 470–7.

Simon, H. A. (1983). *Reason in Human Affairs* (Oxford: Basil Blackwell).

Smircich, L. (1983). 'Organization as Shared Meaning', in L. R. Pondy, P. J. Frost, G. Morgan, and T. C. Dandridge (eds.), *Organizational Symbolism* (Greenwich, Conn.: JAI Press), 55–65.

Smith-Doerr, L., J. O. Owen-Smith, K. W. Koput, and W. W. Powell (1999). 'Networks and Knowledge Production: Collaboration and Patenting in Biotechnology', in R. Th. A. J. Leenders and S. M. Gabbay, *Corporate Social Capital and Liability* (Dordrecht: Kluwer).

Smith Ring, P. and A. H. van de Ven (1994). 'Developmental Processes of Cooperative Interorganizational Relationships', *Academy of Management Review*, 19/1: 90–118.

Smolensky, P. (1988). 'On the Proper Treatment of Connectionism', *Behavioral and Brain Sciences*, 11: 1–74.

Spender, J. C. (1989). *Industry Recipes* (Oxford: Basil Blackwell).

Stinchcombe, A. L. (1990). *Information and Organizations* (Berkeley, CA: University of California Press).

Stoelhorst, J. W. (1997). 'In Search of a Dynamic Theory of the Firm' (Twente University, the Netherlands, doctoral dissertation).

Storper, M. (1997). *The Regional World: Territorial Development in a Global Economy* (New York: Gilford Press).

Streissler, E. W. (1973). 'To What Extent was the Austrian School Marginalist?', in R. D. C. Black *et al.* (eds.), *The Marginal Revolution in Economics: Interpretation and Evaluation* (Durham, NC: Duke University Press).

Teece, D. J. (1986). 'Profiting from Technological Innovation: Implications for Integration, Collaboration, Licensing and Public Policy, *Research Policy*, 15: 285–305.

Teece, D. J. (1988). 'Technological Change and the Nature of the Firm', in G. Dosi, C. Freeman, R. Nelson, G. Silverberg, and L. Soete (eds.), *Technical Change and Economic Theory* (London: Pinter).

Thiel, C. (1965). *Sinn und Bedeutung in der Logic Gottlob Freges* (Meisenheim am Glan: Anton Hain).

Thompson, J. D. (1967). *Organizations in Action* (New York: McGraw-Hill).

Thurik, A. R. (1996). 'Small Firms, Entrepreneurship and Economic Growth', in P. H. Admiraal (ed.), *Small Business in the Modern Economy* (Oxford: Basil Blackwell), 126–52.

Toffler, A. (1970). *Future Shock* (London: Pan Books).

Tushman, M. L. and E. Romanelli (1985). 'Organizational Evolution: A Metamorphosis Model of Convergence and Reorientation', in B. A. Staw and L. L. Cummings (eds.), *Research in Organizational Behavior* (Greenwich, Conn.: JAI Press), 171–222.

—— and P. Anderson (1986). 'Technological Discontinuitties and Organizational Environments', *Administrative Science Quarterly*, 31: 439–65.

Unger, B. (1999). 'Innovation Systems and Innovative Performance: Voice Systems', unpublished paper presented at a NIAS Workshop, Wassenaar, the Netherlands, 16 June.

Utterback, J. and F. Suarez (1993). 'Innovation, Competition and Industry Structure', *Research Policy*, 22: 1–21.

Vaughn, K. I. (1994). *Austrian Economics in America* (Cambridge: Cambridge University Press).

Van de Ven, A. H., and R. Garnd (1988). 'A Framework for Understanding the Emergence of New Industries, in R. S. Rosembloom and R. A. Burgelman (eds.), Research on Technological Innovation, Management and Policy, iv (Greenwich, CT: JAI Press).

Veblen, T. B. (1919). *The Place of Science in Modern Civilisation and Other Essays* (New York: Huebsch).

Vernon, R. (1966). 'International Investment and International Trade in the Product Cycle', *Quarterly Journal of Economics*: 80.

Volberda, H. W. (1998). *Building the Flexible Firm* (Oxford: Oxford University Press).

Voort, X. van der (1999). *Knowledge Conversion in Information Systems: The Case of the Dutch Army*, Report by the Faculty of Management and Organization, Groningen University, PO Box 800, 9700 AV Groningen, the Netherlands.

Vossen, R. W. (1996). 'R & D Decisions, Firm Structure and Market Structure' (PhD School SOM, doctoral dissertation), Labyrinth Publications, PO Box 662, 2900 AR Capelle a/d IJssel, Netherlands.

—— and B. Nooteboom (1996). 'Firm Size and Participation in R & D', in A. Kleinknecht (ed.), *Determinants of Innovation: The Message from New Indicators* (London: Macmillan), 155–68.

Vries, J. de and A. van der Woude (1995). *Nederland 1500–1518* (*The Netherlands 1500–1815*) (Amsterdam: Balans).

Vromen, J. J. (1995). *Economic Evolution: An Enquiry into the Foundations of New Institutional Economics* (London: Routledge).

Vuyk, R. (1981). *Overview and Critique of Piaget's Genetic Epistemology* I (London: Academic Press).

Vygotsky (1962). *Thought and Language*, ed. and tr. E. Hanfmann and G. Varkar (Cambridge, MA: MIT Press).

Walker, W. (1993). 'National Innovation Systems: Britain', in R. R. Nelson, *National Innovation Systems* (Oxford: Oxford University Press), 158–91.

Weick, K. F. (1979). *The Social Psychology of Organizing* (Reading, MA: Addison–Wesley).

—— (1995). *Sensemaking in Organisations* (Thousand Oaks, CA: Sage).

—— and K. H. Roberts (1993). 'Collective Mind in Organizations', *Administrative Science Quarterly*, 39, repr. in M. D. Cohen and L. S. Sproull (eds.) (1996), *Organizational Learning* (London: Sage), 330–58.

Weinberg, N. M. (1990). '*Innovation, Competition and Small Business*' (Erasmus University, Rotterdam doctoral dissertation) (Alblasserdam, Netherlands: Haveka).

Weintraub, E. R. (1988). 'The Neo-Walrasian Program is Progressive', in N. de Marchi (ed.), *The Popperian Legacy in Economics* (Cambridge: Cambridge University Press).

Werner, H. and B. Kaplan (1963). *Symbol Formation* (NY: Wiley).

Whitley, R. (1998). 'Internationalisation and Varieties of Capitalism: The Limited Effects of Cross-national Coordination of Economic Activities on the Nature of Business Systems', *Review of International Political Economy*, 5: 445–81.

—— (1999). *Divergent Capitalisms: The Social Structuring and Change of Business Systems* (Oxford: Oxford University Press).

Williams, B. (1988). 'Formal Structures and Social Reality', in D. Gambetta (ed.), Trust: Making and Breaking of Cooperative Relations (Oxford: Blackwell), 3–13.

Williamson, O. E. (1975). *Markets and Hierarchies: Analysis and Anti-trust Implications* (New York: The Free Press).

—— (1985). *The Economic Institutions of Capitalism: Firms, Markets, Relational Contracting* (New York: The Free Press).

—— (1993). 'Calculativeness, Trust and Economic Organization', *Journal of Law and Economics*, 36: 453–86.

Winograd, T. (1980). 'What Does It Mean to Understand Language?', *Cognitive Science*, 4: 209–41.

Winter, S. G. (1964). 'Economic "Natural Selection" and the Theory of the Firm', *Yale Economic Essays*, 4: 225–72.

—— (1982). 'An Essay on the Theory of Production', in S. H. Hymans (ed.) *Economics and the World Around It* (Ann Arbor, MI: University of Michigan Press).

Witt, U. (1993*a*). 'Turning Austrian Economics into an Evolutionary Theory', in B. J. Caldwell and S. Boehm (eds.), *Austrian Economics: Tensions and New Directions* (Boston / Dordrecht: Kluwer), 215–43.

—— (ed.) (1993*b*). *Evolutionary Economics* (Aldershot: Edward Elgar).

—— (1998*a*). 'Do Entrepreneurs Need Firms?', unpublished paper for the workshop 'Recent Developments in Austrian Economics', Max-Planck Institut zur Erforschung von Wirtschaftssystemen, Jena, 7–8 August.

—— (1998*b*). 'Between Entrepreneurial Leadership and Managerial Governance: The Contingent Ontogeny of the Firm Organization', unpublished paper for the DRUID Conference, Bornholm, 9–11 June.

Wittgenstein, L. (1976). *Philosophical Investigations* (Oxford: Basil Blackwell); first published 1953.

de Woot, P., A. Heyvaert, and F. Martou (1978). 'Strategic Management: An Empirical Study of 168 Belgian Firms', *International Studies of Management and Organization*, 7: 60–75.

Wyatt, S. (1985). The Role of Small Firms in Innovative Activity, *Economia & Politica Industriale*.

Yelle, L. E. (1979). 'The Learning Curve: Historical Review and Comprehensive Survey', *Decision Sciences*, 10: 302–28.

ZANFEI, A. (1996). 'Technology and the Changing Organization of Transnational Firms', unpublished paper for the EMOT Workshop, Durham, NC, 28–30 June.

ZELENY, M. (1998). 'On the Social Nature of Autopoietic Systems', in L. Khalil and K. E. Boulding, *Evolution, Order and Complexity* (London: Routledge), 122–45.

ZUCKER, L. G. (1986). 'Production of Trust: Institutional Sources of Economic Structure 1840–1920', in B. A. Staw and L. L. Cummings, *Research in Organisational Behaviour*, VIII, 53–111.

ZUSCOVITCH, E. (1994). 'Sustainable Differentiation: Economic Dynamism and Social Norms', unpublished paper for the Joseph A. Schumpeter Conference, Münster, 19–21 August.

Index